CENTER
FOR
CREATIVE
PHOTOGRAPHY

A look at the building that houses the Center for Creative Photography offers only a suggestion about what goes on within the walls. The architects made sure that the main entryway—off a busy pedestrian route in the University of Arizona's arts quadrant—would draw visitors easily to galleries, library, bookstore, lecture hall, and then upstairs past visual points of interest to areas for quiet examination of photographs and for archival research. This intentional progression from sidewalk to exhibition space to private study area allows for a variety of events and programming while accommodating different ways of experiencing photography. Exhibitions, lecture series, symposia, workshops, teacher training, group and individual tours are all ways the public can use the Center. And an international audience experiences the Center, not through these physical spaces, but through publications such as the scholarly journal, catalogs, the newsletter, and through traveling exhibitions originating at the Center.

Behind the walls and at the heart of the publications and exhibitions are the collections and archives. These art works and research materials, forming the quiet core of the Center, were acquired incrementally over the twenty-five years of the Center's history. They tell many stories of photography including the histories, the biographies of its practitioners, the evolution of its processes, and the impact of its institutions. Together the collections and archives make possible the invisible behind-the-scenes explorations and discoveries that have made the institution one of the world's foremost centers for the appreciation and study of photography.

ORIGINAL SOURCES

Art and Archives
at the Center for Creative Photography

edited by
Amy Rule
Nancy Solomon

research assistance by
Leon Zimlich

Center for Creative
Photography
The University of Arizona

www.creativephotography.org

The Center's web site offers ever changing information about current exhibitions and programs, new publications, rights and reproductions, traveling exhibition schedules, and how to make appointments to use the Research Center and PrintViewing facilities. Also featured are materials designed to take advantage of Internet capabilities: online guides for educators, finding aids to archival materials, lists of prints in the Photograph Collection accompanied by basic searching tools, and the University of Arizona Library's Sabio gateway to books and periodicals in the CCP Library. Improvements in searching capabilities are implemented as they are developed, and information provided in the datablocks in this book is updated as additional photographs and archival materials are accessioned. Books, catalogs, and monographs published by the Center can be ordered from the museum store. Visit www.creativephotography.org to keep up to date about the Center's holdings and activities.

Publication of this book was made possible by a grant from The Henry Luce Foundation through its American Collections Enhancement Initiative.

ISBN 0-938262-37-8—hardcover
ISBN 0-938262-38-6—softcover

Table of Contents

Introduction and Acknowledgments   17 – 25
   by Amy Rule

Ansel Adams and the Founding of the Center   34 – 35
   by John P. Schaefer

Ansel Adams   36 – 41
   by Amy Rule

Lola Alvarez Bravo   42 – 45
   by Cristina Cuevas-Wolf

Artists' Books   46 – 49
   by Nancy Solomon

Richard Avedon   50 – 52
   by Mark Williams

Louis Carlos Bernal   53 – 55
   by Timothy Troy

Josef Breitenbach   56 – 62
   by Marcia Tiede

Francis J. Bruguière   63 – 65
   by James Enyeart

Harry Callahan   66 – 71
   by Harold Jones

William Christenberry   72 – 75
   by April Watson

Edward S. Curtis   76 – 78
   by Timothy Troy

Louise Dahl-Wolfe   79 – 84
   by Jennifer S. Edwards

Andreas Feininger   85 – 88
by Stuart Alexander

French Photography   89 – 91
by Marcia Tiede

German Photography   92 – 93
by Marcia Tiede

Ralph Gibson   94 – 100
by Nancy Solomon

Laura Gilpin   101 – 103
by Timothy Troy

Judith Golden   104 – 106
by Cass Fey

Group f/64   107 – 110
by David Peeler

Charles Harbutt   111 – 113
by Roxane Ramos

Robert Heinecken   114 – 117
by Stephanie Lipscomb

Japanese Photography   118 – 120
by Terence Pitts

Margrethe Mather   121 – 124
by Sarah J. Moore

Mexican Photography   125 – 126
by Terence Pitts

Hansel Mieth and Otto Hagel   127 – 131
by Sally Stein

Kozo Miyoshi   132 – 134
by Dustin Leavitt

Tina Modotti   135 – 137
by Sarah J. Moore

William Mortensen   138 – 142
by Larry Lytle

Beaumont and Nancy Newhall   143 – 148
by Keith McElroy

Sonya Noskowiak   149 – 152
by Darsie Alexander

Marion Palfi   153 – 157
by Betsi Meissner

Mickey Pallas   158 – 159
by Dena McDuffie

Photo League   160 – 163
by Betsi Meissner

Aaron Siskind   164 – 167
by Maria Antonella Pelizzari

Henry Holmes Smith   168 – 171
by Leon Zimlich

W. Eugene Smith   172 – 177
by William S. Johnson

Frederick Sommer   178 – 185
by Nancy Solomon

Southworth & Hawes   186 – 189
by Ellwood C. Parry III

Spanish Photography   190 – 191
by Terence Pitts

Peter Stackpole   192 – 194
by Roxane Ramos

Paul Strand   195 – 199
by Maria Antonella Pelizzari

Teaching in a Collection   200 – 203
by Carol Flax

Travel Albums   204 – 208
    by Alison Nordström

Arthur Tress   209 – 211
    by Amy Rule

Tseng Kwong Chi   212 – 213
    by Terence Pitts

Jerry N. Uelsmann   214 – 217
    by Roxane Ramos

Willard Van Dyke   218 – 221
    by James Enyeart

Laura Volkerding   222 – 225
    by Marcia Tiede

Todd Walker   226 – 229
    by Nancy Solomon

Water in the West   230 – 234
    by Leon Zimlich

Todd Webb   235 – 237
    by Terence Pitts

Brett Weston   238 – 241
    by Dianne Nilsen

Edward Weston   242 – 248
    by Terence Pitts

Garry Winogrand   249 – 252
    by James Enyeart

Ylla   253 – 255
    by Timothy Troy

Datablocks   262 – 396

List of Illustrations   401 – 417

About the Authors   418 – 422

Index   423 – 445

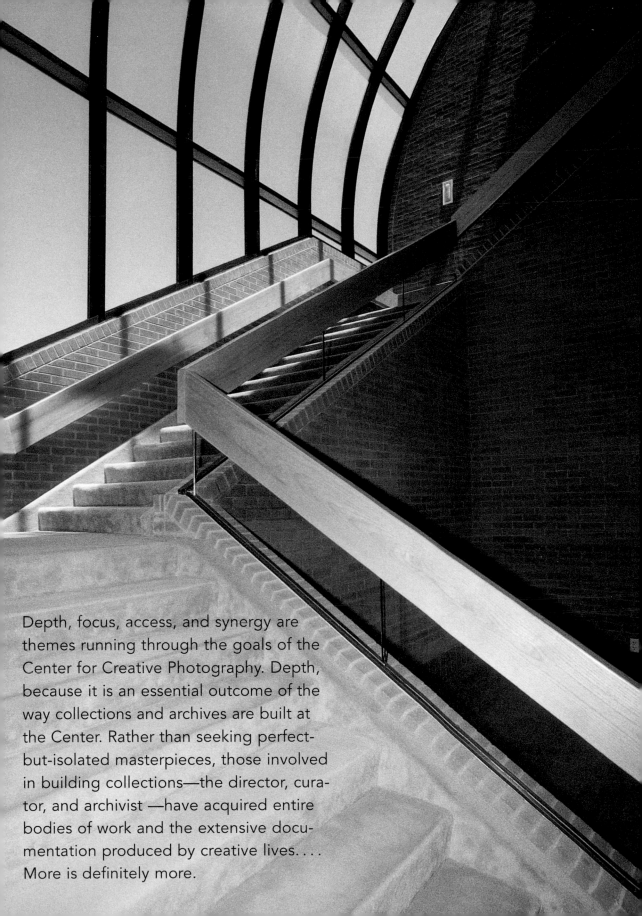

Depth, focus, access, and synergy are themes running through the goals of the Center for Creative Photography. Depth, because it is an essential outcome of the way collections and archives are built at the Center. Rather than seeking perfect-but-isolated masterpieces, those involved in building collections—the director, curator, and archivist —have acquired entire bodies of work and the extensive documentation produced by creative lives. . . . More is definitely more.

GALLERY HOURS:
MONDAY - FRIDAY
9 TO 5
WEEKENDS, NOON TO 5

LIBRARY HOURS:
MONDAY - FRIDAY
10 TO 5
SUNDAY, NOON TO 5

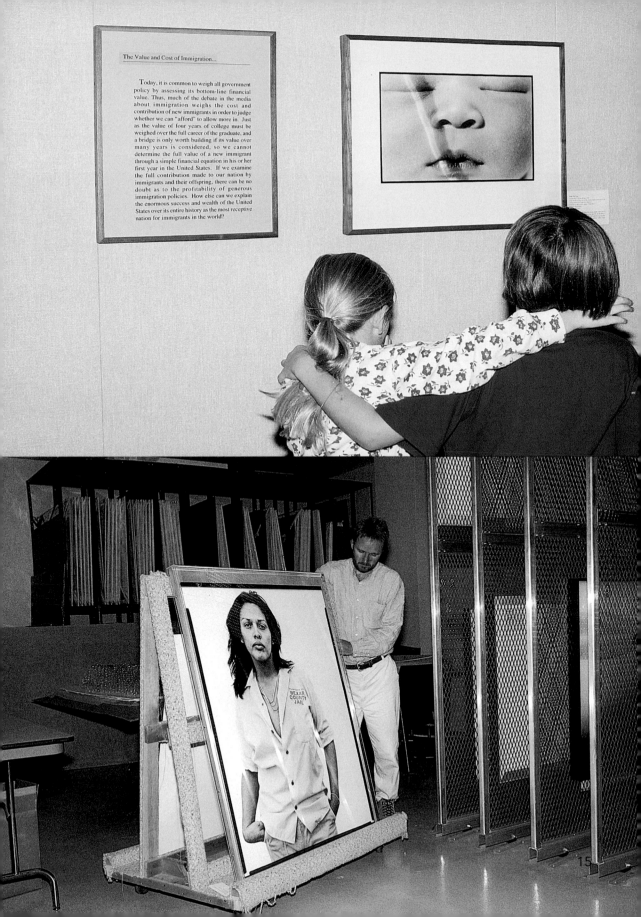

The Value and Cost of Immigration...

Today, it is common to weigh all government policy by assessing its bottom-line financial value. Thus, much of the debate in the media about immigration weighs the cost and contribution of new immigrants in order to judge whether we can "afford" to allow more in. Just as the value of four years of college must be weighed over the full career of the graduate, and a bridge is only worth building if its value over many years is considered, so we cannot determine the full value of a new immigrant through a simple financial equation in his or her first year in the United States. If we examine the full contribution made to our nation by immigrants and their offspring, there can be no doubt as to the profitability of generous immigration policies. How else can we explain the enormous success and wealth of the United States over its entire history as the most receptive nation for immigrants in the world?

ROBERT C. BISHOP: *Aspen Photographers Conference, Hotel Jerome, Aspen, Colorado*, 1951

Left to right:

Lying on floor: Will Connell, Wayne Miller

Seated in second row: Milly Kaeser, Ansel Adams, Dorothea Lange, Walter Paepcke, Berenice Abbott, Frederick Sommer, Nancy Newhall, Beaumont Newhall

Back row: Herbert Bayer, Eliot Porter, Joella Bayer, Aline Porter, Mrs. Paul Vanderbilt, Minor White, Mrs. Steele [secretary to Paepcke], John Morris, Ferenc Berko, Laura Gilpin, Fritz Kaeser, Paul Vanderbilt

Introduction

by Amy Rule

A look at the John P. Schaefer Building housing the Center for Creative Photography only barely suggests what goes on within the walls. The architects made sure that the main entryway—off a busy pedestrian route in the University of Arizona's arts quadrant—would draw visitors easily to galleries, library, bookstore, lecture hall, and then upstairs past visual points of interest to areas for quiet examination of photographs and for archival research. This intentional progression from sidewalk to exhibition space to private study area allows for a variety of events and programming while accommodating different ways of experiencing photography. Exhibitions, lecture series, symposia, workshops, teacher training, group and individual tours are some of the ways the public can use the Center. An international audience experiences the Center, of course not through these physical spaces, but through publications such as the scholarly journal, catalogs, the newsletter, and through traveling exhibitions originating at the Center.

Behind the walls and at the heart of the publications and exhibitions are the collections and archives. These art works and research materials, forming the quiet core of the Center, were acquired incrementally over the twenty-five years of the Center's history. They tell many stories of photography including the histories, the biographies of its practitioners, the evolution of its processes, and the impact of its institutions. Together the collections and archives make possible the invisible behind-the-scenes explorations and discoveries that have made the institution one of the world's foremost centers for the appreciation and study of photography.

This book provides a snapshot of the collections and archives of the Center as they exist at the beginning of the twenty-first century, and a guidebook to future explorations. A good snapshot provides information, incites curiosity and imagination, and promises that there is more to be seen. A good guidebook provides maps, but also inspires the confidence to turn the dotted lines into real paths and shorelines. The design of this book is intended to do these things as well as to look good and feel good in the hand. Visitors at the Center can take home a souvenir of their experience in the building. Scholars will consult the book for its densely packed data about the most significant collections. Collectors can consult it to learn more about the artists in their own collections. Potential researchers can use it to plan research trips. Beyond and above such practical uses, however, this book embodies the idea that there is no one right way to see and appreciate photography. Multiple voices speak *through* the collections—if we are attuned to hearing them—and many voices speak *about* the collections to inspire us, enlighten us, and cause us to think with healthy skepticism about how we know what we know about photography.

Thirty-two authors have contributed essays to this book. They are a diverse group, but what they have in common is the shared experience of direct contact with the collections and archives. Some present a lofty, encompassing vantage point, while others

Receipt for cleaning a piece of bloodstained velvet. Inscription by Margrethe Mather,
"a poetic cleaning bill?" 1923
Edward Weston Archive

Envelope with deconstructed postage stamp collage, drawing, and lettering
by Keith Smith, 1975
Robert Heinecken Archive

are as intimate and particular as a friendship will dictate. Individually, they celebrate the excitement of discovery and of personal encounters with photography. Taken as a whole they comprise a multifaceted view of the collections at the Center for Creative Photography.

The book begins with a text by Dr. John P. Schaefer, who as a young university president had a unique opportunity to establish a new kind of place for photography. Texts were also contributed by each of the Center's three past directors: Harold Jones, James Enyeart, and Terence Pitts. Center staff members Cass Fey, Dustin Leavitt, Betsi Meissner, Dianne Nilsen, Roxane Ramos, and Marcia Tiede wrote essays that are the product of their opportunity not only to see great numbers of photographs at the Center but also to come to know them over time. Each one writes from intimate knowledge, yet from a different perspective. Many former staff members have contributed essays on subjects especially close to them. William S. Johnson, the first archivist to work on the massive W. Eugene Smith Archive, has written movingly on his subject. Tim Troy, who for many years developed the book and magazine collections while serving as librarian, has added several essays based on his wide and eclectic interests in photography. Other former staff members who worked on specific projects have provided essays: Mark Williams, former registrar of the Richard Avedon Archive; April Watson, who assisted with our William Christenberry exhibition; Stuart Alexander, who worked on the Andreas Feininger Archive and wrote for an issue of *The Archive*; and Dena McDuffie, who organized the Mickey Pallas Archive. Nancy Solomon, who worked closely with photographers on publishing projects during her twenty-year term as the Center's editor, has written on subjects related to books and book making. Scholars, some of them recipients of the Ansel Adams Visiting Research Fellowship, have contributed essays reflecting a synthesis of fresh, raw research and conclusions drawn from extensive reading and looking. These authors include: Darsie Alexander, Cristina Cuevas-Wolfe, Larry Lytle, Alison Nordström, David Peeler, Maria Antonella Pelizzari, and Sally Stein.

Students and faculty of the University of Arizona enjoy an especially close relationship with the Center, and for this book some of them have contributed essays growing out of opportunities to conduct primary research. Stephanie Lipscomb and Jennifer Edwards have written on the subjects of their master's theses, Robert Heinecken and Louise Dahl-Wolfe respectively. Dr. Lee Parry's essay on a remarkable daguerreotype is an outcome of his extensive research on nineteenth-century American arts and culture. Dr. Sarah Moore followed her interest in women photographers to produce essays on Tina Modotti and Margrethe Mather. Carol Flax, artist/instructor in electronic arts, blends comments from her photography students with her own tribute to the power of encountering original works of art. Dr. Keith McElroy, a former student of Beaumont Newhall, writes on both the Newhalls in an essay combining telling, human details with a reminder of the great importance of this photographic team.

The second half of this book consists of blocks of data—condensed bundles of information describing the photograph collection, research materials, related information concerning publications, collections at other institutions, and some copyright information. As a special convenience to the reader, the "highlights" field emphasizes in a necessarily subjective manner remarkable, rare, or otherwise special aspects of the material. A datablock has been written for each artist represented in the collection

Betty and Todd Walker
GAINESVILLE FLORIDA 1972

from Betty and Todd Walker, 1972

KIRTTI-STAMBHA AT VADNAGAR.
[To face page 136, Vol. II.

Season Greetings from Vadnagar – We will be here soon. – The Heineckens

Toran gateways or
Kirtti - Stambhas were
common adjuncts to
Hindu temples as well as to
Vol II   Buddhist
Fergusson p 136   Stupas

from Robert Heinecken, ca. 1975

A
Happy New Year
1975

Eikoh Hosoe

from Eikoh Hosoe, 1975

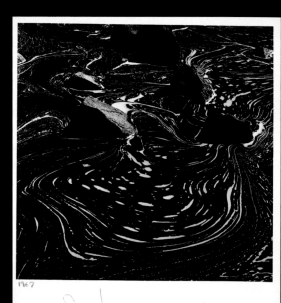

1967

Jay!
Dear Wynn, thanks for your photograph and the note. Happy Holidays and happy working. Joe

from Joseph Jachna, 1970s

from Jack Welpott, 1972

from Marilynn and Jerry Uelsmann, 1972

from Brett Weston, 1975

Holiday greeting cards
sent to Wynn Bullock
Wynn Bullock Archive

from Judy Dater, 1969

HARRY CALLAHAN: Portraits of Aaron Siskind, 1951
Portion of contact sheet
Harry Callahan Archive

either by ten or more works or by a significant amount of research materials, and for special discrete collections formed by individuals such as Ansel and Virginia Adams, Wynn Bullock, and Julia Corson, or thematic collections such as the Postcard Collection.

Following the datablocks are lists of the photographs reproduced in this book along with complete identification. Throughout the book, photographs in the collection have been reproduced in color whenever possible. Letters, ephemera, negatives, and other research materials are reproduced on black pages.

The book concludes with an extensive index including references from the essays, footnotes, datablocks, and captions.

While describing the collections and archives of the Center, the fascination is in unique details, but equally so in common threads. Another guidebook might have been organized to emphasize genre, style, geography, or chronology, but in our decision to simply use the most neutral of organizing principles—alphabetization—we sought to leave room for the reader to see his or her own themes. At the root of all we do at the Center is the desire to show the mysterious creative process as it is expressed through photography and to capture the means to study the ongoing process of photographic history. Because the creative process is often intangible, spontaneous, complicated, and protracted, our methods for documenting it must be ingenious and permissive. Ingenious, because evidence can take many forms and always exists in an active state or continuum that is sometimes hard to dissect. Permissive, because the line between vanguardism and marginalism can be difficult to define. Several generations may be needed to find an audience for a work of art or to understand an intellectual force.

As with many contemporary arts institutions, the Center's collections and archives developed with the direct participation of artists. Beginning with the work of five living master photographers all between the ages of 63 and 73 (Ansel Adams, Wynn Bullock, Harry Callahan, Aaron Siskind, and Frederick Sommer), the collection has grown to include the archives of over fifty artists—some deceased, some at the end of their careers, some enjoying a resurgence of interest in their work, and some younger artists with years of creativity before them. This leads to a tension not yet fully explored or exploited. On one side is an institution's natural tendency to limit the transgressive nature of the artist, and to shape a safe identity that can be described within the bounds of cataloging and inventory systems and justified within a collection policy. Yet the artist has goals beyond the security and preservation afforded by the institution, and by participating in the creation of the historic record achieves the desired immortality and control over which particular history is preserved. In instances where the artist and the Center work together, the definitions of archive may expand to include warehouse, show window, and plant for production.

Depth, focus, access, and synergy are themes running through the goals of the Center for Creative Photography. Depth, because it is an essential outcome of the way collections and archives are built at the Center. Rather than seeking perfect-but-isolated masterpieces, those involved in building collections—the director, curator, and archivist —have acquired entire bodies of work and the extensive documentation produced by creative lives. Rather than one beautiful portrait of Alfred Stieglitz by Dorothy Norman, we have hundreds of her prints showing him in different states of mind, times of day, and postures. This allows us to compare the totality of her effort to complete a portrait of Stieglitz with the selective works she chose to publish and exhibit. Our insights are taken to a deeper level when we examine the verso of her prints and read the comments Stieglitz wrote there. Another example of depth is illustrated with the reproduction of three variants of Paul Strand's *The Family, Luzzara, Italy*, 1953. Instead of studying only the well-known and published version of Strand's most important postwar work, researchers can consult the entire Strand collection for different croppings, different human dynamics, and different effects. More is definitely more.

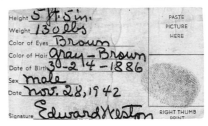

Identity card with Edward Weston's fingerprint, 1942
Edward Weston Archive

Focus is often the unexpected gift of an unguarded moment viewing collections. The supremely fascinating concreteness of Edward Weston's thumbprint is simultaneously a symbol of uniqueness and mortality. The texture screen favored by William Mortensen is revealed to be a photograph of his own pen and ink cross-hatching laboriously filling a page, signature-like and rhythmic as a heartbeat. Focus is the byproduct of working with original objects, art works or manuscripts, and of making oneself accessible to the tangible, physical immediacy of the encounter.

Access to the collections and archives is at the core of the Center's mission. As possibilities for electronic access increase, it becomes easier to present our constituents with information about the collections in the form of searchable cataloging records, finding aids, and descriptions of exhibitions and publications. The Center also increases remote access to collection information through its participation in the Art Museum Image Consortium (AMICO), but it does so with the conviction that authentic experience with art cannot be transferred through surrogates and that the cultural value of the art experience will not decrease over time. This book's captions, datablocks, essays, and illustrations are signposts back to the original objects. They must serve as catalysts in the many cases where space or timing did not allow fuller descriptions. John Gutmann's archive, for example, only recently arrived, has yet to be organized, cataloged, or exhibited. Its presence in this book demonstrates how the Center's collections are in a constant state of evolution, from the new and disorganized to the fully cataloged and accessible

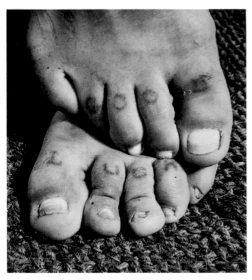

JOHN GUTMANN: *"Good Luck" Toes*, 1945

archives. We could not ignore our new collections, but their latent importance can only be suggested.

The most powerful theme that emerges throughout the collections and archives is that of synergy. The relationships among collections multiply as each small addition brings its own interconnections and overlapping relevancies. The complex web of friendships among photographers suggests synergistic flow in many directions. We find Keith Smith's letters in Robert Heinecken's archive, just down the aisle from the archive of Judith Golden, a student of Smith and a colleague of Heinecken. Wynn Bullock's extensive archive contains boxes of photographic greeting cards sent to him by dozens of photographers who sent meticulously prepared photographs as holiday tokens. Who knew that such dissimilar artists as Heinecken and Bullock would be connected through the evidence of a fanciful handmade greeting card?

Examples abound in this book of ways in which the sum is greater than any of its parts. Marianne Moore's comment in a letter to Edward Weston that "the ferocity of the designation, Wild Cat Hill, is an exhilaration" is the tantalizing hint of her poetic consciousness always at work. Margrethe Mather's inscription on a cleaner's receipt for blood-stained velvet demonstrates the poetic consciousness of a visual artist. Synergy can also be manifest in connections that jump across time and place. Contiguous collections and

CARLETON WATKINS: *Yosemite Falls, 2630 feet. Early Shed Built Near Black's Hotel*, 1861
Stereoview from Watkins' Pacific coast series. Image made during Watkins's first visit to Yosemite
Gift of Virginia Adams

24

MINOR WHITE: *Lake Almanor, California*, April 4, 1947

archives make such discoveries possible. Carleton Watkins photographed a cabin at the foot of Yosemite Falls in 1861, and seeing it through a stereoviewer, we are nailed into consciousness of the moment through the raking afternoon light accentuating each splinter and board of the rough cabin walls. We are no less present in a particular moment of stillness and clarity in Minor White's photograph of sharply delineated splintered wood, taken in 1947.

Finally, synergy can show itself in the image of a moment congested with portent as it is in the group portrait leading off this introduction. The Aspen Photographers Conference of 1951 brought together more than twenty of the top American photographers of the day at an event sponsored by the Aspen Institute of Humanistic Studies. We study the faces of Frederick Sommer, Minor White, Berenice Abbott, and Dorothea Lange as they pose in the lobby of the Hotel Jerome, hamming it up and laughing. Their ten days of discussions led to the founding of the immensely influential magazine *Aperture* that appeared in April of the following year. It is fitting to illustrate this on the first page of our book because so much of what was going on in the 1950s with this core group of people kicked off the chain of events resulting in the photography world of the 1970s, the founding of the Center, and the photography world as we know it today—receptive audiences, reflective critics, supportive institutions, take-a-chance publishers, and the network of artists that make up the collections and archives of the Center for Creative Photography.

Acknowledgments

This book is the product of mingling the ideas from many people with the hard work and dedication of many more. Terence Pitts, Nancy Lutz, Trudy Wilner Stack and I formed the initial group that brainstormed ideas for a book. Leon Zimlich provided indefatigable research assistance. Dianne Nilsen and Denise Gosé produced the hundreds of perfect color transparencies necessary to the plan, and did this while also providing photographic services for dozens of other projects. The Center's staff, especially Leslie Calmes, Roxane Ramos, and Marcia Tiede, gave the project their support and enthusiasm over the very long time it took to complete it. Peter C. Jones and Richard Misrach provided design suggestions at crucial moments in the process. Nancy Solomon edited and designed the book with her usual sensitivity, patience, and optimism. Uncountable numbers of colleagues across the country offered responses to my question, "What does a good collection guide look like?"

Finally, this book could not have come into being without the generous support of The Henry Luce Foundation. The Foundation's inspired objective of increasing the visibility of art collections throughout the country through the American Collections Enhancement Initiative will have monumental impact in our time. We are honored and pleased to be a part of this project.

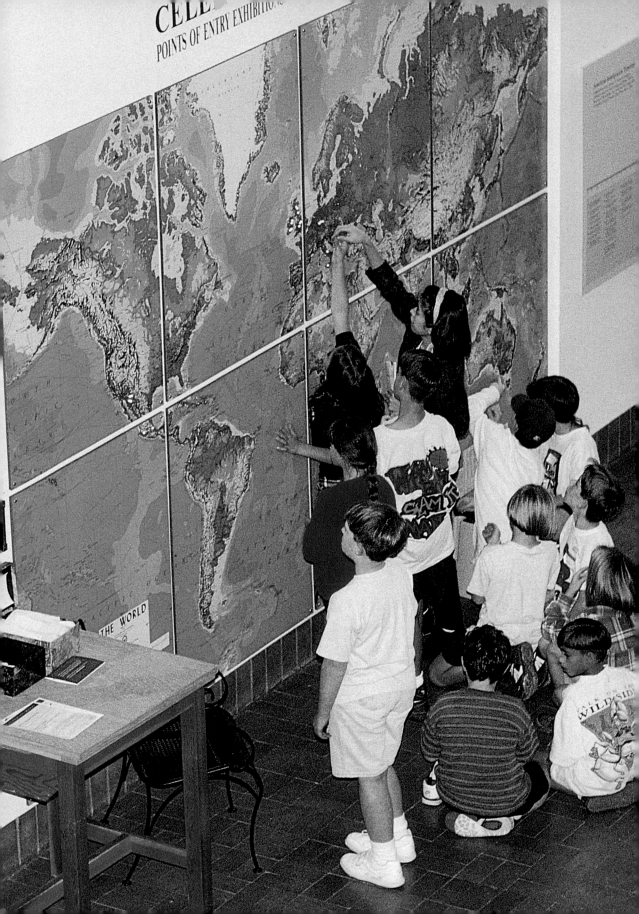

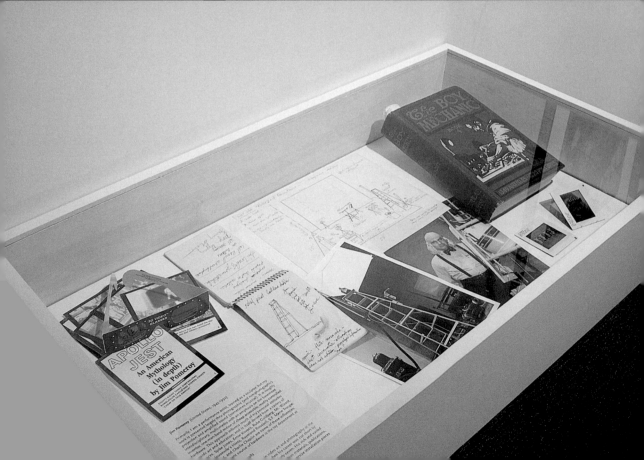

As with many institutions, the Center's collections and archives have developed with the direct participation of artists. Beginning with the work of five living master photographers all between the ages of 63 and 73, the collection has grown to include the archives of over fifty artists; some at the end of their careers, some enjoying a resurgence of interest in their work, and some younger artists with years of creativity before them. This leads to a tension not yet fully explored or exploited. On one side is an institution's natural tendency to limit the transgressive nature of the artist, shaping a safe identity that can be described within the bounds of cataloging and inventory systems and justified within a collection policy. The artist has goals beyond the security and preservation afforded by the institution, and by participating in the creation of the historic record achieves the desired immortality and control over which particular history is preserved. In instances where the artist and the institution work together, the definitions of archive may expand to include warehouse, show window, and plant for production.

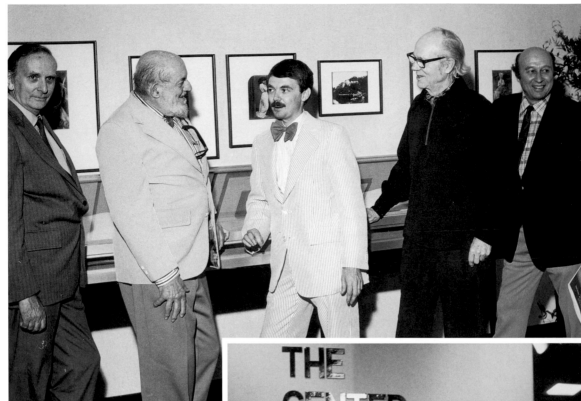

RAY MANLEY:
Left to right: Frederick Sommer,
Ansel Adams, Harold Jones, Wynn
Bullock, and Harry Callahan at
opening exhibition of the CCP,
1975

Dr. John P. Schaefer and Ansel
Adams at opening exhibition of
the CCP, 1975
CCP Archive

Ansel Adams and the Founding of the Center

by John P. Schaefer

The Center for Creative Photography is the product of the vision of one of the medium's greatest masters, Ansel Adams (1902–1984), and my conviction as university president that photography is a key element of the art and literature of our times. During the opening of a one-man exhibition of Ansel's photographs at the University of Arizona's Museum of Art, I ventured to ask him if he would be interested in placing the archives of his work at the University. Ansel, though somewhat surprised by the direct nature of my suggestion, responded by saying that he was not interested in having his work stand as an isolated collection. If, however, the University were willing to think in broader terms and include the works of many other photographers, he would be interested in exploring the possibilities. What followed was an invitation to visit him at his home in Carmel.

Conversations with Ansel in December of 1974 were a revelation as he shared his own history in photography, in conservation, in writing and teaching with me. I, in turn, put forth ideas about what I believed the University was and could become, and why photography deserved the serious attention of students and scholars alike. We spoke of archives, teaching programs, seminars, visiting scholars, collecting and preservation, publication, the creation of exhibitions; over the course of days the concept of the Center for Creative Photography was born.

With invaluable input from William A. Turnage, Beaumont Newhall, David Laird (University Librarian), and Harold Jones, the initial concept of the Center was refined and expanded. Harry Callahan, Wynn Bullock, Frederick Sommer, and Aaron Siskind joined with Ansel to found the first archives of the Center. W. Eugene Smith soon joined the University's faculty. Paul Strand contributed much of his work, and the archive of Edward Weston was later added to the growing collections.

Within a year the Center became an international presence in the field of photography. It remains an active "work in progress," awaiting its next photograph, a key letter, significant memorabilia, a run of magazines, a rare book—all of which are vital to a living and growing archive.

Ansel was a dreamer and a visionary, but unlike so many others, his ideas guided his actions and his actions led to accomplishments. His advocacy of photography defined it as an art form with apologies due to no one. His writings and the examples of his own work dominated modern photography and shaped much of the medium as we know it. Ansel's images of "wilderness" became a symbol and a motivating force in the conservation movement. His dedication to quality led to a revolution in the reproduction of images in photographic books. The images of Manzanar, an internment camp for Japanese Americans, were a reflection of his social conscience. With the exception of Stieglitz, no artist has done more to move photography into the forefront of galleries and museums.

Ansel was a caring human being and a delight to be with. His sense of humor, charm, intelligence, and sensitivity were manifest in his work and life. Without him the Center would have been little more than a fond wish.

ANSEL ADAMS: *White Branches, Mono Lake, California*, 1947

Ansel Adams

by Amy Rule

When I began working as the Center's archivist in 1981, a mural-sized print of Ansel Adams's *Monolith, The Face of Half Dome, Yosemite Valley* was hanging on the wall in director Jim Enyeart's office. Visitors didn't get much of a view of the photograph because it faced Jim's desk where he could see it, but occasionally when I was in his office for a meeting I took a chair to the side of the desk and from that vantage point I could look at *Monolith* as much as I wanted to. The office space was small, but the ceiling was high. The dark cliff face rushed upwards toward the purity of the featureless sky. During breaks in the conversation I relished the nobility and peace of that photograph and seemed to feel the coldness of the Sierra air. I never asked Jim what he thought of the image, but with time I came to feel that its choice was superbly appropriate. Ansel said this was the first negative he previsualized. This was the image he imagined, created with the use of a red filter, and finally printed to match his heightened experience of Half Dome. This photograph stands for a turning point in Adams's creative life and in the evolution of contemporary photography.

As time went on, and I became ever more intimately familiar with the Ansel Adams Archive, I came to feel that there were other icons of significant moments not only in his photographs but also in his personal papers. It may be that his entire archive is in itself an icon of a moment in the history of photography. An archivist rarely finds the "smoking gun" piece of evidence, but as a result of working with a collection begins to feel physical and psychological closeness to the subject. We may, in fact, come to see practically every piece of paper as a potent clue and have to work against dangerously romanticizing our conclusions. It is tempting to believe and to want to prove that an artist's life contains a consistency discernible both in the creative process and in the biography. How easy to see openness and honesty in Edward Weston's round schoolbook cursive, a good match for his philosophy of voluntary simplicity. In contrast, when I first saw Ansel's handwriting, I didn't know what I was looking at. It was surely the most idiosyncratic script I had ever tried to decipher. Young Ansel's difficulty with formal schooling, his hyperactivity, and his later success as an autodidact explain why his handwriting shows scant impact of any formal handwriting lessons. Does his writing also demonstrate his innate reluctance to follow convention, to do it his own way? I think it is a mistake to read too much into it, but as soon as I became more familiar with Ansel's unique handwriting, my appreciation of even his most widely published photographs increased.

This uniqueness is hard on the reader impatient to read lots of letters and get on with the research, however, and anyone who works with the papers in the Ansel Adams Archive becomes grateful for the invention of the typewriter. I would nominate Ansel's typewriters as iconic artifacts in his archive. Not only did Ansel prefer the typewriter over the pen, but he joyfully exploited the typewriter's possibilities as an artistic tool, using colored ribbons and all the signs and symbols available on the keyboard for the

ANSEL ADAMS:
*Gravestone Carving and Lichens, New England
Cemetery, Concord, Massachusetts, ca. 1965*

many letters and postcards he produced every day. Perhaps he first began to appreciate the typewriter at the 1915 Panama Pacific International Exposition where the manager of the Underwood display taught him the secrets of the device. Later in his life, he remembered this event and retold the story and perhaps thought about how his life spanned technologies from typewriters to computers. Throughout his adult life, Ansel owned many typewriters, desk models and portables that he carried in his car, and onto trains and airplanes when he traveled further afield. The Olivettis and Remingtons show up in the informal portraits of him, making it obvious that the typewriter came with Ansel as did his hat and his camera. Three typewriters now rest in his archive along with a tape recording of the sound of him typing. No one has yet done the research of linking particular typewriters to particular letters, but given the impact Ansel's letters had on his world—on photographers, politicians, and curators—this would be an interesting endeavor.

Ansel's archive tells us that, whether from vanity, honesty, or compulsiveness, he wanted us to know a lot about him. He saved his papers, at first through benign neglect, and later through an active process of collating, sorting, and organizing, so that the papers evolved into one of the most important and historically relevant photographic archives in existence. The first researcher to use them was Nancy Newhall, who was writing *The Eloquent Light*. Today, they are consulted more frequently than any other archive at the Center. Ansel's staff did the actual organizing and filing, even typing handwritten items for clarity and copying cross-references, but Ansel did the saving.[1] Perhaps he realized early on how the transit of his life was intersecting many other important lives, and foresaw how his personal archive would become truly the record of many associations and friendships. He must have believed that truth (rather than the devil) resides in the details. Certainly his meticulous approach to exposing film, to printing photographs, and to preserving decisions in his exposure and printing records indicates his trust in detail. His home in Carmel incorporated a concrete bunker built into the hillside where he stored his negatives and other precious archival items—further evidence of his passion for preservation.

The result today is 120 shelves full of boxes containing more than 30,000 pages of correspondence. Was the world smaller then, or did Ansel really know almost every figure of cultural importance? Sixty years of letter writing includes names such as Bill Brandt, Brassaï, Alvin Langdon Coburn, Jean Cocteau, Buckminster Fuller, and on through the alphabet. If a researcher began reading letters to and from Beaumont and Nancy Newhall, and read one page every minute, it would take about a week with no lunch breaks to get through every letter. But of course, that kind of research is not productive. Time is needed to thoughtfully digest the content, to rest the eyes, and to take notes. A lot of time is necessary to do original research in archives and to know what questions to ask. Since a selection of Ansel's letters became widely available through publication in 1988 of *Ansel Adams: Letters and Images, 1916–1984*, the use of the letters in his archive has somewhat decreased. The demand for published resources is high, but it must still contend with copyright laws which, being what they are, allow little chance for every letter, manuscript, or negative in Ansel's vast files to be published or digitized for online access.

The reality is that research will continue to rely on the original sources. There are more than 40,000 negatives in the archive. Extensive activity files contain information about how frequently Ansel had his piano tuned, how much Grabhorn Press charged to print the Taos Pueblo book, how he advertised his short-lived San Francisco art gallery, what changes were made to galleys for his major books, what was recorded in Sierra Club minutes, and thousands of other topics. His files reveal the interconnectedness of the photographic world just as other archives at the Center (such as the Water in the West Project) reveal how Ansel's legacy for environmental consciousness lives on. Assuming that future scholarship will not be satisfied with the known, and will inevitably seek the unknown, we can conclude that the magnitude of the collection will furnish fertile ground for many generations to come.

Some avenues of historical research are forced to rely on just a few available sources, usually biased, and often second- or thirdhand. Contemporary historians face different problems, often having too much undifferentiated information from too many sources. There is so much information in the Ansel Adams Archive that it is easy to overlook what might not be there. Quantity can overwhelm. The rare and subtly important things can become insignificant beneath an overburden of unimportant things. But these are just challenges for scholarship which must learn new strategies for efficiency and for evaluating aesthetic and historic value as it grapples with largesse. The important questions about Ansel's career will be answered after the sifting of not only the records he preserved, but after mining the archives of his friends and associates Edward Weston, Brett Weston, Wynn Bullock, Harry Callahan, and the others whose archives also reside at the Center.

John Szarkowski has written that Ansel's photographs "have enlarged our visceral knowledge of things that we do not understand."[2] The same thing could be said about his archive. Memory being a notoriously unreliable witness, we are fortunate to have an archive of tangible, evocative, contradictory, poignant, and specific artifacts of a life in photography to help us understand a time we did not live, and to appreciate a vision unique in photography. In its vastness and complexity, as well as its centrality to so many issues and personalities in photography, the Ansel Adams Archive is the perfectly representative building block on which to have begun the Center.

1 Thanks to Andrea Stillman, who became Ansel's assistant in the 1970s, for supplying information about the organization of Ansel's papers. Andrea also shares my interest in Ansel's typewriters. Years ago, she began collecting information about the purchase of each typewriter. She also noted letters in which Ansel wrote about his typewriter. Her file is in the Ansel Adams Archive.

2 John Szarkowski, *Ansel Adams at 100* (Boston: Little, Brown and Company in association with the San Francisco Museum of Modern Art, 2001), p. 18.

Ticket book for
Panama Pacific International Exposition
San Francisco, 1915
Ansel Adams Archive

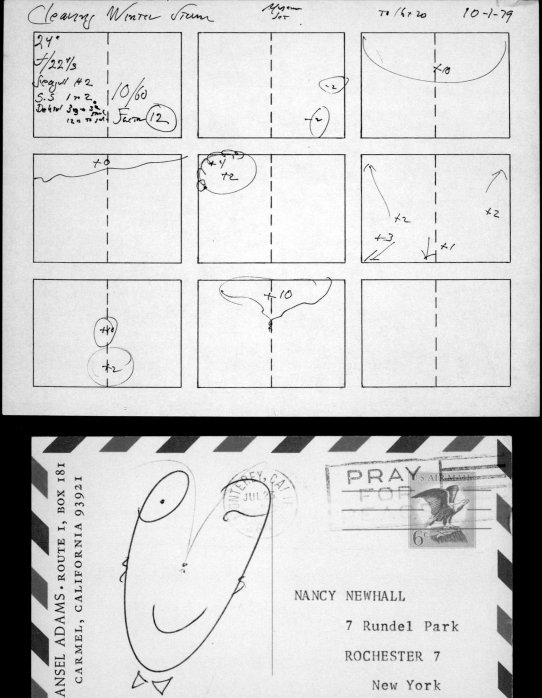

Above: Printing instructions for *Clearing Winter Storm*, museum set, negative #1-YW-82
Below: Postcard from Ansel Adams to Nancy Newhall with drawing by Adams, 23 July 1964
Ansel Adams Archive

LOLA ALVAREZ BRAVO: *En su propia cárcel,* ca. 1950

Lola Alvarez Bravo

by Cristina Cuevas-Wolf

Lola Alvarez Bravo (1907–1993), who is much celebrated in Mexico, has only recently begun to garner attention in Europe and the United States. Her photographic contribution is pivotal in bridging the revolutionary spirit of two distinct decades and setting an important precedent for contemporary women photographers in Mexico.

Alvarez Bravo turned to photography at the end of the 1920s, a decade enamored with Mexican folkways. Her introduction to photography took place alongside her husband, Manuel Alvarez Bravo, whom she married in 1924 and who achieved an international renown for his figurative, at times surreal, images of a Mexico caught between tradition and modernity. For three years, from 1924 to 1927, Manuel and Lola lived in Oaxaca, where Manuel worked as an accountant at the State Accounting Office. Together they spent their leisure time exploring the indigenous cultures and peoples of the region. It was here that Lola began to develop and print photographs under Manuel's tutelage. Their interdependent manner of working—from the selection of the subject and its composition to the final tripping of the shutter—has made it difficult to discern at times which photographs from the late 1920s are his or hers. For each, photography was the means to represent their individual visions of the country and its people.

Through Diego Rivera's murals for the Secretaria de Educación Pública (Ministry of Public Education) Lola Alvarez Bravo gained insight into her culture and drew inspiration for her photography. Long before moving to Oaxaca, she visited the Ministry of Public Education and saw the mural of the looms. It was not until later that she understood the meaning of that mural and took in Rivera's sense of composition, light, and form. Along with Manuel, she became the chosen photographer of the Mexican muralist's work in the 1930s.

Edward Weston may have left an indelible imprint on the look of modern photography in Mexico with his emphasis on formal precision and the effects of light and of contrasts. The power of the indigenous subject matter that attracted both the Mexican muralists and photographers lent photography a place and purpose in the country's revolutionary struggle. This is significant since there was no forum in Mexico in which to debate the social potential of photography, in contrast to such contemporary forums found in photographic journals in the Soviet Union.

Upon their return to Mexico City in 1927, Manuel and Lola Alvarez Bravo met leading painters, poets, and musicians of their time. The art scene pulsated anew with rebellious strife. The Treinta-Treintista art movement transformed propaganda posters into powerful weapons. The intellectual and literary group of *Los Contemporaneos* [The Contemporaries] delved into aesthetic reverie. In contrast, the politically charged *Liga de escritores y artistas revolucionarios* [LEAR, The League of Revolutionary Artists and Writers] unified the artistic scene in 1935. It adopted the principles of the Popular Front, turned pro-government, and became an important mediator in creating jobs for artists. No artist at this time could afford not to belong.

Upon separating from Manuel in 1934, Lola embarked upon an independent life and career as a full-time photographer. Her first job came when Héctor Pérez Martínez appointed her chief photographer for *El Maestro Rural*, a monthly magazine published by the Ministry of Public Education for elementary school teachers. It was in the pages of this magazine that Alvarez Bravo's camera images wed the humanist sensibilities of the 1920s with the image of the masses of the 1930s. Her photographs render sympathetic images of mestizo and Indian women in her signature direct, portrait-like style to promote the unifying role of women in society. Such directness gives way to photographic essays that use innovative camera angles to reveal a collective spirit among young men working to improve themselves through technical education, young women dancing, or young athletes training. The well-known image of raised fists in solidarity is transformed into raised children's hands reaching up to grasp hold of a new elementary schoolbook.

Alvarez Bravo's awareness of and engagement with constructivist photographic forms stems from her involvement with the LEAR. As a member of this group, Alvarez Bravo helped organize the film club together with painter, engraver, and photographers Emilio Amero and Manuel Alvarez Bravo. This "cine-club" screened, among other works, films by Sergei Eisenstein and Dziga Vertov, which the Soviet government discreetly lent. In 1931, the Salon de Arte in Mexico City hosted an exhibition of contemporary graphics organized by Gabriel Fernández Ledesma, and the LEAR's own magazine, *Frente a Frente* (1934–1938), demonstrated an awareness of German and, to a lesser extent, Soviet graphics. This visual, moral and political climate led Alvarez Bravo to experiment with photomontage and constructivist photography in the pages of *El Maestro Rural* and, in the process, to revalidate Mexico's revolutionary national image.

In the midst of this intellectual and artistic tumult, Alvarez Bravo came in contact with prominent photographers of her time—Tina Modotti, Paul Strand, Sergei Eisenstein, and Henri Cartier-Bresson. She photographed her friends who were the leading painters, musicians, poets, intellectuals, and politicians of her time, leaving behind a portrait of a generation that shaped Mexico's revolutionary culture. Her photographic work also captures the state of modernity and modernization in Mexico of the 1930s and 1940s. Although Alvarez Bravo felt a certain estrangement towards modern formalism, she continued to use photomontage and innovative camera angles in other aspects of her work in the 1940s and 1950s, which speaks to her fascination with modernity and its creative possibilities.

Women photographers in Mexico have proven to possess a singular ingenuity. Tina Modotti might have been the only woman photojournalist working for *El Machete* in the 1920s, and Alvarez Bravo the only woman following government ministers on their official tours, and hiking up her skirts to climb oil derricks for such magazines as *Vea, Voz, Avance, Futuro*, and *Espacio*, but their courage blazed a trail for contemporary women photographers in Mexico. As a teacher of photography at the Academy of San Carlos in 1948, Alvarez Bravo played a direct role in encouraging a young American photographer to come into her own, namely Mariana Yampolsky. This fruitful student–teacher relationship overcame the shortage of supplies and inadequate equipment to achieve a proficiency in creative photography.

Lola Alvarez Bravo's contribution to photography and the arts is extensive and is encapsulated in the large collection of negatives held at the Center. This collection represents her professional work, what she called her "little jobs." They reveal her way of working, her disregard for dates, and her own organizational logic. Among her professional work, one will find those certain photographs that pleased her and reflected her personal views. As Olivier Debroise has pointed out, "photographs that somehow did not fit within her more rigid assignments."

The University of Arizona Library holds the volumes of *El Maestro Rural* that contain Alvarez Bravo's photographic work. These holdings provide insight into Alvarez Bravo's professional work, which has yet to be fully researched and analyzed.

Artists' Books

by Nancy Solomon

Taken together, the artists' books in the Library, Research Center, and Photograph Collection form a diverse study collection, offering hundreds of examples. The artists may use the physical form of the book, or the sequencing of pages, or unique texts and other surprises to communicate with the "reader." This is an intimate medium, made to be experienced by the reader/viewer/perceiver, who turns the pages and senses the interaction of the paper, printing, text, and binding. Often bookworks come literally from the hands of the artist into the hands of the viewer.

Most artists who create books reject the look-but-don't-touch philosophy that dominates the art world in favor of a direct tactile interaction between the artist and the viewer. No matter where the books are housed at the Center, the opportunity to see the material is more like using a library than viewing work in a gallery or museum exhibition. These books are accessible.

Library

The backbone of the CCP Library's collection is housed in the Rare Book Room. Artists' books are listed under both title and author in the University of Arizona Library's online catalog. In addition, the Library of Congress subject heading ARTISTS BOOKS leads to nearly five hundred of these titles (slightly more than half of the approximately 850 artists' books in the Center's Library).

CLARISSA T. SLIGH: *What's Happening with Momma?*, 1988

Many of these were produced in editions by publishers specializing in artists' books:

For instance, Clarissa Sligh's *What's Happening with Momma*? is from the Women's Studio Workshop. The book is an accordion-folded, silk-screened series die-cut in the shape of a house with peaked roofs; the letterpress-printed texts about a girl's confusion when her mother leaves home to have a baby are also accordion-folded and attached to each room/page as if they were steps. The book is printed on both sides and can stand upright as a sculpture.

Bill Burke's *I Want to Take Picture,* published by Nexus Press, takes advantage of the ease of integrating photographic images with text in offset lithography to capture his impressions of Cambodia. Burke presents a collection of found objects, texts, and his photographs in a scrapbook format to make powerful statements about both the conflict in southeast Asia and his own visit to the region a decade later.

The Visual Studies Workshop offset production, *Life in a Book*, by F. Deschamps, explores photographic reality through images, sequencing, and the form of the book itself: a hat changes size in different contexts, a person is trapped in the gutter of the book, and plays on words are given a very literal photographic interpretation.

Because artists' books must be experienced to be fully appreciated, artists use different strategies to get their work into viewers' hands. Some artists take control of the entire publishing process:

Todd Walker, a photographer and a master printer, conceived of and produced books in editions of several hundred under his own Thumbprint Press imprint: such as, *A Few Notes: Selected from Lesson A of Wilson's Photographics; Enthusiasm Strengthens; See;* and *For Nothing Changes: Democritus, on the Other Side, Burst Laughing.*

Susan kae Grant makes small editions with the care that normally

SUSAN KAE GRANT: *Giving Fear a Proper Name: Detroit*, 1984

goes into making one-of-a-kind pieces. Her *Giving Fear a Proper Name: Detroit* was made in a limited edition of fifteen. The texts are letterpress printed on pink papers integrated with actual photographs that have been cut and impaled with pins and other real objects—like a black satin quilted heart and pouches of real human teeth and fingernails—all combined in a carefully crafted pink leather binding with a pink satin bookmark sewn in and weighted with a tiny toy gun. The book combines the soft, lovely feminine with tormented fear in a tactile and powerful expression.

Tucson has an active book arts community, and the CCP Library collection reflects that, including works by many of those artists, such as Judith Golden, Beata Wehr, and Todd Walker. Some are unique, such as Wehr's *Relocation Continued*, which expresses the Polish-born artist's yearning for a sense of home—a yearning intensified by her keen sensitivity to the materials that she uses to create a house on every page.

In contrast are the quick photocopied books presented in a wide variety of formats.

These books stress ideas over craft, and the ideas can be highly personal, from considering the nature of dust to determining whether your colleague is a space alien.

The Center's Library holdings began as a collection of artists' books that use photography in some way. Later, a broader range of artists' bookworks were added, increasing their usefulness as a study collection. Special Collections of the University of Arizona Library also has examples of artists' books and the beautiful book as a fine art.

Photograph Collection

Books in the CCP Photograph Collection tend to be one-of-a-kind like Judith Golden's *Masks*, 1974–84, or especially fragile work. These can be seen with staff assistance via the Center's PrintViewing program.

Four examples of Keith Smith's elaborate and engaging books are in the collection. *Book 118*, an octagonal book, is an experience unfolding from a continuous accordion binding into a large irregular shape; the sequence combines color photographs of babies machine-sewn onto the page together with black-and-white photographs of stone sculptures. From the Aaron Siskind Collection is Smith's tour de force *Book 91*, in which strings are pulled through holes in page after rigid page, creating changing patterns of string and their shadows.

Elisa Gittings's delicate *Rock's Words* is an intaglio book with double spines, enticing us to overlay her translucent photographic etchings of rocks and surprisingly related female human forms.

Wooden Book is an early work by former Tucsonan Pamela Moore. A sequence of four gum bichromate photographs deconstruct the image of a young girl until she becomes just a silhouette with all the patterns in her clothing scattered around her. Each print is mounted on a small wooden panel and hinged to the others, folding like a screen into a soft pink leather pouch.

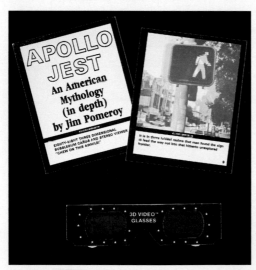

JIM POMEROY:
Apollo Jest: An American Mythology (in depth), 1983

Research Center Archives

More extensive examination of artists' books is possible by appointment in three individual artists' archives in the Research Center.

In the Irene Shwachman Archive, this artist's creative process can be examined in the many iterations of *Now You Know: This Is Serious Photography*, 1987. She experimented with different page sizes, starting with a large maquette in 1978. By 1981, the book had shrunk to its final size. She cut photographs, used sequences of transparent and translucent pages in combination with opaque pages, and played with a mirror page and a photo-booth theme. The book evolved over several years.

Ultimately, a National Endowment for the Arts award enabled Shwachman to use a com-

IRENE SHWACHMAN: Maquette for artist's book *Now You Know: This Is Serious Photography*, n.d.

mercial printer to produce the book. The bids from the printer indicate the limitations commercial processes imposed on the book—even while making it possible to bring the project to fruition as a printed edition. A metal spiral binding allowed Shwachman to maintain the playful spirit of her original ideas—keeping her sequences of mirror, see-through, and translucent pages, alongside printed photographs. She controlled the placement of each page. Shwachman integrated mezzotint-screened black pages, silk-screen on transparent pages, and hand-coloring with conventional offset lithography. From the start, her text was borrowed, tongue-in-cheek, from the promotional materials of an old portrait studio in New York. Over the years, the text evolved too, becoming simpler, more apt. In the end, *Now You Know: This Is Serious Photography* is masterful, a playful but serious commentary on the elements of photography—light, image, and paper.

The Jim Pomeroy Archive reflects his interest in artists' books from two perspectives. An avid promoter of bookworks, Pomeroy organized an exhibition from his personal collection. The Pomeroy archive includes his own bookworks and his collection of thirty-four bookworks by other artists. Surprisingly, there is little overlap between the titles in Pomeroy's collection and those in the Center's Library, thus expanding the examples one can see from the history of artists' books. Pomeroy's collection begins in 1964 with Ed Ruscha's *Various Small Fires and Milk* and continues through his own *Apollo Jest: An American Mythology (in depth)*, 1983—a series of eighty-eight 3-D bubble gum cards commenting on the space program, which he was assembling in the year of his death.

Pomeroy also built a reference library on stereo photography to get the technical knowledge he needed to develop stereo installations and bookworks throughout his career. He explored three kinds of stereographic viewing: ViewMaster in *Jim Pomeroy: Stereo View*, anaglyph stereo cards that are viewed with red-and-green stereo glasses in *Apollo Jest*, and side-by-side stereo pairs presented in *Seeing Double*, published by the California Museum of Photography, Riverside.

The Todd Walker Archive includes special hardcover editions of his books that he bound by hand in cloth and marbled paper, which he made himself choosing both the colors and the swirl patterns.

RICHARD AVEDON: *Cesar Chavez, Founder, United Farm Workers, Keene, California, 6-27-76*
From the portfolio *Rolling Stone: The Family*, 1976

Richard Avedon

by Mark Williams

The portraits by Richard Avedon (b. 1923) remind us that faces are a subject of limitless fascination. Perhaps we first learn this as infants lying in our mother's lap gazing up at her face. In this moment the observer enjoys the absolute adoration of the observed and is itself the subject of study and delight. Words have no place in our enjoyment of faces in those early years, and even later in life, when we try to describe a face, we are limited by what language can do. Visual artists, however, can explore the expressive qualities of their media to create portraits that speak to us, haunt us, and move us in unexpected ways. Avedon's tender yet powerful image of Cesar Chavez is such an example. This artist looks headlong into the humanity and pathos of each of his subjects, whether they are plain or elegant, fraught with emotion or serenely self-contained. In the 1950s Avedon took fashion photography out of the studio and onto the streets of Paris. His early fashion work is filled with vitality and movement, anticipating the free-spirited culture of the 1960s and 1970s which he continued to reveal and inspire. Avedon's portraiture simultaneously documented the icons of our changing culture from Eisenhower to Frank Zappa. He photographed the civil rights and antiwar movements and documented the political landscape of the 1970s in a portfolio titled *The Family* commissioned by *Rolling Stone* magazine. He welcomed in the last decade of the century by documenting the destruction of the Berlin Wall. The Richard Avedon Archive at the CCP includes all of these works.

Our experience of juxtaposition—the coexistence of dramatic opposites—is central to our time and our culture. Avedon is the undisputed master of juxtaposition, challenging us with images of the exquisite beauty of our potential and the often-sobering reality of our limitations. Each new body of work, from his first publication, *Observations*, and his first one-man exhibition at the Smithsonian Institution, through his most recent publications, has asked the viewer to confront the pervasive dichotomies of modern life. The images reproduced in this book are representative of the kind of juxtapositions Avedon presents throughout his work. His photograph of Elise Daniels encapsulates our longing for glamour and the insecurity and opacity experienced within it. With all its energy and elegance, that photograph is connected through Avedon's passionate and unflinching vision with the serenely noble portrait of Chavez. The worlds of fashion and political struggle are united through their shared human predicament.

Emerging from the diversity of Avedon's work is the undeniable political nature of much of it. As the photographer of the famous and powerful, Avedon offers us a rare glimpse into the shadows of power and fame. He has at the same time given image to the disenfranchised and unheralded, often placing images of power in direct relationship to images from the margins of society. Through the experience of Avedon's work we are forced to wrestle with our own complicity with the struggles these opposing images represent.

Avedon's *In the American West* series challenges our ability to gaze upon ourselves

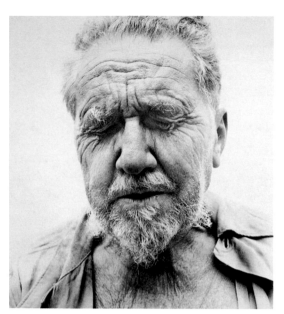

RICHARD AVEDON:
Ezra Pound, Poet, June 30, 1958, Rutherford, New Jersey, 1958

without the veil of our heroic self-image. His straightforward depictions confront and contradict romantic notions of what a westerner looks like. He looks beyond the idealistic images of John Ford westerns to the faces of the men and women of the real west, where we see a complex reality bound up in the beautiful and the humble, the heroic and the tragic, where the truth of real faces is juxtaposed with unknowable stories that a photograph cannot explain.

One of the fundamental objectives of the CCP is to study photographers within their field and their times. Avedon's archive offers the possibility to experience hundreds of fine prints with examples from each of his major bodies of work. The growing files of ephemera, research materials, publications, and other documentation of a prolific and varied career are the result of a long-term collaboration between the artist and the CCP to build a deep and unique resource for future exploration.

Louis Carlos Bernal

by Timothy Troy

I have felt a great deal of anger and anxiety in my life and I have used photography as an outlet for these frustrations. My images have always dealt with the inner battle of my soul.

Louis Carlos Bernal

Bernal (1941–1993) was born in Douglas, Arizona, and grew up in Phoenix. After completing his M.F.A. at Arizona State University in 1972, he joined the faculty of Pima Community College in Tucson where he remained for the duration of his career, developing and heading its photography program.

In 1978 while documenting the barrio neighborhoods of Tucson, Bernal came across a small, apparently abandoned house. It was the home of an elderly woman, and everything within was as she had left it when she'd been taken abruptly away to a nursing home. He searched for the old lady, found her, and asked her permission to photograph the interior of her house—the tops of her desk and commode, notes on her bulletin board framing a religious image, and so on. The finished tableaux series became known as *The Benitez Suite*, and it is one of Bernal's most sensitive bodies of work. Though subsequently lauded for his color photography, Bernal, at this point in his career, was worried about the lack of permanence of color. Also, he believed that the kind of intimate portrait he wanted to create of the old woman was only possible through black and white.

In 1979, Bernal, along with four other photographers—Morrie Camhi, Abigail Heyman, Roger Minick, and Neal Slavin—received funding from the Mexican American Legal Defense and Educational Fund to photograph Mexican American life. In the accompanying exhibition catalog entitled *Espejo: Reflections of the Mexican American*, Bernal said: "The MALDEF project has allowed me to explore the essence of my being, I wanted to convey what I found—the new sense of pride, the new awareness that is flowering both within myself and within the community." He and others of the period described this new sensibility as Chicanismo. The Center for Creative Photography is the official repository for the photographs and documentation of the Espejo project.

Bernal was one of ten photographers selected by the Los Angeles Olympic Organizing Committee in 1984 to document the Summer Olympic Games. He said at the time: "My job will not only be that of a photographer of athletes. In addition, I shall leave behind the record that the photographic lens of an Hispanic registered the comings and goings of ordinary people during those two months." His photographs from this project do just that: they are less about the Olympic games and Olympic athletes and more about the people of the city of Los Angeles.

On 24 October 1989, Bernal was struck by a car in Tucson while riding his bicycle to work. He remained in a coma, unable to communicate and needing round-the-clock

LOUIS CARLOS BERNAL: *Dos Mujeres, Douglas, Arizona*, 1978
From the group exhibition *Espejo*

care, for nearly four years. Bernal died on his birthday, 18 August 1993. He was fifty-two years old.

"My images speak of the religious and family ties I have experienced as a Chicano," he had written earlier. "I have concerned myself with the mysticism of the Southwest and the strength of the spiritual and cultural values of the barrio." Ethnicity, in fact, dominates the largest part of his work, his hundreds of images of ordinary people in and outside their homes in barrios from Texas to Los Angeles. "The responsibility of a Chicano artist is to feed the soul of his people," Bernal said. He saw an urgency to his work, to document the lives of people whose ancestral neighborhoods were being bulldozed in the name of urban renewal. He said at the time: "It is my hope that my images provide some small contribution to my people—*La Raza*."

Bernal's great success was his ability to take pictures of people in situ and have them be at ease with him as a photographer. The subjects are relaxed, and we are relaxed and grateful that we have been allowed into their community. We are outsiders still, but Bernal has brought us with him, and therefore our presence is less intrusive. There remains that sense that these are "his" people, and Bernal himself said that in so many words. Bernal's mission—perhaps his possessiveness—was understandable in the time period within which he was working. It was the height of the La Raza movement, and La Raza was articulating a response to a hundred plus years of every conceivable kind of oppression and repression at the hands of the Anglo. The artist, Louis Carlos Bernal, was genuinely engaged in the struggle.

JOSEF BREITENBACH: *Sybille Binder and Paul Robeson, Role Portrait in Othello*, ca. 1932

Josef Breitenbach

by Marcia Tiede

The career of Josef Breitenbach (1896–1984) spans five decades, beginning in his native Germany where his family ran a wine business in Munich. His earliest images were taken during trips for the family business—landscapes and architectural studies from Munich, Paris, and the Tyrol. The wine business failed around 1930, and Breitenbach became a portrait photographer, noted especially for photographing Munich's actors. In 1933 he was obliged to relocate to Paris after a visit from Nazi officials, as much due to his leftist associations as to his being Jewish. Here he established himself within a circle of German expatriates and achieved some success again as a portraitist of renowned artists and writers, such as Bertolt Brecht, James Joyce, Aristide Maillol, and Max Ernst. He served as a Paris photographer for the British International News Agency and became a member of the Société française de la photographie and the Royal Photographic Society. He continued other themes that he had begun in Germany—plant studies and landscapes, architecture, and some nudes.

In Paris, Breitenbach experimented in a surrealist manner (techniques such as unusual toning and montage). In his archive are installation shots of the International Surrealism Exhibition held in Paris in 1938 that included work by Salvador Dali and Man Ray. One of the more unusual moments of his career was devising a way to photograph odors, made manifest through a technique developed by French botanist Henri Devaux, by floating fine powder on a layer of mercury in the presence of a pungent sample such as a flower or coffee bean. Breitenbach later gained some attention in relation to this technique, but failed to promote it as being of scientific merit.

Like several other photographers whose archives are housed at the Center (Hansel Mieth and Otto Hagel, Andreas Feininger, John Gutmann, Marion Palfi, Hans Namuth), Breitenbach was part of the flight of Europeans to New York before and at the beginning of World War II. His own departure was negotiated in 1941 from one of the work camps in France where he had been interned for a year and a half. Unlike many of his fellow émigré photographers, however, he never achieved real success after relocating, despite extensive networking efforts—perhaps, it has been suggested, due to his extremely independent nature, and also due to a certain high-manneredness, a tendency to inflate how he represented himself. Whereas Philippe Halsman and Feininger quickly parlayed their work into successful careers for *Life* magazine, and André Kertész and Lisette Model similarly found sustenance as staff photographers for magazines until they could achieve public recognition of their own work, Breitenbach struggled to support himself as a portrait photographer and by a handful of commissions for *Fortune* and other magazines throughout the 1940s. He again made portraits of some people he had known in Paris—the printmaker Karl Schrag and Max Ernst—as well as Josef Albers at Black Mountain College in North Carolina. Breitenbach was invited by Albers to guest lecture at Black Mountain in 1944, along with Barbara Morgan. He eventually

Above: Identity card, 1938
Below: Pocket diary, 1936
Josef Breitenbach Archive

AFFIDAVIT IN LIEU OF PASSPORT

REPUBLIC OF FRANCE!
DEPARTMENT OF BOUCHES DU RHONE
CITY OF MARSEILLE
CONSULATE OF THE UNITED STATES
   OF AMERICA

} SS.

Before me, Myles STANDISH   Vice Consul of the United States of America, in and for the district of Marseille, France, duly commissioned and qualified, personally appeared Josef BREITENBACH who, being duly sworn, deposes and says :

That his full name is Josef BREITENBACH and resides at 28, rue Mirabeau, Agen (Lot et Garonne) France

That he was born on April 3,1896 at Munich, Germany

That he is single, married to

That he is the bearer of no valid passport or other document for travel to the United States because. he has lost his German nationality and owing to present international conditions, is unable to obtain a valid travel document.

That this affidavit has been executed to serve in lieu of a passport to allow him to proceed to the United States.

DESCRIPTION :

Height : 5'7"
Weight : 160 lbs
Hair : black
Eyes : hazel
Marks : none
Complexion : medium

Josef Breitenbach
Josef Breitenbach

PHOTOGRAPH ATTACHED

CONSULAR SERVICE

Subscribed and sworn to before me this 29th day of April, 1941.

Myles Standish
Myles Standish
Vice Consul of the United States
of America.

Service No. 4332
Fee Prescribed

Affadavit in Lieu of Passport allowing Breitenbach to travel to the United States, April 1941
Josef Breitenbach Archive

obtained teaching positions at Cooper Union in 1946, and at the New School for Social Research (where Model, Palfi and W. Eugene Smith also taught) in 1949. Namuth, who had studied under him in Paris, did so again at the New School.

Breitenbach continued to teach photography until he was in his seventies, and as a teacher was well regarded. He achieved some professional recognition during his first decade in the United States: inclusion in exhibitions at the Museum of Modern Art in 1947, 1948, and 1950, and a one-person show at the Smithsonian in 1950. He also developed an important historical collection of photography that he used in teaching. But in many ways he seemed to be at a standstill. His portraiture no longer displayed his earlier experimentation, and his efforts to get various book projects published failed. Whether for lack of funds, time, or interest, there is a real paucity of images of the American landscape or city in his work, given that he spent the last four and a half decades of his life in this country. Aside from trips for commercial purposes, his only cross-country trips were to teach in North Carolina and Florida in 1944, and for a holiday in Colorado in 1947. He did make shorter trips, to photograph in the Adirondacks, Niagara Falls, and other rural areas not far from New York City.

JOSEF BREITENBACH AND HENRI DEVAUX:
Rose Petal Exhaling Its Fragrance, 1937–39

Instead, Breitenbach experimented with abstract photograms—an ongoing aspect of his interest in surrealism. He used this technique in teaching, and also briefly as a source for textile patterns. There are also some examples of surrealist still lifes, negative prints, and bas-relief prints (superimposing a positive and a negative to create an image with exaggerated delineation and contrast). And from the late 1940s until around 1960 Breitenbach developed the body of work that he is most notorious for today, though not during his life—an extended series of nudes, made mostly at two nudist camps in New Jersey, owned and frequented by German-Americans. Breitenbach made nude images throughout his life—a result of his ongoing obsession with the female form and of his numerous personal relationships. Incredibly, given the length and diversity of his career, the three books published about Breitenbach since his death all focus upon a single session one day in Munich in 1933, when he photographed a nude female model along with his formally attired male friend.

In the nudist camps Breitenbach was free to photograph children as well as women—some swimming or playing tennis, others posing easily and even proudly for him—perched in a tree like a latter-day nymph, standing by a cornfield or on a forest path, lying in meadow grass. His subjects, almost exclusively female, were not necessarily the embodiment of stereotypical beauty. It is said that Breitenbach considered this his best work. If so, it was not timely: the American sensibility could not appreciate it then, and probably still has trouble with it today—though now for the reason that this was a man choosing to photograph nude women and girls, rather than for the more prudish attitudes prevalent in the 1950s, when male control over the camera's point of view, in itself, would probably not have been questioned. A more specialized grouping within this body of work is what he called "This Beautiful Landscape," images of female genitalia, which were explicitly a reflection of his relationship with the subjects—a sort of personal catalog, an assemblage of fetishes.

JOSEF BREITENBACH: Untitled, ca. 1950.

From 1952 to 1953 Breitenbach served as photographer for the United Nations Korean Relief Agency (UNKRA), and from that pivotal event began a regular summer routine of trips to Asia, during free time from teaching, to photograph for sponsors such as UNICEF, UNESCO, IBM, and Standard Oil. He visited most of the countries of Asia, with Japan being a favorite cornerstone destination of each trip. He collected oriental artworks for his personal collection and as gifts. A selection of his Korean images constituted the first exhibition at Helen Gee's Limelight Gallery (by mere happenstance, since an intended exhibition by Robert Frank fell through); and one image was included in Steichen's blockbuster show *The Family of Man* at the Museum of Modern Art the following year.

Breitenbach thrived on this last phase of his career; as he wrote to a friend, "I feel to be in the middle of the stream of life. The continuously renewing experience of a culture so different from everything I saw before. . . is mine. I feel old enough to understand it and ripe enough to enjoy it. . . .To be at the height of my life." He always found occasion to make his own images as well as the ones necessary to satisfy his business obligations. Breitenbach did almost no reportage in the United States, except in the context of a couple of commercial projects; hardly a single American is recorded in his work aside from formal portrait or nude study. Yet most of his imagery from Asia is of people, especially women and children—going to market, on the street, at temples, in health clinics or schools, working in fields. His efforts to promote his Asian work met with only limited success: a cover story in *Aperture* magazine in 1965 and publication of his only realized book, *Women of Asia*, in 1968.

In 1965, Breitenbach had a retrospective at the Münchner Stadtmuseum, which also acquired his collection of historical photography in 1979 and published a major book on that collection. In 1983, the year before his death, he gave his "archives"—a set of perhaps two hundred photographs—to that museum, and a Breitenbach Foundation was created there. A centennial exhibition of his work took place in 1996 in Munich and Halle, initiated by T. O. Immisch of the Staatliche Galerie Moritzburg Halle. The companion monograph includes works reproduced from the Center's collection, and research derived from the archive. But there seems still today to be little awareness of the Center's extensive Josef Breitenbach Archive, acquired in 1989; it is not mentioned in recent French and German biographical outlines of his career. The depth of this archive is all the more remarkable given the difficult circumstances of Breitenbach's departure from Europe.

Francis Joseph Bruguière (1879–1945) exemplified the spirit of American avant-garde photography in the 1920s and 1930s. His experimental images of cut paper, light abstractions, and multiple exposures were so exclusively devoted to the abstract elements of photography—light, form, and multiple in-camera images—that the resulting abstractions eluded his American peers, including Alfred Stieglitz and his circle of followers, the Photo-Secessionists. Although a member of the Photo-Secession himself, Bruguière was never very active in the group, exhibiting with them only once. After 1919 he rejected the painterly soft focus works that he and his close friend, Frank Eugene, among others, were producing. While Paul Strand had moved toward a new reality for photography—"brutally direct" in Stieglitz's words—Bruguière had begun to reject reality altogether.

It was Frank Eugene who introduced Bruguière to Stieglitz by way of a letter in 1908[1] in which he wrote to Stieglitz,—"be good to him—he has fine qualities— . . . he has the right feeling concerning art matters." Bruguière visited Eugene in Europe in 1912 and 1913. They traveled together to Venice where they visited several futurists like Prestini. Although they remained in correspondence they did not see each other again until 1927 and 1929 when Bruguière had exhibitions in Paris and Berlin. Bruguière's only major exhibition in New York, where he had moved from San Francisco in 1918, also took place in 1927 at the Art Center. Following his introduction to the futurists, Bruguière moved quickly to experiments of his own. The work he produced during the 1920s was more in keeping with the European interest in experimental photographic expressions than with the Stieglitz circle whose modernist evolution remained tied to reality. Bruguière's friends described him as charming and quiet, yet openly disdainful of social and intellectual affectations. In 1923, Bruguière wrote to Sadakichi Hartmann: "Things go about the same . . . I never see painters or photographers. Better luck for me."[2] What Bruguière failed to mention in his letter to his friend was that in 1922 he met Rosalinde Fuller, an English actress appearing on Broadway, whom he had fallen in love with and for whom he had left his family. They remained together until his death in 1945. During their time in New York from 1922 to 1928, Bruguière and Fuller embarked upon numerous multiple exposure experiments, portraits and nude studies of her. But the most compelling of these experiments was for a series Bruguière titled *The Way*. The series included a young German dancer, Sebastian Droste, and Fuller as the sole actors before Bruguière's camera. The photographs were intended as still images for a fantastic surreal film that was never made. Droste died of a brain hemorrhage in 1925. It was at this time that Bruguière began his cut-paper abstractions, which became his dominant imagery for the rest of his life. Bruguière and Fuller moved to London in 1928.

FRANCIS J. BRUGUIÈRE: *Experiment*, ca. 1925

In 1929, Bruguière published twenty-four new photographs in his first major book, *Beyond This Point*, with a text by Lance Sieveking. In 1930 he finally produced a film, which has become one of the earliest modernist abstractions in the history of film. Titled *Light Rhythms*, the film was based on cut-paper abstractions, which remained stationary while different light sources changed position, animating the static forms. Bruguière's film and light abstractions may be seen in relation to the concurrent films of Man Ray and Hans Richter. Between 1930 and 1940 he used a variety of other methods (straight, Sabattier effect, cliché-verre, relief printing) to expand his visual vocabulary of surreal and abstract imagery. From this and earlier work Bruguière's contributions may be seen as the precursor to a number of artists including Edward Steichen, Wynn Bullock, Frederick Sommer, and Henry Holmes Smith, all of whom were familiar with Bruguière's work.

FRANCIS J. BRUGUIÈRE:
"Few Are Chosen," 1931

Bruguière's legacy as one of photography's first abstract surrealists is best expressed in the words of the critic, John Mason Brown, who wrote for the *Boston Evening Transcript* on 9 April 1927 (Bruguière's first major exhibition review) that "unquestionably they have something in common with the modernist school in painting. But the exciting truth is that, regardless of faint similarities to current strivings in other art forms, they stand definitely and bravely by themselves as important victories for the camera."

Had it not been for Rosalinde Fuller, Bruguière's life's work might have slipped away, as did awareness of his contributions until the early 1970s when I published a monograph on his life and work. Following Bruguière's death in 1945, Fuller carefully stored away his negatives, prints, and the original negative of his film *Light Rhythms*. She continued with her career as a stage actress in Britain, receiving a distinction of honor (M.B.E.) from the Queen toward the end of her life. She and Bruguière had always lived comfortably, but had not prepared for old age. Through the patronage of Roxanne Malone and myself, Lee Witkin, and Sam Wagstaff, Fuller was able to live out the last years of her life with renewed comfort and lived to see Bruguière take his richly deserved place in history.

1 Beinecke Library, Stieglitz Archive, 15 September 1908.

2 In a letter from Bruguière to Sadakichi Hartmann, dated 24 September 1923, New York, from the Wistaria Hartmann Linton Collection, University of California, Riverside.

HARRY CALLAHAN: *Chicago, ca. 1952*

Harry Callahan

by Harold Jones

One of my students sent me an article from one of Chicago's newspapers written a few days after Harry Callahan (1912–1999) passed away. The article said Harry was "one of the most influential photographers of the twentieth century." Harry was a quiet restless midwesterner who was proud of the level of respect his work achieved. And he taught others who came after him to follow their own path to life's poetry and visions.

I first discovered Callahan's work when, as a young art student in 1965, I saw his "Black Book" published by El Mochuelo Gallery.[1] The book was superbly printed and showed the range of Harry's precise excursions through photography. I treasured the book but it never occurred to me that someday in the future I would represent him at LIGHT Gallery, New York, and years later, invite him to have a home for his work and archive at the Center for Creative Photography in Tucson.

Often, when I visited Harry in Providence during the LIGHT years, we would sit in his studio/office on the top floor and there would be stacks of several months' worth of proof prints from Harry's latest excursions. Harry proofed everything. Sometimes he would lament that there wasn't anything good in the stacks. The prints recorded the search but not yet the spark that Harry was looking for. He was a purely intuitive photographer who photographed through an idea until his feelings for the subject matter spoke clearly through the photograph. And the process of getting there was a primary part of Harry's restless rambles.

Reading copies of Harry's letters[2] in the Todd Webb Archive of the Center for Creative Photography is a melancholy and fascinating experience for me. Fascinating because it is like listening to Harry's mind as he shared his life's experiences and uncertainties with his old friend from the Detroit days. Todd Webb was a member of the Detroit Camera Club at the time Ansel Adams visited the club and gave some workshops for a few days in 1941. No letters exist from those days but of those workshops Harry has said, "It is Ansel that freed me."[3] Copies of Harry's letters to Webb, written years later, often mention Harry's continuing restless search for photographs.

The only thing I do is walk—I walk about 2 miles a day—it works off my nervousness and relaxes me to photograph.[4]

I've enjoyed being in the east but have been restless—wanting to see as much of it as I can—and wanting to photograph. My photography suffered because I do more looking than photographing.[5]

It wasn't until I read the copies of Harry's letters to Todd Webb that I found out that income from the print sales for the "Black Book" was used by Harry and Eleanor to help buy their house on Benefit Street in Providence, Rhode Island. The same house where

Exhibition of photographs

harry callahan

10 november thru 29 november 1947

SEVEN FIFTY STUDIO

750 north dearborn street superior 3622
mary jo slick   merry renk   olive oliver
noon to 8 p.m. monday thru friday

Exhibition announcement: Seven Fifty Studio, Chicago, 1947
Harry Callahan Archive

HARRY CALLAHAN:
Individual images cut from original contact sheet. Probably used in
selection of images for *Peachtree Street* series, Atlanta, ca. 1990
Harry Callahan Archive

HARRY CALLAHAN: *Eleanor, 1949*

Harry and I used to sit on the top floor drinking bourbon and looking at his latest photographs.

The people who are publishing [the El Mochuelo book] *also have a gallery in Santa Barbara and they bought the photos in the book. The book will have 126 photos. I got $2500 which is enough for the down payment.*[6] [This also tells us a bit about the photography market in 1963.]

In the same letter he writes about his struggle to photograph.

My photography doesn't go too well. I really haven't adjusted yet or as usual don't know what I am doing.[7]

In a letter later that November I found a clue about why the reproductions in the El Mochuelo book are so fine.

The first proofs were very poor so I went down there [to Meridan Press, Meridan, Connecticut] *and pointed it out—they came up with far better ones.*[8]

And some of the letters tell of other ways that buying a house affected his life. In January 1964:

I am doing some assignments to get enough for closing costs on our house. The assignments are low pay pleasurable but extremely time consuming.[9]

In June when they had moved in and began renovating the house, photography was still in the front of his mind.

HARRY CALLAHAN:
Eleanor and Barbara, Chicago, 1954

We are living in the 4th floor of our house amidst rubble. Without a bath and hot water. We do have an electric frying pan and a refrigerator and toilet.

I hope to have the darkroom going in about a week. My Hallmark show has been pushed up to August 15 and I don't know whether or not I'll make it or not. I'm certainly worried.[10]

And in September:

I had no idea what it is to restore an old house. The workmen were here at 8:00 am and were here till about 8:00 pm. I was trying to print and keep sane—they did get my darkroom ready pretty soon.[11]

Harry did get his Hallmark Gallery show ready on time. And it was a great success. Edward Steichen, a supporter of Harry's and an admirer of his work, was among those who attended the reception and celebratory dinner. (Correspondence to Harry from Hallmark can be found in his archive at the Center for Creative Photography.)

I remember once Harry told me he was no poet. He meant with words. But to a great many he was a poet—his poems were made for the eyes to feel and minds to see. He made photographs that speak of integrity, faith, wonder, and surprise. He showed us the magic of photography that makes possible the eloquence of seeing.

1 El Mochuelo Gallery, Santa Barbara, California, 1964.

2 Originals are in the collection of the Department of Photography, Museum of Modern Art, New York.

3 John Szarkowski, *Harry Callahan*, Museum of Modern Art and Aperture, New York, 1976, p. 11.

4 Undated letter (1961–1963) to Todd Webb, Todd Webb Archive.

5 28 May 1962 letter to Todd Webb. Todd Webb Archive.

6 8 November 1963 letter to Todd Webb. Todd Webb Archive.

7 8 November 1963 letter to Todd Webb. Todd Webb Archive.

8 21 November 1963 letter to Todd Webb. Todd Webb Archive.

9 28 January 1964 letter to Todd Webb. Todd Webb Archive.

10 2 June 1964 letter to Todd Webb. Todd Webb Archive.

11 September 1964 letter to Todd Webb. Todd Webb Archive.

WILLIAM CHRISTENBERRY: *Church, between Greensboro and Marion, Alabama*, 1973
From *The Alabama Box*, 1980

William Christenberry

by April Watson

There, lying on the barrel in front of me, looking vaguely like a piece of worn harness, was an object which I slowly recognized as once beloved to me. It was a stereopticon. It belonged in the parlor, on the lower shelf of the round table in the middle of the room, with the Bible on the top. It belonged to Sunday and to summertime.

From *Kin*, by Eudora Welty[1]

I think that oftentimes art can make an outsider look back on something he has never been a part of, and make him feel like he has always been a part of it.

William Christenberry[2]

With polite Southern pride, William Christenberry (b. 1936) will often say that he can tell you a story about every work of art he has ever made. It is an irresistible invitation for any first-time visitors, particularly those from points north and west of Christenberry's childhood home in Hale County, Alabama. Here, the seeds of his artistic inspiration were, and continue to be, sown. With a twinkle in his eye, Christenberry's tales unfold: accounts of a hoop snake in kudzu; Gypsies and an abandoned store-turned-palmist building; a hooded Klansman standing terrible and silent at the top of a stairwell; a woman whose egg carton flowers decorate unmarked graves. Gourd trees, rust-ravaged signs, red dirt, rickety ladders, tar-tacked walls, and hooded forms appear time and again in various transfigurations, comprising Christenberry's visual lexicon. His stories, sparked by these and other motifs in the paintings, drawings, sculpture, photographs, found objects, and installations that constitute his life's work, enlarge and expand the experience of seeing. As when reading a work by Eudora Welty, one is easily seduced by the romance of imagery that speaks of the humor, pleasure, hardship, terror, and love of place. Yet one is always aware of deeper dimensions, of something culturally and spiritually more intense, that exists just beneath. Like Welty's "stereopticon," noted in the passage above, Christenberry's motifs are objects "once beloved" operating simultaneously as catalysts for the recollection of a specific time and place, and as metaphors for the mutable, often tragic, nature of memory itself. Christenberry looks "back on something" through the eyes of someone intensely formed by one place, and who has long since lived someplace else.

The impossibility of reducing the manifold nature of Christenberry's work holds true as well when attempting to describe the artist himself. Pilgrim, documentarian, collector, and creator, his roles as an artist are multiple, shaped by a myriad of personal and cultural experiences. Christenberry's need to make things, to put his hands in the service of his invention, stems in part from family tradition. Though neither of his parents, William and Willard, made a living from their creative endeavors, both worked extensively with handicrafts and encouraged Bill in his formal education as an artist.

Christenberry began his academic training in 1954 at the University of Alabama, Tuscaloosa, where he concentrated on painting, earning a B.F.A. in 1958 and an M.F.A. the following year. Coming of artistic age in the era of abstract expressionism and pop art, Christenberry assimilated the ideas and techniques of both without siding with either camp. Taken, too, with the work of earlier surrealists and dadaists, while also immersing himself in the writing of William Faulkner, Carson McCullers, and Thomas Mann, among others, Christenberry absorbed a diverse range of artistic and literary influences. During this time, Christenberry also began to make simple snapshot photographs with a Brownie camera to aid his painting.

After graduating, Christenberry's advisor, Melville Price, encouraged him to get out of Alabama. Christenberry left his teaching position in Tuscaloosa, and in 1961 moved to New York. He remained there for one year, working various jobs to support himself while suffering a frustrating creative dry spell. Three months into his stay, he met the photographer Walker Evans, whose images of Hale County in *Let Us Now Praise Famous Men* had made a profound impact on Christenberry. Evans took kindly to the younger artist, facilitating a job for him at Time-Life through his connections as editor of *Fortune* magazine. They met often, with Evans serving as both a friend and mentor to Christenberry and encouraging him to consider his Brownie snapshots as serious photographs. When Christenberry left New York to take a teaching position at Memphis State, he took with him the City's artistic stimulus, an invigorated confidence, new directions for his work, and a friendship with Evans that would last a lifetime.

Upon returning to the South in 1962, Christenberry began to address in his work the most difficult aspect of his white Southern heritage: the Ku Klux Klan. At a faculty art exhibition in 1963, Christenberry exhibited two paintings, *Hate I* and *Hate II*, that dealt with the Klan. Criticized by administrators who felt the subject inappropriate, Christenberry found himself at the center of a controversy that follows him to the present day. Though he destroyed the paintings, Christenberry could not shake the need to pursue the Klan material as a vital part of his work.

In 1963, Christenberry made his first Klan dolls—GI Joe figures adorned in regal satin robes—and began to assemble *The Klan Room*. Now grown into a claustrophobic installation of several hundred drawings, paintings, sculptures, photographs, Klan ephemera, and assorted found objects, *The Klan Room* is an obsession as bedeviling as it is cathartic for the artist. As seen most readily in the transmutation of his Klan dolls from lavishly robed moveable puppets to bound, gagged, and tortured hooded forms, Christenberry's reaction to the evil of the Klan moves from a more distanced exploration of the brotherhood's seductive trappings to an exorcism akin to voodoo ritual. It is a vexing engagement with a terrible side of human nature that remains with the artist as a wound he cannot heal yet refuses to ignore, despite admonitions that it "is not the proper concern of an artist or of art."

By the time Christenberry left the South in 1964 to teach at the Corcoran School of Art in Washington, D.C., his visual vocabulary was well in place. The call to Alabama remained strong, and in that year he began his annual pilgrimage to Hale County, returning with relics of home that provide creative sustenance between visits. Weathered metal advertising placards, hand-painted wooden signs, hollowed-out gourds, and bags of Alabama red dirt are among the treasures that travel back with the artist to his studio. The sojourns also provide Christenberry with the opportunity to photograph, year after year, the same country churches, dilapidated storefronts, abandoned warehouses, and simple graveyards that haunt his memory. Working with both his Brownie camera and, since 1977, an 8x10-inch Deardorff view camera, Christenberry makes his photographs with little deviation in exposure or vantage point. The photographs occupy an integral intermediary point for the artist

WILLIAM CHRISTENBERRY:
5¢ Sign, Demopolis, Alabama, 1976

relative to his work in other media. Removed one step from reality, they exist simultaneously in past and present time, often outlasting their subjects to become documents of a swiftly disappearing material world. Further, they serve as springboards for the subjects' reconfiguration in drawings and three-dimensional structures. Without the photographs, Christenberry's ongoing series—his *Building Constructions, Southern Monuments, Dream Buildings*, and Klan tableaux—would seem somehow unhinged; too far removed from the terrain that so fervently informs his imagination.

As the landscape and people of Hale County change with disquieting facility, Christenberry feels his connections to the place with ever-greater intensity. At the same time, his work of the past five years reflects an increased removal from specificity of detail to abstraction of form. *The Dream Buildings*, begun in 1979 as richly textured and colorful cube-based structures, now soar as slender white obelisks that pierce the air. Ink wash drawings of buildings once readily recognized as a tenant or dogtrot house have become ghost forms, where negative space defines edges and shapes dissolve into blackness. Though figures have never appeared as primary subjects in Christenberry's art, their implied presence through vernacular signifiers and the specific arrangement of things is always tangible. Yet, as time progresses, even those markers grow more distant, as the artist faces his own mortality with ever-greater urgency.

Again, the words of Eudora Welty come to mind, her narrator speaking as a grown woman revealing her thoughts upon leaving a childhood home revisited after many years:

> *There was the house, floating on the swimming dust of evening, its gathered, safe-shaped mass darkening . . . The last gleam of sunset, except for the threadbare curtain of wisteria, could be seen going on behind. The cows were lowing. The dust was in windings, the roads in their own shapes in the air, the exhalations of where the people all had come from.*[3]

1 Reprinted in Eudora Welty, *The Bride of the Innisfallen and Other Stories* (New York: Harcourt Brace Jovanovich, Inc., 1955), p. 140.

2 Bill Christenberry as quoted in Thomas W. Southall, *Of Time and Place: Walker Evans and William Christenberry* (San Francisco and Fort Worth: Friends of Photography and Amon Carter Museum, 1990), p. 62.

3 Welty, p. 154.

EDWARD S. CURTIS: *Cheyenne,* ca. 1900–10

Edward S. Curtis

by Timothy Troy

Arguably as famous a photographer as Ansel Adams in the minds of many Americans, Edward S. Curtis (1868–1952) has left an enormous legacy of magnificent prints and rapidly escalating market prices. The former was his ardent goal; the latter would astonish him. He died in 1952 disheartened and nearly penniless, his life's work, *The North American Indian*, all but forgotten.

A half-dozen years into the new twentieth century, Curtis, an energetic, young studio photographer and mountain guide in Seattle, launched a photographic project the scope and obsessiveness of which remains unparalleled in the history of the medium. The cultures of the vanquished natives of the North American continent, Curtis had determined, would soon die out. He decided he would create a photographic record of them for the world, and in many ways—thirty years, tens of thousands of miles, and forty thousand prints later—he succeeded in doing just that.

With extraordinary energy and perseverance (and best wishes from none other than Theodore Roosevelt), Curtis crisscrossed North America to record the lives of Native Americans in over eighty different tribes and bands west of the Mississippi and north into Alaska and the Bering Strait. He saw his images as "transcriptions for future generations that they might behold the Indian as nearly lifelike as possible." By all accounts Curtis was a gifted field worker for his time, developing for the most part an easy rapport with the people he visited and establishing lasting friendships. He met and photographed many of the grand old warriors, Chief Joseph and Geronimo among them, and he was deeply moved by his subjects. Much less known than his photographic work, Curtis and his crews collected more than ten thousand wax cylinder recordings of music, stories, and myths in dozens of indigenous languages. These are now housed at the Library of Congress. He lectured tirelessly to raise money for his project and was rewarded with sporadic infusions of large amounts of money from the likes of J. Pierpont Morgan. He even made a feature-length film about the Kwakiutl Indians of the Pacific Northwest entitled *In the Land of the Headhunters*—a huge, costly, Hollywood-esque production which Curtis futilely hoped would help him finance his bigger Indian project. Indeed, Curtis—later in life—worked in Hollywood as a still photographer.

One of Curtis's problems was that he came late to the photography of the American Indian. Dozens of other capable photographers, like Ben Wittick, Timothy O'Sullivan, William Bell, and William Henry Jackson, had preceded him into the American West in the last half of the nineteenth century, particularly when the federal government launched great geological and geographical surveys. Scientists, artists, and photographers accompanied these expeditions to record all that they observed.

With little more than a third-grade education, Curtis, although he was a successful society portrait photographer in Seattle, was not exposed to the more sophisticated new trends in field anthropology being developed by people like Franz Boas. Curtis's was very much an infatuated involvement with his subjects; his images, for the most part, come from a romantic tradition of the photography of native peoples as exotic subjects. Though he was able to persuade Frederick Webb Hodge, Chief of the Bureau of American Ethnology, to become his editor, many academicians were understandably critical of Curtis's zeal. He was—when all is said and done—an artist-adventurer who had thrown himself into the middle of their profession.

In 1982, Christopher Lyman published, through the Smithsonian Institution, *The Vanishing Race and Other Illusions: Photographs of Indians by Edward Curtis*. It was the first critical exposé of Curtis's often-dubious practices in "ethnographical" photography. Not always finding his subjects in the kinds of traditional dress he envisioned that they should be wearing, Curtis traveled with a chest full of appropriate "authentic" costumes. Subsequently, individuals from tribes far apart in miles and cultural belief sometimes appear in the exact same outfit. At Curtis's direction, his studio staff (headed for years by the superb technician, Adolph Muhr) regularly doctored glass plates and final prints. Unwanted objects, such as automobiles, were removed.

In all fairness to Curtis, the practice of staging photographs among native peoples was not something unique to him. The whole process in the nineteenth century of engaging in what historians now call "the photography of the other" was nearly always daunting both for the photographer and for the subject, *l'exotique*, who, after all, had to sit or stand frozen for long periods of time in front of a large, bulky, black box that seemed to be gaping with a single eye. There is more often than not a wariness, if not terror or hostility, in the expressions of those being photographed.

By Curtis's time, at the outset of the twentieth century, the photographic process was less cumbersome and the subjects—most of them—were all too aware of "white men" and their cameras. Curtis's natives are often smiling; sometimes they appear slightly bored. But mostly, just beneath the surface, there seems to be a sad resignation. Wariness has become weariness in the countenances of the old men.

Ironically, the images in *The North American Indian*—as hauntingly lit and memorable as they are—are, in the final analysis, ethnographically nearly worthless, or, at best, are flawed as evidential records of "pre-contact" indigenous cultures. The "way of life" that Curtis had sorely wanted to find and record had evolved through the process of acculturation into something quite different, and he was forced to recreate his romantic conceptions of the "way it must have been."

Interestingly for researchers, two complete sets of *The North American Indian* are housed on the University of Arizona campus, one in Special Collections of the University of Arizona Library, and one in the Arizona State Museum. This is remarkable given the fact that, of the approximately three hundred sets printed in Curtis's time, it is estimated that only about one hundred remain unpillaged. The complete sets consist of twenty volumes of text each illustrated with small photogravures (approximately fifteen hundred prints total in the twenty volumes). Accompanying each text volume is a portfolio of thirty-six or more larger photogravures. An intact set therefore contains close to twenty-five hundred images.

Louise Dahl-Wolfe

by Jennifer Edwards

Louise Dahl-Wolfe (1895–1989) is best known as a fashion photographer. Her tenure at *Harper's Bazaar* from 1936 until 1958, a period when the journal was at the vanguard of dramatic changes to the style and content of women's magazines, provided her with this particular prestige. Although she is generally recognized for her astute and early use of color photography to illustrate fashion, a closer examination of Dahl-Wolfe's black-and-white photography at the Center for Creative Photography reveals a much more complex photographer. Through the masterful combination of artistic skill, art historical knowledge, cultural consciousness, and aesthetic refinement, Dahl-Wolfe created images that surpass mere advertising work and constitute important contributions to the history of photography.

Dahl-Wolfe's early art training and mentors helped to establish her aesthetic awareness and interest in photography. She enrolled at the San Francisco Art Institute in 1914 and studied design, composition, art history, anatomy, light values, and color theory. As a young painter, Dahl-Wolfe became discouraged when one of her teachers criticized her work, and around 1919 she started to translate all she had previously learned into photography. She cites Annie Brigman as her primary photographic inspiration, although Consuelo Kanaga, whom she met through Brigman, had a greater influence by teaching Dahl-Wolfe how to balance commercial work with independent creativity. The two photographers often took pictures of the San Francisco Bay area together and, beginning in 1927, did the same in Italy and North Africa. Beyond practicing photography, Dahl-Wolfe's yearlong journey throughout France, Austria, Germany, Hungary, Italy, and Tunisia allowed her to learn about other cultures, view significant works of art, and nurture her independent spirit. She also met the man who became her husband for over fifty-six years, Meyer (Mike) Wolfe, a painter and sculptor who provided her with constant creative and professional support.

In 1932, Dahl-Wolfe returned with her husband to his home state of Tennessee. While there, she photographed rural life during the Great Depression. In addition to being sympathetic portraits, these images illustrate Dahl-Wolfe's aesthetic concerns. By photographing on a daily basis, she could concentrate on making various lighting conditions, still-life objects, and backgrounds benefit her subject via both visual and material information. These images were responsible for launching her into commercial photography when Frank Crowninshield, publisher of *Vanity Fair*, printed some in his magazine. Beaumont Newhall also incorporated four of the Tennessee pictures as examples of straight photographic portraiture in *Photography 1839–1937*, the first major American photography exhibition held at the Museum of Modern Art.

Joining the staff of *Harper's Bazaar* as a fashion photographer in 1936, Dahl-Wolfe arrived at an ideal time; major changes in magazine publishing and fashion photography were underway, and there was ample room for individual creative innovations. Carmel

LOUISE DAHL-WOLFE: *Japanese Bath, Betty Threat, Model*, 1954

Snow, the editor-in-chief, was adamant about maintaining high standards of quality and laying out the magazine to insure each issue's distinctive visual pace. Born and educated in Europe, Alexey Brodovitch, who Snow hired as art director, brought revolutionary design transformations to the pages of *Harper's Bazaar*. He understood the importance of contemporary art ideas in commercial design for capturing the reader's attention and creating a dynamic, unified work. Brodovitch also believed photography was a key component of the new appearance of *Harper's Bazaar* and instilled in his photography staff the need to turn to both past and contemporary art for inspiration.

As a newcomer to the field, Dahl-Wolfe initially looked to the fashion work of photographers such as Martin Munkacsi and Man Ray for photographic sources, though she quickly began to draw upon her own vast knowledge and experience to create her signature style. For example, Munkacsi was one of the first photographers to illustrate fashion on women active in the outdoors. Dahl-Wolfe did not accept Munkacsi's outdoor scenes simply because they were the latest style in photography, but rather because they represented contemporary cultural trends. Women were becoming more active and could travel; therefore, they needed appropriate attire. Dahl-Wolfe's modernist aesthetic sensibilities were important in featuring contemporary backgrounds and considering compositional relationships between the model, setting, and camera frame. She often capitalized on forms and patterns found in nature or on location that were similar to those illustrated in art; floor tiles, mirrors, and architecture reflected qualities of European art movements such as cubism and constructivism. Taking a cue from Man Ray, she sometimes used works of art to magnify a fashion's design or its contemporary relevance: several shoots were at the Museum of Modern Art. Over time, she learned how a simple piece of paper placed in a model's hands could simulate both a key visual element and an art object.

Dahl-Wolfe's photographs are similar to theater in two ways. Visually, her studio images often appear as a well-ordered series of stage settings and props. She went to great lengths to produce such scenes. Some shoots involved elaborate set design with painted backdrops, such as one depicting Chinese calligraphy created by Mike Wolfe or, in another case, a complete recreation of a Japanese bath. The photographic results of such efforts varied between an artificial stage effect in the former to a more natural film screen quality in the latter. Professionally, Dahl-Wolfe also directed all stages of photographic production. This freedom extended to working out of her own studio and having a voice in the final placement of her images. The only predetermined components were the specific garments and celebrities assigned to her to photograph. Much of this was possible because Snow and Brodovitch had the utmost confidence that the photographers they hired were talented and fully capable of contributing to the exciting new character of *Harper's Bazaar* if given complete creative license. Her position as one of the magazine's primary photographers is demonstrated upon examining the volume and content of the work she produced, including a majority of assignments depicting premier fashion designs and celebrities.

In addition to documenting current fashions and art, some of Dahl-Wolfe's most notable imagery was due to the subject rather than her artistic influence. She photographed her contemporaries from literature, fashion, art, photography, film, and theater.

Pages from handwritten diary of Dahl-Wolfe's travels in Italy and Greece with small gelatin silver prints made in Venice, 1927

Harper's Bazaar press pass for the 1939 New York World's Fair

Visual index to Louise Dahl-Wolfe's photographs for *Harper's Bazaar* magazine, January 1941

LOUISE DAHL-WOLFE:
Edward Hopper, Standing, 1933

Carson McCullers, Gabrielle (Coco) Chanel, Jean Cocteau, Margaret Bourke-White, Ingrid Bergman, and Paul Robeson are just a few examples of her more famous subjects. There were instances when women who modeled for Dahl-Wolfe became named personalities with their own careers, as was the case with Lisa Fonssagrives (later Mrs. Irving Penn). Dahl-Wolfe also claimed that one of the *Harper's Bazaar* covers she photographed was responsible for launching Lauren Bacall's Hollywood career.

Overall, Dahl-Wolfe's photographs are straightforward and in clear focus to illustrate detailed craftsmanship, elegant design, and expressive portraits. Strong elements of design and composition became her most distinguishable trademarks. After over twenty years of developing her own photographic style, she chose to leave *Harper's Bazaar* when the new art director tried to exert his creative influence on her work. Although she continued to work for magazines such as *Sports Illustrated* and *Vogue,* she remained wary of the future of commercial photography and officially retired in 1960. Dahl-Wolfe was a strong-willed woman who chose to give up her career rather than relinquish the creative freedom she had coveted for her entire life as a photographer.

Although confident as a photographer, Dahl-Wolfe declared she was not an artist. In apparent contrast to this conviction, she acknowledged that her work was artistic by donating her entire monochrome collection to the Center for Creative Photography, an institution dedicated to photography as a form of art. Exploration of this collection from as many different vantage points as possible will result in the discovery of outstanding photographic examples that challenge our attitudes about art, photography, and commercial images.

Andreas Feininger

by Stuart Alexander

Although the photographer Dennis Stock posed for *The Photojournalist* as part of a series of symbolic portraits of various professions, it could well be a self-portrait of Andreas Feininger (1906–1999). It serves as a metaphor for Feininger's career in photography. A bold, clear, and direct presentation of a man's head, his face merged with a camera, it reflects the characteristics of Feininger's style. It also demonstrates his close identification with the medium—a life immersed in photography.

Andreas Feininger was the oldest of three sons of the New York born painter Lyonel Feininger. Born in Paris and raised in Germany, Andreas Feininger studied cabinetmaking at the Bauhaus and architecture in Zerbst. Certainly, his creative sensibility began at home. Living and studying at the Bauhaus, he absorbed the attitude toward experimentation that contributed to the "New Photography," the use of extreme close-ups, negative printing, severe angles and perspectives. He wrote, "I always strive to produce images which show the viewer more than he would (and often could) have seen had he been confronted with my subject in reality."

ANDREAS FEININGER:
The Photojournalist Dennis Stock, Winner of the LIFE Young Photographers Contest, 1951

Changing economic and political circumstances took him to Paris for a brief time and then to Sweden in 1933 where he found that, because of his American citizenship, practicing architecture was forbidden to him. He quickly filled the need there for a good architectural photographer and began to refine his craft.

He moved to New York in 1939 and shortly afterward met the charismatic and powerful associate editor of *Life* magazine, Wilson Hicks. From 1941 to 1962, Feininger completed a prodigious number of assignments for the magazine, well over three hundred. Hicks also provided him with the opportunity to produce *New York* (1945), his first influential book of photographs of the city. Included are some of the finest pictures he ever made. Feininger had ideas about the vitality, density, and excitement of the city he wanted to communicate. There were difficult visual problems to solve. He used his cabinetmaking skills to perfect a super-telephoto camera

ANDREAS FEININGER: *Midtown Manhattan Seen from Weehawken, New Jersey, 1942*

that he had first experimented with to portray the giant ships in Stockholm harbor in proper perspective to the buildings in the background. He put this equipment to brilliant use in New York in pictures, such as the one of the ocean liner *United States* passing before the Manhattan skyline and the foreshortened crowds on Fifth Avenue. These pictures have been copied so many times they are clichés now, but when they were first presented to millions of *Life* readers they were a revelation. From the early sixties until the end of his life, Andreas Feininger remained true to his beginnings and spent the better part of his time working independently on his book projects.

His fascination and curiosity about the world drove him. He loved cities, particularly New York where he lived and to which he devoted several of his books, but he spent nearly half of the year surrounded by nature at his country home in Connecticut. Many of his books are devoted to forms in nature. This passion took him all over the world to photograph for his book *Trees*. The researcher will note that his archive includes feathers, shells, and stones that he gathered and photographed.

Feininger wrote, "good presentation means three things: clarity, simplicity and organization. I found this most easy to accomplish by keeping my means and equipment simple." But that did not prevent him from using exotic fish-eye lenses or building his own elaborate super-telephoto lenses out of interlocking wooden boxes if he needed them to create precisely the image he believed would convey the quintessence of his subject.

Feininger is one of those rare figures to influence generations of photographers all over the world as much through his writing about how to effectively use the medium as through his images themselves. He authored well over forty books; some have been translated into more than a dozen languages. From his first book in 1934, and over the ensuing sixty-plus years, a large proportion of his titles are instructive manuals on how to make better pictures. For more than fifteen years he wrote a monthly article for *Modern Photography* magazine. They are never plain how-to texts. He stresses using a creative imagination to get the maximum out of the tools at hand. His prose is as clear and straightforward as the poetry of his photographs.

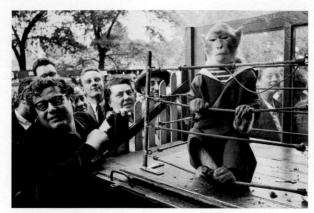

ROBERT DOISNEAU: *Les animaux supérieurs*, 1954

in 1974 and 1976 at the end of his career (with a side jaunt to England) were his only trips to Europe. Brassaï had visited Adams in 1973 in California, and Plossu also visited him that year.

The personal collection of Aaron Siskind includes two photographs by Lucien Clergue, and two toned vegetal studies by Denis Brihat. Edward Weston's collection of works by others includes four photographs by Daniel Masclet, whose "grande rencontre" with Weston in 1933 changed the direction of his career.

The experimental, surreal emphasis of photography in France is illustrated in the CCP's collection by American-born Man Ray's 1931 portfolio of photograms, *Électricité*, commissioned by Paris's electric utility company; by two hand-colored images from German-born Hans Bellmer's 1930s series *Les Jeux de la Poupée*; by a superimposed

image of the Pont Marie by Denise Colomb from 1950; a solarized 1948 portrait by Maurice Tabard; and by ten chemically altered and toned images by Jean-Pierre Sudre from his 1979 series *Végétal & Insectes*. This tradition is most recently represented with a toned photogram by Patrick Bailly-Maître-Grand, from his series *Les Nipponnes d'eau*; and by a toned paper-negative image from Laurent Millet's *Petite Machine Littorale* series. One may also mention in this context the work of the Belgian photographer Pierre Cordier, whose "chemigrammes" or chemically altered photograms were mostly received as part of the Aaron Siskind Collection. The Center has the collaborative portfolio by Pablo Picasso and French photographer André Villers, *Diurnes* (1962), that consists of thirty collaged photograms in a case silkscreened by Picasso.

The Center's only research collection of a French photographer is that

BRASSAÏ: *Le passage cloute*, 1937

JEAN-PIERRE SUDRE: Untitled, 1979
From the series *Végétal & Insectes*

of Bernard Plossu, begun in 1983 while he was living in New Mexico, shortly before his return to France. Plossu's peripatetic career began when he accompanied a group to Mexico in 1965/66 as photographer, though he had virtually no experience at the time. Born in Vietnam, he first visited Niger with his father when he was thirteen; he is enamored of arid regions, "le jardin de poussière," as one of his many books is titled. His dropped-horizon, intimate, playful, often out-of-focus views contrast dramatically with the formal, exacting images of Paul Strand, whose geographic trajectory Plossu overlaps. The fine print collection includes all of Plossu's images reproduced in *The African Desert*, published by The University of Arizona Press in 1987 with royalties to benefit CARE's drought relief efforts. There are also four of his prints rendered in the four-color Fresson process, and toned images from New Mexico and North Africa. The Center also has a sizable representation of images by Philippe Salaün, who formerly printed for Plossu.

GISÈLE FREUND: *Hôtel du Châtelet, Paris*, 1952

German Photography

by Marcia Tiede

The Center's collection of German photography represents more than forty photographers covering the entire twentieth century. Perhaps the highlight of the Center's German holdings is a significant group of prints by Bauhaus students and faculty—Lotte Beese, Katt Both, Hannes Meyer, Heinz Loew, Umbo, and others—as well as other experimental German photographers of the late 1920s and early 1930s—Franz Roh,

FLORIS M. NEUSÜSS: *Engel*, 1967

Werner Rohde, and Friedrich Seidenstucker. This group of fifty-eight vintage prints was acquired from the Rudolf Kicken Galerie (Cologne) in 1982. The Umbo work includes later images made while traveling through the United States in 1952. The CCP also has Umbo's portfolio of ten photographs published in 1980, the year of his death.

The holdings of Bauhaus-related materials continue with sixty-nine photographs by Herbert Bayer generously donated by the artist. This collection originally constituted a traveling exhibition sponsored by ARCO in the late 1970s. Bayer spent the years 1921 through 1928 at the Bauhaus, first as a student, then a faculty member in several areas. From 1928 until his emigration to the United States a decade later, he worked in advertising and exhibition design, while still pursuing his own photography. With the exception of one image, this collection concentrates on the period from 1925 to 1937.

The Center's early twentieth-century German collection includes three bromoil and bromoil transfer prints by Heinrich Kühn from 1910 and circa 1920, acquired also from the Rudolf Kicken Galerie. Kühn is also represented in the CCP's holdings of *Camera Work*, along with Theodor and Oscar Hofmeister. The CCP has six vintage prints by August Sander from the 1920s and early 1930s, mostly obtained through the Halsted Gallery; and a nude study by Wilhelm von Gloeden made in Taormina, Sicily, around 1900. Karl

WERNER ROHDE: *Karneval*, ca. 1928

LOTTE BEESE: Untitled [Hannes Meyer], ca. 1928

Blossfeldt's portfolio of twelve magnified plant studies from 1900 to 1928, produced by Galerie Wilde in Cologne, 1975, was an early acquisition.

Recent German photography in the Center's collection includes a steel plant triptych by Bernd and Hilla Becher; thirty photograms by Floris M. Neusüss from the 1960s to the 1980s; two traumatized self-portraits by Hermann Försterling; several images by Bastienne Schmidt, including one from her series *Vivir la Muerte*; and an image by Max Becher and his American collaborator Andrea Robbins. Six images made in the early 1980s by Stefan Diller were acquired as part of the Ansel and Virginia Adams Collection. Other contemporary German photographers with minor holdings at the CCP are Verena von Gagern, Arno Jansen, Klaus Kammerichs, Andreas Müller-Pohle, Sigmar Polke, Heinrich Riebesehl, Thomas Ruff, and Peter von zur Muehlen.

A related high point of the CCP's collections is a cluster of extensive archives of German émigré photographers who came to the United States before and during World War II. These include Josef Breitenbach, John Gutmann, Hansel Mieth and Otto Hagel, Marion Palfi, Adolf Fassbender, and Andreas Feininger. The CCP has, as well, smaller collections of work by German-born photographers such as Ruth Bernhard, Yolla Niclas Sachs, Ruth-Marion Baruch, and Hans Namuth. Fritz Henle, who emigrated from Germany to the United States in 1936 and worked for *Life* and *Harper's Bazaar* magazines between 1937 and 1950, is represented by over seventy prints, including a selection from his one-person exhibition at the Witkin Gallery in 1980; his diverse works include a few industrial images made in Germany in 1930, and postwar images of Krupp Works, mostly from 1964. Frederick Sommer and Sonya Noskowiak, both of German parentage and raised in South America (Brazil and Chile), are also represented by substantial collections.

RALPH GIBSON: *Complutensian Polyglot Bible, Pierpont Morgan Library,* 2000

Ralph Gibson (b. 1939) is such an articulate artist that we can almost present this essay in his own words. Unlike many artists who do not like to talk about their art, Gibson enjoys discussing and writing about his work. During Gibson's quarter-century relationship with the Center, the Ralph Gibson Archive has grown beyond a fine print collection to include writings, correspondence, business records, videotapes, and press sheets and design plans from his publishing projects. His life and work can be examined from different perspectives.

Captured on videotape in the gallery talk on 4 May 2001, for his exhibition *Ex Libris*, Gibson said:

> *My relationship with the Center started in 1975 when Harold Jones came to visit me in my studio. He was founding director [of the Center]. He said he would like to make an archive.*
>
> *I said, "I'm only thirty. I'm so young to have an archive."*
>
> *He said, "Well, the reason we're inviting you to have an archive [is that] we don't know anything about the creative process in living art photographers. Most archives are of dead masters. We want to start with living masters."*
>
> *Of course, saying something like that to me opened a very wide vista. I took it very seriously.*
>
> *Through thick and thin, I've always wanted to be a photographer. I still want to be a photographer. And I know I'm only as good as my next photograph. I profoundly believe that. That is my modus operandi, my raison d'être. Of course, it is encouraging to see these works on the wall. It does give me strength to hold the new book in my hands. But, I've shot about ten rolls here in Tucson in the last few days. I'm very anxious to go home and develop them. Because that is the real barometer— that's how we know we're still there.*
>
> *Marcel Duchamp said, "An artist owes it to his or her work to get it out, to get it seen."*
>
> *I use the book as that. This show is exclusive. It's only going to be around for a month or two. The book is going to be around for a long time. . . . I decided to make a book about a dreamer— The Somnambulist. I was thirty . . . I had already been a photographer for thirteen years. I had to self-publish it to get it right.*
>
> *The book was very successful. It established me in a very small field— art photography. I was known. I went from starving. My cameras were pawned. And in about three months I was starting to be invited to lecture and shows and things like that.*
>
> *I discovered by following my own inner needs. By taking the pictures that I wanted to take, that I needed to take, I was going to have a career. I could make*

a living just doing my thing. Now it's forty years later. I'm sixty-two. I still feel the same way— I am only as good as my next photograph.[1]

The CCP Research Center includes hundreds of videotapes of public presentations, commercial tapes about specific artists, and interviews with photographers by knowl-

edgeable Center staff members. These began when the opening of the Center was recorded in black and white on a half-inch open-reel tape deck and continued through 3/4-inch U-matic interviews, to camcorder documentation of public presentations. These tapes capture both image and sound and are made in the spirit of oral histories. Most are unedited raw footage intended for research use in the Center. Tapes are duplicated for preservation and playback in current tape formats in the Center's Library.

In 1987 when Gibson came to work with us on *Ralph Gibson: Early Work*, issue 24 of *The Archive*, we recorded an interview by then-Director James Enyeart, who worked with Gibson on his archive for twelve years. Enyeart asked why there were so few words in his books.

Ralph Gibson Gallery Talk on 4 May 2001

The reason that I don't put words — I am interested in visual syntax. I am interested in the language of photography. I know that there is something that photography can say that hasn't been said and I personally believe that in so saying a definition of the medium that I can accept will be informed.[2]

Gibson's photography books were so crucial to his career that he discussed them in the CCP tapes made fourteen years apart. I had read that Gibson spent three years preparing grids and layouts for *The Somnambulist*[3] and had always been interested in Lustrum's position in the history of the photographic book. Hearing his tapes again prompted me to examine the material from Lustrum Press, which Gibson co-founded, in the Center's Research Center. One large storage box is devoted to Gibson's first book *The Somnambulist*. Among the loose press proofs, I found a handwritten diary, on a folded press sheet, describing what he learned day by day at the printer's—about his work and reproducing it.

Oct. 26 [1970], 9:30 am

Here at Rapid for the second day — one form almost done already — Neil, my pressman, on this book is a superb lithographer—

. . .

I couldn't sleep last night. Dreams of the printing of the book or else just plain tossing + turning around thinking of the project.

. . .

I expected to be exhausted but wasn't. In fact being here at Rapid, overseeing my own job, discovering the pitfalls of my sloppy technique, etc. is really a good experience. This is a tremendously exciting job.

. . .

Oct. 28, 10:30

Now I'm certain that the single spot varnish was the way to go — The images are pulsing on the page — Deep, rich black. Varnishing isn't easy — Perfect register is mandatory or the images will ghost just like in the duo-tone — I've learned a tremendous amount about how it can <u>extend</u> the feeling of a photograph — whereas I've always felt that reproduced images could be superior, actually are superior to the original, I had never seen my own work so treated — I'm really very happy and also feel that the few discrepancies I had noticed + lamented throughout the job are not really so severe and even noticeable as I had made them appear within my head — It's all O.K.

This spot varnish process has drawn my attention to the relationship of whites to blacks in my work. The way my eye relates to both colors + what it does with them. Obviously there are far more areas of black than white in my vision, and the space that I'm so interested in looking [at] is to be gotten thru my use of Black as POSITIVE space rather than as a negative — (The way most photographers do it!).

. . .

As I see these varnished sheets come of[f] the press + appreciate their beautiful tones, I realize that "My Satisfaction is Complete."[4]

On the 1987 tape, James Enyeart asked, "What does it mean to have an archive?"

Gibson responded: "It's highly layered. Looking at photography, remembering my life. It lent a great deal of purpose. I wouldn't have taken care."

Having seen Atget's scribbles in French about his chemistry, Gibson mentioned how intrigued he was by the potential scholarly use of his ephemera. Clearly though, it was the photograph collection that captured Gibson's attention, particularly because he knew he would be encountering his early work again for *The Archive* project.

Gibson dreamed about his archive:

I had a big dream about all my life's work—a very unpleasant dream. It had to do with looking at work that came from a difficult time in my life.

I used to think I was making a great sacrifice. I now realize that to have done anything else would have been the sacrifice. In the course of making this noble decision, I passed through a lot of very difficult times. Times of great stress. Times of great anxiety and dissatisfaction. I clung to my work as my only sense of myself I could possibly see. There was no other sense of self. There was no home. I never reckoned that I would have the life I have now. I was prepared to settle for considerably less like some of our great American masters—Callahan, Siskind, Sommer; they are the guys who paid the price for my generation.[5]

From the oral history materials on videotape alone, one can learn about Gibson's uncomfortable Catholic boyhood, his early desire to be a photojournalist, and what he learned as an assistant to Dorothea Lange. Although Gibson is known for the quality

Ralph Gibson's *Hands Over Prow*, 1969, was the cover image for his first Lustrum Press book — *The Somnambulist*

What it does with them - Obviously there
are far more areas of Black than white
in my vision, and the space that I'm
so interested in looking is to be gotten thru
my use of Black as a POSITIVE space
rather than as a negative — (The
way most photographers did!)

⊣⊢

As I see these varnished
sheets come of the press & appreciate
their beautiful tones, I realize
that "My Satisfaction is Complete!"

Above: Page from Gibson's handwritten diary describing his experience press checking
   The Somnambulist at Rapid Printers in 1970
Below: Press sheets from *The Somnambulist*
Ralph Gibson Archive

of his silver prints, one can also see and hear an artist who embraced commercial technologies for artistic purposes and broader communication, right down to integrating digital imaging into his creative process for his newest work in both the *Ex Libris* Iris prints and book.

If materials about the artist offer additional levels of understanding, they do not present the whole picture. Gibson himself stated the caveat concerning this type of inquiry: "The artist and the art are quite separate entities." The Ralph Gibson Archive also provides the opportunity to see the more than three hundred prints themselves: his nudes, abstractions of European architecture, faces, and books; and photographs with recurring motifs, such as the human hand, captured gesture, and explorations of light and shadow.

1 Ralph Gibson, *Ex Libris* exhibition gallery talk, videotape (Tucson: Center for Creative Photography, 4 May 2001).

2 "Ralph Gibson Interviewed by James Enyeart," videotape (Tucson: Center for Creative Photography, 1987).

3 Thomas Dugan, "Ralph Gibson," in *Photography between Covers* (Rochester, New York: Light Impressions, 1979), p. 50.

4 Ralph Gibson, handwritten diary on a folded press sheet, 26–28 October 1970, Ralph Gibson Archive, Center for Creative Photography.

5 "Ralph Gibson Interviewed by James Enyeart."

Laura Gilpin

by Timothy Troy

Spanning nearly seventy years, the photographic career of Laura Gilpin (1891–1979) was one of struggle and determination, of disappointment and jubilation. She was in every sense a pioneer—a woman in a genre that was dominated by men. To follow her life from her early pictorialist years as a student in the Clarence White School between 1916 and 1918 to her final projects in the 1970s is, in effect, to study the history and stylistic breadth of twentieth-century photography itself. She was an accomplished craftswoman as well as an extraordinarily gifted artist. Over the years she experimented with many photographic techniques using a wide range of processes, cameras, and lenses. She is still considered by many who know her work to be one of the greatest masters of platinum printing.

Gilpin was born in Colorado. She was sent East to boarding schools and attended the New England Conservatory of Music briefly. But, with the exception of these few years and those spent in New York studying with Max Weber, Paul Anderson, and others, she lived and photographed in the American West, particularly Colorado and New Mexico, and in Mexico. She is probably best known now for her work among the Navajo and Pueblo Indians and for her documentation of the great Mayan prehistoric sites of the Yucatan, but she was also an exceptional portraitist and architectural photographer.

Remarkably resourceful, Gilpin never shied away from supporting herself through commercial photographic work and brought to those remunerative assignments the same dedication and discipline she did to her own artistic projects. When her family fell on hard times before World War I, she established a poultry business and later, with her lifelong friend Elizabeth Forster, owned a turkey ranch outside of Colorado Springs. From 1942 to 1944 she found work as a photographer for the Boeing company in Wichita, Kansas, taking pictures of B-29 bombers, aircraft workers, and visiting dignitaries. She would have preferred working for Roy Stryker in the Office of War Information, but he turned her down saying that he thought the photographs of Pueblo Indians she had sent him were too much in the soft-focus, romantic tradition of an earlier photographic era.

Gilpin should be remembered as much for her remarkable sense of book artistry as she is for her photography. Her professional life essentially consisted of a series of challenging book projects for which she struggled constantly to find support and publishers. Starting with a series of informational brochures on the Pike's Peak region and Mesa Verde National Park, Gilpin not only took the photographs for her publications but also often designed them and researched and wrote the accompanying texts. *The Pueblos: A Camera Chronicle* was published in 1941, followed *by Temples in Yucatan: A Camera Chronicle of Chichen Itza* in 1948 and *The Rio Grande: River of Destiny* in 1949. The quality of the images in these books remains remarkable even as one views them more than fifty years after their publication. The published reproductions, however, were never of the superb quality of the original prints. Indeed, not until after her death—in *Laura Gilpin: Early Work*, published by the CCP in 1981, and in Martha Sandweiss's biography,

LAURA GILPIN: *Cornice—Temple of Kukulcan, Chichen Itza, Yucatan, 1932*

Laura Gilpin, An Enduring Grace—do we see illustrations approximating the tonal beauty of her actual photographs. Gilpin's texts were generally authoritative, though she was sometimes criticized for broad generalizations about native American people, a falling back on cultural relativism which had become passé.

In 1968 after many years of work and travel, Gilpin finally published perhaps her finest book, *The Enduring Navaho*. Beginning in 1930 she and Betsy Forster had travelled as often as possible into the Four Corners region of the Southwest to photograph Anasazi ruins and desert and canyon landscapes. They had seen there, too, for the first time the Navajo people. In 1931, Forster took a position as a field nurse in Red Rock in the heart of the Navajo reservation, and over a period of several years, both women developed lasting friendships with people in and near the small community. Intervening years and other projects did not dissuade Gilpin from envisioning a major work on the Navajo, but like Edward Curtis before her, she had to continually struggle for sponsors and a publisher for her project. Having moved to Santa Fe in 1945, she continued to support herself and Betsy, who had become an invalid, through slide lectures, contract work with museums in Santa Fe, publishing commercial postcards and Christmas cards, and selling images to magazines and stock agencies.

The Enduring Navaho was finally published in 1968 after eighteen years of perseverance on Gilpin's part. It is a wonderfully integrated book of texts and images, portraits and landscapes. As if in contradiction to Edward Curtis's sense of the "vanishing" Indian, the book is a testament to Gilpin's sense—arrived at over many years of journeying to and from Navajo country—that these were a people who could endure and retain most of their culture in the face of apparently overwhelming odds.

In speaking to Martha Sandweiss, Gilpin's biographer, the anthropologist and photographer John Collier, Jr., said: "Laura was a photographer in the grand tradition and a profound humanist, which is often the case with fine photographers. Her winning point was that she never let photography as a craft come between Laura and the Navajos . . . [her] accomplishment remains her extreme emotional bridge between her subject and herself THROUGH the lens of her camera."

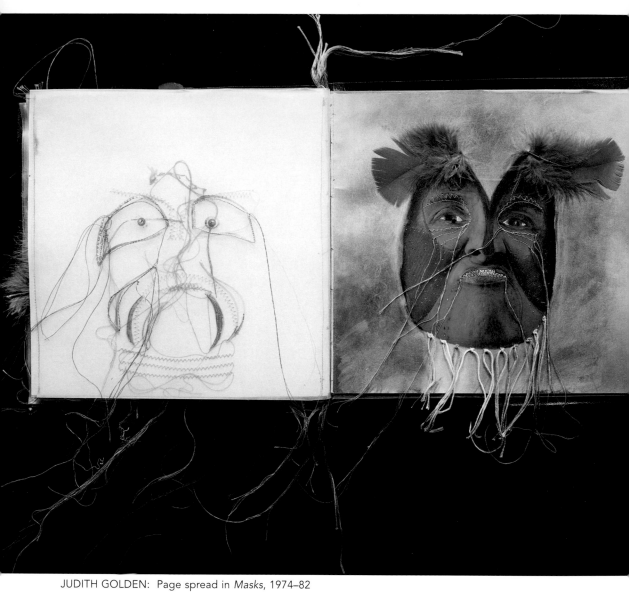

JUDITH GOLDEN: Page spread in *Masks*, 1974–82

Judith Golden

by Cass Fey

Few things serve a museum educator as well as an original object that stimulates the imagination and eagerly encourages exploration by all who view it, regardless of their age or experience. The artist's book, *Masks, 1974–1982*, by Judith Golden (b. 1934), is that kind of remarkable resource. Turning the pages of *Masks* to reveal its rich and unexpected imagery has motivated elementary students to burst into spontaneous applause—their expectations of what a photograph should or could be forever changed. Advanced high school art classes have studied this piece in preparation for creating their own portraits; they are keenly observant of Golden's engagement with color, use of unconventional materials, and of her vigorous embellishment of the print surface. This work has also inspired compelling reflective essays, written by university English students who analyzed the work for what it communicates regarding issues such as identity, illusion, and transformation.

The concept of a photograph representing more than a point-and-shoot capturing of a moment is new territory for most classes visiting the Center, as is the experience of viewing an artist's book. The museum's galleries and PrintViewing area attract art classes of all levels, but by far the majority of students have little knowledge of fine art photography. They come to discover what they can learn from studying photographs as conveyors of creative expression and meaning. Seeing *Masks*, comprised of a sequence of self-portraits that have been imaginatively assembled, stitched, and remade by the artist's hand, gives new insights into the photographer's role as inventor, explorer, and insightful communicator. While hearing about the artist and viewing her work, students learn that the treatment and presentation of the images and the sequence and construction of the book represent Golden's personal views and vision, which have been formed through cultural, social, and aesthetic influences.

Trained as a printmaker and painter, Golden has never been interested in making traditional imagery: her work is known for its innovative alternative techniques and for its combinations of photography and mixed media. She began incorporating photographs into printmaking pieces while studying at the School of the Art Institute of Chicago in the late 1960s. When her focus changed to photography, she continued working the print surface by hand, intuitively coloring with oils and pastels, and layering with textures and collage. A book arts class with Keith Smith, and another class requiring her to "make art with a machine," led Golden to include sewing techniques in her work. This was natural for someone who had enjoyed sewing her own clothes, as her mother had before her. At the University of California, Davis, where she earned her M.F.A. in 1975, Golden found a more relaxed attitude toward art. There she was introduced to the found objects, brilliant colors, and humor of "Funk" art and, as a result, her own work became larger, brighter, and more playful.

For some time, issues of illusion and reality in photography have been at the heart

JUDITH GOLDEN: *Persona #10*, 1983
From the *Persona Series*, 1982–85

of Golden's work. In *Masks*, she incorporated long, flowing threads and feathers—actual materials rather than the illusion of textures and objects seen in the image. By design, collage elements move and occupy three-dimensional space in contrast to a static, flat print. Golden is well aware of the power of the photograph to suggest to viewers that they are seeing something real. When looking at a photograph of a chair, for instance, she explains that someone is more likely to say, "This is a chair," rather than, "This is a photograph of a chair," as is often the case when discussing other media. Golden contradicts this notion of photographic "reality" by applying real materials to the mechanically produced print.

The artist's interest in disguise, fantasy, and transformation has been influenced by many ideas such as natural cycles, rituals, societal roles and expectations, theatrical masks, and identity issues. After moving to Tucson in 1981 to teach at the University of Arizona, she began studying the ceremonial paint and masks of native cultures, which "conceal the individual self but reveal the universal spirit." In her own culture, "the facades people wear" to assume specific social roles are especially relevant. Each day we adjust and vary facial expressions and attitudes when relating to different people in order to fit in, assert individuality, communicate feelings, or present another aspect of our identity. These issues have resurfaced and evolved through portrait sequences such as *Chameleon* series (1975–76), *Magazine Make-Over* series (1976), *Persona* series (1982–85), *Cycles* series (1983–85), and *The Elements* (1986).

Observers are inevitably drawn into the enchanting scenario created in *Masks* while viewing its progression of increasingly larger and more lavishly decorated images. At first, they are intrigued by the exuberant expressiveness of Golden's work. By the time the plain black cover of the book has closed, students have witnessed a complex and complete metamorphosis, from recognizable portrait to mysterious magical being. In the end, through examining Golden's artistic vision, which extends far beyond the photographic surface and frame, viewers begin to understand and appreciate the ability of photography to delight, inspire, enrich, and inform.

Group f/64

by David Peeler

Group f/64 was a collection of San Francisco Bay Area photographers who, for a time in the early 1930s, shared a certain aesthetic outlook and exhibited their works together. The designation 'f/64' referred to one of the smallest lens settings then available, a technical adjustment providing exceptional clarity from an image's foreground to its background; as such, the name 'Group f/64' was an example of the tendency among twentieth-century photographers and critics to use seemingly cryptic nomenclature for what are sometimes rather simple orientations—sharpness, in the case of Group f/64.

There were six principal photographers in Group f/64. These were Ansel Adams and Willard Van Dyke, its founders; the group's aesthetic progenitor, Edward Weston; Sonya Noskowiak, Weston's protégée and live-in companion; Weston's son Brett Weston; and the well-established San Francisco photographer Imogen Cunningham. Other members included John Paul Edwards and Henry Swift—both only briefly worked in photography. Also associated with the Group were Consuelo Kanaga and Alma Lavenson, who went on to distinguished careers in photography, and Preston Holder, who became an academic anthropologist.

ANSEL ADAMS:
Boards and Thistles, South San Francisco, 1932

The Group's primary exhibition was an eighty-image show held at the M. H. de Young Memorial Museum in San Francisco from 15 November to 31 December 1932. Although there were a few landscapes in that exhibition, the tendency was toward closely focused, decontextualized images of organic subjects like plants or vegetables, or similarly composed photographs of industrial or mechanical subjects like chains or wheels. These and other f/64 images were thoroughly within a modernist photographic aesthetic, with shallow spaces, fragmentary treatments, an intense regard for the subject's physicality, a sharp rejection of narrative, and an insistence upon the purity of the photographic medium. These were qualities of what was known as straight photography, and they set the f/64 practitioners apart from the older aesthetic of pictorial photography, which was noted for techniques and expressions borrowed from painting,

Adams - 1958

In a joint interview (with dorothea Lange and Imogen Cunningham) published in U.S. Camera in August, 1955 ("Interview with Three Greats"), you told the interviewer, Herm Lenz, that you had thought about organizing a group like F:64 for two years before it happened. Was it soft-focus Pictorialism which motivated your interest in straight photography in 1930, or something more specific?

I think it was more the desire on my part to see a group formed to express the excitment of the "new approach" rather than just as a protest towards the fuzzy Pictorialism of the day. Perhaps anyone embarking on a new track subconsciously needs the support of others- hence the formation of groups, societies, and parties in all aspects of life.

AA

Adams - 1958

Any other comments you would care to make regarding Group F:64, 'straight' photography, or your own association with these principles, would be appreciated.

No- nothing in particular. The effect of Group f/64 wqs very considerable- yet hard to pin down to any one example . As I said, it is good that it did not last long enough to become a "cult".

AA

Adams - 1958

Can you trace the disbanding of Group F:64 to any single event or reason? Was it when Edward Weston withdrew from the Group? When Willard Van Dyke moved east? When the gallery at 166 Geary Street run by you and Joseph Danysh closed?

I think Group f/64 disbanded as a logical final step- it accomplished its purpose and there was no need for repetition. In fact, continuation might well have reduced its effectiveness. Edward Weston's withdrawel might have initiated the trend, but I think it would have occured anyway.

AA

Notecards with questions about Group *f/64* from George Craven, answers by Ansel Adams, 1958
George Craven Archive

an inclination toward softly focused images, and a penchant for photographs that told stories.

In their statements, the f/64 photographers styled themselves as innovators, the vanguard of a new rebellion against pictorial motifs. But this was not quite the case. For a least a quarter of a century there had been similar calls for straight photography and rejections of pictorialism in East Coast photographic circles; and during the 1910s and 1920s, Eastern photographers such as Alfred Stieglitz and Paul Strand produced images anticipating many features of the f/64 works. Yet none of this lessened the intensity of the f/64 photographers' claims, nor the breathlessness of some of their West Coast viewers. Indeed, the California pictorial photographer William Mortensen took deep offense at these new photographs. He engaged Adams in an impassioned and even snippish (on both sides) debate over the merits of straight photography, an exchange that seems almost comic given that straight photography had existed and been accepted for decades.

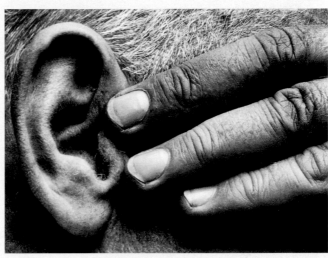

BRETT WESTON: *Three Fingers and an Ear*, 1929

Much of the intensity was self-conscious posturing on the part of the f/64 photographers. With the exception of Weston and Cunningham, most were younger artists who had come to straight photography relatively recently. With the heat and loudness of their proclamations, the f/64 photographers positioned themselves as avant-garde innovators, cutting-edge artists who deserved attention because they offered freshness in contrast to an overworked and stale expression. Additionally, there was a geographic dimension to the f/64 rhetoric, for these photographers trumpeted the significance of West Coast photography, suggesting that it was as serious and meaningful as East Coast work, and that San Francisco was just as much an art center as was New York.

But there was more than self-promotion in the f/64 photographers' presentation of themselves as radicals. Weston, Adams, and some of the others liked to think of themselves as beyond politics but in their f/64 tropes and in their other activities of the 1930s, these artists evinced some of the radical accoutrements found among other creative Americans during that tumultuous decade of petitions, demonstrations, and declarations. It is easy to see why the photographers were affected by their times. The f/64 exhibition came during the horrible winter of 1932/33, when the Great Depression was at its worst and when people suffered terrible catastrophes both human and natural. Many Americans were drawn to the Left—particularly in the photographers' neighborhood. The Bay Area was a particularly intense center of radicalization, giving rise to the bitter San Francisco General Strike of 1934, which for a time seemed to herald the arrival of open class struggle in the United States. The photographers were not immune to these developments, and in 1932, shortly before Group f/64 was formed, Weston found himself drawn to a meeting of the Communist Party's John Reed Club, a gathering where he was saluted as "Comrade" Weston. Shortly thereafter, when the f/64 photographers composed the defining proclamation of their group, they affected a radical tone that was virtually de rigueur among emergent arts and letters groups of the 1930s, calling their document the "Group f/64 Manifesto," and described themselves as engaged in a battle against a "tide of oppressive pictorialism."

Group f/64 was short-lived. Slightly more than five years after the 1932 exhibition, Van Dyke wrote that "Group f/64 no longer exists as a group of photographers exhibiting together with a common point of view." Such evanescence was perhaps natural given the qualities and circumstances that brought the photographers together. Many of their ties were more personal than programmatic, and although they shared a certain photographic persuasion or orientation, they were bound by something more like imprecisely expressed consensus than by a carefully articulated creed. Indeed, it was with remarkable speed that many of them left behind the concerns that they had displayed in the winter of 1932. In 1933, Adams traveled east for his first meeting with Stieglitz and then temporarily laid aside his camera to open a gallery in a move that was clearly imitative of Stieglitz's New York career. Van Dyke left f/64 imagery, took up the much less aestheticized motifs of documentary photography, and then went even farther afield to make political films. Similarly, in 1934 Kanaga moved to New York where she photographed for the New Masses and Daily Worker. Even Weston, who had been such a model for the others, soon abandoned his highly selective and closely focused studies of natural objects and began a massive project of photographing the West's expansive landscapes.

In its brief historical moment, Group f/64 achieved a concise and ultimately well-recognized expression. They may not have been together long, but the photographers of Group f/64 established a resonating standard for their contemporaries and successors. And thanks in large part to Weston, Adams, and the others, West Coast photography enjoyed heightened status in the American art community—a photography distinct from but not inferior to images made in the East.

Charles Harbutt

by Roxane Ramos

If looking at the work of Charles Harbutt (b. 1935) conjures a certain déjà vu, a been-there-seen-that feeling, there are good reasons. For many years a Magnum photographer, Harbutt documented some of the most memorable moments and movements of the late 1950s and 1960s—JFK's funeral, civil rights rumblings, anti-war protests, revolutionary Cuba. It is equally true to say these images are etched on our collective consciousness because Harbutt and others photographed them. Yet even when his work shifted from photojournalism to more personal explorations—from assignments to assignations—there is something familiar about the work. To call Harbutt a "voice of a generation" might have some validity, infused as the early photographs are with irony and even a veiled moral outrage. But his later scrutiny of his surroundings mark him more as

the incarnation of a sensibility, that of the modern American making sense of the post-World War II deluge—consumerism, media bombardment, urban isolation. We "recognize" Harbutt's images because they resonate in some deep, alienated, distinctly American recess within us.

CHARLES HARBUTT:
Riverdale Balcony, Riverdale, New York, 1968

There is no such thing as a neutral image. Harbutt himself explored the challenges of his medium and grappled with the relationship between reality and image, attempting to reproduce one with the other. As Harbutt acknowledges in his 1973 "Travelog" essay, a photograph does not simply record reality; it also reveals something of the imagination and sensitivities of the photographer. His photographs have shown us this all along—they are documents not only of historic events and street scenes, but of political and existential inquiry. Throughout his career, Harbutt has selected and rendered images that compel the viewer to identify with an "outsider" perspective—the disenfranchised, the exploited, the lonely.

Formally, Harbutt's work resides at the intersection where the decisive moment meets film noir. Like Cartier-Bresson before him, Harbutt was trained on the "frontlines," accustomed to the rigors and constraints of "action shots" and continued to work with a certain economy of gesture. The photographs reveal an impulsive urge to catch the image when all conditions—lighting, subjects, crop—are precisely, spontaneously right. Yet even though some photographs are happy "accidents," Harbutt's picture making is consistently shaped by his intuition and keen observation.

The compositions themselves reference the cinematic artistry of 1940s gangster films with its claustrophobic framing, disjointed juxtapositions, rich shadows, and incongruous sense of scale. Bodies are severed by the cut of the frame. Architectural details

CHARLES HARBUTT: *Scrivener, Wall Street, New York, 1970*

—beams, escalators, partitions—isolate individuals from the larger environment or press down on them ominously. Like those film noir heroes, Harbutt's subjects don't "fit."

Even when Harbutt shoots landscapes or street scenes, an incongruity is evident. There is a Harbutt image from 1963 depicting a small town street. If we have any doubt that this is Anywhere, USA, the Stars and Stripes cut across the foreground, splitting the scene in two. The message could be "Long may she wave," but probably not. Look closer. The streets are empty; the windows are dark. No one is home in this land. The photograph bespeaks a menacing peacefulness and passivity. It is a social critique without words.

There are echoes of Robert Frank and portents of Bastienne Schmidt. The viewer is forced to confront the contradictions inherent in this "land of the free." It is possible to draw affiliations with any number of photographers (there is, for example, a 1978 catalog comparing Harbutt's work with that of Kertész), but Harbutt's more relevant comrade-in-art is a painter, Edward Hopper.

CHARLES HARBUTT:
Boys Smoking in Car, Reform School, New York, 1963

Social observers both, Harbutt and Hopper are bound by an aesthetic and thematic solidarity. Both artists specialize in the vacant landscape—blocks of shadow or wall, intimidating stretches of brick or highway—and the lone figure—leaning expectantly out a window, slumped in a hotel doorway, silhouetted by harsh office light. Both depict ostensibly banal scenarios and imbue every room and road with emotional intensity. And both employ voyeuristic perspectives, "invading" private moments, devoid of self-consciousness, to illuminate the longing—our longing, an American longing—behind the facade.

Through our twenty-first-century eyes, Hopper's renderings seem fairly provincial, focusing on white New Englanders exclusively; this was the world Hopper inhabited. Harbutt, too, works within the world he knows, but it has been a wider journey, extending beyond United States borders to Cuba and Mexico. But wherever he takes his camera, Harbutt, like Hopper, is interested primarily in the human condition—a thwarted, relentless state—and only incidentally in Americana.

For this reason, Harbutt's photographs, like Hopper's paintings, still feel timely and apt. The sites and scenes may reveal regional and period restrictions, but the subjects themselves—expectation, desolation, alienation, desire—are universal and timeless. In a sense, Harbutt has picked up where Hopper left off (Hopper died in 1967), offering contemporary takes on the loneliness and disconnection behind the bravado, his own particular perspective on the state of the union, the news behind the news. And who is better positioned to make these observations than the artist, separated always from the rest of the world by a canvas or lens, watching? Harbutt has not really stopped reporting; he has merely changed the nature of his investigation. In 1969, he edited a Magnum compilation called *America in Crisis*. With his seemingly laconic, yet vigilant eye, Harbutt prods the dark underbelly of the American dream, laying bare the shadows behind American optimism and "opportunity." He is still on the frontlines, sending in stories.

ROBERT HEINECKEN: *Recto/Verso #3,* 1989
From the portfolio *Recto/Verso,* 1989

Robert Heinecken

by Stephanie Lipscomb

Cultural saboteur. Situationist prankster. *Enfant terrible* of photography. Chauvinist. The artist Robert Heinecken (b. 1931) has received many labels during his forty-year career. Yet, it has always been difficult to call him a "photographer" in the strict sense of the word, because he rarely uses a camera to make his pictures. Nor does he practice straight photography. Rather, Heinecken works on the fringes of the photographic medium—and in the margins of what might be considered acceptable subject matter for art—as an artist who only uses photography as a means to an end, but not as the end itself.

Heinecken's subject matter addresses sexuality, violence, politics, and social stratification. By pulling images from the mass media (television, magazines, mail order catalogs, and pornography), he creates work that is instantly recognizable. By manipulating this material, he invests it with a meaning that betrays its original purpose and thus uses the media's own strategies to expose and critique it. The results, while frequently humorous and absurd, flirt precariously with issues of sex and violence, consumerism, and culture. Heinecken's obsessive fondness for the materials of his craft—the pages of pornography, advertising, and fashion—has aroused considerable criticism and raised questions about his success in provoking inquiry or whether he is simply promoting the media's agenda. Undeterred, Heinecken has practiced his art consistently since 1960, showing his work and lecturing in the United States, Europe, and Japan. He retired after thirty years on the faculty of the University of California in Los Angeles in 1991. His career was the subject of a major retrospective at the Museum of Contemporary Art in Chicago in 1999. He lives and works in Chicago with his wife, the artist Joyce Neimanas.

Robert Heinecken was born in Denver, Colorado, the only child of a Lutheran minister. In 1942 the family moved to Southern California, where Heinecken attended public high school and then community college in Riverside, earning an Associate's Degree in Art in 1951. For the next two years, Heinecken studied at the University of California, Los Angeles. He dropped out in 1953 to enlist in the United States Navy, where he learned to fly airplanes. In 1954 he joined the Marine Corps as a fighter pilot. When he was discharged with the rank of Captain in 1957, Heinecken, like many others in his generation, returned to the university to complete his education on the GI Bill. He earned a B.A. degree in art in 1959 and an M.A. the following year. While in school, Heinecken concentrated mostly on printmaking, but by the end of his graduate study, he was introduced to photography and to the pre-Pop Art ideas of Robert Rauschenberg and other artists who were incorporating photographic imagery into their art. As part of his final exhibition in graduate school, Heinecken showed both straight etchings and more "experimental" etchings in which he incorporated typographic material from newspapers and magazines.

In 1960, Heinecken was appointed as an instructor in the Department of Art at UCLA, teaching drawing, design, and printmaking. Within two years he had initiated a photographic curriculum for the department and was appointed Assistant Professor in 1962, overseeing a regular series of courses in undergraduate photography. Over the next three decades, Heinecken's influence as a teacher was profound; he encouraged his students to approach art—and particularly photography—in the same spirit of experimentation and risk with which he approached his own work. Fostered in part by social and political events occurring outside the university at the time—the Vietnam war, the rise of the women's movement, and the growth of the counterculture—the classroom became a place for dialogue and self-evaluation: an "interpretive community" composed of university level photography instructors and their students engaged in a continual process of art-making and critique. In 1965, at a meeting of the Society for Photographic Education in Chicago, Heinecken delivered a paper titled "Manipulative Photography" in which he described a philosophy of art practice out of which he worked and taught:

The chief aim of art is in the refinement of a person's relationship to his existence, a continuing process that is accomplished through his work. In making photographs, or in any other similar poetic endeavor, the formal means or structure towards that refinement must be completely open ended and have the definite possibility of taking diverse manipulative direction as well as an invariable one, provided that intense personal commitment is the result.

When Heinecken emerged in the Southern California art scene in the mid-1960s, he was one of a growing number of artists who had begun to incorporate photographs and other mass-media images into their art as a way to renegotiate the nature and meaning of contemporary art. In the 1950s the assemblage artist Wallace Berman recognized and developed the potential of photograph-as-object: an element that could be used as raw material for art-making rather than as an artificial window on the world. Other Los Angeles artists, like Edward Ruscha and John Baldessari, practiced photography not as photography but as a medium of conceptual art. Affirmed and inspired by these new approaches, Heinecken seized the opportunity to transform a medium restrained at one time by the purist principles of the zone system into one increasingly entwined with the signs and symbols of American consumerism, fashion, and even pornography. By confronting popular culture imagery in this way, Heinecken began to illustrate photographically what was only beginning to be articulated at that time: that photographic "truth" was inevitably informed by and subject to cultural definition. At every stage Heinecken reminds us of photography's pervasiveness and its significance as a medium of transformation.

Many of Heinecken's ideas stem from a fundamental interest in randomness, chance, and arbitrary relationships. In much of his early work, such as in the series *Are You Rea* (1964–68), Heinecken reveals the cultural significance of two images coinciding. In this work, Heinecken placed a magazine page on a sheet of photographic paper and exposed it in the same way as a contact print made from a negative. Because of the thinness of the magazine page, the visual information from both the recto and verso

ROBERT HEINECKEN:
Facing pages in altered *Time* magazine, "150 Years of Photo Journalism," showing Dorothea Lange's *Migrant Mother*, Robert Capa's *Death of a Loyalist Soldier*, and Joe Rosenthal's *Iwo Jima*, 1989

sides appears on the single surface of the processed print, revealing provocative—yet arbitrary—juxtapositions. Heinecken's cut-up or otherwise altered magazines, which he began making in 1968 and frequently returned to, cleverly transpose parts of images from one page onto the next, demonstrating the myriad ways information—and the unsuspecting viewer—can be manipulated by printed media. His series entitled *He:/She:* (1977–79) places handwritten dialogues between a man and a woman below the images in several SX-70 Polaroid prints, exploring ways text and image inform and subvert each other and commenting on gender relationships. His elaborate, life-size collage figures in his more recent *Shiva* series meticulously combine Western mass-media images with the ancient religious symbolism of Eastern culture.

The Center's collection of post-1960s Japanese photography was effectively started in 1978 with the acquisition of four photographs by Jun Morinaga and fifty photographs by Ryuzo Kitahara, which were included in the archive of W. Eugene Smith on his death. Smith had spent a year in Japan in 1961–62, commissioned by the Japanese industrial firm Hitachi, Ltd. to photograph all aspects of the company for their publications. Morinaga served as an assistant to Smith during part of this time, and Smith noted in an introduction to one of Morinaga's books: "There are few photographs that profoundly move me, that change my life. Jun Morinaga's photographs did both." Later, in the early 1970s, Smith returned several times to Japan in the course of his documentary project on the disastrous results of industrial mercury pollution on the fishing village of Minamata, in collaboration with his wife Aileen Miyoko Smith. It was during this time that Kitahara, who was also photographing environmental pollution, sent Smith some of his own photographs.

The Center's Japanese collection began to grow in earnest in the 1980s with acquisition of works by Eikoh Hosoe from several of his important series—*Man and Woman*, *Embrace*, *Barakei* (Ordeal by Roses), *Kamaitachi*, and others. In 1988 and 1990, an important pair of acquisition grants from Hitachi America Ltd. permitted the Center to acquire more than eighty works by eighteen living Japanese photographers, allowing

EIKOH HOSOE: *Man and Woman, #24*, 1960
From the series *Man and Woman*, 1959–60

the Center's collection to begin with World War II. Included in this acquisition was Hosoe's series *Kimono*, evoking phases of a woman's life.

The Hitachi Collection of Contemporary Japanese Photography also includes works by the following: Taku Aramasa (Japanese immigration to South America); Masahisa Fukase (mostly from his somber *Black Bird* series); Yasuhiro Ishimoto; Miyako Ishiuchi; Kikuji Kawada; Hiroh Kikai; Norio Kobayashi (*Suburbs of Tokyo*); Michiko Kon; Kozo Miyoshi; Ittetsu Morishita (*Hibakusha—Hathuko Tominaga*, about a Hiroshima survivor); Daido Moriyama; Ikko Narahara (from his *Japanesque* series made at the Zen Buddhist Sojiji Temple); Takashi Sekiguchi (a grid of colored eggs, from his *Uzura* or "quail" series); Toshio Shibata (constructed road landscapes); Issei Suda; Yoshiyasu Suzuka (praying hands, and larger-than-life portraits from his *Face to Face* series); Shomei Tomatsu; and Hiroshi Yamazaki (bulb-exposure seascapes in the series *The Sun Is Longing for the Sea*).

IKKO NARAHARA: *Japanesque #46, Sojiji, Japan,* 1969

Kaiso, a portfolio of twenty dye transfer prints by Japanese-American photographer Mihoko Yamagata, was acquired by the CCP in 1989 with funds from the Willard Van Dyke Memorial Fund for Documentary Photography. The images form a fragmented portrait of her hospitalized Japanese grandmother, and their accompanying narratives describe memories of youth, marriage, and wartime Japan.

In 1991, a Japanese government Overseas Training Program for Artists award brought Tokyo-based photographer Kozo Miyoshi to the United States to become an artist-in-residence at the Center. His stay was extended when he received a Konica Prize in 1993. His five-year relationship with the Center resulted in another noteworthy addition to the collection.

In the 1990s the Center acquired Hiroshi Sugimoto's photolithograph portfolio of fifty of his precisely bisected seascapes, *Time Exposed*, as well as a large original photograph by him that was part of the CCP's 1998 exhibition *Sea Change*. The newest additions to the Japanese collection include small still lifes by Masao Yamamoto from his series *A Box of Ku*, and individual prints by Yoshihiko Ito, Kenji Hosoe (son of Eikoh Hosoe), and Kenji Nakahashi.

DAIDO MORIYAMA: *Ferryboats, Tsugaru Strait*, 1971

One recent acquisition brings the Center's Japanese collection full-circle. Ruiko Yoshida, a student at Columbia University in the 1960s, had assisted W. Eugene Smith with the preparation of *Japan—A Chapter of Image* (1963) for Hitachi. In 1997, Ms. Yoshida presented the Center with a group of seventeen of her photographs that Smith had once selected for publication in his never-realized magazine, *Sensorium*.

JUN MORINAGA: Untitled, ca. 1963
From book *River, Its Shadow of Shadows*, 1978

Margrethe Mather

by Sarah J. Moore

Margaret [as her friends called her] herself has remained an enigma. It is as though she came from nowhere, basked briefly in Weston's reflected glory (then for almost a decade shared an obscure, often secret life with me) and finally disappeared from the world of photography all together.[1]

So recalled William Justema about the nearly ten years he spent as the companion, collaborator, and model of Margrethe Mather (1885–1952). Enigma, indeed. By all indications, Mather was an active figure in the intellectual, artistic, and bohemian circles of Los Angeles during the 1920s: she exhibited widely including in Los Angeles, San Francisco, Oakland, Pittsburgh, Seattle, New York, Boston, and Mexico City; her works were often cited in the contemporary press for their spare compositions and elegance and were reproduced in such distinguished venues as *Pictorial Photography in America*, published in five volumes by the Pictorial Photographers of America between 1920 and 1929; she was a founding member of the Camera Pictorialists of Los Angeles, whose annual salons from the late 1910s through the 1940s were among the most enduring and respected exhibitions of pictorial photography; her circle of acquaintances included such prominent writers, artists, photographers, and critics as Johan Hagemeyer, Edward Weston, Sadakichi Hartmann, Robo de Richey, Tina Modotti, Emma Goldman, Margaret Anderson, Charles Gerrard, Carl Sandburg, Clarence B. McGehee, Alfred Kreymborg, and Arthur F. Kales. And yet disappear she did; the last years of her life were distinguished by physical decline and increasing isolation. Perhaps even more pernicious was Mather's disappearance from the historical record, her work slipping into virtual obscurity for nearly half a century.

What can account for a career whose currency in the 1920s is matched by only occasional and largely biographical references in contemporary sources? Is it the expansive shadow of Edward Weston, her longtime friend, studio and business partner, and creator of a series of evocative nudes of Mather? Is it the indelicacies of (photographic) history that have privileged the achievements of the so-called modernist photographers at the expense of pictorialists whose works were considered *retardataire* and aesthetically bankrupt by the 1920s? Is it Mather herself, whose eccentricities are suggested by her less-than-conventional biography and whose frankly eroticized images of William Justema, her junior by more than fifteen years, were without precedent?

Although his comment may be apocryphal, Weston wrote of Mather in his Daybooks from Mexico: "[she was] the first important person in my life."[2] Indeed, Mather was among the earliest artists with whom Weston collaborated; the two met in 1912/1913 at the Los Angeles Camera Club. At the time, Weston had a photographic studio in Tropico (now Glendale), a suburb of Los Angeles, and was working in the prevailing pictorial style. Mather and Weston shared an interest in the art of photography and sought to

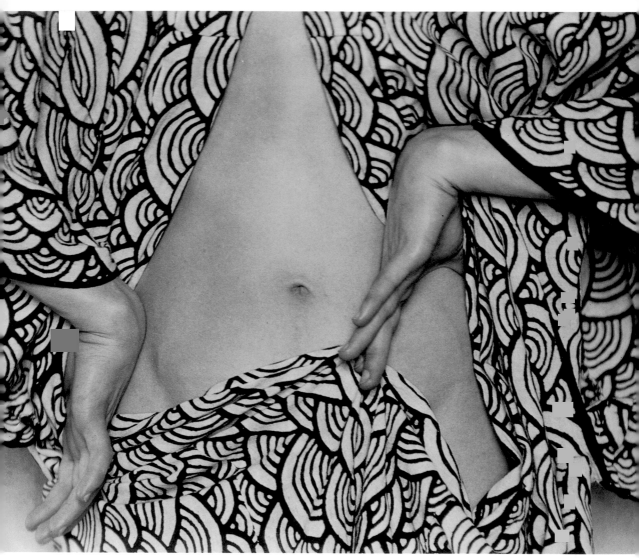

MARGRETHE MATHER: *Semi-Nude* [Billy Justema wearing kimono], ca. 1923

incorporate Japanese aesthetics into their work through spare, asymmetrical compositions and an emphasis on formal relations. That Mather and Weston were charter members of the Camera Pictorialists of Los Angeles in 1914 suggests that each was committed to the formal promotion and display of pictorial photography. As early as 1917, Mather and Weston began to exhibit together; by 1921 they had collaborated on several photographs including portraits and evocative, soft-focus figure studies. In addition to moving in the same artistic circles, Mather shared Weston's studio as both photographer and assistant and there created such memorable images as the double portrait of Weston and Johan Hagemeyer, 1921.

Although Mather posed for Weston as early as 1912/1913 and was the subject of such self-consciously pictorial portraits as *Prologue to a Sad Spring*, 1920, the most sustained body of work as Weston's model was in 1923 with a series of nudes taken at Hermosa Beach. This series of images attempts to merge formalism and eroticism, anticipating Weston's nudes of Tina Modotti in Mexico, and marks the beginning of the end of Mather's close collaboration with Weston. Although Mather maintained Weston's studio during his first trip to Mexico, continued to exhibit occasionally with Weston, notably in Mexico City in 1922, and was invited by Weston to participate in such important exhibitions as *Film und Foto* in Stuttgart, 1929, she became increasingly involved in exhibitions and publications of pictorial photography in Los Angeles, including acting as a juror, with photographer Arthur F. Kales, for the annual salons of the Japanese Camera Pictorialists of California, which began in 1923 and were widely regarded for "advancing abstract pictorialism."[3] Moreover, in 1921, Mather met William Justema with whom she began a decade-long collaboration that resulted in a series of photographic works whose embrace of abstraction and eroticism was without precedent by women photographers of the period.

Justema's lithe and slender youthful body provided Mather with the perfect site to explore her interest in the aesthetics of photography and the potential of the camera to flatten space and transform objects into abstract shapes. Fragments of Justema's nude body—torso, shoulders, hands, legs—are isolated against neutral backgrounds and manipulated into languorous rhythms and linear patterns. Empty space and an economy of detail enhance the quality of abstraction. In spite of their elegant formalism, Mather's photographs of Justema are not exercises in abstract patterning, nor are they distinguished by their objectivity or their distance from the subject. Rather, Mather's empathetic gaze and ability to give visual form to an emotional and (one suspects) physical identification with the subject lend these photographs a degree of intimacy and eroticism that addresses the boundary between representation and lived experience. The untitled view of Billy Justema in man's summer kimono, ca. 1923, is an elegantly conceived image that frames the nude torso of Justema with a geometric-patterned kimono and hands gracefully arranged to mirror the slight swell of his belly and groin. Evocative of leisure, sensual languor, and an intimacy borne by physical contact, Mather creates an image of feminized masculinity that is visually compelling and erotically charged. In addition to her images of Justema, Mather photographed erotic drawings by Justema, which they sold in portfolios to augment the rather modest income on which the two artists/collaborators lived.

In 1929, the year of the stock market crash, William Justema was working as a designer in San Francisco and was hired as decorator at the M. H. de Young Memorial Museum in Golden Gate Park to assist with a major renovation. In 1930, he arranged for an exhibition shown there of photographs by Mather and himself entitled *Patterns by Photography* in which everyday objects—gloves, clam shells, ivory combs, tickertape, cherries, cigarettes—were photographed at close range against a neutral background so as to create elegant rhythmic patterns. As Justema recalled, "this was not to be salon photography but to show how the camera might contribute to the field of decorative design."[4] Paralleling a series of photographs that were made for a joint application to the Guggenheim Foundation in 1925—their ultimately unfunded project was called "The Exposé of Form"—the images were distinguished by their exploitation of the camera's ability to transform mundane objects into abstract patterns, an aesthetic strategy that was being practiced by many photographers of the period. Although Mather continued to photograph sporadically during the early 1930s, the de Young exhibition in July 1931 marked the end of her collaboration with Justema; by the late 1930s, Mather apparently abandoned the medium altogether.

During the first three decades of the twentieth century, American photography sought to define itself: first within the context of fine art and second within the context of the medium's specific properties. The former struggle is often identified with pictorialism, a photographic practice that sought to elevate the status of photography from the mechanical and commercial to that of fine art through the emulation of techniques and imitation of styles popular in painting from the period. Modernist photographic practice, by contrast, assumed the fine art status of photography and exploited the unique qualities of the medium—its potential to flatten space and create abstract formal patterns—through sharply focused, unmanipulated images. Although pictorialism continued to be widely practiced throughout the 1930s and many so-called pictorialists, such as Mather, embraced modernist concerns to varying degrees, formalist modernism emerged as the dominant mode and assumed a tone of moral superiority that endured, largely unchecked, for decades. It was not until the late 1970s and early 1980s that critics and historians of photography began to look again at the medium's history in an attempt to expand its purview and question these assumptions. The history of pictorialism, in particular, has profited from this revisionist activity, restoring complexity and richness to a period that had been stunningly oversimplified in previous accounts. The cavernous gaps created by an historical model that pitted the modernists against the pictorialists are being mined not simply to add new names, such as Mather's, to the litany, but to reinsert the photographs within the dynamic cultural, historical, and aesthetic context in which they were produced, exhibited, and discussed.

1 William Justema, "Margaret: A Memoir," in *Margrethe Mather*, *Center for Creative Photography* 11 (1979), pp. 7–8.

2 Edward Weston, *The Daybooks of Edward Weston: Volume I, Mexico* (Rochester: The George Eastman House, 1961), p. 145.

3 Sigismund Blumann, "Our Japanese Brother Artists," *Camera Craft* (March 1925), p. 109.

4 Justema, *Mather*, p. 18.

Mexican Photography

by Terence Pitts

Twentieth-century Mexican art and photography was deeply rooted in the social issues and aesthetic changes that erupted from the Mexican Revolution, prompting artists to turn to daily life, the artisanship of the peasantry, and the ancient mythologies of Mexico's pre-Columbian peoples for new imagery and artistic styles.

The Center's long commitment to twentieth-century Mexican photography is both a function of Tucson's close proximity to Mexico (less than one hundred kilometers) and

GRACIELA ITURBIDE: *El Sacrificio, La Mixteca*, 1992

the influence that Mexico and its photographers have had over the course of American photography throughout much of that century. Beginning with Edward Weston, who lived in Mexico most of the time between 1923 and 1926, the history, culture, and landscape of Mexico has played an important role in American art. Countless American writers, musicians, and visual artists have found inspiration there, including a number of the photographers represented by archives or significant print holdings in the Center's collection. In addition to Edward Weston, the list includes his son Brett Weston, Paul Strand, Aaron Siskind, Todd Webb, Max Yavno, Van Deren Coke, Rosalind Solomon, Danny Lyon, Linda Connor, and others.

The Center's first involvement with Mexican photography came in 1979, with an exhibition it organized called *Contemporary Photography in Mexico: 9 Photographers*. Acquisitions from each of the nine photographers in the exhibition laid the groundwork for a collection that now numbers approximately six hundred photographs by nearly twenty photographers.

The first generation of post-revolution era photography is represented at the Center with a number of important works by Manuel Alvarez Bravo and by the archive of his

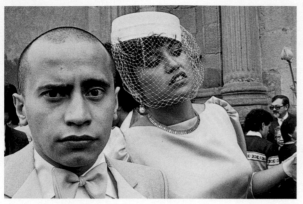

PEDRO MEYER: *La boda en Coyoacán*, 1983

first wife, Lola Alvarez Bravo, which includes more than 175 of her prints. In their differing ways, they laid the foundation that would form the base for Mexican photography for the rest of the century. The two Alvarez Bravos used a combination of twentieth-century aesthetic approaches and centuries-old iconography to penetrate the contradictory history and spirit of Mexico. Faced with a country increasingly conflicted by a profound and graceful stoicism and fearful violence, of great thinkers and vast illiteracy, Manuel and Lola tried to find a new visual language that would resonate with both Mexicos. Whether the subject was the landscape, a nude form, a still life, or a lone figure walking down a street, their photographs transformed the ordinary into powerful symbols and archetypes.

Between them, Lola and Manuel Alvarez Bravo touched the lives and careers of succeeding generations of younger photographers, several of whom are featured in the Center's collection. Mariana Yampolsky, an American artist who moved to Mexico in 1944 and eventually became a Mexican citizen, was a close associate of Lola Alvarez Bravo. For more than a half century, Yampolsky has poetically paid homage to the cultural genius of Mexico as expressed in the country's popular architecture and rich folk traditions. Her work also includes a strong body of portraits of Mexican artists and intellectuals.

FLOR GARDUÑO: *Arból de Yalalag, Yalalag, Mexico*, 1983

Rafael Doniz, Flor Garduño, Graciela Iturbide, Pedro Meyer, José Angel Rodríguez, and Jesús Sánchez Uribe represent a generation of photographers that emerged in the late 1970s to expand upon the possibilities set out by Manuel Alvarez Bravo, with whom they were students and assistants. As Mexico continues its rapid change from a heavily rural and dispersed population to one of the densest urban populations on the planet, the villages and life of Mexico's indigenous peoples serve as the subject for extended photographic investigations by nearly all of these photographers. The Center also houses more than 150 photographs by Manuel Carrillo that survey his poetic form of photojournalism.

Hansel Mieth and Otto Hagel

by Sally Stein

Though their names do not figure in most histories of photography, Hansel Mieth (1909–1998) and Otto Hagel (1909–1973) were German émigrés who made notable contributions to the development of photojournalism and committed social documentary in the United States while sharing together a fantastically varied life in which photography figured more or less prominently as the times and political climate changed. In the heyday of American photojournalism, both were extremely active. Mieth became a staff photographer for *Life* within the magazine's first year of publication, joining the quite small cadre of Bourke-White, Eisenstaedt, Stackpole, Hoffman, McAvoy, and Mydans. Her work was a staple in *Life* for the next decade; and one of her pictures, the portrait of a half-submerged monkey, made for a 1939 picture story on animals transported to the Puerto Rican island of Santiago for medical experimentation, came to enjoy the status of a *Life* classic that was frequently reprinted, often with a caption that explained the animal's fierce look as a response to noisy females rather than captivity.

The strange success of that photograph is especially ironic since Mieth and Hagel led lives that demonstrated a fervent commitment to social and political independence rather than commercial and cultural success. Though Hagel between the late 1930s and the mid-1940s produced major photo stories for *Life* and *Fortune*, he guarded his status as a freelancer and took every opportunity to work outside mainstream media channels, especially for unions. In the first half of the 1930s, Hagel made an independent film on the labor conditions of California cotton pickers who had just engaged in one major strike; the film was lost after his apartment was raided during the San Francisco General Strike of 1934, and it only resurfaced under the title "A Century of Progress" in the 1970s, at which time it came to be regarded as a pioneering effort in social documentary filmmaking in support of labor struggles. After the mysterious disappearance of his first film, Hagel concentrated on photography while continuing to focus on labor struggles. Along with other progressive San Francisco-based photographers (including Horace Bristol), Hagel covered the violent Salinas lettuce strike of 1936, and it is his picture of armed vigilantes that was reproduced in Lange and Taylor's *An American Exodus* (1939) to show the force of reaction with which farm labor had to contend in California. Meanwhile, Hagel had continued to cover the ongoing struggle of waterfront workers in the port of San Francisco, and his photographs (along with a few uncredited photographs by Mieth) form the basis of *Men and Ships* (1937), the pictorial published by the Pacific Maritime Federation to commemorate its hard-earned victory for West Coast dockworkers. In this case Hagel's graphic work seems to alternately appropriate the punchy visual style of *Life* and the political montage sensibility of *AIZ* (the innovative German–communist pictorial that featured covers by John Heartfield).

Neither Mieth nor Hagel were willing to renounce their politics to succeed in mainstream media, and both preferred living in California over life on the East Coast. In the early 1940s, Mieth continued work for *Life* out of the San Francisco office, but by the

HANSEL MIETH: *Young Man Sleeping in Box Car, 1936*

end of the war their relations with Time Inc. became strained with the rise of anti-communism. The Hollywood blacklist is relatively well known; the Red Scare's impact on the major East Coast publishers is a history that remains to be told. The experience of Hagel and Mieth is doubtless just one element in a larger story. Work grew scarce after both resisted Time Inc.'s pressure that they testify before the House Un-American Activities Committee. Instead, Mieth and Hagel moved north of San Francisco to try their hand at farming near the historic home of Jack London, the writer whose paeans to a life of independence had first drawn these young German vagabonds to search for greater freedom in the United States.

Between the 1950s and the 1970s, they continued to photograph and to combine their photographic work with writing (and also painting in Mieth's case). But these endeavors necessarily had to adapt to the demands of raising animals for a living; moreover, in the political climate of the Cold War, there were few receptive outlets for their socially engaged work, even though Hagel had the honor of having one of his postwar photographs featured with a full-page enlargement in Steichen's *Family of Man* (1955).

In the 1950s, only two photographic essays they initiated were featured in *Life* and both of these stories were toned down or sanitized. They published a collaborative essay in the 26 June 1950 issue of *Life* on their return to Fellbach, the village outside Stuttgart where both were raised until their teens when they began to wander across two continents in search of personal and social freedom. The project focused on the pernicious legacy of the Nazi era and the difficult postwar efforts at reconstruction but made no reference to the way both photojournalists had their own freedom to travel restricted as suspected communists in their adopted country.

Their 14 November 1955 essay, ironically titled "The Simple Life," offered a self-documentation about their lives as independent farmers trying to make a living working the land. Here they avoided stating that their return to the land was only half-voluntary after work for magazines became scarce, nor did they mention in conjunction with the story's most dramatic photograph of a bonfire of diseased chicken carcasses that they suspected government officials may have contaminated their livestock as part of an effort to harass unrepentant leftists.

If Mieth and Hagel had ever harbored illusions that they could gain a mass audience for photographic exposés without compromising their political viewpoints, they abandoned those illusions by the mid-1950s and concentrated on smaller, local venues to present their perspectives. The last major publication Hagel worked on was a trade-union sequel to the earlier pictorial on the waterfront struggles. In 1963, he once again collaborated with the Longshoreman's and Warehouseman's Unions of the Pacific Maritime Association to produce *Men and Machines*. The book aimed to explain the state of longshoring following the historic mechanization and modernization agreement in which the unions sought to protect the rank and file while agreeing to adapt to the labor-saving processes of containerization. Three decades later, that book remains a significant publication for both labor history and documentary books; it is also a testament to the extremely critical perspective Hagel maintained throughout his life. Shortly after publication, Hagel delivered the sharpest judgment on this work: "the trouble is that *Men and Machines* does not really touch the core of the problem, except in the very

OTTO HAGEL: *New York Stock Exchange, 1938*

last page, on my insistence [which briefly addressed the growing pool of young workers competing for a drastically reduced number of jobs]. The real problem is this: what is happening in our society, when the machine can do the job better and faster than before. . . .Where is the milestone that says, so far, and no farther? There is no such thing as a milestone on a toboggan (ride). This little problem we have to leave to the future."[1]

For the next decade in Hagel's case, and for an additional quarter century in Mieth's case, they remained activists, exploring with younger generations how photography, past and present, by themselves and by others, might serve struggles for social justice. For Hagel and Mieth, photography was always an instrument for communication, understanding, and change. At a time when the practice of photography has increasingly focused on art, their lives and lifelong work in which photography was always a means, not an end, offer an illuminating counter model.

Their archive, which the Center received in 1998, includes books, correspondence, tear sheets, contact prints, negatives, and slides (Hagel was an early user of color for photographic essays in *Fortune* and *Life*), some exhibition material, the maquette for *Men and Machines,* and manuscript material. It includes an unpublished autobiography by Mieth recounting a life that spanned two continents, nine decades, the worlds of magazines in their prime, and small-scale farming in an era of increasing agribusiness in the state of California. What continues through all those changes is the commitment of two free spirits to balance, if not reconcile, the personal quest for liberation with the commitment to remain engaged witnesses of massive struggles of social transformation. It should be no surprise that they lived with contradictions and suffered from them, but their determination to face such contradictions made their lives and the documents they produced immensely compelling.

1 From a letter by Hagel to friends identified as John and Barbara, dated 11 March 1964.

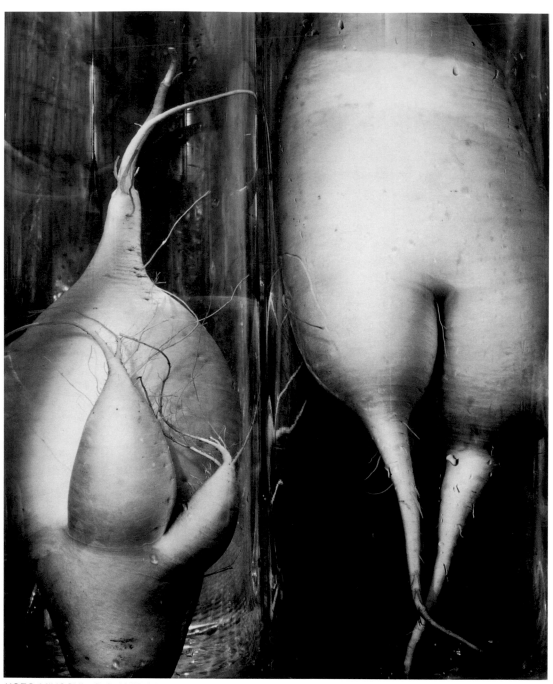

KOZO MIYOSHI: *B-6*, 1987–91
From the series *Roots* *<NE>*

Kozo Miyoshi

by Dustin W. Leavitt

A cursory inventory of traditional Japanese art reveals an inclination toward a vernacular that appeals to the senses more than it provokes the critical intellect, and a manner that is broadly sentimental. In the West, sentimentality and decorativeness still suggest superficiality and arouse the condemnation of Western intellectuals. In Japan, however, mass appeal bears no such shibboleths for, it must be remembered, Japan's is a culture of consensus, and where, in an environment of critical acceptance, simple beauty and uninquiring sentimentality have achieved a certain profundity.

All this in mind, it is interesting to note with what alacrity the Japanese photographer Kozo Miyoshi (b. 1947) introduces candid sentimentalism to the deliberate medium of serious large format photography. The result, at least for the Western audience, is a body of work that exhibits both emotional subtlety and intellectual acuity, yet is supremely accessible and nonsectarian in its appeal.

Miyoshi, who I got to know well in the early 1990s when he was artist-in-residence at the Center for Creative Photography, was born in rural Chiba Prefecture, just south of Tokyo. His father was a horticulturist, and it was in homage to the glass hothouses around which he grew up that the recently matured photographer conceived his two most noteworthy early photographic series, *Roots <NE>* and *Conservatory*, during the 1980s. *Roots <NE>*, still Miyoshi's best-known series, is nevertheless atypical of his work for its snug thematic focus. It records the incremental decay of a pair of daikon radishes contained in large glass jars over an extended period of time, invoking the poignancy—which one must unavoidably label sublime—of life in fleeting transition. That this is a venerable and very Japanese theme is no accident.

Like *Roots <NE>*, Miyoshi's *Conservatory* series depicts a world circumscribed by glass. Interestingly, given the suggestive coincidence of family greenhouses and encapsulation themes, these are the only series dominated by interiors. The balance of Miyoshi's work, up to the present, portrays the larger world outdoors and tends more and more to record without discrimination whatever happens to lie before the lens at any given moment, the photographer allowing subjectivity as a principle, rather than picture making as a decisive act, to guide his hand. I have watched him set up his camera (the capacity for almost infinite detail is perhaps the most compelling reason Miyoshi works exclusively with an 8x10 Deardorff view camera) and inadvertently nudge it off frame by a few degrees, yet—when informed about the error—merely shrug and make the exposure anyway. More than any other I know, Miyoshi believes in the power of *photography* over the often illusory power of the photographer.

Miyoshi always works in series, which serve more as organization strategies than subterranean themes. Often his series are subject oriented and may be very specific, as with *Airfields*, *Chapel*, and his codicil to *Conservatory*, photographs of public botanical gardens in nearly all of the fifty United States, which he completed in 1994 under the auspices of a very prestigious Konica Prize. Just as often, his subjects may be broad, as with *Innocents*, *Picture Show*, or *Southwest*. Some barely avoid being maudlin (*Innocents*, *Route 66*), while others (*Roots <NE>*, *Chapel*, *Cactus*) are cryptically cerebral. Typically, however, Miyoshi's photographs are simply original, well observed, and skillfully crafted. They reveal a soul unencumbered by cynicism or self-doubt.

Which brings us back to my original point—how art in the Japanese tradition, of which Miyoshi is thoroughly (if not entirely) a part, is both formalistic and sentimental. Formalism—picturing the world according to visual paradigms that are acknowledged universally within a specific culture, using appropriate signs and marks to bear and consign information—is a hallmark of Japanese art. Its pictorial application is obvious to anyone with eyes to see. Similarly, Japanese literature depends upon an ancient codex of images that represent small philosophical worlds, as, for example, when the insertion of *sakura*, cherry blossom, into a Japanese narrative necessarily, in one fell stroke, introduces an ideological motif, intact and fully formed, regarding the transitory nature of life. It is here that Miyoshi's photography departs from the Japanese art tradition. Photography, by its very nature, relies heavily upon the illusion of reality to make it viable. Furthermore, Miyoshi's release of control to the nature of the medium itself, allowing (if not desiring) anything in the world that occurs beyond the photographer's jurisdiction to occupy the frame, is far from typically Japanese. His passion (or even, perhaps, his dispassion) is the world itself, exactly as it is.

I am reminded, by way of example, of one winter morning, in Taos, New Mexico, when we set up the Deardorff in front of the old church at Ranchos de Taos for the obligatory, archetypical large format photograph. Miyoshi's first exposure was not of the church at all, but rather of the highway passing by in the other direction. The second exposure was equally unconventional for, rather than striving to replicate the great, iconic photographs of previous decades by tortuously wringing the camera's bellows in order to crop out all the undesirable modern incursions—telephone wires, signage, parked cars—Miyoshi welcomed them and, what is more, waited politely for a family of tourists to enter the frame who were just as politely waiting for him to take his shot.

Miyoshi's sentimentalism is where he is at his most Japanese, however. It is difficult to define the term for Western audiences, who are conditioned to hear it only as a slur. Yet, it is just too accurate a label to abandon. Japanese culture is sentimental, both in the worst sense and in the best. At one end of the spectrum it is the hatchery of an endlessly replenished clutch of cuddly creatures so cloying, so bizarre, they don't have time to *become* kitsch because they are born that way—the Pokemon phenomenon alone bears sufficient evidence for the case to be laid to rest. At the other end of the spectrum lies sentimentality as emotion undiminished by skepticism or self-analysis, a kind of faith, a kind of ingenuousness, a kind of purity that is steadfastly certain. For all Japan's modern bafflements, this immaculate sentimentality is, for me, what remains utterly Japanese. And it is what lies at the heart of Kozo Miyoshi's experience. It is that which informs him as an artist—a profound emotional attachment to the world and its inhabitants that is unconditional and impartial, a sensibility he reveals with eloquence, subtlety, and grace.

Tina Modotti

by Sarah J. Moore

In a 1928 article entitled "The Photographs of Tina Modotti: Revolutionary Anecdotes," Cuban writer Marti Casanovas wrote, "Tina Modotti's photographs have a double pathos, and because of this they excite great passions: for their purely artistic creation, in the aesthetic and formalist sense, and for their social transcendence, their propaganda directed to the service of one human ideal." Inserting the photographic work of Modotti (1896–1942) within contemporary discourse about the tension between art making and political action, Casanovas argued that images such as *Bandolier, Corn, Sickle*, which had appeared in 1927 in *Mexican Folkways*, a Spanish–English language journal published in Mexico City that featured articles on Mexican art and folk traditions, demonstrated that socially engaged art did not preclude aesthetic quality nor did aesthetics, by definition, diminish the potency of political meaning and resonance. That Casanovas's article appeared in the first issue of *30–30*,[1] a journal sponsored by Treinta-Treintista, an organization of politically engaged artists working against increasingly reactionary forces in the Mexican government, suggests the degree to which Modotti's work intersected with current debates on how art functioned as an agent of political change in post-revolutionary Mexico.

Indeed, Casanovas was not the only observer to note the polemical nature of Modotti's photography that seemed to embrace two distinct muses: modernist aesthetics and revolutionary rhetoric. Coincident with Modotti's first one-person exhibition in Mexico City in late 1929, for example, Mexican muralist David Alfaro Siqueiros gave a public lecture entitled "The First Revolutionary Photographic Exhibit in Mexico,"[2] in which he located Modotti's work on an historical trajectory of political art. Modotti herself published a statement on her photography to accompany the exhibition (the statement also appeared in *Mexican Folkways*[3]), in which she obliquely addressed the collision between art and radical politics. Bristling at the terms "art" and "artistic" to describe her socially committed work, Modotti argued that good photography, as she called it, embraced the inherent limitations and advantages of the medium and was "the most eloquent, the most direct means for fixing, for registering the present epoch."

The late 1920s was a critical period in Modotti's brief photographic career that spanned scarcely a decade and was distinguished by her self-conscious collapsing of the barriers between political engagement and image making. Unlike her works in the early 1920s, such as *Cloth Folds* (also called *Texture and Shadow*) and *Telegraph Wires*, that suggested the preeminence of formalist aesthetics perhaps attributable to her involvement with and indebtedness to Edward Weston, with whom she then lived and worked, Modotti's commitment to radical politics rose to the surface of her photographs in the late 1920s. *Worker's Parade*, first published in *Mexican Folkways* in 1926 and reprinted in a number of journals with variant titles, and *Worker Reading El Machete*, for example, specifically addressed the role of the worker and the revolutionary ideal of

TINA MODOTTI: *Circus Tent*, 1924

universal literacy. That the worker is shown reading *El Machete* was not without significance. The newspaper, founded in 1922, was dedicated to workers and peasants; in 1925 it became the official organ of Mexico's Communist Party, which Modotti joined in 1927.

By the late 1920s and early 1930s, Modotti's work was available to an ever widening and international audience through numerous publications and exhibitions. In the summer of 1926, Modotti and Weston traveled throughout Mexico photographing decorative arts for a commission Weston received from American anthropologist Anita Brenner. From the literally hundreds of photographs that were taken during the fifteen-week sojourn, seventy were used as illustrations for Brenner's book *Idols Behind Altars*, published in English for an American audience in 1929. In addition to her photographs being published in such journals as *El Machete*, *Mexican Folkways*, and *30–30*; *New Masses*, and *Creative Arts*; and *L'Art Vivant*, and being displayed in exhibitions in Los Angeles, Berkeley, Guadalajara, and Mexico City, Modotti undertook the ponderous task of documenting the work of the Mexican muralists Diego Rivera and others for publication in *Mexican Folkways* and subsequent monographs. This project suggests Modotti's deep commitment to the potency of political art in the public arena as an agent of social change and, as the art historian Sarah Lowe has noted, "had a significant impact on the art of the 1930s: her photographs were reproduced in art magazines and political journals throughout the world and thereby gave international visibility to the muralists whose work was inaccessible except to those who could travel to Mexico."[4]

Finally, the late 1920s were a period of intense personal tragedy and impending political exile from Mexico. Exiled Cuban revolutionary Julio Antonio Mella was murdered in Mexico City in January 1929. Modotti, his lover and companion at the time of the murder, was falsely charged with his violent death and was promptly arrested. Although she was acquitted a week after the murder, her name and reputation had been publicly smeared in the periodical press, she remained under constant police surveillance, and was faced with the imminent threat of deportation. Most perniciously, the political turmoil that defined her life in 1929 effectively brought her career as a photographer to an end. That Modotti was arrested after an assassination attempt on the life of the recently inaugurated president, Pascual Ortiz Rubio, was detained for two weeks, and then given two days to leave the country only six weeks after her first one-person exhibition in Mexico City in December 1929 is perhaps only the most obvious demonstration of the collision between politics and art that characterized Modotti's brief but passionate photographic career. As Casanovas concluded, "Tina Modotti has made of photography a genuine art, and has placed this wonderful tool . . . in the service of the revolution. This is perhaps her greatest achievement and glory."[5]

1 Marti Casanovas, "Revolutionary Anecdotes," in *30–30* (July 1928), pp. 4–5.

2 Amy Stark [Rule], ed., "The Letters of Edward Weston and Tina Modotti," *The Archive* 22 (January 1986), p. 62.

3 *Mexican Folkways* (October–December 1929), pp. 96–98.

4 Sarah M. Lowe, *Tina Modotti Photographs* (New York: Harry N. Abrams, 1996), p. 37.

5 Casanovas, p. 5.

WILLIAM MORTENSEN: *Torse*, ca. 1935
From the portfolio *Pictorial Photography*, ca. 1935

William Mortensen

by Larry Lytle

In 1979, I attended an exhibition of the work of American photographer William Mortensen (1897–1965). I was mesmerized and baffled by his images, which looked nothing like any photography that I had ever seen.

For thirteen years I tracked down books and articles written by Mortensen, yet never again saw any of his amazing prints. My interest and passion grew to learn more about this man and his incredible work. I could find very little reference to him in general photographic histories. Except for a couple of monographs on West Coast pictorialism and the essays by A. D. Coleman, there were very few writings about Mortensen or reproductions of his images. I decided to attempt to write a biography of this historically underrepresented artist.

Consulting the *Index to American Photographic Collections*, I found that the Center for Creative Photography with its sizable collection of Mortensen material was at the top of the list. Coincidentally, the Center's William Mortensen Archive contained many of the same photographs that I had seen in the exhibition in 1979.

My first day at the Center I was struck by a strange dichotomy. It seemed a morgue of items securely entombed. Boxes and flats were brought out on a cart by the archivist. A feeling of respectful quiet settled over me as I opened those boxes and looked at the belongings of one so long dead—a person I had thought about for so long. But conversely, after my examination, I had a chance to see the Research Center for what it was. Behind that quietude, I found a bustling community of people dedicated to patient nurturing and protection of all those artifacts. They conserve, catalog, index, and restore all those objects before they ever reach the hands of the researcher.

Our connection between the past and the present depends upon the resources they preserve, providing us with the clues and puzzle pieces that help us put together the picture of a person, event or movement. I realized that an archive is a library of things more than books, though the Center does have a great photography book library. Without these repositories I would be searching the world to collect enough meaningful material. Without a committed and professional staff, like those I have encountered at the Center, research would be a grim, joyless task. Now, even with all the time spent there, I still feel overwhelmed with the volume of prints, letters, scrapbooks, and other mementos that constitute Mortensen's archive. His wife Myrdith and his friend, model, and co-author George Dunham had both contributed (thank God!) what they possessed to create, respectively, the Mortensen and Dunham archives.

I have encountered so many unexpected and interesting things—both personal and public. Some of the personal effects were a note/sketch book that Mortensen kept from his short trip to Greece in 1920 (with wonderful drawings, notes, and journal entries), postcards to his parents from Los Angeles when he moved there in 1921 (one telling them of his work on a film and the people he was getting to know), a scrapbook

STATEMENT

 CAMERA CRAFT PUBLISHING CO.

95 MINNA STREET   SAN FRANCISCO 5, CALIFORNIA

Date...... Feb 15,1952 ....

WILLIAM MORTENSEN
903 Coast Blvd
Laguna Beach, California

Royalties on books sold during the ~~Terms: NET CASH. No discount.~~
month of January,1952

55	Command To Look	@	.37½	$20.63
37	Monsters & Madonnas	@	.60	22.20
195	Pictorial Lighting	@	.50	97.50
✗170	Print Finishing*	@	.52½	89.25
194	Flash in Modern Phgy	@	.37½	72.75
64	New Proj. Control	@	.35	22.40
210	The Model	@	.82½	173.25
82	Outdoor Portraiture	@	.57½	47.15
				$545.13
	George Dunham	1/3		181.71
				363.42

*now out of print

ℛ1

1st International Colour Print Exhibition
THE CAMERA CLUB, LONDON.
"The Bandit"
This Photograph was accepted and
hung at the above exhibition.

November, 1950.

exhibited at
the b.y.m.c. union
camera club
boston, massachusetts

JUL 19

Exhibited at
THE
CAMERA CLUB
OF
PHILADELPHIA

CRYSTAL CITY
CAMERA CLUB
CORNING N.Y.

Exhibited
BY THE...
SEATTLE
PHOTOGRAPHIC
SOCIETY

SEATTLE :: :: WASHINGTON

EXHIBITED
AT OUR
GALLERY

THE
CLEVELAND PHOTOGRAPHIC
SOCIETY
CLEVELAND OHIO

EXHIBITED BY
THE
Raytar
CAMERA CLUB
ROCHESTER, NEW YORK, U. S. A.

exhibited at
READING CAMERA CLUB
READING, PENNA.

EXHIBITED
LANSING
Camera Club

EXHIBITED
BY THE MINIATURE
CAMERA CLUB ▶▶▶
OF NEW YORK ▶▶▶

Exhibited by
The BOSTON Y.M.C.
UNION
CAMERA CLUB

Organized 1908

MAR 1940

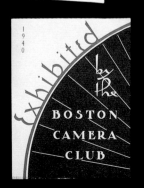

1940

Exhibited
by
the
BOSTON
CAMERA
CLUB

Exhibited by
HOUSTON
CAMERA
CLUB

hcc

HOUSTON,
TEXAS

Salon exhibition labels, various dates
William Mortensen Archive

WILLIAM MORTENSEN:
Untitled [George Dunham], n.d.

assembled by Myrdith containing personal memorabilia, and photographs of Mortensen in his uniform—a stateside soldier in World War I.

Concerning his life as an artist, writer and teacher, I found newspaper articles describing his work in Laguna Beach, California (where he spent the remaining thirty-four years of his life and produced his best work), school brochures outlining the course of study offered by the Mortensen School of Photography (possibly the first school of photography on the West Coast), reams of original manuscripts of his books and articles (published and unpublished), and a large collection of his prints (experimental and exhibition quality). Of course I am listing but a trifle of what is to be found in the archive. It would have taken untold frustrating years of first finding, then begging private collectors for access to uncover what I found on just my first visit to the Research Center.[1]

Admittedly I am a neophyte researcher and naively believed when I began this journey that one or two trips to the Center would suffice. I have made eight trips so far and expect to make several more. A journey is a good way to describe the research process. One must physically travel to the environment that houses the archive, and then once there, settled in, laptop opened, one must mentally travel to the past life and thoughts of another person. I realized by about the fourth trip that I would need to investigate other archives to cross-check ideas and information. I don't know quite when I will be finished. Already I feel the tug of new projects, new investigations.

Biographical research is a life-changing experience. It challenges preconceived ideas about the past and gives unexpected insight into both the subject and oneself. I have grown to understand how important primary research is and how much like detective work it is. Over the past six years I have uncovered new bits of information, adding to what is already at the Center. Besides the excitement of discovery, I feel a real satisfaction contributing a few more small pieces of data that add to the context of another's history. After I have gone, this material in its boxes and flats will be there for the next person curious about the life of William Mortensen.

1 In the time I have been doing my research, three of his former students have donated some of their Mortensen holdings; see the Grey Silva, Robert Balcomb, and Anson Beman collections.

Beaumont and Nancy Newhall

by Keith McElroy

Beaumont (1908–1993) and Nancy (1908–1974) Newhall were New Englanders to the core and as a partnership devoted their lives together from 1936 until Nancy's death to gaining recognition for photography as a fine art. In retrospect Beaumont judged the exhibition and catalog they generated for the Museum of Modern Art exhibition, *Photography 1839–1937*, to be their most important contribution.[1] They spent their honeymoon acquiring prints for this project. Together they generated a continuous barrage of publications that greatly influenced the growing acceptance of art photography. Beaumont was the disciplined and diligent researcher; Nancy was a wordsmith, crafting prose to celebrate her passion for the beautiful in the medium. At the end of the century their pursuits seem so obvious and essential, but they were carried out in a climate that was often indifferent and unsupportive. In Beaumont's autobiography, *Focus*, published in the year of his death, he confessed his frustrated desire to dedicate himself to art photography: "Continuing to investigate the history of photography, although fascinating in the past, from the vantage point of a world war [II] seemed a dry and uninspiring academic pursuit."[2]

During Beaumont's military service, Nancy continued the project as acting curator of photography, mounting fifteen exhibitions as the Museum of Modern Art convulsed with political intrigues. The Board of Directors included several members who opposed the inclusion of photography as an art medium. Beaumont resumed his position as curator of photography at MoMA only to be informed that the Board had appointed Edward Steichen as director of photography. After he resigned his position in 1946, the Newhalls pursued a series of freelance writing and research interests, and in 1947 Beaumont received his first Guggenheim fellowship (a second in 1975). Nancy continued her collaboration with Paul Strand on *Time in New England* (published 1950). During the summers of 1946 through 1948, Beaumont taught at Black Mountain College where the legendary faculty included Joseph Albers, Walter Gropius, Buckminster Fuller, John Cage, and Merce Cunningham. He also taught at the Institute of Design in Chicago, which had been founded by Moholy-Nagy. In the fall of 1948, Beaumont was appointed Curator of Photography for the newly opened George Eastman House in Rochester, New York, where he was to serve as Director from 1958 to 1971. During these years he built the collections and the reputation of the institution into the preeminent photographic museum in the world and expanded the literature on the history of the medium more than any other scholar. He also occasionally taught courses at the Rochester Institute of Technology from 1954 to 1968 and at the State University of New York at Buffalo from 1968 to 1971.

In 1971, when Beaumont Newhall retired from his position at the George Eastman House and joined the faculty at the University of New Mexico, he lined one wall of his spacious office with the row of tall metal file cabinets that housed the clippings, catalogs,

THE MUSEUM OF MODERN ART

NEW YORK

11 WEST 53rd STREET
TELEPHONE: CIRCLE 5-8900
CABLES: MODERNART, NEW-YORK

BEAUMONT NEWHALL, CURATOR OF PHOTOGRAPHY

8 October 1942

Dear Edward and Charis,

I was feeling fairly torn up yesterday morning, having said goodbye to Beau three hours earlier, while the moon was still shining. We had a strange and wonderful two weeks together; the atmosphere of an Army school is curiously juvenile and at the same time terrifying. I was feeling that the best job I could do in this crisis was to stick to Beau and be the perfect Army Wife. And then as I came in the door they told me there was a large wooden box from Weston! Bless you for timing its arrival when you did! I tore off my coat and unscrewed the lid and starting lifting out 74 platinums. An honest and beautiful selection of the early work of E. Weston. In fact, the first third of the great Weston show. I defy anybody to open that package and not indulge in dreams of the Weston show. We'll probably show a selection of the platinums this winter, and the temptation to add to it from Dave's collection, and the Museum's, and our own, and then write to you for more is very great. To wait for peace---! And yet it needs the concerted powers of all of us, and leisure, and the cash, for it must be the Weston show and its impact must be authoritative.

The platinums are registered as an extended loan and in due time you will receive a list of them. Your generosity in offering them all to us is something I appreciate more everytime I look at them, but so much has happened and so much is likely to happen that I feel you'd better keep the ownership of them for the duration. Only please reserve us a chance to keep some of them when the time comes for you to want them back. Beau explained to you, I think, about war risk insurance: there isn't any for works of art; and things can be insured only while on exhibition. As soon as the prints are listed and boxed, they will be kept with our other treasures as safely as possible. Sad that the paste has stained some of them at the top. Is there anything that can be done about it?

What news from you? A nice long letter is due you; this one has to be xP (sorry about my homemade typing!) chiefly business. We have no home, we live in suitcases and under our hats generally. Euripides is living in the country and I hope he likes it. Beau is coming Saturday for a brief glimpse of things, and shall I have something to show him! Also a nice little print room, praise the lord, with fresh paint, and a new blond print table, & grey velvet curtains, and everything proper about it.

Much love, and do write all the news.

Nancy

oct 26

Letter from Nancy Newhall to Edward Weston, written while she was working on his Museum of Modern Art retrospective, 8 October 1942

41 West 53 St., New York 19, N. Y.

15 July 1946

Dear Edward:

We are all saddened by the death of Stieglitz. The end came quickly and, we believe, cleanly. He had a heart attack on Saturday before last. We dropped into an American Place after lunch and found him there alone, lying on the cot in the little room, very weak and low. The doctor had just come. We stayed with him until some people came, for we were shocked that he was entirely alone. He talked, almost in a whisper. We didn't want him to talk, but he couldn't keep still. When other people came, we left. Nancy went back later in the afternoon. Mellquist and Zohler took him home. On Sunday we went around with flowers. He was better, but we could not see him. On Tuesday we heard that he was sitting up. Then on Wednesday he had a stroke and lost consciousness, from which he never recovered. He died in the hospital on Friday night.

It was inevitable and it happened in a clean way, but it has left us all with empty feelings in our hearts. He was a tremendous inspiration to Nancy and to myself, and we shall always treasure the moments which we spent with him.

I found out about the photograph for Milton Greene and I had the Museum send you a wire. I hope that we can distribute the things, but unless they are here next week, I'm afraid that we will not be here to do it.

Here are two letters for you which I found at the Museum. Amusing that Mexico is discovering your work again through the New York show! Had a nice note from Merle; glad he had a visit with you.

More soon. Best to all the clan that are within hailing distance.

Yours,

Beaumont

BEAUMONT NEWHALL: *Henri Cartier-Bresson, New York, 1946*

and notes from which he had and would continue to publish. By that time these materials had already reached the public via some 632 books, articles, and reviews.[3] These files included texts on his other loves—film, ship models, and cooking. Newhall was a serious gourmand and took great pride not only as an accomplished chef but also in the book and 234 articles on wines and food preparation that he had published. Even Nancy had been drawn into writing several entries under his column title, "Epicure Corner." She was, in addition, author of over eighty books, catalogs, and articles.

Especially after Nancy's death in 1974, Beaumont became retrospective about their place in the formation of the history of photography. He made copies of her correspondence with Ansel Adams for the Center for Creative Photography's Ansel Adams Archive. He participated in various formal and informal discussions about the nature of future histories of the medium. In the 1970s the widening circle of a new generation of well-trained professionals was giving serious consideration to the interpretation of photography. Newhall's *History of Photography* and its modernist's vision of art photography was frequently challenged. It was, however, the universal constant against which each revisionist's insights were tested. Within this climate he came to the task of the final edition of his famous text published in 1982. He was acutely aware of its historical contribution; the dilemma was whether to try to reflect the complexity of the state of the discipline or to make the necessary corrections and adjustments while retaining its original assumptions. His decision was to accept his historical contribution and to leave his basic thesis intact. During this time he was sometimes portrayed as defending an outmoded position, and various statements that he made about new trends were used to justify this image. His graduate students, however, knew him to be ever supportive of their work and tolerant of their search for new directions and methodologies.

Beaumont became concerned about how the papers and library he had assembled could be made available to serve future researchers in the subject areas he and Nancy had pioneered. He envisioned the files to be a research tool and not merely their vintage collections. B. G. Burr was the first of several graduate students employed to help bring these many files into some useful order through a system of indexing on file cards. Meridel Rubenstein distilled this intention: "He saw his research as fodder, there to start little fires, to give away, to fuel further inquiry."[4] To this end, while continuing to acquire new materials, he disposed of first editions, rare books, and vintage prints, replacing them with more recent copies: his legacy would be intellectual not antiquarian. The main body of the Newhalls' collected papers and manuscripts, which are now at the Getty Research Institute (acc.# 920060), are estimated at 54,115 items in 256 boxes occupying sixty linear feet of shelving.

Although Beaumont Newhall taught various courses in academic institutions throughout his career, his outlook was never that of a career academic. He did, however, take great pride in being in on the foundation of the first graduate program in the History of Photography at the University of New Mexico. In the large undergraduate program in photography and art history, his lecture courses were popular, attracting large enrollments, and had to be cast for a different audience than he had previously confronted, as he said, one that had already read his text.[5] He developed lectures with great care and taped each one with a portable recorder. His initial approach was more that of a writer scripting the presentation, but he began experimenting with more dramatic techniques for capturing the attention of the audience. As he came to the climax of topics such as Alfred Stieglitz and Edward Weston, the authentic emotion in his voice broke through the professorial New England mannerisms. His graduate seminars were crowded and focused on broad subjects. He was from the beginning frustrated by library holdings that lacked the depth he had come to take for granted. To insure that his students could read the original texts he considered essential, a three-ring binder of photocopies was placed on reserve. He continued to edit and make additions until the evolved contents of that much used binder became *Photography: Essays and Images*, which he published in 1980 for the benefit of other students of the medium. After retirement from the University of New Mexico, he was named a Professor Emeritus, received an honorary Ph.D. from Harvard University, and was named a John D. and Catherine T. MacArthur Foundation Fellow.

With the move to New Mexico, Beaumont returned to the practice of photography. After his marriage to Christi Yates Newhall in 1975, she among others in his circle encouraged him to consider exhibiting his own work. A small exhibition at UNM was curated by his museum practices students, and he agreed to his first one-person public exhibition, which opened at the Kay Bonfoey Gallery in Tucson, Arizona, in 1978. Ms. Bonfoey was the aunt of Christi Newhall, and the gallery, set in gardens of natural vegetation, was ideally scaled for the fifty medium-size prints that were professionally printed. Much to his surprise, the Center for Creative Photography purchased twelve images to add to the two prints that came to the CCP as part of the Ansel and Virginia Adams Collection, one which was part of the *New Mexico Portfolio* (1976), and a Polaroid portrait of Strand by Newhall in the Paul Strand Collection. The CCP subsequently acquired one print in 1983 and four in 1986. Eight prints by Nancy also entered CCP in the Adams collection. The positive reception for his creative work and his introduction to David Scheinbaum, who became printer, dealer, and traveling companion, led to subsequent, one-person exhibitions in New York, Vienna, Los Angeles, San Francisco, Carmel, Denver, Honolulu, Rochester, Albuquerque (two), Santa Fe (four), and elsewhere. The success in these venues resulted in acquisitions by numerous important collections including The Victoria and Albert Museum and The Museum of Modern Art, and ultimately led to the publication of *In Plain Sight*, 1983.[6]

1 Beaumont Newhall, *Focus: Memoirs of a Life in Photography* (Boston: Little, Brown and Company, 1993), p. 253.

2 Newhall, *Focus*, pp. 248–49, 251.

3 Van Deren Coke and Thomas Barrow, checklist published on Beaumont's retirement.

4 Steven Yates, *Beaumont Newhall: Colleagues and Friends* (Santa Fe: Museum of Fine Arts, Museum of New Mexico, 1992).

5 Newhall, *Focus*, p. 239.

6 Eleven images from the Center for Creative Photography collection are reproduced in *Beaumont Newhall, In Plain Sight* (Layton, Utah: Peregrine Smith Books, 1983).

Sonya Noskowiak

by Darsie Alexander

Miss N. [is] leaving for San Francisco in a few days. . . . Told me yesterday that she is interested in photography and wants to go on with it. . . . It seems a joke to me. . . . Illusions of youth![1]

Johan Hagemeyer's journal entry
about photographer Sonya Noskowiak
29 September 1926

When photographer and horticulturist Johan Hagemeyer hired Sonya Noskowiak (1900–1975) as a studio assistant in 1925, he could not have fathomed a future that included her participation in the landmark Group f/64 exhibition at the de Young Museum of San Francisco in 1932 and a career that brought early notoriety among the press and public alike. Nor did Noskowiak, born in Leipzig, Germany, and raised in Chile, appear to have great ambitions as a photographic artist. But within just five years, Noskowiak's nascent interest produced a small but singular body of work—impressive enough to stand on its own alongside that of Edward Weston and Ansel Adams.

Noskowiak's personal background did not foreshadow a career in photography, though it undoubtedly had a bearing on how she processed the world visually. She learned about the physical beauty and harsh reality of the land from her father, a gardener and sometime landscape designer, and this would later serve her photographic interests.[2] After spending her childhood moving from one location to another while her father sought work, first in Chile, then Panama, then California, Noskowiak finally struck out on her own at nineteen by moving to San Francisco. She enrolled in secretarial school and later was employed at Johan Hagemeyer's Carmel studio. Here Noskowiak made her first contact with photography, and the possibilities of her future began to unfold.

Through Hagemeyer, Noskowiak met Edward Weston, and her work in photography began in earnest. From 1929 to 1935[3] they had a close personal and professional relationship; she lived with him as a companion, model, and surrogate mother to his children. He offered her artistic and technical expertise, and shared in the enthusiasm of her first successes. By 1930, Weston was already a mature artist with a clearly defined mission. The stark beauty of photography, Weston claimed, came from the precision of the lens, not from the self-conscious pursuit of "artistic effects."[4] He inspired Noskowiak to notice the visual potential of her surroundings and taught her the rudiments of transforming them with her camera.

Noskowiak was attracted to bold feats of urban engineering, symbolic of the modern age—the giant pylons of city bridges, curving highways, and massive water tanks. The power of these structures, both physical and visual, underscored Noskowiak's aesthetic interpretation. She often adopted a low vantage point, tilting her camera to exaggerate the stunning architectural profiles of her subjects. In a photograph of a lighthouse interior from 1931, Noskowiak creates a dynamic and disorienting composition by looking

SONYA NOSKOWIAK: *Calla Lily*, 1930

up into a tower of prismatic glass. As in other images of the same period, Noskowiak establishes a visual tension by means of extreme contrasts of light and shadow. Here a mass of lighthouse machinery becomes an angular black form against a backdrop of white light. By focusing on the place where light enters and is emitted, Noskowiak underscores the function of this building while heightening its visual drama.

Noskowiak fixed her lens on the recurring patterns of nature. Like Weston, she concentrated on discrete objects photographed at close range: the inside of a flower, the veins of a plant, the lined surface of a rock. The effect was to magnify and abstract nature, allowing its physical properties to become the basis for her compositions. She was keenly aware of the shapes prescribed by organic forms, and how they would translate photographically. With only two options for orienting her prints—horizontally and vertically—she chose carefully, rarely going against the natural features of what lay before her. By working in such close proximity to nature, she discovered its many structural similarities. Seen through Noskowiak's eye, the back of a leaf might resemble the veined hand of an old person, or eroded sand evoke the wing of a bird. By creating visual parallels between distinct objects, Noskowiak uses photography to suggest the coherence of the natural world.

Critical attention came early for Noskowiak. By the middle 1930s, her work had appeared at the de Young Museum, and at the Ansel Adams, Denny Watrous, and Willard Van Dyke galleries. Seeking to distinguish her work from those of her male counterparts, writers like Dora Hagemeyer emphasized Noskowiak's feminine vision, the "delicate loveliness" of her prints. In a similar vein, Willard Van Dyke told Noskowiak that her photographs "are beautiful, sensitive, and very fine in their feminine approach. I like the size. It makes them intimate."[5] Though such praise was undoubtedly welcome, it frequently overlooked some of the most obvious qualities of Noskowiak's work—its powerful simplicity and complete lack of sentimentality.

When Noskowiak's relationship with Weston broke apart in 1935, her life and work changed considerably. Eager to leave Carmel, she moved back to San Francisco, where she established a portrait studio and worked for the Federal Art Project, a division of the Works Progress Administration, from 1936 to 1937. The FAP, like the Farm Security Administration, was a government-sponsored agency that employed photographers to document the conditions of the time for a fixed income each month. Whether or not the social concerns of the FAP caused the shift in Noskowiak's work is open to question. But by the mid-1930s, she was photographing in a new way, replacing her intimate studies of nature with far more expansive and frequently distant views of rural and urban landscapes. Behind the stylistic shift was a conceptual one. The land was no longer perceived in strictly poetic or aesthetic terms but as a place where people lived and worked. Although human subjects are largely absent from these images, their labors are not. Working wharves, harvested fields, and stacked timber appear as constant reminders of human presence. Such images are presented with a direct matter-of-factness, devoid of a moral or philosophical tone. Where Noskowiak had once rejected all references to a broader context or reality in her works, she became increasingly inclusive and specific, using the camera to describe rather than fragment her surroundings.

San Francisco was a good place for Noskowiak, full of possibilities. Many of Noskowiak's friends were there, as well as a small but important community of women

SONYA NOSKOWIAK:
Untitled [Golden Gate Bridge], 1930s

artists—including Imogen Cunningham, Dorothea Lange, and Alma Lavenson. Noskowiak took advantage of her experience in portrait photography to open a studio on Union Street and attracted a distinguished clientele of artists, writers, actors, and musicians. She had learned the art of portrait photography in Carmel and knew how to exploit the subtleties of posing to evoke particular moods or emotions. Her ability to allude to her sitters' interior world was matched by her understanding of and admiration for the beauty of exteriors. She could not resist casting those with striking features in a dramatic light, often photographing the lines of the neck or face as she might a stunning ornament or piece of sculpture.

Business was always somewhat precarious for Noskowiak, however. She sometimes held several jobs at once and had little time for creative work. Though dating Noskowiak's prints can be difficult, it seems likely that she stopped making artistic photographs sometime in the mid-1940s, perhaps not long after working for the FAP. Commercial work ensued throughout the 1950s, but business plummeted in the early 1960s. In 1965 she was diagnosed with bone cancer and died ten years later in Marin County.

Noskowiak's career in photography took many turns, some spurred on by artistic decisions and others by personal circumstances. Noskowiak herself viewed her years with Edward Weston as a high point, and this was true artistically as well. Her work from this period reflects her seriousness about photography and related problems of form, light, and composition. However, Noskowiak's work continued to advance after she and Weston parted ways, and showed great insight into the social landscape of post-Depression era America. Noskowiak always photographed what she knew best without indulging in sentiment or narrative. California, her adopted home, inspired her finest efforts and tied her to a rich tradition of photography in the American West.

1 Johan Hagemeyer Archive, Center for Creative Photography.

2 Information about Noskowiak's childhood was obtained from an interview with her sister, Jadwiga Babcock, on 21 July 1994.

3 According to her sister, Noskowiak's friendship with Weston began in 1927, though this is yet to be confirmed.

4 Edward Weston, entry for 15 March 1930 in *The Daybooks of Edward Weston* (Millerton, New York Aperture, 1973), p.147.

5 Letter from Willard Van Dyke to Sonya Noskowiak, 4 September 1933, in *Sonya Noskowiak Archive*, *Guide Series* 5 (Center for Creative Photography, 1979).

Marion Palfi

by Betsi Meissner

By the mid- to late 1940s, émigré Marion Palfi (1907–1978) was fully integrated into American life. In only five short years, she had become an American citizen, established herself as an independent photographer, made contacts in the field, and was earning a modest living. She pursued her socially oriented photographic interests with courage and self-confidence until her death in 1978, and never forgot the discrimination that initially drove her away from her life in Berlin and Amsterdam.

Little is known about Palfi's early work in the United States and even less about her formative years abroad. Over the course of her career in this country, which spanned from the 1940s to the 1970s, she undertook a number of photographic studies that were intensive, all-consuming, and somewhat controversial. Many of them took years to complete. Only one, *Suffer Little Children*, was published, though a number of her photographs appeared in various pamphlets, brochures, and liberal-minded journals of the day. She was particularly sensitive to political and economic changes, having witnessed

the rise of a fascist government in Germany in the 1930s, and based many of her major life decisions on the political tide, in both Europe and America. This is evident in her choices of projects, many of which intersected with current news events.

MARION PALFI: Untitled, 1967–69
From the series *First I Liked the Whites, I Gave Them Fruits*

Palfi disliked using the term documentarian and referred to herself as a social research photographer. She believed documentary related only to factual information, devoid of the in-depth investigation and aesthetic considerations she found to be essential in her own work. In the manner of a photojournalist, she knew that bearing witness was the only acceptable option. Her photographs go beyond the superficiality of interesting subject matter to create visual statements of concern and caring within desperate situations. Her mission was to record the powerless and the disenfranchised as well as the isolated and the disinherited, in order to bring about improvement in their lives regardless of personal danger to the photographer.

Marion Palfi was born to an upper middle-class family in Berlin. A beautiful face and physique prompted lucrative modeling and acting careers, but political changes and a life reassessment resulted in her renouncement of a life in privileged German society. After a two-year apprenticeship at a traditional portrait studio in Berlin, she opened her

MARION PALFI: Untitled, 1955–57
From the series *You Have Never Been Old*

own studio and made a living in portraiture and occasional journalism assignments. As the political situation in Germany deteriorated, Palfi moved to Amsterdam and remained there until 1940, when she emigrated to the United States.

Her new home in New York provided an excellent foundation for her photographic ideology. The desire to acknowledge those in the margins of society and highlight their achievements culminated in a 1944–1945 project entitled "Great American Artists of Minority Groups." Photographs of Japanese-Irish ballet dancer Sono Osato, Jewish sculptor Chaim Gross, conductor and musician Dean Dixon, Spanish-American poster artist Leon Helguera, and poet Langston Hughes were included. Through her interaction with notable celebrities of New York while researching the project, Palfi established a circle of friends and acquaintances that she would call upon for support throughout her life. They included John Collier, Sr., Eleanor Roosevelt, Edward Steichen, Lisette Model, and Langston Hughes and his aunt, Toy Harper. Her close ties with Hughes resulted in ongoing

MARION PALFI: Untitled, 1949
From the series *There Is No More Time*

connections with the black community. These individuals helped Palfi to consolidate thoughts and ideas, and gave her a strong foundation of encouragement as she struggled to inspire others to take action through her imagery. Her stylistic tendencies, her modes of expression and presentation, and the subjects she chose are reminiscent of the work of the Farm Security Administration (FSA) photographers. In fact, her research methods and plans of action echo the shooting scripts FSA organizer Roy Stryker designed and dispensed to his photographers during the 1930s.

1948 was a particularly rewarding year as a number of Palfi photographs were featured with those of Morris Engel, Herbert Matter, and Arnold Newman at the Photo League in an exhibition entitled *A Closer Look: Four Photographers*. Palfi rented the darkroom facilities at the League, joined the organization, and eventually taught a photography class there.

For much of her career, Marion Palfi was modestly subsidized by various government and social work agencies and special interest groups. She received four major awards in her lifetime: a Julius Rosenwald Fellowship in 1946 to pursue work on race relations, a Taconic Foundation grant in 1963 to study segregation in the South, a John Simon Guggenheim Memorial Fellowship in 1967 to follow the relocation of Native Americans, and a grant from the National Endowment for the Arts in 1974 to look at this country's prison system. For the most part, however, she fronted her own money from commissioned work for the research projects dear to her.

Social documentary moved out of favor as a method of photographic expression in the late 1940s and early 1950s, suffering the ravages of McCarthyism and Cold

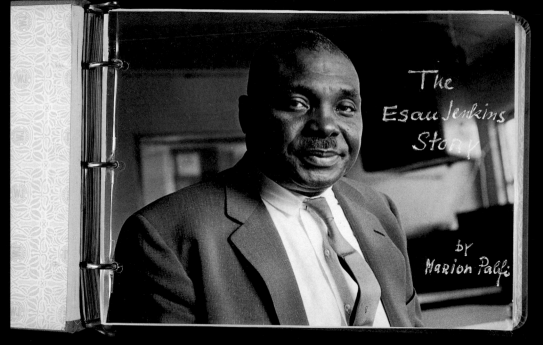

Title page of maquette for unpublished book "The Esau Jenkins Story," 1964/66

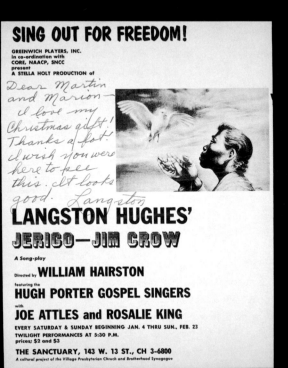

Handwritten note from Langston Hughes to Marion Palfi on handbill for his play *Jerico–Jim Crow*, n.d.

Cover of the premier issue of *Ebony* magazine, November 1945, with Palfi's photograph from the Henry Street Settlement in New York

All Items from the Marion Palfi Archive

War politics on one hand, and the aesthetic sea change of abstract expressionism on the other. Adding to its displacement in the media was the advent of a technical innovation known as television, where the most immediate events could be captured and broadcast. For Palfi, however, social documentary, or as she referred to it, social research, remained her photography of choice.

As we enter a new century, many of the issues Marion Palfi addressed in her imagery twenty-five to fifty years ago remain relevant issues in our society today. These include—under the larger rubric of civil rights—the divisive issues of racism, Native American living conditions and relocation, juvenile delinquency, the psychological aspects of aging and housing for the aged, the infringement of prison inmates' rights, the devastating effects of child neglect and abuse, the rise of gangs, and the persistence of poverty and slums. Addressing social conditions that challenged tidy notions of The American Dream as it guided so many immigrants to the shores of the United States, Palfi exposed struggle and injustice, true impediments to concepts such as life, liberty, and the pursuit of happiness.

MICKEY PALLAS: *Hula Hoopers, Chicago, 1958*

Mickey Pallas

by Dena McDuffie

The older I get, the less impressed I am by fame, fortune, and beauty. Instead, I find myself admiring the people who spend their lives doing what they want, doing it well, and having a ball doing it. Perhaps that's why I so admire Mickey Pallas (1916–1997).

Born in Belvidere, Illinois, the son of Rumanian Jewish immigrants, Mickey grew up poor in Chicago. He lived for a time in a home for orphans where he made lifelong friends, was bar mitzvahed, and learned to take pictures. He once called photography "the best thing that ever happened to me." When he finished high school, at the height of the Great Depression, Mickey set out on his own. He worked in a dry cleaning store, drove a truck, worked the assembly line at Studebaker, and was a union organizer in the food and tobacco industry. He married in 1937; he and wife Millie had two children. In his spare time, he led a band, "Mickey Pallas and His International Famous Orchestra."

All the while, he was taking pictures, honing his skills with a camera along with his insight into human nature. His early images are typical of beginning photographers: weddings, babies, and bar mitzvahs. But before long, Pallas counted *Ebony*, *Playboy*, and *Sepia* magazines, ABC-TV (most notably Studs Terkel's "Studs' Place" and "Morris B. Sachs' Amateur Hour"), Standard Oil, Encyclopedia Britannica, and the Harlem Globetrotters among his clients.

In 1959, displeased with the quality of photographic processing available in the Chicago area, Pallas founded Gamma Photo Labs. Gamma began as a two-man operation and grew to 125 employees, quickly becoming one of the largest labs in the country. By the time he sold Gamma to the Weiman Company in 1972, Pallas was a wealthy man.

Pallas decided to pursue a longtime dream. He opened a fine photography gallery in Chicago, the Center for Photographic Arts, in 1973—with galleries, a bookstore, darkrooms, and a research library for Chicago photographers. Despite good publicity and sterling intentions, the Center lasted less than a year. Pallas estimated huge losses. During the 1970s, Pallas opened two other galleries, but neither proved successful.

In 1979, Pallas suffered a stroke, the first of several that would eventually take his life. After several years of inactivity, he hired Janet Ginsburg to help organize the huge collection of photographs he had created. Ginsburg saw his potential as a fine artist and, in 1986, curated *Mickey Pallas: Photographs 1945–1960*, the first retrospective exhibition of Pallas's work, with Kenneth Burkhart of the Chicago Office of Fine Art.

In 1985, after a long struggle with cancer, Millie Pallas died. The following year, Mickey met and soon married Pat Zimmerman. The couple lived in Palm Springs for the next ten years, then moved to Scottsdale, Arizona, where Mickey died in 1997.

I met Mickey and Pat Pallas while I was organizing his archive at the CCP. Although he had suffered strokes and heart surgery and had lost much of his short-term memory and his hearing, his spirits were still high. He loved to tease, to joke, and to sing Yiddish songs in his wobbly voice. And he loved to laugh. He once told me, in a hushed tone as though he was entrusting me with a wonderful secret, "I had a lot of fun."

Photo League

by Betsi Meissner

Humanistic. Socially relevant. Politically charged. These are some of the words we now use to describe the Photo League. Concerned with nurturing a photographic sensitivity that would uncompromisingly reflect society, the League sought to use the photograph as an instrument for social change. As such, content and form were to become intimately linked.

Based in New York from 1936 to 1951, the League's origins can be traced to the 1930 formation of a politically leftist group known as the Film and Photo League, which had in turn been created as a cultural wing or offshoot of the Workers International Relief (WIR). A radically liberal Red Cross organization headquartered in Berlin before Hitler's rise to power, the function of the WIR was to offer international aid to laborers during worker strikes. The WIR organized the Worker's Camera Leagues in New York City to promote the efforts and causes of the class struggle. The photographs produced appeared in alternative publications such as *New Masses* and *Daily Worker*.[1]

JEROME LIEBLING: *Boy and Car, New York City*, 1949
From the portfolio *Jerome Liebling Photographs*, 1976

In the spring of 1930, the New York Camera League expanded to include film production. The new Film and Photo League's goal was "to struggle against and expose reactionary film; to produce documentary films reflecting the lives and struggles of the American worker; to spread and popularize the great artistic and revolutionary Soviet productions."[2]

Controversy frequently erupted among members beginning in 1934 regarding subject matter and production, leading to a formal division two years later. Still photographers reformed as the Photo League. A number of the filmmakers, including Ralph Steiner and Paul Strand, reorganized to form Frontier Films. An amiable relationship existed between the two organizations with Frontier members appearing at the League as lecturers and panelists, and their film productions were featured occasionally. The goals of the Photo League changed slightly to "put the camera back into the hands of honest photographers, who . . . use[d] it to photograph America."[3]

WALTER ROSENBLUM:
Women and Baby Carriage, Pitt Street, New York, 1938

The Photo League served as a self-sufficient forum for social documentary, relying on membership dues and fees from classes and lectures for operating expenses. It did not cater to pictorialist, experimental, or contemporary schools of work, but welcomed and encouraged those who chose to photograph the external world as directly and as realistically as possible. The amateur and professional photographer members sought to elevate the status and meaning of photography and to increase social awareness and reform by integrating formal elements of design and visual aesthetics with powerful and sympathetic evidence of the human condition. This credo can best be observed in League members' preference for street photography and documentary over other genres. Group photographic projects included studies of New York's Harlem, the Lower East Side and other ethnic neighborhoods, the lives and economic needs of children, civil defense (police and firemen etc.), and the changing cityscape. Membership in and association with the League hinged on a keen interest in socially relevant issues, and not simply on a matter of photographic style.

LEWIS W. HINE: *Bowery Mission Bread Line, 2 A.M.*, 1907
From the portfolio *Lewis W. Hine, 1874–1940*, 1942

League headquarters were low profile, occupying a New York loft space that consisted of two rooms, a lobby, a gallery space, and darkroom. Membership enabled use of the darkroom and participation in one of the most active and wide-ranging photographic groups in America. Seeking to be distinctive amid the myriad of contemporary camera clubs, the League offered basic and advanced photography classes—this at a time when no such courses were offered in trade schools, colleges, or universities. By 1938 the school had expanded to include documentary workshops featuring guest lecturers such as Paul Strand and Berenice Abbott. League members organized approximately six exhibitions per year; these ranged from solo to group shows and involved both members and invited guests. Notably, photographs by Lisette Model and photo montages by John Heartfield made their American debuts at the

```
April 4
Present: Siskind, Mendelsohn, Engel, Corsini, Lyon, Kleinman,
Lester, Schiffman, Kosofsky, Prom.

Fortune Magazine is interested in our Harlem Document prints, as
they are planning a series on New York life.  Columbia University
is also interested in exhibiting our Document pictures, but the
show will probably not be held before the Fall.  The New Masses
is giving the Portrait of a Tenement a two-page spread.
The Teachers' Union will be able to get us into a Harlem school
so that we may take pictures of overcrowding.
Our Park Avenue Series is missing.
Engel brought in some new laundry pictures.  A portrait of the owner
was very dramatic, but not well lighted or printed.  We filed two
prints of workers at the machines, one very simple and natural, the
other more striking.
Mendelsohn's picture of the Stanford White houses was so harshly
printed and the shadows were so dense that he was asked to make
a softer print.
Carter bought a switchblade knife, for photographic purposes.
```

Minutes from meeting of Photo League group working on the *Harlem Document*,
4 April [1940?]
Aaron Siskind Archive

League. A newsletter, known as *Photo Notes*, was produced sixty-five times over the years, and included member information, updates, lecture and debate calendars as well as photographer's tips. Among the noted lecturers who spoke at the League were Ansel Adams, Margaret Bourke-White, Robert Frank, and W. Eugene Smith. Major social events took place about every six months and frequently featured entertainers such as Pete Seeger and Woody Guthrie (who lived upstairs from the League). The headquarters itself served as an informal meeting place and remained open every evening and weekends.

League members admired and sought input from a number of photographers whom they regarded as 'honest,' those involved in social investigation and also persistent in uncovering candid moments. These included the photographers of the 1930s project conducted by the Farm Security Administration as well as Berenice Abbott, Alfred Stieglitz, Paul Strand, and Edward Weston. The League also served as caretaker of the Lewis Hine Memorial Collection. Prints from Hine's negatives were sold in small portfolios (fifty portfolios of five prints each—one of which is in the CCP collection) to raise money for sorting and cataloguing the collection after Hine's son gave the League control of the photographic estate.

Most of the members who joined before the end of World War II were first generation Americans born in the first quarter of the twentieth century. Many stood in firm agreement with the political beliefs of the liberal intelligentsia and were vehemently

SANDRA WEINER:
East 26th Street, New York, NY, 1948

anti-Fascist. Few were aware of the Photo League's Berlin origins and believed the group had been founded in 1936 rather than reorganized.

Just as politics played an important role in the formation of the Photo League, politics were to be the ultimate undoing of it. The search for and persecution of those individuals and organizations with possible Communist ties became the pervading task of Senator Joseph McCarthy in the late 1940s. In December 1947, the Photo League was declared subversive and placed on the United States Department of Justice blacklist by the Attorney General. As the concept of socially informed documentary photography also came under attack, a number of eminent photographers defied the charges and joined in support of the League, inflating the membership ranks to over one hundred, but governmental pressure and the resulting fears of an anxious general public eventually overwhelmed the organization. It dissolved in the summer of 1951.

Documentary photography, and specifically social documentary, suffered a severe blow. It would not again become a popular and active pursuit for groups of photographers until the 1960s.

Over the course of its fifteen-year existence, the Photo League attracted the participation of virtually every major photographer who traveled to or lived in New York. It was a unique place where photographers could come together to share, explore, and nurture their ideas through impassioned discourse and collective work.

Approximately three hundred artists' names can be linked to the Photo League through the *Photo Notes* newsletters. The Center has one or more photographs by forty-three of these photographers, including major archival collections of League members Ansel Adams, Richard Avedon, Sid Grossman, Marion Palfi, Aaron Siskind, W. Eugene Smith, Paul Strand, Todd Webb, Dan Weiner, Edward Weston, Max Yavno, and Ylla. Other members and associates represented in the photograph collection include Berenice Abbott, Alexander Alland, Lou Bernstein, Rudolph Burckhardt, Jack Delano, Eliot Elisofon, Morris Engel, Robert S. Harrah, Fritz Henle, Lewis Hine, Consuelo Kanaga, Sy Kattelson, Erika Klopfer Stone, Dorothea Lange, Jerome Liebling, Lisette Model, Barbara Morgan, Beaumont Newhall, Nancy Newhall, Arnold Newman, Ruth Orkin, Walter Rosenblum, Arthur Rothstein, Yolla Niclas Sachs, Ben Shahn, Louis Stettner, Lou Stoumen, John Vachon, David Vestal, and Minor White.

1 Anne Tucker, "The Photo League: Photography as a Social Force," *Modern Photography* 43:9 (September 1979), p. 90.

2 Ibid. Quoted by Tucker from *Experimental Cinema* (February 1931).

3 Ibid, p. 92. Quoted from *Photo Notes* (August 1938).

AARON SISKIND: *Remembering Joseph Cornell in Merida 12, 1975*

Aaron Siskind

by Maria Antonella Pelizzari

In 1978, during an interview at the Center for Creative Photography, Aaron Siskind (1903–1991) explained his need to take pictures, observing that "a photograph, like any work of art, is something that you have to enter into . . . like a dream." Siskind, who began to use the camera in the early 1930s in New York City as a documentary photographer, was profoundly interested in photography as a visual language that could convey the metaphors, symbols, and substance of dreams. This abstract and even surrealist approach to photography has often puzzled Siskind's critics and historians who have interpreted his photographs as though they were the work of an abstract expressionist painter instead of investigating the particular nature of Siskind's photographic language.

If Siskind received inspiration and professional encouragement from the community of abstract expressionists in New York in the 1940s, it is still limiting to see his pictures as formal abstractions of objects found in the world. Siskind's main concern was not abstraction in photography. Through the camera lens, he intended to find a poetic language that could link experience with memory, sight with surprise, common objects with unknown signs. As Siskind's most acknowledged critic, Carl Chiarenza, has explained, "for him the photograph was a visual construction equivalent to the verbal construction of poetry and the sound construction of music."[1]

Siskind played piano and wrote poetry before he realized that he could be more successful with a camera than with a notepad. His background was in literature, and he recognized as his most important influences the writings of Marcel Proust, James Joyce, T. S. Eliot, and, most important, the poetry of William Blake. Like Blake, Siskind was concerned with the basic duality of life, with the tension between good and evil, the body and the spirit, imprisonment and freedom, connection and isolation, illusion and truth. This tension permeates all his work, even as he explores a variety of genres, from architectural photography to still life, from social documentary to abstraction. The body of work that most clearly illustrates this tension was produced in his mid-career in 1954, and titled *Terrors and Pleasures of Levitation*. Inspired by the scene of young divers in Lake Michigan near Chicago, Siskind photographed their bodies floating in midair, in the sublime moment of suspension between earth and sky. Strictly photographic for its capacity to capture movement, this group of images appears like the creation of a new calligraphy, in which the human body is a signifier of weight and gravity in photographic verses on freedom and lightness.

Floating and mysterious figures like the divers can be identified throughout Siskind's work. Even his early documentary photographs in New York City in the 1930s suggest a symbolic nature rather than a social commentary. In 1932, he joined the Film and Photo League, a photographic organization that was most concerned with social reform and documentary essays. Siskind did not embrace the organization's credo but attended lectures and discussed photography in what was the main venue at that time. His largest body of work from this period was produced with the Feature Group at the League and titled *Harlem Document*. In this body of work, Siskind engaged with his students on the meaning of documentary photography, on photography as the result of an idea, and on the formal construction of a picture through the photographer's own perception and feeling.

From this engagement with documentary practice grew Siskind's exploration of photography as a way "to see the world clean and fresh and alive,"[2] free and independent from factual information and careful planning. He was first struck by this experience in 1944 at the New England fishing village of Gloucester, when he began to photograph discarded objects on the beach and found him-

AARON SISKIND:
Terrors and Pleasures of Levitation 94, 1961

self "involved in the relationships of [those] objects, so much that the pictures turned out to be deeply moving and personal experiences." Realizing that "subject matter, as such, had ceased to be of primary importance," he let his personal responses guide the choice of subjects and shapes, thus starting to compose his own visual poems through organic debris and objects in transformation. While the subject matter shifted from seaweed and discarded gloves to writings on the wall, graffiti, and natural formations, his involvement with photography as a means to unconscious response did not change until the end of his life.

From the mid-1950s on, Siskind tested these ideas about picture making also through his travels abroad (to Mexico, Italy, Greece, Peru). Most frequently, he traveled to experience that "freshness" of perception that he had felt in Gloucester, moving through foreign-speaking crowds in a state of surprise, stimulated by his own feeling of estrangement and isolation. He recognized in distant countries like Mexico and Italy signs of decay, religion, and of organic transformation from life to death. His renderings of Roman statues on the Appian Way, like his images of mummies at Guanajuato, are reminders of his early fascination with discarded objects, resting in the world in a state of temporary flux.

Likewise, Siskind's memories were stimulated by foreign sites. He dedicated bodies of work in Italy and Mexico to his friends Franz Kline and Joseph Cornell. These homages confirm Siskind's picture making as a process of memory retrieval. The experience of travel excited his perception, enabling him to recognize in foreign shapes familiar ones, and vice versa.

Siskind's unique contribution to the history of twentieth-century photography was not only as a picture maker but also as a teacher. Together with Harry Callahan, he formed the core curricula of the first master's degree in photography at the Chicago Institute of Design, beginning to teach there in the fall of 1951. That same year he taught photography at Black Mountain College. Later, in 1971, he joined the Department of Photography at the Rhode Island School of Design. He was active during the early years of the Society for Photographic Education, in rendering photography a new field of discussion and in implementing educational activities. His teaching, together with his humanistic belief in photography as an instrument of self-knowledge, makes him a towering figure in the history of American photography and culture.

1 Carl Chiarenza, "Form and Content in the Early Work of Aaron Siskind," in *Photography: Current Perspectives*, (Rochester: Light Impressions, 1978), p. 188.

2 Aaron Siskind, "The Drama of Objects" (1945), in Nathan Lyons, *Photographers on Photography* (Englewood Cliffs, New Jersey: Prentice Hall, 1966).

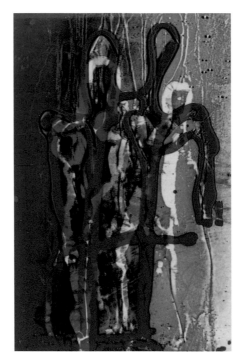

HENRY HOLMES SMITH:
Royal Pair, 1951/1982

Henry Holmes Smith

by Leon Zimlich

The enactment of the GI Bill at the close of World War II led to a burgeoning of programs of higher learning in the United States. Photography began to be taught in the fine arts departments of colleges and universities. Among the artists leading the photographic community into academia was Henry Holmes Smith (1909–1986), who taught at Indiana University from 1947 to 1976. There, Smith offered the first university course in the history of photography; was a founding member of the Society for Photographic Education; and wrote endlessly about photography and the place of the photographer in society. An inspiring teacher, he taught generations of photographers who have gone on to teach others and at the same time, he created significant photography of his own. As a leader within a developing community of fine art photographers, teachers, and critics, Henry Holmes Smith played a pivotal role in forming the ways we think about photography now.

Henry Holmes Smith joined the faculty of Indiana University in 1947, but his teaching began before the war at the New Bauhaus. Members of the Association of Arts and Industries, an organization of Chicago area manufacturers, wanted a school of design in the United States to contribute to the needs of American industry. They persuaded László Moholy-Nagy, an émigré from Nazi Germany and a former master at the original Bauhaus school, to establish The New Bauhaus American School of Design in Chicago. Modeled after the original Bauhaus school of design in Germany (1919–33), the Chicago school was short-lived, lasting only a year. It was revived to become first the School of Design and then finally the Institute of Design, where Harry Callahan, Aaron Siskind, and Arthur Siegel taught.

At the Bauhaus, as well as at the New Bauhaus, photography was not practiced as a separate art but as one of a number of tools available to a designer. No preconceptions limited how the medium should be used. Consequently, students of the school experimented. This freedom from a dogmatic view of photography appealed to Smith. As a student at Ohio State University, he admired Moholy-Nagy's teachings about photography, particularly for their views on the role the arts played in life.

Smith was working in the darkrooms of the Marshall Field department store portrait studio in Chicago when Moholy-Nagy began to organize the New Bauhaus. Smith wrote Moholy-Nagy regarding his own experiments with color photography and was later invited to design the darkrooms for the school. Building the new darkrooms led to the opportunity to teach as well. Smith worked with Gyorgy Kepes, who ran the photography program during the single year that the New Bauhaus operated (1937–38), before financial difficulties forced its closure.

The end of New Bauhaus allowed Smith to pursue other interests. He was a prolific writer, producing perhaps more fiction and nonfiction than photographs, and it was as a writer that he had the broadest influence over the photographic community. In 1939, on the recommendation of Moholy-Nagy, *Minicam* magazine hired Smith to write an article on photographic solarization. This eventually led to a position as an associate editor of the magazine, where he stayed until inducted into the United States Army in 1942. But his experience there was dissatisfying.

The mediocrity of the popular photographic press and the control it and photographic manufacturers exercised over the medium provoked in Smith the desire for a community of professional fine art photographers, that would control the conditions of its work. That desire, shared by others, remained with him when he returned from the war in 1945. The founding of *Aperture* by Minor White, Beaumont and Nancy Newhall, Ansel Adams, and others in 1951 provided a forum for that fledgling community. Smith was a frequent contributor to the journal and became a regional editor in 1960. In *Aperture* he published a seminal series of essays on the subject of interpreting, or reading, photographs, beginning in 1953 with

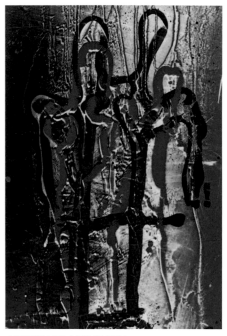

HENRY HOLMES SMITH
Royal Pair, 8, 1951/1982

"The Photograph and Its Readers" and continuing through "Image, Obscurity, and Interpretation" in 1957.

The idea that photographs could be read was but one aspect of the trend in postwar photography toward subjectivism. Another was the rise of photography as an academic discipline, which helped shift the emphasis from documentary, prevalent in the Depression era and throughout the war, to a more individual expression of the photographer's state of mind. Two leaders in this direction were Minor White and Henry Holmes Smith.

This impulse in Smith's work might be seen in his early dissatisfaction with the formal education he received at Illinois State Normal University, the Art Institute of Chicago, and Ohio State University, where he graduated in 1933 with a degree in art education. At each of these institutions Smith found that art education was plagued by dogmatic, rote-teaching methods and artistic practice that was neither encouraging nor accepting of personal expression that departed from the mainstream. Nevertheless, he did find encouragement in the work of other artists, such as the photographs of Francis Bruguière published in the 1920s, which inspired Smith through their play with light. In László Moholy-Nagy he found an example to guide his development as an artist in society.

Arguing that the essence of photography was the manipulation of light, Smith adopted a variety of techniques, including combination printing, multiple exposures and photomontage, which were traditionally anathema to straight photography. He evolved a photogram-like technique using refractive substances such as water and syrup on glass, sometimes in combination with dye-transfer color printing, to produce cameraless but nevertheless figurative images.

His technique was suited to his subject matter—the metaphysical, mythical, fundamental relationship of man to god, parent to child. For example, the black-and-white image *Mother and Son*, 1951, inquires into both that familial relationship and the Greek myth of Oedipus. Free from dictates of method and straight photography, he explored numerous variations of *Royal Pair*, experimenting in both black-and-white gelatin silver printing and dye-transfer color imagery.

Over the course of thirty years, from 1947 to his retirement in 1977, Smith taught several generations of students, among them Jack Welpott, Betty Hahn, Jerry Uelsmann, and Robert Fichter, who have themselves gone on to teach still more students. That their work demonstrates such a wide variety of techniques and purposes is a testament to Smith's ability to prod his students toward self-expression rather than a slavish adherence to tradition. Smith's interest in building a community of thinking professionals who would control the discourse surrounding fine art photography led to his organizing numerous exhibitions, workshops, and publication. These included a 1956 workshop on interpreting photographs, and a 1962 panel on teaching photography, which was a beginning toward the creation of the Society for Photographic Education.

W. EUGENE SMITH: Untitled [Haiti], 1958–59

W. Eugene Smith

by William S. Johnson

W. Eugene Smith (1918–1978) passionately believed that photographs could change individual lives, influence public opinion, play a central role in the affairs of men and nations, and even affect the course of human history. He also passionately believed that the most beautiful photograph was the most moving photograph—and thus the best photograph to accomplish this aim.

So Smith believed that it was both aesthetically necessary and morally imperative for a photojournalist to create the most beautiful, most powerful, and most significant work of art possible out of the events of their daily occupation. And he struggled to transform every photographic "story" from a mundane informational narrative essay about a particular event or activity into a poetic vehicle for the creative interpretation of the human condition.

From the very beginning of his career, his relentless energy and drive, his commitment, his undoubted skills and talents, and, most particularly, his extraordinary photographs, had made Smith a phenomenon, then a legend in his field. In the pragmatic world of professional photojournalism, Smith's impassioned stance was admired and extolled as the better part of the discipline's ethical potential and simultaneously denigrated as impractical and obstructionist. Smith was frequently admired and castigated in the same breath by his fellow professionals. His professional activities and his private exploits were an active part of the stories and legends that circulated throughout the fabric of the photographic community. Smith became a celebrity and a taste-maker: whether he liked it or not, his reputation lent weight and substance to what he did, what he said, or how he photographed.

Briefly, during the anti-Communist hysteria of the Cold War, Smith attempted to turn this reputation to political use in support of the rights of those photographers of the New York Photo League under attack by the United States Attorney General's Office. This muddled effort failed and Smith permanently turned away from any form of organized political activity, but he never shook himself free from his self-imposed responsibility to define the ethical and aesthetic dimensions of his discipline. Smith often found this responsibility to be a burden and came to believe that the only way that he could meet this burden was by providing an ideal model through the strength of his own work and the correctness of his own professional decisions.

Thus there were few casual photographic opportunities for Smith, as almost anything he photographed might (with some grace, a little luck, and a lot of hard work and emotional anguish) be transformed into a work of art. It must have been a little like being on a baseball team involved in a tight pennant race, where everything or anything in every game could make or break the season for the team. Of course, the emotional toll of constantly living within this heightened state of tension was enormous —very wearing on Smith and also tough on those around him.

The amazing thing is not how often Smith failed to transform his everyday assignments into expressive art during the course of his career, but how many times he succeeded. During World War II, his essays—all only published in fragmented form—about the carrier warfare in the South Pacific, the wounded soldiers in "Hospital on Leyte," and the Japanese civilians in the refugee camps, as well as his photographs of the battles of Saipan, Iwo Jima, and Okinawa, were extraordinary in their demonstration of personal daring, humane compassion and emotional intensity.

After the war Smith's essays in *Life* magazine, from "Folk Singers," published in 1947, followed by the historic "Country Doctor" in 1948, then "Taft and Ohio" in 1949, and "Great Britain" in 1950, to the classic "Spanish Village," "Recording Artists," "Nurse Midwife," all published in 1951, through the 1952 essay "Chaplin at Work" to "A Man of Mercy," his 1954 essay on Albert Schweitzer, were often seen as key markers in the post-war growth of humanistic photojournalism. They also are extraordinary examples of the fluidly evolving vision of a major artist struggling to expand the boundaries of his personal style and to enlarge his grasp over the complexities of his chosen discipline—which was the art of the narrative photographic essay.

After leaving *Life* in 1954 over a dispute involving what he thought to be an editorial misuse of his photographs that damaged his effort to achieve a heightened awareness of the photographic essay as a means of expression, Smith became involved in a long, confused, and ultimately personally disastrous project called the "Pittsburgh" essay. Hired to provide some contemporary views for a chapter in a visual book celebrating the one hundredth anniversary of the city of Pittsburgh, Smith, still smarting from his battles with *Life* and believing that the fullest emotional potential of the photographic essay had not yet been achieved, independently and unilaterally attempted to transform this commercial assignment into an epic visual poem that he hoped would be similar in its scope, dimensions, and impact to Walt Whitman's *Leaves of Grass*.

He hoped that the "Pittsburgh" essay would be groundbreaking, that it would be so powerful and so persuasive that it would compel the photographic community at large to expand its understanding and raise its standards about the aesthetic potentials of the photographic essay form. This effort, to Smith's mind, failed. And it failed in reality as well, as the photographic community accepted the part of the "Pittsburgh" essay that finally reached publication with mixed praise, but with little overt comprehension or concern for the issues that had been driving Smith so hard for so many years. This issue upon which Smith had foundered his career and damaged his personal life was simply not that important for the general community, and Smith's inarticulate efforts to effect a sweeping change within his discipline were either misconstrued or misunderstood.

Smith then went into a period of retrenchment, moving into a downtown loft in New York and living and working among the anti-establishment New York arts underground that was then fermenting towards a paradigm shift in the arts, cultural, and social scenery of America during the 1950s and 1960s. There Smith's art continued to evolve as he shifted away from the rhetorical public style that had served him so well as a photojournalist and found his way into a more intimate and personal photographic vision.

During the next decade Smith continued to generate work that was extraordinary in its richness, complexity, and power. This included his essays on the musicians and visual

W. EUGENE SMITH: *Earl Hines*, 1964

artists living around him in New York City, his documentation of the social unrest and political protests of the 1960s, and what he once called his "greatest unpublished essay," which was the work he made between 1958 and 1959 about bringing some form of modern medical treatment to the insane in Haiti.

Most of this work was never completely realized, and it was seldom publicly seen in any extensive form. Nevertheless, individual photographs from the larger bodies of work were published, and these continued to uphold and extend Smith's reputation throughout the newer generations within the photographic community. And as the adherents of the practice of photography as a means of private, personal expression grew in number and in influence within the overall photographic community, Smith's beautiful photographs and the continuing stories of his artistic dedication served to gather even more legends around his name.

Curiously, the two most completely realized bodies of work that Smith accomplished during the final years of his career took place not in the United States, but in Japan. The first started out as a commercial job for the Hitachi corporation, one of the industrial giants of the burgeoning Japanese industry. Hired in 1961 to make photographs for what was, in essence, a company's annual report, Smith transformed that job into his first full-length book titled *Japan: A Chapter of Image*, which he himself photographed, edited, and wrote. Once again Smith attempted to create an evocative essay that went beyond the literal depiction of the corporation's activities to express his own poetic responses to the colors and character of Japan. The book, divided between these two poles, is not completely successful. But the body of photographic work that Smith generated during his yearlong visit to Japan is extraordinary in its vigor, range, and complexity.

In 1971, Smith returned to Japan again, and he and his new Japanese–American wife Aileen joined an ongoing citizen's protest movement against industrial pollution then occurring in the small city of Minamata. For four years the Smiths demonstrated in and photographed these intensifying protest activities and their political consequences, and they organized exhibitions and created articles and essays that were published in Japan and throughout the world. This work culminated with the publication of the book *Minamata*, the final and most successful book-length photographic essay that Smith accomplished. *Minamata*, with its dramatic message, its impassioned humanity, and its powerful photographs, became one of the first popular works to focus worldwide attention on the problems of industrial pollution and potential ecological damage. The ambition of this venture and its successful completion brought Smith's reputation back out of the shadows that had surrounded his middle career. W. Eugene Smith's work was once again widely acclaimed as the apex of humanistic photography.

WAKE UP AMERICA

15 years ago the Ku Klux Klan distributed
millions of hand-bills like this!

COMMUNISM

Destroys Free Government
and all its Institutions

COMMUNISM
WILL NOT BE
TOLERATED

KU KLUX KLAN
RIDES AGAIN

(This is copy of original (reduced)

The KU KLUX KLAN has never stopped its fight on COMMUNISM.

The CONGRESS of the U. S. laughed — They investigated — reported that there were no COMMUNISTS in America.

Today the government itself has awakened to the real danger facing us.

The conviction of spies has been so numerous that we hear no more about "Red Herring."

COMMUNISM is being taught in our PUBLIC SCHOOLS.
(Ask your children)

COMMUNISM is being taught openly in OUR COLLEGES.

COMMUNISTS are in key positions in many of our LABOR UNIONS.

COMMUNISTIC ideas are being fed to you and your children thru the Motion Pictures.

Even some of our Preachers have COMMUNISTIC ideas and are including them in their SERMONS.

THE KU KLUX KLAN is fighting against Negro Domination to protect our WHITE WOMANHOOD — to uphold the kind of DEMORACY given to us by our FORE-FATHERS.

PRO COMMUNIST The Anti-Defamation League of the B-nai B'rith calls Gentiles "Goyin." (which means cattle) and seeks by block negro voting, smear tactics to build Jewish Communist Dictatorship in the United States. THIS WE MUST PREVENT.

THE KU KLUX KLAN is fighting COMMUNISM and all other ISMS except PURE AMERICANISM.

If interested in our crusade write

POST OFFICE BOX 231, LEESVILLE, S. C.

ASSOCIATION OF CAROLINA KLANS

Ku Klux Klan handbill published by the Association of
Carolina Klans. Collected by W. Eugene Smith while trav-
eling in the South for his Nurse Midwife essay, ca. 1954
W. Eugene Smith Archive

Contact sheet made of 2¼-inch negatives and notebook from the "Country Doctor" essay, 1948
W. Eugene Smith Archive

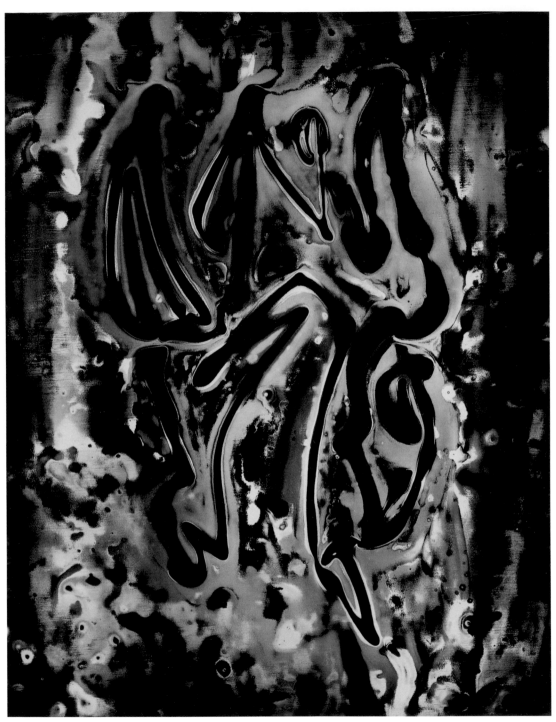

FREDERICK SOMMER: *Smoke on Glass*, 1962

Frederick Sommer

by Nancy Solomon

Art and photography order our visual perception
Aesthetic logic is the ordering of our feelings

Choice and chance
Structure art
And nature[1]

Frederick Sommer (1905–1999) was an international intellectual and artist before he became a photographer. Born in Italy in 1905 of a Swiss mother and a German father, he trained in landscape architecture at Cornell University in Ithaca, New York, and completed his first projects in Rio de Janeiro, Brazil. He could read and converse in German, Italian, English, Portuguese, and French. From the beginning his work was anchored by a strong sense of structure, an order he found in nature. He was already accomplished in drawing and painting when seeing work by Edward Weston whetted his interest in photography.

An aura of myth surrounded Sommer and his work as a photographer. His choice to live in the remote Prescott, Arizona; his highly selected oeuvre; a few tantalizing published writings; and his ability to attain the long tonal mid-range of platinum in silver prints—all contributed to his status as a legendary photographer.

Although choosing to live outside major art hubs, Sommer remained in touch with important figures in the world of photography as an art form. He visited Alfred Stieglitz for a week in 1935. After seeing Edward Weston's photographs and visiting him in California, Sommer bought a Century Universal 8x10-inch view camera. The Westons then visited in Prescott in 1938 during their Guggenheim-funded travel in Arizona. Sommer met Charles Sheeler in 1940 and was a close friend of Max Ernst, who later moved to Sedona, Arizona. Sommer's photographs were presented in *Aperture* in the 1950s, and a special issue was devoted to his work in 1962. Henry Holmes Smith used Sommer's *Sacred Wood* in his early explorations into "reading" photographs.

As a man of his own ideas, Sommer was not interested in the conventional museum presentation in which a curator or critic looks back over an artist's lifetime work. His response to curatorial initiatives was usually "pretend I'm dead." He did not want to participate. Yet, Frederick Sommer was intimately involved in the Center's publication of a pair of books in 1984: *Sommer·Images* and *Sommer·Words*. What drew him to this project was a unique publishing concept devised by then-Director James Enyeart: "[The] Books…are devoted to an artist's integral participation in the content and design. These books reinforce the concept that books as visual instruments can be meaningful as conventional monographs and that by allowing artists to speak directly through a book format of their own creation, we learn more than is printed on the page."[2]

FREDERICK SOMMER: *Valise d'Adam*, 1949

The Frederick Sommer Archive contains four 8x10-inch films for *Valise d'Adam*, 1949. Two are negatives and two are thin film positives. Both negatives are fairly dense. Note that the camera shifted slightly between exposures: the photograph in the Center's collection shows more of the background wall on the right revealing a vertical sequence of four more holes in the wall.

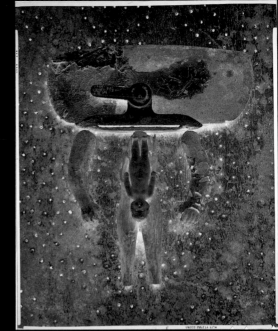

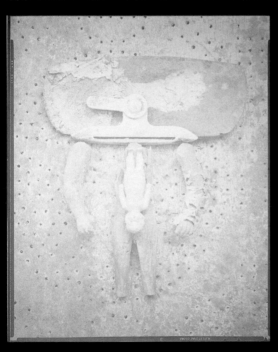

Sommer's film holders were bored with identifying pinholes, which are in the upper left margin of the negatives [see enlargement beside the negatives] as 4+1 and 4+3 configurations, respectively. He also painted Agfa Crocein Scarlet dye directly on the emulsions, adding density to different thin areas on each negative.

A call to Naomi Lyons, printer for Sommer since 1985, explained more. Sommer with printer Alex Jamison devised a system of using a film positive as an out-of-focus mask by suspending it on glass one inch above the negative in the contact frame. The film positives were both made from the 4+3 negative. Because the negatives were so similar, the film positive from the one could be used to mask either. They considered applying for a patent for this unique system. According to Lyons, Sommer made fine prints from both negatives but usually printed from the 4+1 negative.

FREDERICK SOMMER: *Paracelsus (paint on cellophane)*, 1959

Frederick Sommer's visual art found expression in drawing and painting before he ever became a photographer. His *cliché verre*, literally "painting on glass," negatives bring this earlier means of expression into his photography. There are at least three different types of *cliché verre* negatives in his archive. *Paracelsus*, 1959, was painted in dusty-rose-colored acrylic medium on cellophane and sandwiched between two sheets of glass. According to Sommer's printer Naomi Lyons, the *cliché verre* negatives were printed with a 5x7-inch Burke and James Solar enlarger. The cellophanes between glass heated and flattened during the printing process. The archive also contains many very fragile, still-rippled negatives painted on cellophane.

Smoke on Glass, 1962, represents Sommer's third type of *cliché verre*. In *Sommer · Words*, he describes his process for making these paintings in soot and grease on a single sheet of glass:

I take a piece of aluminum foil and draw on it....The next move...is to take these foils and smoke them over a candle. Having deposited the soot on foil, the next step is to grease a piece of glass lightly. Once I have done this, it becomes easy to take the soot that is on the aluminum foil and press it onto the glass....If all goes well (and it sometimes does), the definition is magnificent; there are no grain problems because soot can out-perform silver images any day.

This project would allow Sommer a forum for his writing as well as his photographs. And he wanted them to be separate and yet together—thus the format of two matching books. Enyeart described how the process would work: "In order for this collaboration with the Center as publisher to take place, it is necessary to have a designer in the tradition of a master craftsperson capable of working with the artist over a period of time; such has been the case with Nancy Solomon and Frederick Sommer."[3]

As intermediary, I experienced his creative process at work—I was both an observer and a participant—seeing when his process was fixed and when it was fluid. Sommer had worked on his texts with a secretary, in that time when computer printouts looked typewritten. He had already thought about the position of every line on the page; our objective, when these texts were transformed into type in a book, was to make it appear on the page as much like the typewritten page as possible. Yet, this was the same mind that devised skipreading—where he read aloud from an existing work (in our book we presented skipreading from Apollinaire's *Zone*) selecting phrasing and words to create a new poetry that was still grounded in the original text, sequences selected from the original order. Hearing him skipreading aloud from a new text to show me how it worked was one of the loveliest moments in the project for me.

The images in the book were selected from photographs already in his archive at the Center and from some works on paper, such as paintings drawn in pigmented glue that looked like musical scores, which were soon to be added to the collection. We were sequencing his Arizona landscapes in which the horizon was outside the picture, making the foreground or middle ground function as the entire picture plane. There were his images of cut-paper constructions, images out of focus to emphasize their monumental features, compositions created of the juicy innards of chickens, portraits, and the collages and abstract works on paper.

We had a stack of 8x10-inch copy prints representing every image in the book and built a sequence, surrounding ourselves in a circle in his living room with pairs of images to be seen together in the spreads of the book. Some of the pairs were dramatic, bringing together unexpected combinations of images. The sequence was exciting but there was one spot where it didn't work. The conceptual gap after one spread was too great. We tried working out of it; moving pairs throughout the book. Ultimately, he decided the sequence could not be fixed. He picked up all the copy prints, shuffled them, threw them down to further alter the sequence, and we started anew with completely different pairs, arriving at the sequence presented in *Sommer · Images*.

One theme that ran through his life and his work was middle tone gray. He painted his house in Zone V gray (chosen from Ansel Adams's zone system). Even his bathtub and fixtures were the same color. This selection carried through into the books, which were bound in gray paper and stamped in a lighter matte gray foil.

When we went to the printer, Prisma Graphic, in Phoenix for three days of press checks, he surprised me again. We had co-designed the books, working within the limitations of the sizes of book printing paper, the size of presses, and the need to isolate color images in one part of the book for cost reasons. All my training in publishing books about fine art has been focused on reproducing the original as faithfully as possible. When we started the duotone press checks, Sommer told the pressman, "You know, I always wanted these to be more gray. You would be doing me a favor if you ran more gray."

I should not have been so surprised. In the companion volume, *Sommer · Words*, he had discussed this very issue:

> *I don't like to make the same thing twice just to store it away. I have ceased think-ing that all prints from the same negative should look alike. It may be that the next time I print, I'm lucky to get two or three prints that in their differences serve other aspects of their possibilities. Creators of images in the past, like Seghers and Rembrandt, had no qualms about making prints that would be difficult to rec-ognize as having been made from the same plate. I haven't pushed my prints to that length because when a photograph is under-printed or over-printed too much, it looks like hell. Fine drawing paper, without anything on it, is more to look at than an empty spot on a piece of photographic paper; the black ink in a fine etching is richer than the black in a photograph. So there are some innate limita-tions. Apart from that, I tend to favor variety between prints. Beautiful variations between prints are assets, not discrepancies.*[4]

After Sommer's death, materials began to arrive at the Center for his archive. Now one can view his negatives. Particularly intriguing are the *cliché verre* negatives that he made to get "some of this need for drawing out of my blood....If all goes well ... the definition is magnificent; there are no grain problems because soot can out-perform silver images any day."[5]

They are fragile beyond what I had imagined—some rippled by the wetness of the ink forty years ago. There are many more *cliché verre* negatives than are represented in prints in the collection. A study collection of original cut paper also exceeds the images we know in his photographs.

His 8x10-inch negatives can be examined. For instance, the dense negatives for his image field landscapes of the Arizona desert allowed long exposures to reveal the pre-cise detail in these photographs. The set of films for *Valise d'Adam* including both neg-atives with positive masks is just one fascinating example of what can be learned from examining a photographer's negatives.

Sometimes a synergy emerges between two different archives. This occurred with the Edward Weston Archive. Weston, who rarely saved correspondence from others, kept a letter from Frederick Sommer, who had recommended a ground glass focusing strategy using a hair, a hole, and a magnifier. Weston's enthusiastic response about this "revolution in focussing" is in Sommer's archive.[6]

1   Frederick Sommer, "Poetry and Logic, 1980–1983," in *Sommer · Words* (Tucson: Center for Creative Photography, 1984), p. 18.
2   James Enyeart, *Sommer · Images* and *Sommer · Words* (Tucson: Center for Creative Photography, 1984), p. 4.
3   Ibid.
4   Frederick Sommer, *Sommer · Words* (Tucson: Center for Creative Photography, 1984), p. 48.
5   Ibid, p. 49.
6   Thanks to CCP archivist Amy Rule for pointing out this connection.

ALBERT SANDS SOUTHWORTH & JOSIAH JOHNSON HAWES: *Sleeping Baby*, 1860
[Overmat removed]

Southworth & Hawes

by Ellwood C. Parry III

Admittedly, when compared to the major collections of Southworth & Hawes daguerreotypes housed in the Metropolitan Museum of Art, New York, the Museum of Fine Arts, Boston, and the George Eastman House, Rochester, the four whole-plate images in the Ansel and Virginia Adams Collection at the Center constitute a very small selection. But they hold special interest because they were acquired by Ansel Adams in the 1930s, and his choices—an elegant portrait of an older woman, a stark portrait of a mature young man seen against a gray, featureless background, a dark, vignetted, oval portrait-in-profile of a young girl, and a stunning image of a sleeping baby—may have been far from random. In fact, they seem to speak volumes about the f/64 group's aesthetics in that era of American photographic history.

Some basic curatorial questions regarding these four 8½x6½-inch plates are easier to answer than others. For example, authenticity is clearly not an issue since their attribution to the famous Boston firm of Southworth & Hawes, which flourished from 1844–1862, is certain. Likewise, their provenance is equally secure. They were part of the huge collection, carefully preserved by Josiah Johnson Hawes until his death in 1901, which his heirs finally began to part with through sales and donations in the 1930s.

Who the four sitters are, on the other hand, and when they posed before the camera in the Southworth & Hawes studio on Tremont Row, Boston, is another matter. "Unidentified" and "circa 1850" are standard notations in the growing literature on America's most expensive and most celebrated daguerreotypists. The *Portrait of a Woman*, for instance, is a variant of the same female subject, wearing the same outfit with lace cap and ties against a dark background as *Unidentified Female*, n.d., a whole plate (also produced in the firm's vignetted or "crayon" portrait style) now in the International Museum of Photography at George Eastman House, Rochester. In the same fashion, no name can be attached to the oval-matted *Profile of a Young Girl* or the *Portrait of a Young Man*, both presumably from the 1850s.

Identification and dating are not a problem, however, with *Sleeping Baby*, the most appealing of these four daguerreotypes. Obviously enough, this image is not a "post mortem." The propped-up angle and the accidental disposition of the arms and legs are enough to prove that this child has not been laid out after death, peacefully and symmetrically, awaiting the camera operator as part of the ritual of final viewing. More to the point, a pair of whole plates—*Edward Hawes, Asleep, with Hands Together* and *Edward Hawes, Asleep, with One Arm Raised*—portraying the same domical-foreheaded, round-cheeked, bow-mouthed child, only slightly older with darker, thicker hair, have recently come to light as part of the David Feigenbaum Collection of Southworth & Hawes daguerreotypes that were put up for auction at Sotheby's, New York, on 27 April 1999. Furthermore, when the glass and mat were removed during a recent conservation examination of *Sleeping Baby*, two things became evident. First of all, the opening in

Verso of daguerreotype, *Sleeping Baby*, showing plate marks, corrosion, and early tape residue

the mat, which had not been changed since Ansel Adams owned it and allowed it to be reproduced by Beaumont Newhall and Charles LeRoy Moore, had unfortunately left a stain where it cut off the out-of-focus portions of the plate. On the other hand, it also became evident that the child's garment had been enhanced with whitish pigment, thereby increasing the contrast between it and the gray tone of the baby's skin as well as the supporting pillow. The one person credited with hand-coloring in the Southworth & Hawes studio is Nancy Southworth Hawes, sister of one partner, wife of the other, and mother of this child, her third and only son.

Since Ansel Adams's quasi-cryptic file cards on two of these daguerreotypes indicate that the images were received from "old Mr. Hawes," it is well worthwhile to piece together what is known about Edward Southworth Hawes, a son who clearly honored but did not follow in his father's profession. Obituaries after his death on 22 November 1942 record that he was eighty-two at the time, meaning that he must have been born during the final few weeks of 1859 or more likely in 1860. Hence a specific date of 1860 can be assigned to this charming image of an infant a few months old, taken by the father and retouched by his mother. As to his later career, it is known that Edward Hawes graduated from Harvard College in 1880 and received a Ph.D. there in 1884 for his thesis, "Summarium usus plautini in enuntiationibus condicionalibus." As an academic, he spent twenty-nine years as a teacher of Greek and Latin in the classical languages department of the Polytechnic Preparatory Country Day School, Brooklyn, New York, ending with his retirement in 1921.[1]

Given this history, it is easy to understand why, after moving back to the family home at 90 Bay State Street, Boston, Edward Southworth Hawes (then in his seventies and receiving full cooperation from his two older sisters) would begin to part with the vast quantities of photographic materials stored in their house, a process that began with the well-documented sale of celebrity daguerreotypes at Holman's Print Shop, Boston, in November 1934. Most of those images of identifiable sitters were acquired by I. N. Phelps Stokes and later donated to the Metropolitan, which exhibited them in 1939 to celebrate the centennial of the announcement of Daguerre's invention.

Exactly when Ansel Adams acquired *Sleeping Baby*, his first Southworth & Hawes plate, is unclear. One can speculate that it was purchased either in New York or on a visit to Boston, possibly from Dr. Hawes himself. But gaining such a treasure certainly belongs to that moment when, in addition to continuing sales at Holman's Print Shop, the now elderly Hawes children made significant donations of daguerreotypes to various museums and various other collectors and scholars, especially Beaumont Newhall, and were eagerly helping to solidify the reputation of Southworth & Hawes as the finest camera operators of the period.

The second acquisition by Ansel Adams appears to have been *Portrait of a Woman*, which has the price of $10 marked on the verso of the frame along with a seal showing that the image was selected for exhibit at the "Grand Central Palace, April 18th–24th, 1938. New York. First International Photographic Exhibition." It is the third and fourth whole plates, *Portrait of a Young Man* and *Profile of a Young Girl*, that Ansel Adams recorded on file cards as received from "old Mr. Hawes"—wording that seems to imply that they came directly from Edward Hawes, whom he knew personally, and may have been gifts, rather than out-of-pocket purchases.

Whatever the case may be, why Ansel Adams wanted a selection of Southworth & Hawes's work seems easy to fathom. After all, his choices demonstrate the varied camera techniques and lighting effects of the Boston partners, famous for their direct, no-nonsense approach to picture making. That unwavering insistence on the fundamentals of photography clearly resonated with members of the f/64 group along with the concept of complete control and previsualization. At the same time, it may be that Ansel Adams was also taken with the idea of owning four images that so forcefully capture four different stages of human life.

1 Obituary, *New York Times* (23 November 1942).

Spanish Photography

by Terence Pitts

JUAN DOLCET: *Empalao*, 1968

MARTA POVO: *Campanet, Mallorca*, 1984
From the series *Light, 182/8*

In the 1980s, with the assistance of grants from the United States–Spanish Joint Committee for Cultural and Educational Cooperation, the Center assembled a small survey collection of approximately forty works by more than twenty living Spanish photographers. The collection represents some of the geographical and aesthetic variety of Spanish photography since the 1950s. One part of the collection traces the strong history of Spanish documentary photography, much of which is centered on portraiture and capturing the unique traditions of secular and religious customs across Spain's regions and villages. The collection begins with works by several photographers whose careers began during the Franco era—Francesc Català-Roca, Gabriel Cualladó, and Juan Dolcet, and from there moves to the work of a more recent generation of photographers who have worked with an acute awareness of the rapidly disappearing nature of local festivals and other cultural activities. The work of photographers such as Cristina García Rodero, Miguel Bergasa, and Ramon Zabalza is simultaneously documentary and highly personal and forms a consciously created archive of portraits and images in contrast to a Spain profoundly homogenized by economic and political changes in the post-Franco, European Union era.

The other part of the collection suggests some of the rich variety of artistic practice that erupted in the post-Franco era. This group ranges

CRISTINA GARCÍA RODERO: *Virgin y Mártir, Brión,* 1978

from the baroquely ornamented images of Sevillano artist Miguel Angel Yañez Polo to the reflective and poetic images of Marta Povo and Koldo Chamorro and the distinctly playful postmodern works of América Sánchez, Jorge Ribalta, and Joan Fontcuberta.

In addition to this collection of Spanish photographs from the second half of the twentieth century, the Center also holds a group of fifty-eight nineteenth-century albumen prints by Jean (Juan) Laurent. Although born in France, Laurent maintained studios both in Paris and Madrid and photographed extensively across Spain, producing primarily architectural studies, images of Spanish commerce, and reproductions of other works of art.

KOLDO CHAMORRO: Untitled, 1980s
From the series *España Mágica*

PETER STACKPOLE: *Watching a load of rivets coming up against the backdrop of San Francisco, 1935*

Peter Stackpole

by Roxane Ramos

Call it luck. Call it destiny. Whatever was behind Peter Stackpole's (1913–1997) fortu-
itous convergence of circumstance and sensibility, we can look back from the other end
of the twentieth century and locate Stackpole at the launching of its three great M's—
media, machinery, and movies. His position as one of the inaugural photographers for
Life magazine has ensured Stackpole a place in photographic history. Along the way,
he amassed two bodies of work that have relevance beyond the world of photography—his documentation of the building of the Bay Bridge and his extensive portfolio
of early Hollywood images.

The son of artists, Stackpole grew up surrounded by houseguests such as Dorothea
Lange, Diego Rivera, and Edward Weston. It is not surprising then that he chose to go
into the family "business." But even with his creative leanings, Stackpole was fascinated
with gadgetry as a child and a favorite pastime was model airplane building. (He posed
with one of his constructions for a Rivera mural.) His early tinkering paved the way for
an ongoing interest in the technical and mechanical underpinnings of his craft. While
others were still chained to their 4x5 Speed Graphics and Graflexes, Stackpole opted
for the new and as yet unembraced 35mm Leica, the portable camera that shaped the
early development of photojournalism. Later in his career, he wrote a column called
"35mm Techniques" for *U.S. Camera* for fifteen years and designed underwater photography equipment from 1941 to 1974.

In 1934, at the tender age of twenty-one, unemployed, curious, and armed with
his trusty Leica, Stackpole edged his way—literally—onto the Bay Bridge, then under
construction. No victim of vertigo, he befriended the workers (perhaps photography is
the sincerest form of flattery) and the supervisor invited him to photograph the work in
progress. San Francisco-Oakland Bay Bridge is still the longest twin-suspension bridge
in the world, and Stackpole's photographs are a testament to the unflappable spirit of
innovation and determination characterizing that era of American growth.

A series of free-lance assignments followed and led to his honorary membership
in the renowned f/64 group. Willard Van Dyke became something of a mentor to the
young photographer. Even so, Stackpole eventually parted ways with f/64. Their aesthetic proved too pristine and reverential for Stackpole, who preferred to photograph
his subjects in context, in all their grandeur or grittiness. He was not precious about
his photographs. He wanted to be in the thick of things, taking risks as well as photographs, the hallmark of a natural-born photojournalist.

When Henry Luce established his ground-breaking "picture" magazine, *Life*, in 1936,
Stackpole was hired as one of its first four photographers (along with Alfred Eisenstaedt,
Margaret Bourke-White, and Thomas McAvoy). He was part of the birth of what we now
refer to as "media culture." His beat was Hollywood and he took to his famous subjects
with the same enthusiasm he brought to the unsung bridge workers.

PETER STACKPOLE:
Alfred Hitchcock at Academy Awards Banquet, 1941

These were not glamour pictures; Stackpole was committed to the candid image. He knew intuitively that the public wanted to see photographs of their movie idols with their hair and shorts down, so to speak. Still, the Hollywood portfolio is filled with examples of carefully constructed public relations shots. Stackpole was the one who photographed Jimmy Stewart's return from World War II, Greer Garson cleaning her swimming pool, and a teen-aged Elizabeth Taylor blowing out her birthday candles. He rubbed elbows with the rich, the famous, and the inebriated without ever losing his own sense of purpose and poise in the work. He must have been quite the charming and tenacious character to get invited to all those parties. Hollywood was a savvy town and used the products of a well-aimed lens.

Even so, it was an age of innocence Stackpole worked in. Thirty years before Warhol uttered his famous quip about fifteen minutes of fame, entire careers were made, plundered, and even wrecked through the power of still and moving pictures. Long before we examined the tolls of technology or the ethics of expansion, we built up, out, and over, water no obstacle to our ingenuity, creating a spectacle of brick and steel documented through the artistry and science of photography.

Stackpole inadvertently left us a legacy of the twentieth century. How was he to know that the building of the Bay Bridge (and the Golden Gate) would foretell a preponderance of cars and sports utility vehicles the likes of which Gold Rush traffic was but an inkling? How could he predict that our fascination with Hollywood icons would grow into an obsession with fame generally and notoriety in particular? *Life* magazine seems quaint and downright down-home by the tabloid standards of today. Stackpole was just shooting, doing what documentary photographers do—catching the world as it rides by, indifferent to us, never to cycle back in precisely the same way again.

Paul Strand

by Maria Antonella Pelizzari

Paul Strand's (1890–1976) work has been the object of many critical analyses seeking to disentangle the mysteries and contradictions of his creative oeuvre. His life and work are characterized by two major phases: one in his native country and the other one, in Europe beginning in 1949, where he lived in France and traveled to various European countries as well as to Africa. This cultural transition appears in his photographs and brings one to wonder whether the foreign countries, and "the old world" in particular, were conducive to a change in his modernist vision and ideals, or if he carried the same ideals everywhere, visualizing them in different forms. The Paul Strand Archive at the CCP, and in particular the correspondence with his American friends and European collaborators, allows one to trace the continuity of Strand's thinking and the depth of his vision.

PAUL STRAND: *Toadstool and Grasses, Maine*, 1928

One key element in Strand's work was a preoccupation with technology as an alienating force from society. In 1922, he expressed this concern, writing that the "new God" of technology, and the photographic machine in particular, ought to be "an instrument of intuitive knowledge" and of creative vision. He recognized that such a result had been achieved by Alfred Stieglitz, whose portraits revealed "the spirit of the individual" by "purely photographic means."[1] Considering Stieglitz as his mentor, Strand shared these ideas and concerns with other American modernist artists in the 1910s and 1920s, in the visual arts as well as in literature. He became acquainted with Stieglitz's 291 gallery and *Camera Work*; he attended the Armory Show in 1913; and around 1915 he was part of Stieglitz's circle of American artists, with Arthur Dove, Georgia O'Keeffe, and John Marin among others.

During these early years, his work is divided between the social documentary and modernist experiments in abstraction. In 1916 and 1919, in Twin Lakes, Connecticut, he photographed architecture and household artifacts in a cubist style, producing a formal image of shapes and shadows, arranging objects in front of the camera. His fascination with the machine is confirmed by an abstract series of photographs of his Akeley camera

PAUL STRAND: *White Sheets, New Orleans, Louisiana*, 1918

(1921), while his portraits of New York passersby, in the mid-1910s, attempt to capture the individual's expression through the unobtrusive presence of the camera operator. In New York he adopted a trick that he later used also in Mexico, attaching a false prism lens to his camera, thus photographing the people without them being aware of it. In Mexico, in 1933, he held his camera as filter between the natives and himself, capturing the pride and beauty of this population. This style of photographic portraiture, emphasizing the honest and straightforward physiognomy of native people, was reiterated by Strand all around the world.

During these years, Strand worked not only in photography, but also in film. In 1920, he collaborated with Charles Sheeler on the film *Manhatta*, inspired by the "Mannahatta," Walt Whitman's passage in *Leaves of Grass* (1860) and suggesting, in its photography and in its subject, the possible transformation of technology back into nature. In the late 1920s and early 1930s, Strand left the city for New Mexico, and then Mexico, becoming interested in wide open landscapes, portraits of natives, and of native dwellings. A film, *The Wave* (1937), was also the outcome of his work in Mexico, filmed in the fishing village of Alvarado, working with a Mexican crew.

Back in New York in 1938, he joined the Film and Photo League as a lecturer, prepared another film, *Native Land* (1942), and worked on a book project with Nancy Newhall, *Time in New England* (1950). The film and the book contain Strand's passionate reflection on the roots of American culture during the difficult years of right-wing reaction and witch-hunting. Strand soon left his country, in his mind carrying to Europe the model of the early organization of American colonies. He channeled this model into his New England project of "the portrait of a village," directly inspired by Edgar Lee Masters's *Spoon River Anthology* (1915–16) and Sherwood Anderson's *Winesburg, Ohio* (1919). The village ideally reflected for Strand the notion of American democracy, built on the idea of a timeless agrarian world, a nonhierarchical community, a quiet neighborhood, a pastoral landscape. It was a notion informed by socialist ideas as well as by a nostalgic view of the American "virgin land." It contained Strand's humanistic vision toward his modern times, caught between the paradigm of a peaceful rural life and the growth of industrialization. It looked back, while promoting a "dynamic realism."

In Italy, Strand searched for the ideal village, following his book publication *La France de Profil* (1952) in collaboration with the writer Claude Roy. While the French book rendered only the physical appearance of the country, from which Strand and his wife Hazel felt quite separate and excluded, the Italian book *Un paese* (1955) reflected Strand's in-depth study of one village, Luzzara, and his close relationship with the native inhabitants. There he could, through the help of a local interpreter, construct his own visual dialogue with the people, their objects of craft and work, and the legendary stories of its landscapes, weaving together their voices with their portraits. This book project was also relevant to the particular collaboration of Strand with the Italian neo-realist screenwriter Cesare Zavattini. Strand had traced similarities between his roots and the Italian collaborator's through films such as *Shoeshine* (1946) and *Bicycle Thief* (1948) being "direct," "truthful," "honest," "dynamic," and viewing Italian film of this period as "a truly democratic medium, able to speak to all men everywhere in the language of understanding and brotherhood."[2]

PAUL STRAND;
The Family, Luzzara, Italy
[three small variants], 1953

The Italian book was followed by other book projects in the Outer Hebrides (*Tir a'Mhurain*, 1962) and in Africa (*Living Egypt*, 1969; *Ghana: An African Portrait*, 1976), where Strand adopted the same formula of the ideal village, portraying the natives through the heroic physiognomy of their activities and work.

Throughout this work, Strand continued to be concerned with a universalist and profound vision of the world—the same that he admired in Stieglitz at the beginning of his career. From that first encounter with the vision of a master photographer, Strand oscillated in his pictures and statements between avant-garde intentions and traditional ideals, between change and timelessness, between the use of the machine and the dream of a machine-less world. These contradictions were his forte, conveying to his photographs a special energy and intensity.

1 Paul Strand, "Photography and the New God," *Broom 3:4* (1922), p. 256.

2 Strand's response to Umberto Barbaro's welcoming address at the Cinema International Conference, Perugia, 1949, is found in the Paul Strand Collection, Center for Creative Photography.

JO ANN CALLIS: *Goldfish and Stringbeans*, 1980
From the portfolio *Jo Ann Callis*, 1984

Teaching in a Collection

by Carol Flax

Seeing genuine prints is an integral process in studying photography. The final print is what the artist strives for. To see all the detail and feel the final object the artist intended is a powerful and memorable experience that the CCP provides.

Nichole Frocheur
University of Arizona photography student

What gives something presence, makes it real for us? In an age of endless production and reproduction, how can we even pose this question? When we speak of art and especially photography, we no longer can necessarily pinpoint one event, one object as the original, as the one.

As a young and impressionable undergraduate student in photography I had an amazing experience. Studying with Jerry McMillan at California State University, Northridge, I spent hours in rapt attention as he spoke about and showed slides of the work of the Southern California photographers of the 1970s. What brought these to life was Jerry's relationship to this work and to these artists. They were his former students, friends, and colleagues. Maybe all young students are similarly impressed when their teachers speak of contemporary artists as their friends and colleagues. But, there was something different here. Jerry made photography come alive in a way few others have for me.

Doing my graduate work at California Institute of the Arts, I was again extremely fortunate to study with amazing artists: Judy Fiskin, Jo Ann Callis, John Divola, and John Brumfield. I felt incredibly privileged to have access to these artists, their experience, their wisdom, their store of knowledge.

As an educator for the past seventeen years, mostly in Los Angeles, I could send my students to a myriad of museums, galleries, lectures, etc. There was a rich array of access to people and ideas. Yet Los Angeles lacked coherence; the photography community I had come of age with no longer existed in the same way. Los Angeles is big and spread out; it wasn't always easy to get students to go to events and even harder to bring events to them.

When I came to the University of Arizona to teach, one of the first things I realized was how wonderful it was to have access to the collection at the Center for Creative Photography. I also discovered that often the students were not aware of this and had not availed themselves of what the CCP had to offer. I teach a contemporary photography history class in which I talk about artists, show slides of their work, and tell anecdotes from my own experience with these people. I like to think all of this gets through to students and is valuable. But, what was truly breathtaking for me with this class, was the first time I brought them into the CCP to view the collection. This was when I truly saw the light of recognition in their eyes.

I asked my students for their thoughts on the collection, if there was one moment, one image, one experience that truly impacted them in their study of photography. Here are some of their replies.

When I was able to see the Atget images of Paris homes I was struck by how seductive his prints were and how much of a voyeur I felt. Being able to see original/vintage prints is a wonderful opportunity. (Jennifer Laffoon, graduate student)

The artists' books at the Center have been the most interesting resource to me. Being able to interact one on one with these art objects has been a great experience and influence. Also, the first year I was here the grads went once a week for a print viewing, which provided a forum that generated ample discussion among us. Diane Arbus, Joel-Peter Witkin and Ruth Thorne-Thompson were some of the artists whose work elicited the most discussion. (Maria Harper, graduate student)

I have enjoyed getting to view original prints as opposed to reproductions and find it particularly interesting to see multiple, slightly different prints from one negative revealing some of the process and thoughts of the artist behind the final choices of presentation. (Carolyn Joslyn, graduate student)

The most amazing connection for me was seeing Lartigue's work. I have loved his childhood photographs of his family for years. The thought of a little boy looking through his camera and taking beautiful, complex pictures of his little eight-year-old's world thrills me. One photograph in particular, of his cousin leaping down the stone steps, is right out of a child's imagination since she appears to be flying, caught by the camera in mid-air. There is nothing like looking at the genuine photograph; you cannot help but envision the artist's hands, in this case a little boy's hands, touching the very same photograph you are touching, and feeling a more intimate connection with the artist than by merely seeing their work.

*   Another artist's work that is almost essential to see in person is the work of Roy DeCarava. His prints are dark and deep and full of detail that is difficult to appreciate in reproduced forms. I found myself feeling with my eyes the textures of the dark details of the smoke filled jazz clubs and smoggy staleness of New York City subway tunnels. The nearly indiscernible forms in the shadows are alive and probe the imagination when DeCarava's work is seen up-close.* (Nichole Frocheur, graduate student)

Working with the collection has made me aware of the progression of photography, from early daguerreotypes to contemporary work. As a graduate student in photography, I feel the Center is a valuable asset to my education. (Jonathan Crumpler, graduate student)

I remember when [conservator] Laura Downey was giving a print-handling lesson, particularly albums. Her example was Eadweard Muybridge's album called The Pacific Coast of Central America and Mexico; The Isthmus of Panama; Guatemala; and the Cultivation and Shipment of Coffee. *One of eight versions known to exist. All were albumen prints and were completely breathtaking. I literally got the chills*

EADWEARD MUYBRIDGE: *Panama Bay by Moonlight*, 1875ñ76

*and the fact that these images were taken over a hundred years ago and still exist—
it was exciting, and I felt like I was traveling back in time.* (Monica Ramirez, undergraduate student)

Recently I went over to the CCP to spend a few hours in the collection before completing this article. I sent over a list of artists whose work I wanted to look at—people
whose work I admire or artists I knew and felt a kinship with. What I was most reminded
of was the power of contrast. This is something that just cannot come through in books
or slides. I spent many moments admiring Judy Fiskin's small, intimate photograph
from the series *Some Art* [anonymous painting county fair]. It has phenomenal presence.
I almost couldn't take my eyes off it. As I went through boxes of prints, it sat on the
table drawing me back over and over. Then I turned to speak to somebody and noticed
a very large, hand-colored print by Kate Breakey sitting on another table. I had never
seen her work before and can't imagine being so drawn to it if I had first seen it in
reproduction. Both of these works acquire much of their power through scale. Breakey's
work has surface detail that can only been seen in the original, especially as I discovered it, uncovered without glass or plastic interrupting my view. I love that my students
and I have the opportunity to know this firsthand.

Travel Albums

by Alison Nordström

Old photograph albums are often the orphan children of great photographic collections. They are difficult to classify, impossible to display, expensive to conserve, and, broken into the single-image components by which "great" photography is usually defined and understood, often contain undistinguished prints of little aesthetic or economic value. How are we to link these tattered and complex things to the received canon of important pictures that has defined institutional purpose? Tellingly, we find nineteenth-century albums as often in libraries, historical societies, archives, and flea markets as in museums.

Family albums may be of interest to genealogists and historians; their portraits show individuals despite the characteristic poses and formats. But what to do with ubiquitous albums of mass-produced photographs that were dutifully purchased and assembled by earnest travelers bent on education and self-improvement? How many brown and faded representations of Della Robbia babies, the Arc de Triomphe, and native types of Cairo, Naples, or Singapore must we save? These middle-sized albumen prints were printed by the tens of thousands, widely sold and eagerly purchased. Like the postcards that had functionally replaced them by the beginning of this century, they served as aides-mémoires, trophies of a visit, and idealized documents of place that affirm and express our most widely held cultural knowledge.

Page spread in album: *Pacific Islands, 1917.*

Left: "Falls near Apia."

Right: "Power Schooner 'Marua' 70 tons," and other snapshots

We may, of course, extract the "best" photographs from crumbling albums. Mammoth plates, for example, are always of interest for their size and novelty, and certain masterpieces by such recognized masters as Beato, Bonfils, Bourne, and Frith have found their way into standard histories and may have further value as illustrations of historical fact and technological triumph. Students of regional history, ethnography, archaeology, costume, and the like may value even obscure images for the information inherent in their content. Romantics, artists, and others less needful of historical truth may find in these ephemeral scraps exactly the stuff of dreams they need for imaginary journeys or thoughts of a golden age.

Beyond these approaches, however, is another that may let these albums speak in other ways. It starts by considering each album, not as a collection, but as a single discrete object, made or acquired by an individual for particular reasons. We often know little or nothing about albums' makers, yet the albums themselves, in their materiality, structure, and indeed the marks of their use over time, may persist as part of a world that will outlive, not only their makers, but us, their current users. Whole albums, more or less intact, offer us the context in which individual photographs were once kept and understood. They show us the way individual travelers understood and remembered their journeys, what they valued, and what they knew.

Let us, then, interrogate a travel album asking who made it and its component parts, how and of what it was constructed; what its value was, has been, and is, and how and why it got from where it was made to where it is now. Because these are albums about journeys, with fixed component parts often assembled in an individual manner, we may also look for narrative in a sequence of pictures, conscious and unconscious meanings

Tattooes Samoan   Mango Tree   C.P. on "Manua"

Power Schooner "Manua" 70 tons   Commandant's House - Pago-Pago

in juxtapositions on a page, and direct expressions from the past in the texts, annotations, drawings, and inclusions that so often accompany the prints. In these idiosyncratic features we may find a dynamic intersection of individual experience and collective memory.

The early travel albums at the Center for Creative Photography demonstrate the degrees of personalization and authorship such things may have. At the end of that continuum are the ready-made books, produced for sale as souvenirs and easily purchased at hotels, stationers, bookshops, and photographers' studios. We find these in the CCP Library Rare Book Room with titles like *Souvenir de Pompei*,[1] a selection of twenty-five uniformly mounted photographs by Giorgio Sommer, *Ilha da Madeira*[2] holding eighteen anonymous lithocollotypes on pages with embossed borders, and the similarly anonymous *Vues d'Ostende*[3] from Librairie Godtfurneau. Of particular interest in this category is *Ricordi di Firenze*,[4] a selection of quite standard 7x9-inch albumen views of landscapes, churches, and paintings by the ubiquitous Fratelli Alinari. The red morocco covers and marbleized endpapers provide a setting, not only for the photographs but for an elaborate title page crediting Alinari & Cook, suggesting a logical commercial relationship between the photographers and the early British purveyors of package tours.

A somewhat more personal arrangement of photographs can be found in the nine volumes assembled in the 1880s by Alice Maude Bovyer Cowell of San Francisco. The wife of a California land and cattle baron, Cowell traveled extensively in Europe, Egypt, and the Holy Land, acquiring photographs along with other souvenirs.[5] The albums are large, luxurious, and expensive objects, half bound in black morocco leather and trimmed and titled in gold. Though their look is very similar, they vary slightly in paper quality and typeface, suggesting that they were made at different times and places. They are

Page spread in album:
Greece, 1880s

Panorama d'Athènes
by Constantin Athanassiou

professionally made, however, suggesting that Cowell may have followed the practice advocated by Baedecker travel guides of selecting first an album and then the photographs that would fill it, the whole to be fabricated overnight and delivered to the purchaser's hotel. We cannot know, then, how much control Cowell had over the serial organization of her images. They contain work by the usual suspects: Alinari and Sommer in Italy, Zangaki and Bonfils in Egypt and Palestine, Gulmez Frères in Constantinople. The photographs are often organized in an order like that of a journey; though the pictures of Egypt may have been bought all at once, they move us from Alexandria to Cairo and then through the Suez canal to Port Said. Their maker has used handwritten annotations to personalize generic pictures, so, for example, sense is made of a vast *Panorama d'Athenes*,[6] by the word "observatory" inked below that building. These albums too, follow certain conventions of order: an image of a statue is followed by its detail; an image of a museum building is followed by a view of its interior; a city is presented first from a distance, often as panorama, and then to images of specific buildings, gates and doorways. Of the three most common kinds of photographs sold to tourists at that time, Cowell adheres to their most common treatment. First and in the greatest number are views, both landscape and architectural. They are followed by reproductions of painting and sculpture, and finally by costume, genre, and type images of stylized local inhabitants. These last are generally smaller and almost always are shown with several on each page.

We must be careful not to assume that an album maker simply replicated an actual itinerary. In one of three albums assembled by a family named Parrish, *Pacific Islands*, 1917,[7] a typed itinerary is pasted inside the book's cover that outlines a trip begun in New York on 10 January and ended there on 7 May, totaling 19,495 miles. This trip includes New Orleans, Seattle, and Vancouver on the outgoing leg and Salt Lake City,

Chicago, and Syracuse on the return, though none of these places is pictured, perhaps as wanting in exoticism or seeming inappropriate in an album with this title. The itinerary details a long stay on the West Coast and a day in Hawaii before a quick voyage through several Polynesian islands and a return to Hawaii for several visits to the outer islands there. The story told by the photographs is somewhat different, however, as they are organized in a straight narrative line that moves only outward, going from California, to all of the Hawaiian Islands, to Fiji, to Samoa, and to Tonga. The visual story takes you out to the Pacific islands without making you come back, a trope found often in escapist literature.

These photographic travel albums are as different from each other as their makers were, yet a consideration of similarities in their structure and form comes close to giving us glimpses of how a photograph was understood in its own time. Once their early contexts of use have ceased to be, albums may be edited, taken apart, recategorized and, even, discarded, but they should not be. Albums as albums are dense with meaning. Their unpacking as objects is a beginning of an entrée into the visualities and consciousnesses of the past.

1 Giorgio Sommer, *Souvenir de Pompei* (Napoli: G. Sommer & Figlio, n.d.).

2 *Ilha da Madeira* (s.l.: s.n., n.d.).

3 *Vues d'Ostende* (Ostende: Librairie Godtfurneau, n.d.).

4 Fratelli Alinari, *Ricordi di Firenze: fotografie* (Firenze: n.d.).

5 Information on Cowell is from the Bancroft Library, University of California, Berkeley, of which she was an alumna, and from personal correspondence with her grandniece, Pat Bovyer Mason, who donated the albums to the CCP in 1992.

6 This album at the CCP is given accession number 79:217:000.

7 This album at the CCP is given accession number 83:125:000.

Arthur Tress

by Amy Rule

Among a small group of photographers who relish words as much as images is Arthur Tress (b. 1940), whose imagery leads us through dreamlands, slowly feeding our recognition of memory and myth. His recent richly colored photographs and early black-and-white images are known from his nine published monographs and from the rare exhibitions of his work. He is an artist at home with complicated narrative structures and the directorial mode of photography, creating elaborately constructed scenes in nature or in the studio that he photographs in series and then sequences into meditations or slowly unfolding fantasies. These projects may involve a picaresque hero who moves through scenes in the guise of the photographer's shadow (as in his *Shadow: A Novel in Photographs* series), or a hero taking the form of a stiff plastic figurine (as in *Requiem for a Paperweight*) tossed by the unpredictable seas of the artist's imagination. At other times the story is controlled by an omnipotent voice located in Tress's accompanying

Objects used by Arthur Tress in his *Fish Tank Sonata* series, 1988–90
Arthur Tress Collection

ARTHUR TRESS: *Whiteface Mountain, New York, 1989*
From the series *Fish Tank Sonata*

Howls echo over the hills
As the lone wolf beckons a friend;
In this wide open country,
Solitude may in fact be his end.

texts (as in the *Fish Tank Sonata*). "You must pay the ferryman/ And he'll take you across/ The stygian waters to/ The Islands of the Lost."

Tress frequently invokes the title of "magician" to describe the role of the photographer, "someone who is more acutely aware of the subliminal 'vibrations' of the everyday world which can call forth hidden emotions or states of feeling that are usually tightly wrapped up in our unconscious states." His interest in the magical and the fantastical developed after studying painting and art history at Bard College, Annandale-on-Hudson, New York, and after traveling through Japan, Mexico, and Europe. He has also worked as a freelance photographer, documenting Appalachia in a book published by the Sierra Club in 1969 and focusing on urban open spaces for the United States Department of Housing and Urban Development. After about 1970, Tress's personal, creative work was increasingly shown in exhibitions and was supported with a grant from the National Endowment for the Arts.

In 1995, the Center brought together all three parts of a fifteen-year project Tress calls *The Wurlitzer Trilogy*. The individual parts had been published and exhibited separately, but they had never been seen together in a gallery setting in the United States. The trilogy—*Teapot Opera, Fish Tank Sonata,* and *Requiem for a Paperweight*—begins with these words, "Before the invention of magic/ there was only the dark sea." Futuristic photographs of a hapless salaryman floating through drifts of uncontrollable information and imagery conclude the trilogy in *Requiem for a Paper-weight*. The actual objects, thrift store and attic artifacts, dustbin and dime store treasures, collected and then photographed by Tress, now reside in archival boxes in the Center's Research Center. Their tangible physical presence and charm will, in their own way, contribute to our understanding of the magically unfolding story of the series.

Tress's photographs include obscure themes and hidden connections. They are a fusion of fairy tale, nostalgia, social commentary, psychosexual exploration, heroic struggle, and an unflagging belief in the power of objects. With the existence of an archive of photographs and research materials—literally the raw materials of the artist's creative process—an almost limitless opportunity exists for future interrogations of source and intent.

ARTHUR TRESS: *The Wurlitzer Trilogy*, Center for Creative Photography, 4 June–10 September 1995

TSENG KWONG CHI: *New York, New York*, 1979
From *The Expeditionary Series*

Tseng Kwong Chi

by Terence Pitts

Born in Hong Kong, Tseng Kwong Chi (1950–1990) immigrated to Canada when he was a teenager. He completed his art education in Paris and moved to New York City in 1978, where he lived and worked until his death in 1990. Beginning in 1979, Tseng Kwong Chi worked on an extended group of photographs variantly called *The Expeditionary Series* or *East Meets West*. In these photographs, Tseng, who referred to himself as an "ambiguous ambassador," portrayed himself in the persona of a visiting official from the People's Republic of China, a country he never visited. Wearing what appears to be a traditional Mao suit, mirrored sunglasses, and a fake I.D. card clipped to his chest pocket, he consistently appears anonymous, impassive, and mysterious as he stands by or contemplates famous tourist sites and monuments from around the world. Closely associated with 1980s performance art, Tseng's decade-long project serves as an extended performance that confronts the long-standing relationship between photography, travel, and colonialism. Tseng's photographs of a Chinese "Everyman" ironically invoke countless images of imperial colonizers and modern-day rulers posing by their latest conquests. This association evolves throughout the series until in the later work an ever more dimunitive photographer poses before the vastness of immense western landscapes. The title *The Expeditionary Series* also suggests the uneasy relationship between the imagery of political power and the souvenirs of cultural tourism.

The Center owns the most complete set of Tseng's print series *East Meets West*. This set of almost eighty large prints was made posthumously by Tseng's printer under the supervision of his estate.

The Center has also acquired his posthumous twelve-print portfolio, *Costumes at The Met*, published in 1997 by the Julie Saul Gallery (New York). As in *The Expeditionary Series*, Tseng appears in the images in his Mao suit and sunglasses, but here as a party-crashing poseur mingling with Halston, Paloma Picasso, and other glitterati at the Metropolitan Museum of Art's "Party of the Year" in 1980.

JERRY N. UELSMANN: Untitled, 1987

Jerry N. Uelsmann

by Roxane Ramos

Storm clouds are gathering in the dining room. A tide is lapping the living room rug. Ceilings become sky and sky becomes water.

The stuff of dreams? A sci-fi movie? An acid flashback? Not to anyone familiar with Jerry Uelsmann's work. For more than forty years, Uelsmann has made photographic improvisation his signature style, manipulating and juxtaposing images from various negatives to arrive at a final print. These are traditional photographs; they were made using standard darkroom techniques. And yet, they defy our collective expectations of what photographs may reasonably depict and fool our eyes with their seamless execution. Is that woman—or rowboat or hamburger—really floating in mid-air?

Such visual incongruities are staples of Uelsmann's photographic universe. A man stepping through a glass door. A house sprouting from the roots of a tree. The consensus of "reality" has never been an obstacle to Uelsmann's engagement of such elusive subject matter as the negotiation between nature and culture, and the search for the self amidst existential weather. Early on, Uelsmann established his own personal lexicon of imagery and motifs—trees, birds, buildings, mirrors, hands, nudes, geometric shapes. He combines and rearranges these building blocks until the composition culminates in a moment of spontaneous revelation. The artistic aim is to express an interior condition, track a private journey, through the iterative process of experimentation. Uelsmann's darkroom is a laboratory and the artist is a scientist/alchemist investigating the realms of his psyche. Though his impulses are autobiographical, his creations, by virtue of trafficking in signs, often resonate on a deeper level for viewers.

That these images are rendered as photographs, rather than, say, paintings, subverts the notion of photography as an objective medium. What we see in a Uelsmann photograph is not the world as it hits the lens, but the world as manipulated and transformed by Uelsmann. Yet this is true of all photographs, even those that seem to project "reality" and "objectivity." What are Ansel Adams's Yosemite pictures but his version of a pristine wilderness? Why are Eugene Smith's documentary photographs sober and Weegee's wacky? There is no such thing as objective reality, only individual interpretations of external events and subject matter.

In a sense, Uelsmann is working in the documentary tradition of a photojournalist, although he is reporting on his internal visions and explorations rather than social conditions or political conflicts. He provides visual evidence of his metaphysical reveries and inquiries, compiling what amount to photographic diaries. Like other documentary work, his photographs are inherently narrative. For some photographers, narrative is conveyed through a series of linked photographs while others distill stories into a single image. Uelsmann straddles these approaches by working in montage, which is both a compressed series and a constructed distillation.

Historically, Uelsmann belongs to the first generation of image makers who acquired their knowledge and developed their techniques in the academy. He studied at the Rochester Institute of Technology where Minor White established his cult of metaphor, inviting the excavation of surface imagery to yield underlying meaning. White's dictum was: "One should not only photograph things for what they are but for what else they are." Later, at Indiana University, Henry Holmes Smith became a mentor and, in characteristic dynamic fashion, pushed Uelsmann to develop his methods and pursue his vision.

These university-educated photographers were influenced by the work of their instructors and peers as well as the course of photographic history. They created images that were not only an expression of an individual style, but also a reaction to previous modes of working. For Uelsmann, this meant rejecting accepted image-making techniques in favor of a looser interpretation of photographic enterprise.

JERRY N. UELSMANN: Untitled, 1979

Not surprisingly, Uelsmann himself has acquired a reputation as an enthusiastic and supportive teacher, instilling in his students the same sense of curiosity, playfulness, and discovery that his instructors fostered in him. Though many photographers are understandably proprietary about their methods, Uelsmann has been open to explaining his techniques to others—the use of multiple enlargers, the assembly of images, the false starts and redirections—and allowed his work to be instructive as well as inspirational. He has created mysterious images, only to demystify them in the service of photographic education.

Decades ago, photographic manipulation was considered deceptive, even degenerate, a violation of documentary integrity or a form of cheating. But what if a photographer wishes to capture an image that does not exist in the external world? In our age of intermingling disciplines and crossover successes, it's easy to overlook the initial audacity of Uelsmann's approach. He not only turned documentary expectations of photography to more personal ends. He challenged the then-prevalent methods of photographic practice. Not for him the sanctity of straight print-making, a method espoused by Ansel Adams and the f/64 group among others. He challenged Weston's purist notion of "pre-visualization," the full construction of a picture before and during exposure. Instead, Uelsmann proposed "post-visualization" as an addendum to these established philosophies of image-making, that is, "the willingness. . . to revisualize the final image at any point in the photographic process."[1] Looking back, we can see that artists such as Uelsmann instigated nothing less than a mutiny, much like the Surrealists before them, and we owe the expansion of photographic endeavor—Kruger's collages,

Skoglund's constructions, Muniz's sugar portraits—to their experimentation and playful irreverence.

Today, Uelsmann's photomontages are not as disorienting as they once were. With the onset of digital photography, we have learned to see differently. We question the veracity of photographs, their intention and subliminal messages. We understand that photographs can be manipulated as can our perspectives. In a time of innovative technologies, conflicting narratives, and simultaneous truths, we have learned that there are multiple realities and no single authority. Uelsmann has even written of the possibility of "invent[ing] a reality."[2] It is this pursuit that has occupied Uelsmann's artistic life and, though his pictures may not conform to the reality of others, they retain an authenticity and conviction all their own. When Uelsmann depicts a tree floating above a lake or flesh turning to stone, it's because somewhere—even if only in his mind's eye—they really are.

1 Uelsmann, "Post-Visualization," *Contemporary Photographer* V:4, 1967.

2 Uelsmann, "Light Notes," in *Landscape Perspectives: Photographic Studies*, edited by Jean Tucker [essays and photographs from exhibition and symposium held at the University of St. Louis, 1986].

WILLARD VAN DYKE: Untitled, 1967

Willard Van Dyke

by James Enyeart

Willard Van Dyke (1906–1986) received his first camera at age twelve. He began to develop a serious interest in making photographs during high school in 1925. In that same year he purchased a 4x5 camera and used the darkroom of his high school sweetheart's father, the Photo Secessionist John Paul Edwards. Edwards became his mentor, sharing his photographic library of both historic and contemporary photography. In 1928, Edwards introduced Van Dyke to Edward Weston and by 1929 the forty-three year old Weston and twenty-three year old Van Dyke became fast friends and, after a short apprentice period, fellow photographers. Van Dyke and Weston photographed together on many occasions until 1935 when Van Dyke gave up photography to move to New York City. His reasons were many, but among them was a desire to get out from under Weston's shadow and to expand his strong sense of social consciousness into other art forms. For a brief time he took up acting, but within a year he was deeply involved in film as a cinematographer.

Van Dyke's innate sense of organization and leadership made it possible for him at age twenty-four to open a gallery at 683 Brockhurst in Oakland, California, in 1930. With the assistance of Mary Jeanette Edwards, he rented Annie Brigman's former home and studio, an urban, barn-like structure, and turned part of it into a gallery for photography, drawing, and prints. It was here in 1932 that he suggested the idea to Weston and Ansel Adams that they form a collaborative group of photographers who shared a common aesthetic interest in straight photography. It was Adams who gave the group the name Group f/64, but it was Van Dyke who organized the loose association and organized the exhibitions. The group included, among others, Weston, Van Dyke, Adams, Noskowiak, Swift, Cunningham, and Edwards. During this period from 1930 to 1935, Van Dyke made the majority of the photographs for which he is remembered. His formation of the Group f/64 had a significant impact on history's assessment of the photographers who participated and helped to establish a tradition in American photography that remains very much a part of contemporary photography.

When Van Dyke moved to New York in 1935 he said there were two individuals he wanted to meet. The first was the director of the Film Library at the Museum of Modern Art, and the second was Ralph Steiner. Van Dyke and Preston Holder had already attempted to make a film in 1934, but it was never finished. Even so, Van Dyke had informed himself about the work of Steiner, who like Strand had worked as both cinematographer and photographer. Within a year he and Steiner were friends and, in 1936, Steiner recommended Van Dyke to Pare Lorenz for his next documentary film. Van Dyke served as cinematographer for Lorenz's film *The River*, now a classic. In 1938, Van Dyke and Steiner directed and photographed the film *The City*, considered today to be among the most important socially conscious documentary films in film history.

When the United States entered World War II, Van Dyke offered his services to the Office of War Information and served as a liaison between OWI and Hollywood writers who provided scripts for American "propaganda" films, as Van Dyke described his work at this time. Between 1940 and 1965 Van Dyke continued to produce documentary films that earned him a place of significance in film history. During that period, in 1947, he directed and photographed a film on Edward Weston, *The Photographer*, for the United States Information Agency, the only film on Weston's work in which the artist appears. During the following eighteen years, Van Dyke produced, directed, and photographed more than fifty films. In 1965, Van Dyke became the Director of the Department of Film at the Museum of Modern Art in New York. During his nine-year tenure (he was forced to retire in 1973 due to a mandatory retirement policy) at the Museum he changed the department from being a "library" to a full department, expanded to include independent film, avant-garde film, and documentary film. Ever on the move, Van Dyke established the Film Program at the Purchase campus of the State University of New York, became Chairman, and retired as Professor Emeritus in 1981. From 1976 to his death in 1986, Van Dyke returned to making photographs and enjoyed several retrospectives of his work and that of the Group f/64.

Willard Van Dyke is an important link to American modernist photography and to the history of socially committed documentary film. The same was true of his friend and mentor, Ralph Steiner, who brought Van Dyke and myself together to discuss and explore the Center for Creative Photography as the place for Van Dyke's archive. The first meeting took place in the early 1980s and we remained in contact until his death. Steiner continued to remind Van Dyke that the Center was the place for his work. Following his death Van Dyke's wife, Barbara, honored Willard's wishes and placed his negatives, correspondence, prints, and related materials at the Center. This important archive cross-fertilizes a number of other archives at the Center—Adams, Weston, Strand, Steiner—broadening the discussion and understanding of photography and film history as interactive arts in the first half of this century. Van Dyke's archive also makes it possible to finally appreciate the depth and breadth of his personal contributions to that history.

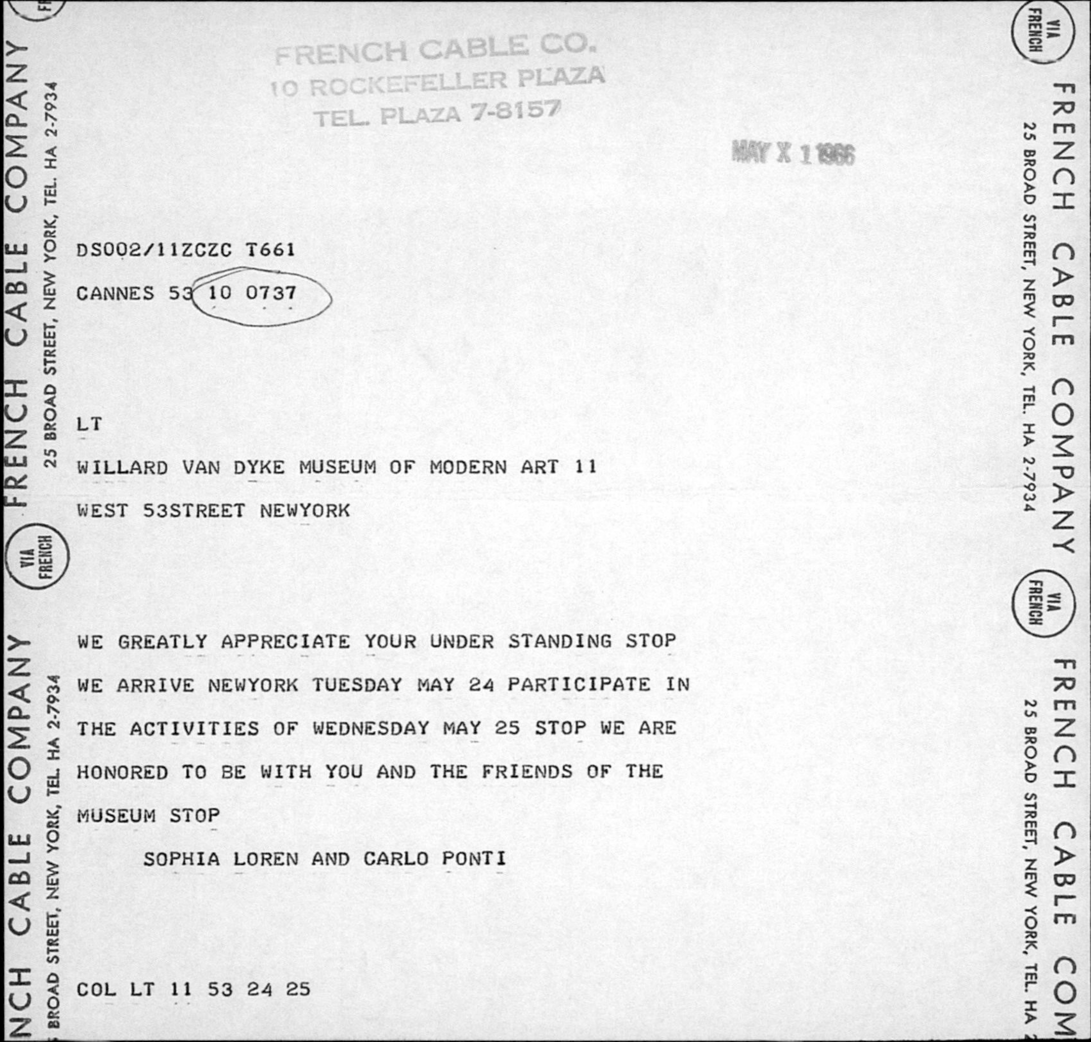

FRENCH CABLE COMPANY
25 BROAD STREET, NEW YORK, TEL. HA 2-7934
VIA FRENCH

FRENCH CABLE CO.
10 ROCKEFELLER PLAZA
TEL. PLAZA 7-8157

MAY X 1 1966

DS002/11ZCZC T661

CANNES 53 10 0737

LT

WILLARD VAN DYKE MUSEUM OF MODERN ART 11

WEST 53STREET NEWYORK

WE GREATLY APPRECIATE YOUR UNDER STANDING STOP

WE ARRIVE NEWYORK TUESDAY MAY 24 PARTICIPATE IN

THE ACTIVITIES OF WEDNESDAY MAY 25 STOP WE ARE

HONORED TO BE WITH YOU AND THE FRIENDS OF THE

MUSEUM STOP

SOPHIA LOREN AND CARLO PONTI

COL LT 11 53 24 25

Telegram from Sophia Loren and Carlo Ponti to Willard Van Dyke at the Museum of Modern Art, n.d.
Willard Van Dyke Archive

LAURA VOLKERDING: *Louisiana*, 1972

Laura Volkerding

by Marcia Tiede

Laura Volkerding (1939–1996) saw her life's work as an ongoing apprenticeship, the pursuit of perfection in a craft. Originally from Louisville, Kentucky, she obtained her graduate degree in printmaking (1961–64) at the Institute of Design in Chicago. After losing most of her printmaking work in a 1972 fire, she devoted herself to photography, which she had been practicing for a decade. She taught printmaking and then photography at the University of Chicago from 1974 to 1980. Her vision was influenced by that of Walker Evans and Art Sinsabaugh; she visited Berenice Abbott and admired the work of Eugène Atget. Her personal collection of photographs includes vintage prints by Aaron Siskind and Joseph Jachna. Volkerding's experience of Chicago as a center of modernist architecture was also formative.

Over thirty years Volkerding progressed from 35mm work to ever larger formats, including a Widelux panoramic camera that she used for a decade, finally abandoning that and smaller view formats for the contemplative clarity of a Deardorff 8x10 view camera. Her early photographic work from the 1960s and 1970s depicted quirky vernacular architecture, campgrounds, and tourist vistas from her summer trips, and wryly observed events and constructs. She experimented with multiple-part works, playing with perspective and discontinuity. Volkerding was involved in the Seagrams-sponsored project to document courthouses across the country in 1978. In 1979 she did two documentary projects: scenes from agricultural communes in China (an unrealized book project) and an exploration of gospel churches in the Chicago area. After this time she seldom photographed human subjects.

In 1980, Volkerding moved to California to become a lecturer in photography at Stanford University, remaining there for the rest of her career. Her search for a personal style, which had earlier vacillated to include images reminiscent of Garry Winogrand or Roger Minick, settled into a consistent quest: she obsessively photographed industrialized waterfronts and other altered terrain. Her previous interest in sculpted landscapes such as gardens continued as well. She used the Widelux, but also began combining contact prints (4x5, 5x7, and a few 8x10-inch) to form precisely contiguous panoramas. Volkerding meticulously pursued the technical demands of these reassembled scenes, ultimately combining up to eight separate images. These panoramic views of rip raps, date groves, and abandoned follies seem to be more a commentary on the forms of our physical endeavors, toward whatever end, than a judgment of damage.

Volkerding had traveled abroad several times since 1968—to Mexico, England, France, Greece, Italy, and Turkey—where she was attracted to copses and cowpaths, and to archaic remnants such as dolmens, abbeys and mosques, cemeteries, and whitewashed adobe. By the mid-1980s she was casting about for a different direction and seeking to make "images driven by architecture and a specific quality of light." (There is a small group of unidentified photographs from around this time, of simple white building facades, a salt mound, and olive tree trunks, labeled by Volkerding only as "White Pictures.") In 1984, the year she got her Deardorff view camera, she went with a friend to the California terra cotta manufacturer Gladding McBean and photographed the workshops. She learned of the Coubertin foundry near Paris when a casting of Rodin's *Gates of Hell* was installed at Stanford and was invited to photograph there the following year.

Through her presence at Coubertin, Volkerding was led to the Compagnons du Devoir, a community of apprentices originating in medieval times, whose craft-based mission resonated with her own sense of devotion to excellence in one's work, espe-

LAURA VOLKERDING: *Coubertin*, 1986

cially that produced by hand. During the last decade of her life she photographed the Compagnons' classrooms and the apprentices' masterpieces; bronze and copper foundries; the workshops of fine woodcarvers, plastermakers, and stonecarvers; and restoration projects in cathedrals and other grand buildings. Often these were long exposures of several minutes. The workspaces are cluttered—or neatly arrayed—with the tools and protective masks and gloves necessary for the work, as well as dense impromptu collages of molds, patterns, design elements, works in progress, and more personal fragments such as graffiti, calendars, and family photos. Volkerding also included backdrops of translucent plastic sheeting, or rays of sunlight from high windows—the filtered or isolating quality of light she liked to pursue. As in her landscapes and other earlier work, Volkerding seems to have been drawn to a certain degree of chaos, to the idea of a logic within random arrangements. Though most of the workshop images were made in France, Volkerding also visited workshops and quarries in Quebec, Tunisia, Spain, Greece, and Italy, and a few in the United States.

The workshop images suggest the presence of the craftsman, though almost never are people portrayed. Volkerding's images seem to describe an ongoing humanity preserved in the work itself—the care with which skills are transmitted to new hands, which in turn devote themselves to restoring the master works of long-passed generations. There are glimpses of personification in the things portrayed as well—a classical sculpture's face floating hauntingly from a poster on a closet, or plaster statues caught in sunlight in an image Volkerding titles *The Dance of the Casts*. Volkerding's titles in general preserve the anonymity of the craftsmen whose spheres of activity are depicted —an absence of ego in keeping with our distinction between "artisan" and "artist," but also a reflection of this work for work's sake, part of a tradition greater than the individual: "I think the lives and work of the Compagnons du Devoir have much to teach us about integrity and about the importance of respect for the past."

LAURA VOLKERDING: *Folly at Santa Rosa Ranch, Coachella Valley*, 1986

Volkerding's first exhibition of the workshop images, held at Stanford in 1986, was executed as printing-out paper prints. The purple-brown tone lends an aura of an earlier time to the work, or may have been incidental to her continued exploration of new techniques. She also made enlarged prints on a warm-tone glossy paper, and then even larger prints of a velvety charcoal quality, on matte Arches Galerie paper—the final rendition of her last and most committed body of work. Volkerding also explored digital imagery, attending a digital photography workshop and sampling the Iris print process at Nash Editions. Volkerding was supported in her many trips to France, Italy, and elsewhere by a Guggenheim fellowship in 1987 and a residency fellowship at the Camargo Foundation in 1993, as well as teaching at Stanford's overseas studies program in Tours. Shortly before her death from a brain tumor at age fifty-six, the Center published *Solomon's Temple: The European Building-Crafts Legacy*, a project that Volkerding had been formulating for several years, and her only monograph. The Reading Room of the Center's Research Center was also named in her honor.

The sizable oeuvre left by Volkerding is remarkable in the context of the CCP's holdings, in that it contains fully three-quarters of all panoramic-format work (both single-image and composite) at the Center; as well as being one of the very few bodies of work by a woman photographer that does not emphasize the traditional female genres of still life, portrait, or figure study. Her landscapes—more than three hundred—make up almost half the landscapes in the Center's collection done by a woman photographer. The handful of spooky large pinhole images of Midi monuments produced during Volkerding's residency at the Camargo Foundation in Cassis, France, during her last year of work are a marvelous addition to the CCP's pinhole holdings. Her printing-out paper prints constitute more than one-third of that technique in the CCP's collection. Her printmaking is represented by a substantial collection of multi-color intaglio prints (many incorporating *chin collé*) and one-color lithographs. Extensive files of personal papers, negatives, and work prints are also included. Regrettably Volkerding, an introspective and dedicated photographer, died before her own work was done and before it received the attention that it deserves.

TODD WALKER: Untitled, 1969

<table>
<tr><td>

Todd Walker

by Nancy Solomon

</td></tr>
</table>

Photographer Todd Walker (1917–1998) was a western original. Born in Utah, he grew up in Los Angeles and moved to Tucson during the seventies. His work resonates with light. In Arizona, it is the brilliant, revealing quality of light in the desert, where his ostensible subjects are the plants, land forms, rocks, even the dirt. His lifelong interest in the human form, particularly heads and female nudes, is revealed in gradations of shadow; he delineates edges as light moves from the brightest highlight through mid-tones to deep shadow.

Todd Walker was that rare combination of a superb technician with an original vision. Because he printed directly on paper, his photographs make a direct tactile connection with the viewer; his work conveys an intimacy with the paper that is simply not possible with out-of-the-box photographic emulsions. Walker was a colorist with his own unique sense of color. Never satisfied with colors available from manufacturers of photographic materials, he mixed his own inks. This skill was honed during his apprenticeship as a teenager in Hollywood painting movie sets; at the end of each workday, he mixed leftover paint to see what new colors he could make. Also sensitive to the tonality reflected from each color, he painted the faux finish for the fireplace in *Citizen Kane*, which was rendered on the set in color to achieve a specific appearance on black-and-white film.

Walker pursued photography as an art form before it offered any financial rewards and before there was much of a support network of other artists working in photography to share ideas with. Like Ansel Adams, Harry Callahan, and others, he supported himself and his family in the 1950s through commercial photography and later through teaching. His own time was dedicated to his own work. Particularly memorable from this period are his nudes—beautiful explorations of form and surface in collotype on paper and Sabattier effect on photographic emulsions.

Walker's most important contribution both to the expression of his own vision and to art was in offset lithography. He brought his entire knowledge of photography to the process of offset lithography and made it into an expressive medium. He explored virtually every aspect from changing the patterns of printing dots to radically lengthening exposures that allowed him to work with any tonal area of an image as line. Here his photographic imagery merges with his innate sense of color. He mixed all his own colors, sometimes printing up to thirty-five colors on one image to achieve what he wanted in a medium that is usually used for mechanical reproduction in a standard set of four colors. His interest in the printing dots prefigured his late work in the emerging pixel-based world of digital photography.

In addition to making single photographs, Walker used sequences of images in portfolios and artists' books. Because he was a printer, he also became a publisher with his own Thumbprint Press. He explored typography and integrating texts and images in

Enthusiasm
Strengthens

by Todd Walker

Title page from *Enthusiasm Strengthens* by Todd Walker, 1987
Todd Walker Collection

TODD WALKER: *Chris, Veiled*, 1970

books like *See* and *For Nothing Changes*. Late in his career Walker taught at Florida State University and the University of Arizona, encouraging student interest in alternative photographic processes and artists' books.

The creative lives of many twentieth-century photographers whose work is in the collections and archives of the Center for Creative Photography continued into their old age. Aaron Siskind, Ansel Adams, Frederick Sommer, and Imogen Cunningham, for instance, photographed in their eighties. In his seventies, Walker continued to grow—absorbing computer photography with the naturalness of an eighteen-year-old raised on television and computers and merging that imagery with his offset lithography. He bought an early Apple computer and spoke directly to it in machine language, rather than using the primitive commercial software available at the time. He even used the computer to generate texts, as in *Enthusiasm Strengthens*. Later, as the capabilities of computers advanced, he integrated video and 3-D imaging in his work.

Walker's work can be seen in several areas of the Center. The Photograph Collection includes fine prints in photo-silkscreen, offset lithography, and standard photographic emulsions. Walker's artists' books can be checked out of the Center's Library, which also holds videotaped interviews by Center staff for reference use in the Library. William S. Johnson and Susan E. Cohen interviewed Walker about his work and ideas in the late 1970s; transcripts from these tapes appear in *One Thing Just Sort of Led to Another*, a book about Walker's work and creative process. In the 1980s, with other Center staff and volunteers, I produced the video *Todd Walker in the Litho Studio*, which captures his working method and the equipment he built himself to make offset lithographs. The Research Center has hardcover editions of his Thumbprint books that he bound himself, wrapped in marbled papers that he made, mixing his own color combinations.

Water in the West

by Leon Zimlich

The Water in the West project began in 1989 as a photographic response to growing concern over water use and allocation in the American West. The project participants recognized that photography, beyond its capacity as art, also provides information and could contribute to public debate on water issues.

PETER GOIN:
Hot Springs at The Needles, Pyramid Lake, Nevada, 1990

Directed by photographer and photoeducator Robert Dawson, and photographic historian and curator Ellen Manchester, the Water in the West group includes photographers Laurie Brown, Gregory Conniff, Terry Evans, Geoff Fricker, Peter Goin, Wanda Hammerbeck, Sant Khalsa, Mark Klett, Ellen Land-Weber, Sharon Stewart, and Martin Stupich. The project is collaborative: members both work together on particular projects and also consult with each other on how the separate projects might proceed. The efforts of Water in the West parallel those of the earlier Photo League in New York, which used photography to contribute to and spark debate on issues of social concern in that city.[1]

The experience of many of its members in similar joint efforts provided a foundation for the success of the Water in the West project. Ellen Manchester and Mark Klett were both members of the Rephotographic Survey Project of 1977–79. Klett was also one of four photographers contributing to the Central Arizona Project Photographic Survey in 1985–86. Robert Dawson worked closely with photographer Stephen Johnson in an extensive survey of water issues in California's Central Valley in the mid-1980s; that work was published in *The Great Central Valley: California's Heartland* (1993). Terry Evans contributed to an NEA-funded photographic survey of Kansas, published as *No Mountains in the Way* (1975).

Whether the boundary between the American West and Midwest is seen as the ninety-eighth meridian or the hundredth, as it has been by various figures, the West has been defined as a region by its aridity. In reporting to Congress in 1876 on the feasibility of implementing the Homestead Act within the western United States, western

230

explorer John Wesley Powell warned that there was not enough water in the arid West to irrigate and open it to extensive farming. Yet, in the ensuing 125 years, much of the West has been developed through the aid of massive water projects in every region—though not without controversy and debate.

In recent years the cost of these efforts has become increasingly evident as the terrain—initially seen as a "wasteland" to be conquered—has been altered and perhaps damaged beyond repair by a century of diverted water, intensive grazing and agricultural use, and accelerating residential development. Waterways, with their fragile riparian corridors, have taken the brunt of this use—being channelized, diverted, dried up through groundwater overdraft, used as toxic dumping zones, and replaced by the sterile passage of canals that sustain no life except at their terminus. For instance, the drying up of the Colorado River delta on Mexico's Gulf of California has affected indigenous and "downstream" water rights. The population of the Sun Belt continues to swell exponentially, with Las Vegas and Phoenix currently among the fastest growing cities. Water in the West members believe that knowledge about water could alter this headlong growth, despite engineering and political feats such as the canal that waters Los Angeles (to the extinction of the Owens Valley), and the dams

TERRY EVANS:
Wheel That Raises Gate for Water Regulation, Cheyenne Bottoms, August 1992
From the series *Western Waters*, No. 21

that form reservoirs and control flows in the Colorado and lesser rivers. Ironically, despite the extent of agricultural and urban growth that has been achieved in the American West, John Wesley Powell's warnings that the arid West could not sustain such development are ringing true.

Photographs from the Water in the West project have been published in numerous books by the individual photographers. Other books represent the larger project: *A River Too Far: The Past and Future of the Arid West* (1991) pairs the photographs with writings about the West and water issues by Marc Reisner, Donald Worster, Wallace Stegner, Roderick Nash, and others; *Arid Waters: Photographs from the Water in the West Project* (1992) includes an extensive essay by Ellen Manchester; and *Western Waters: Photographs by Gregory Conniff, Terry Evans, and Wanda Hammerbeck* (1996) has an essay by John Pultz.

The Water in the West group has been aggressive in presenting their work in exhibition and contributing to symposia on water issues. Water in the West has attempted to

SHARON STEWART:
El Cerrito y la Acequia Madre: Diggin' Ditch, 1993

transcend the usual definition of a photographic exhibition by including presentations of related materials that provide a context for the photographs, such as historical photographs, notes, and contact sheets.

Water in the West project members:

Robert Dawson, a faculty member at City College of San Francisco, has photographed extensively in the Central Valley of California, documenting the shifting patterns of water and land use there, and has also worked in collaboration with Peter Goin, photographing in the region of Reno, Nevada, particularly along the Truckee River watershed between Lake Tahoe and Pyramid Lake.

Ellen Manchester's writing on photography in the West, as published in *Arid Waters* (1992), places the work of Water in the West within an historical context and joins it to the larger effort to document water issues in the West, such as in the writings of Donald Worster and Marc Reisner. She guest-curated the de Young Museum in San Francisco's exhibition and book *Facing Eden: 100 Years of Landscape Art in the Bay Area* (1995).

Laurie Brown has photographed excavated, reconfigured sites in southern California and waterfront living in Las Vegas. Her series of composite images, *Divining Western Waters*, pairs her own contemporary panoramic images of the Southwest with stereographic views made earlier in the century. Though not a rephotographic project, this series makes a comparison between current and past attitudes toward the landscape and its resources as well as the technologies applied to those resources. Another book, *Recent Terrains: Terraforming the American West*, was published by The Johns Hopkins University Press in 2000.

Gregory Conniff has photographed water systems in the North and South Dakota and worked in collaboration with Terry Evans to photograph the Cheyenne Bottoms in Kansas, where the needs of agriculture and the competing demands of wetlands, a seasonal home to migratory waterfowl, have strained the Arkansas River and the Ogallala aquifer. That work was published in John Pultz's *Western Waters* (1996).

Terry Evans's work has centered on water use and management on the prairie in Kansas, and more recently upon remnants of the defense industry in Illinois. Her aerial and

LAURIE BROWN: *Convergence #9*, 1995
From the series *Divining Western Waters*

groundbased landscape photographs have been published in her books *Prairie: Images of Ground and Sky* (1986) and *The Inhabited Prairie* (1998).

Geoff Fricker documents efforts to restore portions of the Sacramento River watershed in northern California. He has also photographed Hawaiian sugar mill ruins and water-works, as well as native Hawaiian ruins, over a twenty-year period—what he refers to as "Water in the Far West."

Peter Goin, who teaches at the University of Nevada, Reno, has photographed water projects in Nevada and New Mexico in addition to his collaboration with Dawson in documenting the Truckee River watershed and Pyramid Lake. Goin's photography at Lake Tahoe was published in *A Rephotographic Survey of Lake Tahoe* (1992). In *Nuclear Land-scapes* (1991), he documented nuclear test sites in Nevada and the Marshall Islands, and the Hanford Nuclear Reservation in Washington state. Recently he published *Humanature* (1996), which addresses the human attempt to control the planet in myriad ways.

Wanda Hammerbeck has photographed at Lake Powell, created by the Glen Canyon Dam on the Colorado River and ironically named after John Wesley Powell who explored the river and canyon. She also documented the way water was used in the growth of Las Vegas, Nevada, and the Owens Valley and the Los Angeles water system. Portions of the latter project were published in *Western Waters* (1996).

Sant Khalsa's Santa Ana River Project documents the construction of the Seven Oaks Dam in San Bernardino County, California, the course of the Santa Ana River through San Bernardino, Riverside, and Orange Counties, and the relationship of river, industry, and development. Khalsa, who teaches at California State University, San Bernardino, has also created several installation art works designed to raise awareness about the human relationship with the environment.

GEOFFREY FRICKER: *Hamakuapoko Mill*, 1979
From the series *Sugar Mills*

Mark Klett's photography is informed by his background in geology and his awareness of the historical context for current land use and attitudes toward the western landscape. A member of the Rephotographic Survey Project of the late 1970s, Klett continues that work with Third View, which visits the rephotographic sites a third time to provide a comparative set of images illustrating both change and constancy. His images show the human presence within, as much as impact upon, the landscape.

Ellen Land-Weber, a faculty member at Humboldt State University in Arcata, California, photographed marshes outside of Arcata. Rather than presenting a story about water misuse and appropriation, Land-Weber's photographs document an innovative project to both recover an abandoned industrial site and to use the natural processes at work in marshlands to treat waste water from the nearby city. Land-Weber also merges traditional landscape photography with digital composite imaging. The digital images combine photographs of the marsh with antique illustrations of various animals, some of them notoriously extinct, coupled with titles redolent of Darwinian principles and current environmental issues.

Sharon Stewart's 1992 survey of village life in El Cerrito, New Mexico (her home), portrays water management strategies that predate the Spanish entrada. There, residents of the community work together to maintain the ditch, or acequia, which provides water for agriculture and livestock, demonstrating tangibly that they are dependent upon each other. Stewart's 1989–1991 photographs from the *Toxic Tour of Texas* series document numerous sites in Texas contaminated by hazardous wastes and the environmental activism of residents whose lives are threatened by the pollution.

Martin Stupich has photographed large-scale mining and water projects throughout the West, primarily in the Columbia River basin in Oregon and Washington, and the Colorado, Salt, and Gila River basins in Arizona. The scale of such projects signals the power of culture to manipulate the landscape.

1 Peter Goin, Ellen Manchester, and Sheppard Fine Art Gallery, *Arid Waters: Photographs from the Water in the West Project* (Reno: University of Nevada Press, 1992), p. 12.

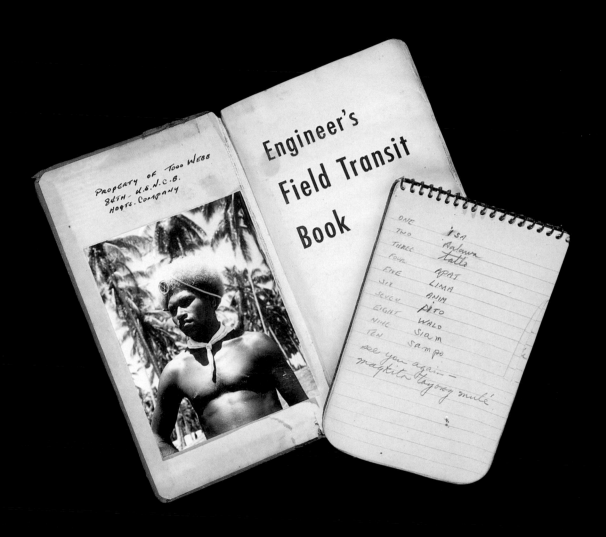

Small notebooks created by Todd Webb while he served in New Guinea during World War II. One records vocabulary and the other contains small photographs.
Todd Webb Archive

TODD WEBB: *Detail, Wall Opposite My Studio Door, Paris*, 1950

As Todd Webb (1905–2000) readily acknowledged, he was saved by the great stock market crash of 1929, which ruined his career in the financial world and propelled him to California to seek gold as the forty-niners had done eighty years before. By the time that photography caught up with him in a serious way in 1938 at the age of thirty-three, he had adventured his way across America and by Pacific sea voyage to another gold mining adventure in Panama. Back in his hometown of Detroit, he started attending camera club meetings, where he took up with fellow novice Harry Callahan and the more experienced Arthur Siegel. In 1941, a ten-day workshop given by Ansel Adams changed Webb's life. Photography became something he wanted to do for the rest of his life.

New York City provided Webb with his first wellspring of inspiration and friendships. During his first brief trip to New York City in 1942, he met Alfred Stieglitz and Dorothy Norman, both of whom would be influential figures in his early career. When he moved there in 1946, after serving as a United States Navy photographer in the South Pacific during the war, he began lifelong friendships with Beaumont and Nancy Newhall and Georgia O'Keeffe. He received some commissions for *Fortune* magazine, then photographed for the Standard Oil Company under Roy Stryker during 1947 and 1948.

Restless and tempted by a commission in Great Britain, Webb crossed the Atlantic in 1949, eventually settling in Paris. From 1949 to 1953, he accepted European assignments from Standard Oil and started working for the newly created United Nations. It was in Paris that he met and married Lucille, another American living abroad.

In 1954, the Webbs moved back to New York and sought new ways to make a living with his photography. He received a Guggenheim fellowship to retrace the path of those who crossed the country a century earlier in search of land and gold. The results of his treks—on foot, by Vespa, and by automobile—were a pair of books written and photographed by Webb on the gold rush trails and remnants of ghost towns: *Gold Strikes and Ghost Towns* and *The Gold Rush Trail and the Road to Oregon*.

A growing friendship with Mitchell Wilder, the first Director of the Amon Carter Museum, led to additional commissions in the 1960s to photograph the nineteenth-century architecture of Texas. Occasional United Nations projects took him to Africa and Mexico. In 1960, the Webbs left New York City to live in Santa Fe, then England, and, once again, France, before finally settling in Maine in 1975.

Throughout his career, Todd Webb responded to every opportunity to produce photographs that demonstrated a strong sense of intimacy and curiosity about the relationship between history, place, and people. Because he was equally at home in the great cities of the world and the wide open spaces of the American landscape, every Todd Webb photograph is a combination of compelling narrative and powerful composition. His style might be described as humanistic documentary, a blend of poetry and reportage, as if he simply could not prevent himself from imbuing his photographs with his own sense of optimism and romance.

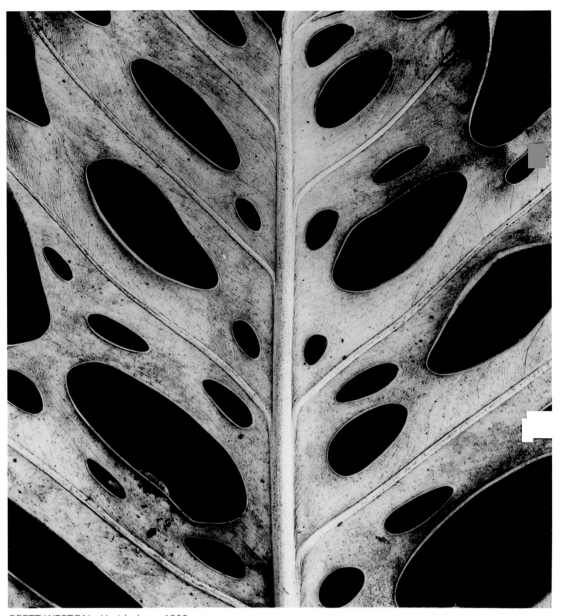

BRETT WESTON: Untitled, ca. 1980s

Brett Weston

by Dianne Nilsen

The sun had not yet risen on a frosty Carmel Valley morning in 1976. I arrived in Brett Weston's (1911–1993) living room during his darkroom break. He had already proofed his latest negatives from our trip down the coast of Oregon and was ready to print. Bowls of dates and roasted almonds waited on the hearth. There I enjoyed, as I would many times over the next two years as his apprentice, sitting by the fire with him and sipping strong black coffee.

Brett's awakening as an artist occurred in the light of a purist approach to photography made classic by his father, friend, and mentor, Edward Weston, who took him to Mexico City as a boy in 1925. His immersion in the medium during those two years inspired the rest of his life. Because of Edward's generosity and encouragement, all the tools of the trade were at Brett's disposal. Equipped with a sharp lens, a well-used Graflex, a sturdy wooden tripod, focusing cloth, and holders loaded with what film Edward could supply, Brett was taught the legendary Weston "by guess and by god" exposure technique and sent off to explore. Unlike Edward, who began as a pictorialist and evolved into a realist, Brett began as a realist and evolved into an abstractionist.

Though he frequently acknowledged the influence his father had on his work and spoke often of his admiration of the photographs of Paul Strand, Charles Sheeler, and Henri Cartier-Bresson, Brett believed other artists influenced his work as much if not more than photographers did. He proclaimed Georgia O'Keeffe to be the greatest American painter. He was a great admirer of paintings by The Blue Four, a group of German expressionists known for the vibrant color and emotion in their paintings. He was moved by the sculptures of Brancusi and Henry Moore.

Brett focused his lifestyle to actualize his desire. With the heart of a child and the wisdom of a sage, he found continual inspiration and fulfillment in photography. He saw the world anew each day. He established disciplined patterns of work and rest. He did what he needed to produce or to inspire his art, and he lived simply if not ascetically.

One day as we prepared lunch, I recall asking myself how a man, who spent several thousand dollars on the brand new camera car in the driveway, had just advised that I was cutting off too much of the root end of the scallion for our salad. As if a Zen riddle, clarity came when I listened to Brett jest with his brothers over who ate which of Edward's immortalized vegetables. The Weston boys had lived leanly most of their lives and food was never taken for granted. The creative quest came with great sacrifice: Brett's camera car and the half-inch of scallion I wasted illustrated a finely tuned survival instinct.

A blazing campfire amidst the Joshua trees and a gang of dusty photographers may have first inspired the big announcement on a moonlit desert night. I heard it often thereafter—at openings, over sumptuous meals with family and friends, print viewing in his living room, or working on the pebbly shores of Point Lobos with workshop students. I certainly heard it while sharing a can of sardines and a beer over a High Sierra

BRETT WESTON: *Skylight, Midtown*, 1947

tailgate lunch. Forever ingrained in my memory, and always delivered with the gesturing gusto he was known and loved for, Brett proclaimed countless times,"On my eightieth birthday I'm going to have a huge bonfire and burn all my negatives." He explained that printing was absolutely personal, and he didn't want anyone else trying to interpret his negatives.

A lifetime later in December of 1991, I found myself driving down the Carmel Valley Road to Brett's former home, where his daughter Erica now lived. Several weeks prior I received an invitation to attend a party in honor of his eightieth birthday. Brett flew in from his home in Hawaii and was meeting me there before the big soiree.

After catching up on our lives in our familiar places by the hearth he asked in his famous California drawl, "So darling, what is this business about the negatives." Wondering if he still planned to burn them on his birthday, I had sent him a letter asking him to consider making a small selection to be preserved in the Center for Creative Photography archives. Trying to outline the archivist's perspective and the value that a selection of the negatives might have for future art historians, I assured him they would never be printed. Days later, I received a response expressing delight that I was coming to the party. No mention of the negatives.

In consideration of my request however, he went on to tell me he had given Cole twelve negatives; each punched with a silver grade-school-style hole punch and marked in grease pencil under a big "X", the exclamation, "No Prints!" Cole, he said, could wave them around at workshops for a few years if he wanted to and eventually place them at the Center. I wasn't sure whether to laugh or cry at his interpretation of my suggestion, so I took a big breath and asked if he had considered the span of his career in the selection. Brett told me to call Cole to see what he had.

Having printed and cared for Edward's work for many years after his death, Cole bemoaned the agony of helping his brother dump several crates full of negatives into the dumpster the day before I arrived. He told me they were then doused generously with water from the garden hose. With thousands left to destroy, Brett had friends lined up to help finish the job, over the next few days. Concerned that the fumes from so many negatives might cause environmental harm, the notion of tossing them into a raging bonfire was reduced to a token shoebox-full he planned to burn in the fireplace at the Stone Pine Inn where his birthday party was to be hosted.

I realized that, if nothing else, I should record the types of film he had used over the years and asked if he might allow me to slice off a variety of his negatives' film notches with his paper cutter before he began destroying them. He agreed. This tiny victory paved the way for a series of spontaneous negotiations over the next few days in a nerve-wracking race against time. Matthias Van Hessemans, the photographer and friend who introduced Brett to Hawaii, joined me in the studio, assisted me, and was a soundboard for ideas as I tried to gently persuade Brett without compromising his convictions or his enjoyment of this special occasion. After the first cut or two, I convinced myself this was archival triage rather than a destructive deed. Brett came in periodically, attempting to lure us back into the living room, chuckling, and calling us mad.

During one of his appearances in the doorway I asked what he thought about my slicing some of the negatives diagonally and preserving both halves. No problem. He said it was fine and joined his other guests again. When the telephone rang a few minutes later, I heard Brett's voice booming that he'd give just thirty minutes of his time. He came back in and announced that someone from the San Francisco *Chronicle* was coming to do an interview and wanted to take pictures of a negative being burned. I handed him several we had already gone through. The picture was published the next day.

As evening approached, I asked Brett how important it was to finish destroying his negatives on his birthday, and if it didn't matter to him, would he allow me a little more time to go through them. He told me to take all the time I wanted. They would be safe there in his studio. As long as they eventually were destroyed, he didn't care. I was enormously relieved, and we spent the next day enjoying ourselves, driving down the coast, meeting friends at Point Lobos, and visiting his family on Wildcat Hill.

I rose at dawn the morning after the party to accompany Brett and his neighbor Iku to the airport. With only a few minutes left to make my final request, I asked Brett what he thought of letting me make a selection of approximately fifty 8x10 negatives to be preserved in their entirety at the Center for Creative Photography. I asked him to imagine how amazing it would be for authors or photographers in the future to hold one of his negatives and consider what it might have been like to produce it. Selecting only negatives that I had seen as signed prints, or that were published in one of his books, I told him I would take them back to the Center and punch holes in a corner of each if he wished, a reminder they were not to be printed. I'd have our archivists send an inventory list so that he would know exactly what I took when I got back. With his blessing, I expressed my gratitude for his trust as we said our farewells at the airport in Monterey.

Back at the Inn, I found Matthias in the dining room with a plastic baggie full of ashes and melted negatives that he had retrieved from the enormous stone fireplace. With only a few hours left before my departure for Tucson; we dashed back and went through several thousand remaining negatives. Discovering a box of 11x14s, I was thrilled to find the last exposure he made—a glowacious agave on Wildcat Hill that I helped him photograph by holding the black side of a focusing cloth as a backdrop.

Underlying Brett Weston's mastery in producing a fine, richly toned gelatin silver print was his ability to recognize dynamic form and the magic evoked by the sheer quality of light. This, along with simple exposure and development techniques, allowed him to transform reality into abstract illusion. Refusing to articulate the meaning in his work, Brett was committed to the idea that art is a visual medium and should speak for itself. He often quipped the same Louis Armstrong quote his father had taped to his writing desk for years: "Man if you gotta ask, you ain't never gonna get to know!"

EDWARD WESTON: *The White Iris*, 1921

<table>
<tr><td>

Edward Weston

by Terence Pitts

</td></tr>
</table>

Edward Weston (1886–1958), perhaps more than anyone else, defined the direction that American art photography would take in the decades immediately following World War I. Over the course of his career, he developed a modernist aesthetic for photography that simultaneously embraced nature and the machine age and that sought to combine personal passions and objective vision. Weston's life and art expressed the American theme of purity and simplicity that extends back through Walt Whitman and Henry David Thoreau to the Puritans.

Weston discovered photography as a teenager, quickly and irrevocably falling in love with the medium. By 1911 he had settled in southern California, just outside Los Angeles, where he set up his own commercial photography studio and married Flora Chandler, with whom he would have four sons: Chandler, Brett, Neil, and Cole.

Too restless and creative to remain solely a commercial photographer, Weston plunged into the international world of amateur artistic photography, almost immediately becoming a successful and respected practitioner of the pictorialist style that defined the art photography of the late nineteenth and early twentieth centuries. For the next decade his work was characterized by softly focused narrative imagery, portraits, and nude studies printed on lush platinum and palladium photographic papers. Simultaneously, Weston became part of the emerging bohemian art scene in Los Angeles, which included dancers, musicians, actors, and other photographers, such as Ramiel McGehee, Johan Hagemeyer, Tina Modotti, and Margrethe Mather, with whom he shared a studio for a while.

In Weston's work of 1918 and 1919, we can begin to see influences from modernist painting. Some images approach pure abstraction while others seem deliberate attempts to adapt the tenets of cubism to photography. A trip that he made to the East Coast in 1922 proved to be the transitional point in Weston's early career. While staying with his sister in Ohio, he made several stunning architectural studies of the Armco Steel Mills. The starkly simple, yet richly detailed Armco images are purely formal studies of the world of modern industry, stripped of pictorialism's narrative and romantic qualities.

From 1923 to 1926, Weston spent most of his time in Mexico City with Tina Modotti, struggling to make a living but participating in the rich artistic life of the revolutionary capital. Increasingly confident in his new straight photographic style, Weston spent the time in Mexico grappling with appropriate subject matter to match. Inspired by the directness and naïve honesty of Mexican folk art, Weston sought to depict both form and passion with a camera. His portraits of friends and fellow artists were heroic, his nude studies became more physically explicit and openly erotic, and his renditions of everyday objects—whether simple folk toys or modern toilets—turned them into objects worthy of contemplation and admiration.

From the moment he returned to the United States, Weston began making work that would fundamentally change the direction of twentieth-century photography in

EDWARD WESTON: *Nude Floating*, 1939

this country. Back in California, Weston sought to translate his Mexican experience into American possibilities. He continued doing nudes and portraits, but turned his passion for making still lifes out of everyday man-made objects into a love for natural objects, such as vegetables, fruits, rocks, shells, and other things that he found in the desert or along the beach. At first, Weston freely intermingled photography of arranged objects and photographing nature in situ. But by 1931 he gave up his own arrangements for nature's. As the early 1930s progressed, Weston's camera pulled back farther and farther from his subjects until he made his first successful landscape since the early days in Mexico, a full decade previously. The landscape would become the main preoccupation for his work from then until he gave up photography in 1948.

The straight, unmannered style of photography that Weston had fought to achieve a decade earlier reached a type of institutional apotheosis in 1932 with the formation of an admittedly informal association of photographers known as Group f/64. The group's subsequent exhibition of their work at the M. H. de Young Art Museum in San Francisco has become one of the watershed moments in American photography, reflecting the

EDWARD WESTON: *Winter Zero Schwartzel's "Bottle Farm," Farmersville, Ohio*, 1941

ascendancy of straight photography over pictorialism. Weston, Adams, and a handful of other West Coast photographers argued that photography's strength should reside in the creation of images of maximum clarity with only the most minimal and cosmetic manipulation in the darkroom.

Weston had had his first glimpse of Point Lobos, the remarkable coastline just south of Carmel, California, in 1928. He fell in love with the stunningly rugged area and ten years later he had a house built there, a small wooden home and darkroom overlooking the Pacific Ocean from a place called Wildcat Hill. In many ways, Point Lobos

exemplifies Weston's strength as a photographer. Here, for twenty years, his photographs transformed the simple, often unremarkable elements of this wild bit of rock outcroppings, tide pools, and hardy trees into images that exalted his love for the natural world.

Dear Frederick —

Enclosed find one buck, balance on acct.

I deeply appreciate work on ground glasses.

Today I adjusted the magnifier as per your suggestion, using hair, and your black writing, seen through thin paper. Had some difficulty because the mag. has quite a depth of focus and my eyes are no longer young (got tired). But all is O.K., and works like a charm. Revolution in focussing!

— I have forgotten your system for centering lens with hole in g.g. no matter how much you swing the back or front you can always line up by adjusting your head! Probably I'm overlooking something quite obvious.

Better return the proof of 3 – 4 x 5's you want. I don't want to guess! I should have numbered them. I have printed N.O. "ovens", Ex Votos — and will try the Tenn. couple next. No hurry on yours, nor mine, please.

After you left, I found that you had left the horsie drawings out on shelf (I had said put in print cabinet, but guess you did not understand). Cat tracks on back, but no damage.

　　　　Saludos Amigos,
　　　　Abrazos, Amor y todo —
　　　　　　　Edward.

Notice!

If you just put "Carmel" as address, letter may get held up a day at least.
Correct : "R.F.D. Carmel —

Letter from Edward Weston to Frederick Sommer, 19 March 1944, discussing a "revolution in focussing!"
Frederick Sommer Archive

Box 262 Prescott. Ariz.
March 23, 1944

Dear Edward:

We returned the proofs in the same mail with last letter. – Hope the drawings are not broken or scratched, a few prints or marks in back don't matter. – Glad you like the focussing set-up. I assume that you remembered to have the ground glass between hair and magnifier when setting magnifier. – You will really be pleased when you see what it can do on subjects that are hard to focus in any light. The centering of lens axis thru hole in g.g. is done without magn. with lens wide open to see if the same amount is visible all around inside lens. Whatever the position of lens in relation to g.g. as long as the axis of lens travels thru hole you can be sure that the center of the lens image alone is being used. This is very important especially with the single elements which have little covering power. I make it a point to always take a glance thru hole without the magn. to see where lens is pointing. It is almost always possible (within reason) to place the swings as needed and still have lens point to center of g.g. this naturally excludes those cases in which front has to be parallel to ground glass and lens raised or lowered in a parallel plane.

Letter from Frederick Sommer to Edward Weston, 23 March 1944, with response to Weston's use of a hair to achieve precise focus
Edward Weston Archive

It took sometime to find out how little I had really exploited the swings before I started to use the hole to check position of lens. Going to this little extra trouble has also the advantage of being able to use magn. on center of image field. — In cases of extreme inclination of lens axis towards g.g. it is no longer possible to use magn. with accuracy since lens axis and magn. axis no longer line up sufficiently, but it is still possible to look thru hole without magnifier to check direction of lens axis. —

I am enclosing the table of relative aperture change **Factors** for working close up. The formula is on back of card. — When you have sometime please send me the formula for Pyro stain. (low sulphite). Also Pyro formula + proportions for low carbonate content.

Please let us know how Charis' mother is doing.

How in hell did this letter get so long!

The best of everything to you both

Frederick

He won the first of two successive fellowships from the John Simon Guggenheim Memorial Foundation in 1938, the first to be awarded to a photographer. He used this time to travel with his second wife, Charis Wilson Weston, photographing extensively around California and the West. In 1941, commissioned by the Limited Editions Club to illustrate Walt Whitman's *Leaves of Grass*, Weston began a photographic tour of the United States that was interrupted by the bombing of Pearl Harbor and the entry of the United States into World War II. After the end of the war and shortly before Parkinson's disease brought about the end of his ability to photograph, Weston experimented with color photography at the urging of the Eastman Kodak Company. Moderately pleased with the results, Weston hoped to be able to explore this new aspect of photography

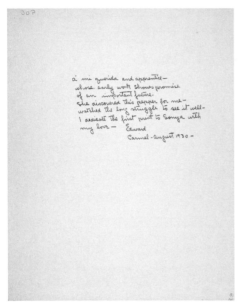

EDWARD WESTON:
verso of *Pepper No. 30*, 1930
Inscription by Weston to Sonya Noskowiak

more. But in 1948, at the age of 62, Weston was forced to retire his camera. Overseeing his son Brett and several darkroom assistants, who did all of the printing, Weston embarked on a review of his entire career, selecting more than eight hundred of his favorite images to print in a limited edition now known as the "project prints."

Weston's writings have proven to be almost as powerful and important as his photographs. The Weston archive includes the extant versions of his Daybooks, which provide insights into his own life and art as well as the intellectual and artistic life of a generation. Whether living in Los Angeles, San Francisco, or Carmel, Weston moved in a wide circle of artists, photographers, architects, dancers, composers, writers, designers, collectors, and other creative people who lived in or were simply visiting California. The archive's extensive correspondence files contain materials relating to Arnold Schoenberg, Richard Neutra, Ansel Adams, Robinson Jeffers, Merle Armitage, Walter Arensberg, Jean Charlot, Tina Modotti, Beaumont and Nancy Newhall, Alfred Stieglitz, Beatrice Wood, and Charles Sheeler, to name only a few.

At the core of the Center's great collection of prints by Edward Weston are more than 1,500 prints acquired with the Edward Weston Archive. These prints, which span his entire life in photography beginning with some landscapes made in 1902 and 1903, are enhanced by many additional prints previously owned by Weston's close friends, including Ansel Adams, Sonya Noskowiak, and Johan Hagemeyer. The Center's Weston holdings are distinguished by a number of unique or very rare works, including early platinum prints and the first print of his work *Pepper Number 30*, inscribed to Sonya Noskowiak, the fellow photographer who was his lover and model at the time and who had brought him the green pepper from the market. The Weston archive also includes Weston's own nearly complete master set of his "project prints."

248

Garry Winogrand

by James Enyeart

Garry Winogrand (1928–1984) first encountered photography in the late 1940s while serving in the Air Force. Then in quick succession, between 1947 and 1951, he explored painting at the City College of the City of New York, painting and photography at Columbia University in New York, and photography with Alexey Brodovitch at the New School for Social Research. Between 1952 and 1969, he made a living as a photojournalist and in advertising. But the moment he discovered the works of Robert Frank and Walker Evans in about 1960, he realized his own passion and potential. He was influenced by the visual intelligence of both photographers, but borrowed little from either. What they took for granted in their own imagery—a distance that, ironically, invoked intimacy and the ability to see lenticularly as if with a glass eye—became in Winogrand's photography both method and vision simultaneously. Frank and Evans conditioned their image making with stylistic refinements, which created visual channels directly accessing subject context in the language of formalism. Winogrand "deconstructed" formalism by accepting the compaction of facts and fiction in the physical world as a way of selecting more, rather than less, to be structured by a photographic rationalization of reality. In a variety of ways he explained to both his critics and his admirers that what he sought from photography was its intelligence more than his own.

In the mid-seventies I commissioned Winogrand, along with a number of other photographers, to work with me on a project. I called him mid-project to discuss the essay I was writing to accompany his photographs. I said that I wanted to describe his work in terms of new documentary work. He shouted back on the telephone, "Documentary? Documentary? Show me a photograph that is not documentary! Let's not overstate the obvious!"

Several events coalesced, over time, to free Winogrand from his lackluster contributions in photojournalism and advertising to become one of the most innovative and tough photographers in the arts of the twentieth century. The first was being named a Guggenheim fellow in 1964, which let him devote himself exclusively to his photography. The second was his inclusion in the exhibition and publication *Toward a Social Landscape* at the George Eastman House in 1966. That international exposure was followed in 1967 by a Museum of Modern Art, New York, exhibition that changed the face of American photography: *New Documents*, which included Diane Arbus, Lee Friedlander, and Garry Winogrand. This was also the moment that John Szarkowski's writing became a disseminating voice for a new era in photography. Finally, Winogrand received two more Guggenheim fellowships in 1969 and 1979.

There has been much speculation about the quality of Winogrand's vision given the knowledge after his death about how many rolls of film he exposed in his lifetime, how many he processed, how many he did not, and whether the enormous numbers of all those rolls of film had bearing on his standing as an artist. Such speculation is entirely

GARRY WINOGRAND: [New York], ca. 1960–61

misdirected if the critical issue is about vision and not method. When Joyce Neimanas was asked by a member of her admiring public how long it took to make a digital image as opposed to a conventional work, she answered, "It takes as long as it takes."

A little over a year before Winogrand died, at the suggestion of Lee Friedlander, he called me on the telephone at the Center for Creative Photography to discuss whether or not the Center would be interested in his life's work then located in his apartment in

New York. We had met on a couple of occasions over prior years, so the discussion was informal and between friends. He said that his lease was up and he could not afford to renew at the price that his landlord was asking for a new lease. He said he wanted the Center to have everything in the apartment from all of his years in New York. He wanted to simply walk away and get on with his life and make photographs.

GARRY WINOGRAND: [Texas], 1964

I suggested that he should consider placing everything on loan, since a gift of what turned out to be 16,000 photographs would not be to his financial advantage. I counseled that someday the tax laws might change to his benefit or that over time I might be able to identify donors to help. He became agitated and said if the Center didn't want everything, then just say so. When I asked what would he do if I said no, he said, "I will just get rid of it." I said yes.

After his archive arrived and I had a chance to survey the prints, I called Winogrand to ask if he had a criterion or a working mark on the prints to identify master or finished prints from work or study prints. He responded, "*You* know the difference." I answered that, yes, I do, but that I would rather fly him out to identify one from the other. He responded, with just a touch of the famous Winogrand wry wit, that it was in my hands now and my problem. I accepted his admonishment as an expression of trust and at the same time could sense in his voice a certain desperation. As it turned out, although he was not fully aware of it at the time, he was fatally ill.

The great number of prints by Garry Winogrand at the Center for Creative Photography, therefore, represent the artist's own assessment and desire to preserve and share a story about the world as he experienced it. It may just be that his prolific style of working was neither pathologic, as some have suggested, nor needful of a rational explanation divisible by some magic set of numbers representing success and failure. He may simply have seen more in more than most.

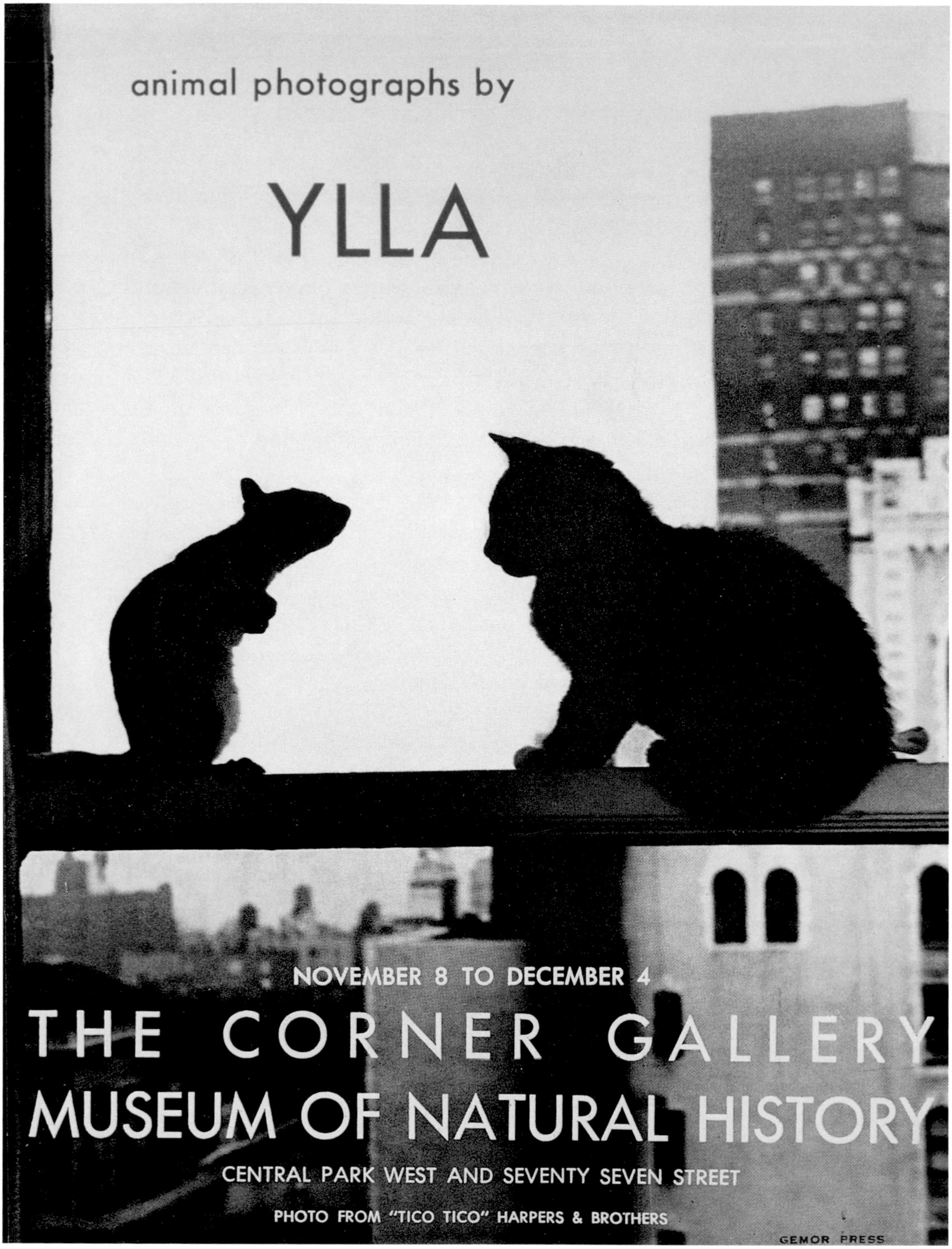

animal photographs by

YLLA

NOVEMBER 8 TO DECEMBER 4

THE CORNER GALLERY
MUSEUM OF NATURAL HISTORY

CENTRAL PARK WEST AND SEVENTY SEVEN STREET

PHOTO FROM "TICO TICO" HARPERS & BROTHERS

GEMOR PRESS

Exhibition announcement, 1950
Ylla Archive

March 28, the Fair at Bharatpur
Incredible atmosphere of festivity, charged with excitement and joy. Upon
arrival, we are taken up to the roof of a building from which we watch this joy-
ous spectacle:
The many dancers, the bullocks decorated in all bright colors, the women
dressed in orange, shy and hiding their faces; the ferris-wheel merry-go-round
turned by a man, and the crowd spotting the Maharaja cannot be controlled,
and cheers and cheers.

Animals in India, with text and photographs by Ylla, appeared posthumously in 1958.

Access to the collections and archives is at the core of the Center's mission. As possibilities for electronic access increase, it becomes easier to present our constituents with information about the collections in the form of searchable cataloging records, finding aids, and descriptions of exhibitions and publications. This book's captions, datablocks, essays, and illustrations are signposts back to the original objects.

The Center's collections are in a constant state of evolution, from the new and disorganized to the fully cataloged and accessible archives.

The most powerful theme that emerges throughout the collections and archives is that of synergy. The relationships among collections multiply as each small addition brings its own interconnections and overlapping relevancies. The complex web of friendships among photographers suggests synergistic flow in many directions.

Focus is often the
unexpected gift of an
unguarded moment
viewing collections.
Focus is the byproduct
of working with original
objects, art works or
manuscripts, and
of making oneself
accessible to the tangi-
ble, physical immediacy
of the encounter.

Gerald S. Ackerman

13 December 1948 – 25 October 1994

Photograph collection: 30 fine prints including 9 platinum and 18 Fresson prints, mostly flower and figure studies

Research materials: The Gerald S. Ackerman Collection (AG 181) contains color transparencies, videotapes, and biographical information. (fraction of a linear foot)

ANSEL ADAMS: *Leaves, Glacier Bay, Alaska*, ca. 1947

Ansel Adams

20 February 1902, San Francisco, California – 23 April 1984, Monterey, California

Photograph collection: more than 2500 fine prints

Research materials: The Ansel Adams Archive (AG 31) holds papers, photographic materials, and memorabilia, 1920s to the present, of Adams, photographer, author, teacher and conservationist. Includes correspondence between Adams and his family, friends, business associates, and other artists; activity files documenting his commercial projects, exhibitions, his associations with the Sierra Club, Friends of Photography, and the Images and Words Workshop; writings, speeches, and interviews; publications with Morgan and Morgan, 5 Associates, and the New York Graphic Society. Also included are printed materials including reproductions of his work in periodicals and books; interviews on audio and videotapes; memorabilia including awards, certificates, cartoons, equipment, and selected items of clothing. Adams's photographic materials include extensive files of negatives, transparencies, work prints, mural prints, and associated technical information. Posthumous materials have been acquired from the Ansel Adams Publishing Rights Trust. (ca. 450 linear feet)

Highlights: Portfolio, *Parmelian Prints of the High Sierras* (1927). Original negatives with associated exposure records; letters from a wide variety of contemporary photographers including Edward Weston, Beaumont and Nancy Newhall, Aaron Siskind, Alfred Stieglitz, and many others; transcripts from the interviews conducted 1972–75 by the Regional Oral History Office at the Bancroft Library, University of California, Berkeley.

The Ansel Adams Miscellaneous Acquisitions Collection (AG 66) holds memorabilia, papers, audiotapes, and photographic materials, 1947 to the present, from a variety of sources. It includes correspondence between Adams and the Polaroid Corporation; a bound compilation of notices, tributes, and editorials relating to his death; and audiotapes and transcripts of a 1979 interview with Adams. (3 linear feet)

The Collection of Ansel and Virginia Adams holds over 2200 photographs gathered by the couple over many years. The photographs, covering 150 years of photographic history, include the work of many photographers with whom Ansel Adams was associated over the years, as well as the work of his students, and historical photographs collected at Best's Studio in Yosemite and in later years.

Highlights: 4 whole-plate daguerreotypes by the Boston photographers Albert Sands Southworth and Josiah Johnson Hawes; images of Yosemite by George Fiske; an album containing photographs by Timothy O'Sullivan and William Bell for the George M. Wheeler survey west of the 100th meridian (1871–1873); works by such photographers as Imogen Cunningham, Arnold Genthe, Lisette Model, Barbara Morgan, Nancy Newhall, Charles Sheeler, Brett Weston, Edward Weston, and Minor White. The Virginia Adams Stereoview Collection, consisting primarily of views of Yosemite, contains 659 photographs by artists such as Edward Anthony,

Charles Bierstadt, Thomas Houseworth, the Kilbourn Brothers, Joseph LeConte, Eadweard Muybridge, C. L. Pond, J. J. Reilly, John P. Soule, Carleton E. Watkins, and many others.

Related information: Many other collections contain materials related to Adams. Of special note: Beaumont and Nancy Newhall Collection (AG 48); Images and Words Workshop Collection (AG 121); Edward Weston Archive (AG 38); Wynn Bullock Archive (AG 10); Arnold Gassan Archive (AG 58); Lectures, Writings and Manuscripts Collection (AG 101).

Rights and restrictions: Copyright to Adams's photographs and writings is held by the Ansel Adams Publishing Rights Trust.

CCP publications: "Ansel Adams: An American Place, 1936," supplement to *The Archive* (1982); "Paul Strand and Ansel Adams: Native Land and Natural Scene," *The Archive* 27 (1990).

David Akiba

b. 7 October 1940, Boston

Photograph collection: 19 fine prints, including 18 in *Charlestown Portfolio*, ca. 1973

Nubar Alexanian

b. 1950, Worcester, Massachusetts

Photograph collection: 62 fine prints including two copies of the *Peruvian Portfolio* created with Stephen Gersh, 1975

Fratelli Alinari

active 1852 to 1920

Photograph collection: 17 gelatin silver (many hand-colored) and albumen prints, mostly reproductions of paintings; also included in group albums

Casey Allen

b. 1924

Photograph collection: 5 fine prints and many study prints

Research materials: The Casey Allen Collection (AG 148) includes audio- and videotape recordings, transcriptions, and research files for Allen's interviews with photographers and other members of the photographic community including Henrietta Brackman, Alexey Brodovitch, Charles Gatewood, Philippe Halsman, John Szarkowski, and many others. Allen was the producer and host of several television programs for WNYC in New York and has authored columns in *Lens on Campus, Studio Photography, New York Times, Popular Photography,* and *Modern Photography* from the 1960s to the 1980s. The collection includes portraits of many of his interview subjects. (16 linear feet)

Related information: The CCP library holds copies of 100 videotaped interviews conducted by Allen with photographers and broadcast as the program *In and Out of Focus* by WNYC in the 1970s.

LOLA ALVAREZ BRAVO: *San Isidro Labrador,* n.d.

Lola Alvarez Bravo

3 April 1907, Lagos de Moreno, Jalisco, Mexico – 31 July 1993, Mexico City, Mexico

Photograph collection: 178 fine prints

Research materials: The bulk of the Lola Alvarez Bravo Collection (AG 154) consists of extensive files of black-and-white negatives in a variety of formats from throughout the photographer's career and includes personal as well as commercial work. Over 2000 of these have been contact printed for research use. A preliminary inventory is available. Some biographical materials, personal papers, and ephemera are also included. (ca. 18 linear feet)

Highlights: Fine prints include portraits of important Mexican cultural figures, such as Frida Kahlo, Diego Rivera, and many others, as well as documentation of rural and urban life in Mexico. Information about the artist's book project *Acapulco,* her work for the magazine *Mexican Folkways,* and her experimental photomontages is included. A few negatives by the photographer's husband, Manuel Alvarez Bravo, were received with this collection.

Rights and restrictions: Copyright to Lola Alvarez Bravo's photographs is owned by the University of Arizona Foundation, Center for Creative Photography.

CCP publication: "Lola Alvarez Bravo: In Her Own Light," *The Archive* 31 (1994).

MANUEL ALVAREZ BRAVO: *La visita*, 1945

Manuel Alvarez Bravo

b. 4 February 1902, Mexico City, Mexico

Photograph collection: 79 fine prints including vintage prints and portfolios from 1974, 1977, and ca. 1979

Research materials: Transcripts of many hours of interviews audiotaped from July to August 1979 are found in the Vivienne Silver Collection (AG 106).

Related information: Correspondence with Manuel Alvarez Bravo is found in the Paul Strand Collection (AG 17), the Robert Heinecken Archive (AG 45), and the Helen Gee/Limelight Gallery Collection (AG 74).

James Anderson

1813 – 1877

Photograph collection: 13 gelatin silver prints of Italian paintings

PAUL L. ANDERSON:
M.G.A. with Camera Work, 1909

Paul L. Anderson

8 October 1880, Trenton, New Jersey –
16 September 1956, Short Hills, New Jersey

Photograph collection: 434 fine prints

Research materials: The Paul L. Anderson Collection (AG 40) contains books and periodicals from Anderson's personal library, many of which contain his annotations on the techniques and practice of photography. (1.5 linear feet)

Highlights: Album of photographs of Ruth Anderson, 1917 to 1924; album of Smith College views, 1935; many chlorobromide, palladium, platinum, gum, and other mixed media prints. Manuscript with instructions for ozobrome sensitizer.

The Collection of Paul L. Anderson includes fourteen issues of *Camera Work* and 56 pictorialist images by Wallace Edwin Dancy, Karl Struss, and others.

CCP publications: "Paul Anderson," *The Archive* 18 (May 1983) and "Paul Anderson," *Guide Series* 7 (1983).

Thomas J. Annan

1829 – 1887

Photograph collection: 28 albumen prints (lacking the 29th) in album *Photographic Views of Loch Katrine*, 1877

E. & H. T. Anthony & Company, New York

Edward Anthony

1818 – 1888

Henry T. Anthony

1814 – 1884

Photograph collection: 72 stereoviews from the Virginia Adams Stereoview Collection

Diane Arbus

14 March 1923, New York –
26 July 1971, New York

Photograph collection: Portfolio, *A Box of Ten Photographs*, 1970, and one image posthumously printed by Neil Selkirk

Research materials: A personal note and a few contact prints are included in the Robert Heinecken Archive (AG 45). Some documentation of the Museum of Modern Art exhibition *New Documents* is contained in the Garry Winogrand Archive (AG 72).

DICK ARENTZ: *Chairs II, Vichy, France*, 1994

Dick Arentz

b. 19 May 1935, Detroit, Michigan

Photograph collection: 49 fine prints, mostly platinum/palladium

Highlight: Portfolio, *The American Southwest,* 1987.

Eugène Atget

12 February 1856, Libourne, France –
4 August 1927, Paris, France

Photograph collection: 28 fine prints

Highlights: Portfolios, *20 Photographs by Eugène Atget,* 1956 (prints by Berenice Abbott); *Le Parc de Saint-Cloud,* 1982.

Eve Arnold

b. 1913, Philadelphia, Pennsylvania

Photograph collection: 12 dye transfer prints in portfolio, *In China,* 1981, and one gelatin silver print in group portfolio, *Ten Photographers,* 1978

RICHARD AVEDON:
*Elise Daniels, Turban by Paulette, Pré-Catelan, Paris,
August 1948*

Richard Avedon

b. 15 May 1923, New York

Photograph collection: 438 fine prints

Research materials: The Richard Avedon Archive (AG 89) includes correspondence, clippings, contact sheets, artifacts, and publications. Artifacts include a shearling coat once slept in by Marilyn Monroe and later used in an *Egoiste* project, and a collection of clippings, ephemera, and drawings once displayed on Avedon's wall. (6 linear feet)

The **Richard Avedon Miscellaneous Acquisitions Collection** (AG 98) contains a variety of materials from different sources. Included are an audiotaped interview and other documentation of the exhibition of *In the American West* at the Amon Carter Museum in 1985. (1.5 linear feet)

Highlights: 13 different series of edition prints, 1946 to 2000, constitute the bulk of the collection. 6 portfolios: *Minneapolis, Alice in Wonderland, Rolling Stone: The Family, Avedon/Paris, Jacob Israel Avedon,* and *The Beatles Portfolio.*

Kurt Baasch

1891, Puerto Cabello, Venezuela –
1964, Baldwin, New York

Photograph collection: 12 fine prints

Research materials: The Kurt Baasch Collection (AG 137) holds the personal papers and photographic materials of Baasch, photographer and horticulturalist. Includes letters from Baasch's friends and associates, Paul Strand and Alfred Stieglitz, as well as clippings and modern contact prints. (2 linear feet)

Robert Balcomb

b. 11 March 1926, Albuquerque, New Mexico

Photograph collection: 19 fine prints

Research materials: The Robert Balcomb Collection (AG 180) contains letters and manuscripts documenting Balcomb's career as a photographer and student of William Mortensen. (1 linear foot)

Highlights: Rolleicord camera that once belonged to William Mortensen; examples of Metalchrome and pigment processes that Balcomb learned from Mortensen.

Lewis Baltz

b. 12 September 1945, Newport Beach, California

Photograph collection: 20 fine prints, including 15 in portfolio, *Nevada,* 1978

Bruce Barnbaum

b. 27 October 1943, Chicago, Illinois

Photograph collection: 24 fine prints, including 10 in portfolio, *Aftermath,* 1979

Susan Barron

b. 1947, Lake Forest, Illinois

Photograph collection: 15 fine prints

Highlights: Portraits of Paul and Hazel Strand and their garden at Orgeval, France, 1975.

Thomas Barrow

b. 24 September 1938, Kansas City, Missouri

Photograph collection: 48 fine prints

Highlights: 2 artist's books, *Trivia* and *Trivia 2*, 1973.

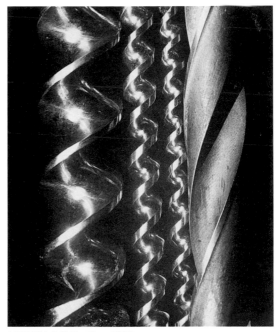

HEINZ LOEW: *Bits*, 1928

Bauhaus Collection

Photograph collection: 31 vintage fine prints

Highlight: Photographs by a variety of Bauhaus artists including Lotte Beese, Erich Consemüller, T. Lux Feininger, Heinz Loew, Lucia Moholy-Nagy, Walter Peterhans, and Umbo, 1924 to 1931.

CCP publications: "Photography and the Bauhaus," *The Archive* 21 (March 1985).

HERBERT BAYER: *View from Pont Transbordeur*, 1928

Herbert Bayer

5 April 1900, Haag, Austria –
30 September 1985, Santa Barbara, California

Photograph collection: 69 gelatin silver prints from the exhibition *Herbert Bayer: Photographic Works*, organized by Leland Rice for the Arco Center for Visual Arts, printed in 1976 by Michaela Allan Murphy, George Eastman House.

Research materials: The Herbert Bayer Collection (AG 25) contains correspondence, writings, publications, memorabilia, negatives, contact sheets, and exhibition installation views. (1.5 linear feet)

William Bell

4 September 1830, Liverpool, England –
28 January 1910, Philadelphia

Photograph collection: 7 albumen prints from *Geographical and Geological Explorations and Surveys West of the 100th Meridian*, *Seasons of 1871, 1872, and 1873* (in the Adams Collection) and 5 individual prints from the Wheeler Survey, 1872.

Research materials: The Terence Pitts/William Bell Collection (AG 166) contains papers related to Pitts's master's thesis "William Bell: Photographs of Utah and Arizona Taken on the 1872 Wheeler Survey," 1982. Includes correspondence, research notes, publications, and copy prints. (0.5 linear foot)

Highlight: Microfilm copy of Timothy O'Sullivan's Wheeler Survey publication.

Rudy Bender

22 February 1937, Miami, Florida – 1991

Will Nordby

b. 1940

Research materials: The Bender/Nordby Collection (AG 151) contains materials related to the collaborations of Rudy Bender (photographer, teacher, writer) and Will Nordby (video and sound editor), who, through their business SynAesthetics, produced widescreen, stereoscopic, multi-media performances in the 1970s such as the quadraphonic *Alternity*. Bender was also the inventor of Quadra Vision and a columnist in *Darkroom Photography* magazine. Their lengthy Wynn Bullock interview was recorded on audiotapes and motion picture film in the last year of Bullock's life. (15 linear feet)

Related information: The Jim Pomeroy Archive (AG 155) documents another multimedia artist.

J. Benor-Kalter

Photograph collection: 12 photogravures in portfolio, *Jerusalem—Twelve Views of the Old City*, 1924, published by The Pro-Jerusalem Society, Jerusalem.

Ferenc Berko

28 January 1916, Nagyvarad, Hungary –
18 March 2000, Aspen, Colorado

Photograph collection: 8 fine prints, 4 of them portraits of photographers

Research materials: The Ferenc Berko Collection (AG 115) contains proof prints, publications, and the 12 postcard set *Early Images, Portfolio I.*

LOUIS CARLOS BERNAL: *Cómoda*, 1977
From the series *Benitez Suite*

Louis Carlos Bernal

18 August 1941, Douglas, Arizona –
18 August 1993, Tucson, Arizona

Photograph collection: 98 fine prints, both black-and-white and color

Research materials: The Espejo Collection (AG 81) contains papers documenting the Espejo project and exhibition, 1977–79, including project records, correspondence, clippings, writings, and publications. (1.25 linear feet)

Highlights: 30 prints in the Espejo project and 7 prints from the Benitez Suite.

Related information: Other contributions to the Espejo project—by Morrie Camhi, Abigail Heyman, Roger Minick and Neal Slavin—are also represented in the CCP collections.

Ruth Bernhard

b. 14 October 1905, Berlin, Germany

Photograph collection: 25 fine prints

Research materials: The Ruth Bernhard Collection (AG 152) contains publications and clippings related to her career. (fraction of a linear foot)

Related information: Letters from Bernhard are contained in the Edward Weston Archive (AG 38).

Dawoud Bey

b. 25 November 1953, New York

Photograph collection: 14 fine prints created for *Indivisible: Stories of American Community*, 2000

Charles Bierstadt

1819, Dusseldorf, Germany – 5 June 1903, Niagara Falls, New York

Photograph collection: 36 stereoviews from the Virginia Adams Stereoview Collection

Big Bend Photo Club

Photograph collection: 7 fine prints by Ben Davis, Victor Schrager, and Melanie Walker

Research materials: The Big Bend Photo Club Collection (AG 16) contains information about this loosely organized group of photographers, primarily students of Todd Walker and Robert Fichter, who were active around Tallahassee, Florida, from 1973 to 1974. They published the *Big Bend Photo News*, a magazine composed of photocopy, offset lithographs, and other media.

Highlight: Audiotape of 1976 lecture by Clarence John Laughlin.

Ilse Bing

23 March 1899, Frankfurt am Main, Germany – 10 March 1998, New York

Photograph collection: 11 fine prints from the 1930s

Philippe Blache

b. September 1948

Photograph collection: 13 fine prints, including 5 from an untitled portfolio of 1975

LUCIENNE BLOCH:
Father [Ernest Bloch] *with Mushrooms, Roveredo.*
Switzerland, 1928

Ernest Bloch

24 July 1880, Geneva, Switzerland – 15 July
1959, Portland, Oregon

Photograph collection: 101 fine prints

Research materials: The Ernest Bloch Archive
(AG 11) includes biographical information;
copies of letters from Alfred Stieglitz, Paul
Strand, and various composers; memorabilia;
photographic equipment such as Bloch's
Polyscop stereo camera; albums of contact
prints; and negatives, 1897 to ca. 1980. Bloch
was the founding director of the Cleveland
Institute of Music, director of the San Francisco
Conservatory of Music, and a professor at the
University of California, Berkeley. The bulk of
this collection consists of small format negatives including stereoviews and transparencies
made between 1897 and 1951. Most of the
negatives have been contact printed for
research use. (12 linear feet)

Highlight: Plaster death mask of Bloch's face.

CCP publication: "Ernest Bloch Archive,"
Guide Series 1 (1979).

KARL BLOSSFELDT: *Blumenbachia hieronymi.*
Geschlossene Samenkapsel, 18mal vergrössert,
1900–28
From the portfolio *Karl Blossfeldt–12 Photographien,*
1975

Karl Blossfeldt

13 June 1865, Schielo, Germany –
9 December 1932, Berlin, Germany

Photograph collection: Portfolio, *Karl Blossfeldt
—12 Photographien,* 1975, with prints from
negatives made between 1900 and 1928.

A. Aubrey Bodine

21 July 1906, Baltimore, Maryland –
28 October 1970, Baltimore, Maryland

Photograph collection: 13 fine prints and many uncataloged work prints

Research materials: The A. Aubrey Bodine Miscellaneous Acquisitions Collection (AG 156) contains materials from various sources related to the career of noted Baltimore pictorialist Bodine. Included are clippings, Bodine's Christmas cards, and exhibition reviews. Of note are the Frank Christopher letters, and publications assembled by Harold A. Williams, author of *Bodine: A Legend in His Time.* (1 linear foot)

Blythe Bohnen

b. 26 July 1940, Evanston, Illinois

Photograph collection: 11 fine prints, self-portraits

Howard Bond

b. 23 July 1931, Napoleon, Ohio

Photograph collection: 33 fine prints, including works from *Portfolio II: Austria*, 1978, *Portfolio III: Victor*, 1980, and *Portfolio IV: Huron River*, 1982

FÉLIX BONFILS: *Les pyramides prises de Gizeh*, n.d.

Félix Bonfils

8 March 1831, St. Hippolyte du Fort, France –
9 April 1885, Alais, France

Photograph collection: 103 albumen prints from the Julia F. Corson Collection

Edouard Boubat

13 September 1923, Paris, France –
30 June 1999, Paris, France

Photograph collection: 23 fine prints, including 15 from portfolio, *Edouard Boubat*, 1981

Alice Boughton

1865, Brooklyn, New York – 22 June 1943, Brookhaven, New York

Photograph collection: 14 platinum, gum platinum, and gelatin silver prints

Harry Bowers

b. 1938, Los Angeles, California

Photograph collection: Portfolio, *Harry Bowers, Ten Photographs*, 1984

Mathew Brady and Company

Photograph collection: 52 modern gelatin silver prints

Highlight: Most of these photographs were printed by Ansel Adams from negatives in the Library of Congress and came to the CCP in the Collection of Ansel and Virginia Adams.

Brassaï (Gyula Halász)

9 September 1899, Brasov, Romania –
8 July 1984, Beaulieu-sur-Mer, France

Photograph collection: 19 fine prints, including *A Portfolio of Ten Photographs by Brassaï*, 1973

Research materials: Letters to Louise Dahl-Wolfe are contained in the Dahl-Wolfe Archive (AG 76).

JOSEF BREITENBACH:
Josef Albers, Black Mountain College, North Carolina, 1944

Josef Breitenbach

3 April 1896, Munich, Germany –
7 October 1984, New York

Photograph collection: More than 2000 fine prints

Research materials: The Josef Breitenbach Archive (AG 90) contains a wide variety of personal papers and photographic materials, 1873–1990, documenting the artist's life and career. It includes letters from family and associates such as Bertolt Brecht, Grace Mayer, and Lucien Goldschmidt. Writings include drafts for published and unpublished articles and files on his book *Women of Asia* (1968). Biographical materials include passports, press passes, and appointment calendars. Exhibition files document his own exhibitions as well as exhibitions he photographed such as the 1938 *Frei Deutsche Kunst* and *5 ans de régime hitlérien*. Education files document Breitenbach's teaching activities at both Cooper Union and the New School for Social Research. His projects to photograph aromas and to document life at Black Mountain College are represented. The archive also includes audiotapes of Breitenbach's lectures, tearsheets, clippings, financial records, negatives in many formats, contact sheets, transparencies, memorabilia, and publications in German, French and English. (74.5 linear feet)

Highlights: Breitenbach's personal collection of photographs is held at the Fotomuseum des Münchner Stadtmuseums, Munich, Germany, but a few items from this collection came to the CCP, including works by Hill and Adamson, Drahomir Ruzicka, and others.

The Breitenbach Miscellaneous Acquisitions Collection (AG 167) holds materials from a variety of sources. It includes correspondence, research materials, exhibition announcements, clippings, publications, and photographic materials. (fraction of a linear foot)

Related information: The CCP holds materials on other émigré photographers who left Germany in the years surrounding the Second World War: Hans Namuth, who studied with Breitenbach in Paris and New York; Andreas Feininger; John Gutmann; Otto Hagel; Hansel Mieth; and Marion Palfi are also represented.

Anne W. Brigman

3 December 1869, Nuuanu Valley, Oahu, Hawaii – 18 February 1950, El Monte, California

Photograph collection: 17 fine prints, including platinum prints and plates from *Camera Work*

Highlight: *The Bubble,* 1905, undated Fresson print by Paul L. Anderson, copied from the *Camera Work* photogravure by Brigman.

DEAN BROWN: Untitled, 1969
From the series *Berlin*, 1969

Dean Brown

10 July 1936, Newport News, Virginia –
8 July 1973, Portland, Maine

Photograph collection: Approximately 2000
black and-white and color prints

Research materials: The Dean Brown Archive
(AG 18) holds papers and photographic materials documenting the photographer's career.
The bulk of the collection consists of contact
sheets, negatives, extensive files of transparencies, dye transfer materials, and work prints.
Also included are diaries and notebooks, letters
to his wife, the artist Carol Brown, exhibition
files, business records, lab notes about the dye
transfer process, assignment files and commercial work done for Time-Life Books, and information about Brown's book *Photographs of the
American Wilderness*, 1976. (64 linear feet)

Highlights: Martin Luther King series, Kodalith
transparencies, tricolor carbon prints (printed
posthumously by Luis Nadeau).

CCP publications: "Dean Brown," *The Archive*
15 (January 1982); "Dean Brown Archive,"
Guide Series 12 (1985).

Laurie Brown

b. 28 December 1937, Austin, Texas

Photograph collection: 74 fine prints including
many in panorama format

Highlight: Portfolio, *Earth Edges*, 1984.

Related information: Water in the West Archive
(AG 172)

Anton Bruehl

11 March 1900, Hawker, South Australia –
10 August 1982, San Francisco, California

Photograph collection: 34 fine prints, including
platinum, gelatin silver, and various color
processes, 1924–37

EXHIBITION

PHOTOGRAPHS & PAINTINGS
BY
FRANCIS BRUGUIERE
THE ART CENTER · 65 EAST 56 STREET
ARRANGED BY THE PICTORIAL PHOTOGRAPHERS OF AMERICA
FROM MARCH 28 UNTIL APRIL 11

Cover of 6-page exhibition brochure, The Art
Center, New York, 1929
Francis J. Bruguière Archive

Francis J. Bruguière

16 October 1879, San Francisco, California –
8 May 1945, London, England

Photograph collection: 4 vintage gelatin silver
prints; 1 plate from *Camera Work*; 282 modern
prints made by James Enyeart from Bruguière's
original negatives

Research materials: The Francis J. Bruguière
Archive (AG 52) holds papers and photographic
materials, 1912–1945, from the career of this
photographer, filmmaker, painter, sculptor, and
designer. The collection includes correspondence, exhibition records, scrapbooks, and
writings. The bulk of the collection consists of
4x5 and 5x7-inch negatives including experimental work, portraits, nudes, architecture, and
landscape views. Modern contact prints of the
negatives were made in 1982. (3 linear feet)

Highlights: Letters from Sadakichi Hartmann
and Frank Eugene; an incomplete 73-page
autobiographical manuscript; materials related
to "Light Rhythms;" a tearsheet from *Camera
Work* inscribed by Alfred Stieglitz; and a 1919
manuscript describing a meeting with
Sadakichi Hartmann and John Burroughs.

Dan Budnik

b. 20 May 1933

Photograph collection: 93 Polacolor 2 prints,
mostly from the Big Mountain Navajo/Hopi
project, 1980s

Research materials: The Dan Budnik Collection
(AG 70) contains activity files, publications, and
proof prints. (0.5 linear foot)

Edna Bullock

20 May 1915, Hollister, California –
14 December 1997, Monterey, California

Photograph collection: 12 fine prints

WYNN BULLOCK: *Old Typewriter*, 1951

Wynn Bullock

18 April 1902, Chicago, Illinois –
16 November 1975, Monterey, California

Photograph collection: 222 fine prints, including 150 prints chosen by Bullock as his representative works

Research materials: The Wynn Bullock Archive (AG 10) holds personal papers, correspondence, exhibition files, technical notes, audiovisual materials, negatives, transparencies, and study prints, 1920–1980, offering extensive information on Bullock's career as photographer, teacher, inventor, and concert singer. Included are notes and diaries; letters from Ansel Adams, Morrie Camhi, Imogen Cunningham, Todd Walker, and many other photographers; documentation of Bullock's experiments with solarization; information about the Friends of Photography; photographic equipment; negative files and index; and selected parts of his personal library. (ca. 80 linear feet)

Highlights: Letters written by Bullock to his mother during an early trip to Europe as a concert singer. Films by Thom Tyson, Fred Paula, and one made by Bullock while he was at the Art Center School in Los Angeles, 1939.

The Collection of Wynn Bullock contains 231 fine prints from a variety of photographers including: Clarence John Laughlin, Geoff Winningham, Antonio A. Fernandez, Edward Weston, Ruth Bernhard, Imogen Cunningham, and Brett Weston.

Related information: The Bender/Nordby Collection (AG 151) contains a lengthy interview with Wynn Bullock made in 1975. Correspondence with Bullock is held in numerous collections at the CCP, including the Ansel Adams Archive (AG 31), the Henry Holmes Smith Archive (AG 32), the Beaumont and Nancy Newhall Collection (AG 48), the Harry Callahan Archive (AG 29), and others.

CCP publications: "Wynn Bullock: American Lyric Tenor," *Center for Creative Photography* 2 (September 1976); "Wynn Bullock Archive," *Guide Series* 6 (1983).

TINA MODOTTI:
*Lou Bunin, Puppet Master, producer of "Hairy Ape,"
with Marionettes,* ca. 1929

Louis Bunin

b. 1905? – [?]

Research materials: The Louis Bunin Collection (AG 146) contains documentation of the career of artist and puppeteer Louis Bunin as photographed by Tina Modotti and others from 1928 until about 1940. Included are clippings, ephemera, and work prints with some views of Eugene O'Neill's play *The Hairy Ape* and the Mexican folk tale *El Conejo Astuto.*

Highlights: 21 photographs by Tina Modotti, including *Hands of the Puppeteer*, which shows Bunin holding controls of puppet.

DEBBIE FLEMING CAFFERY: Untitled, October 1985
From the series *Polly*

Debbie Fleming Caffery

b. 6 March 1948, New Iberia, Louisiana

Photograph collection: 55 fine prints, including 21 created for *Indivisible: Stories of American Community,* 2000

Highlight: 30 images from series *Polly,* 1984–90.

Bill Burke

b. 8 April 1943, Derby, Connecticut

Photograph collection: 35 fine prints, including 31 created for *Indivisible: Stories of American Community,* 2000

HARRY CALLAHAN: *Detroit*, 1943

Harry Callahan

22 October 1912, Detroit, Michigan –
15 March 1999, Atlanta, Georgia

Photograph collection: 91 fine prints plus several hundred study prints and early vintage prints

Research materials: The Harry Callahan Archive (AG 29) is one of the five founding collections at CCP. It holds extensive documentation of Callahan's life and career through his personal papers and correspondence, biographical materials, his black-and-white negatives, color transparencies, a large number of work prints, exhibition and publication files, as well as audiovisual materials. Included are letters, 1940s to 1990s, from friends, curators, publishers, photographers, and others such as Edward Steichen, John Szarkowski, and Peter Bunnell. The exhibition files date from 1947 to the 1990s and include installation views, clippings, ephemera, and checklists. The bulk of the collection consists of work prints, negatives, and transparencies. (ca. 80 linear feet)

Highlights: Correspondence with Light Gallery, New York; rare images from Callahan's early street photography in Detroit and Chicago; negatives and contact prints from collage series.

The Harry Callahan Miscellaneous Acquisitions Collection (AG 96) contains a copy of a film made by Jim Dow in 1967.

CCP publication: "Harry Callahan: Early Street Photography, 1943–1945," *The Archive* 28 (1990).

281

Jo Ann Callis

b. 25 November 1940, Cincinnati, Ohio

Photograph collection: 32 fine prints, including *Dye Transfer Portfolio,* 1984

Camera Work (magazine)

Photograph collection: All issues of this magazine are housed with the photograph collection rather than in the CCP Library. The CCP holds issues from 1903 to 1917; numbers 2, 3, 5–17, 19–21, 25, 27, 28, 34–37, 39, 42–44, 46, 47, 49, 50, and special issues including the Steichen supplement, 1906.

Carol Cameron

active 1970s

Photograph collection: 35 prints in 3 artist's books

Morrie Camhi

16 August 1928, New York – 27 August 1999, Petaluma, California

Photograph collection: 95 fine prints

Highlights: 30 prints from the *Espejo* project, 1977–78; 48 prints from *The Prison Experience,* 1989; 13 prints from *Jews of Greece* series, 1980.

LUCY CAPEHART:
Sarah Natani in Her Sheep Corral, Table Mesa near Shiprock, New Mexico, 1999 [original in color]

Lucy Capehart

b. 22 May 1952

Photograph collection: 18 fine prints, including 17 created for *Indivisible: Stories of American Community,* 2000

Paul Caponigro

b. 7 December 1932, Boston

Photograph collection: 110 fine prints

Research materials: 600 catalog cards with mounted copy prints of Caponigro's photographs, 1957 to 1970, made to test various Polaroid film products.

Highlights: Portfolios, *Portfolio One,* 1962; *Portfolio II,* 1973; *Stonehenge,* 1978.

William J. Carpenter

b. 1861 – d. [?]

Photograph collection: 12 collotypes of Navajo subjects, 1914

Manuel Carrillo

17 January 1906, Mexico City –
20 January 1989, Mexico City

Photograph collection: 153 fine prints, including 15 in portfolio, *Manuel Carrillo*, 1981

Henri Cartier-Bresson

b. 22 August 1908, Chanteloup, France

Photograph collection: 12 fine prints

Eduardo Castanho

Photograph collection: Portfolio, *Eduardo Castanho: 23 Photographs in 5 Series*, 1982

Walter Chappell

8 June 1925, Portland, Oregon –
8 August 2000, Santa Fe, New Mexico

Photograph collection: 14 fine prints, including 10 in portfolio, *Metaflora*, 1980

Research materials: The Walter Chappell Collection (AG 118) contains research materials collected by Chappell related to the career of Hawaiian photographer Ray Jerome Baker.

CARL CHIARENZA: *Noumenon 256*, 1984/85

Carl Chiarenza

b. 5 September 1935, Rochester, New York

Photograph collection: 12 fine prints, including 2 triptychs from 1993

Research materials: The Carl Chiarenza Collection (AG 87) contains research materials prepared by Chiarenza for his Ph.D. dissertation *Terrors and Pleasures: The Life and Work of Aaron Siskind* (1973) and his subsequent book. Included are taped interviews, bibliographies, exhibition lists, correspondence, copy negatives, book galleys, clippings, and manuscripts. Also included are files on *Contemporary Photographer* magazine, edited by Chiarenza from 1966 to 1968. (12.75 linear feet)

William Christenberry

b. 5 November 1936, Tuscaloosa, Alabama

Photograph collection: 144 fine prints

Highlights: Portfolio/assemblage, *The Alabama Box*, 1980; portfolio, *KKK*, 1982.

Related information: Additional material related to the Ku Klux Klan is contained in the W. Eugene Smith Archive (AG 33).

CCP publication: *Christenberry: Reconstruction: The Art of William Christenberry* (1996). Texts by Trudy Wilner Stack and Allen Tullos. (Jackson, Mississippi: University Press of Mississippi; Tucson: Center for Creative Photography, 1996).

Mark Citret

b. 21 March 1949, Buffalo, New York

Photograph collection: 15 fine prints, including portfolio, *Halcott Center, Twelve Photographs,* 1976

LARRY CLARK: Untitled [Billy Mann], 1963
From the portfolio *Tulsa*, 1980

Larry Clark

b. 19 January 1943, Tulsa, Oklahoma

Photograph collection: 50 fine prints in portfolio, *Tulsa*, 1980

Clatworthy Colorvues

Research materials: The Clatworthy Colorvues Collection (AG 12) contains documentation of the *Evidence* project carried out by Mike Mandel and Larry Sultan in Santa Cruz, California, between 1975 and 1977. Included are correspondence, activity files, memorabilia, and manuscripts. Mandel's *Baseball Photographers Trading Cards* project is discussed in a letter and essay. (fraction of a linear foot)

Highlight: Robert Forth's original manuscript for "The Circumstantial and the Evident" used as afterword in *Evidence*.

Lucien Clergue

b. 14 August 1934, Arles, France

Photograph collection: 45 fine prints

Highlights: 12 Fresson 4-color prints in portfolio, *Jeux de l'été*, 1980; 10 gelatin silver prints and 10 Fresson monochrome prints in portfolio, *Caco au Grand Herbier*, 1978.

William Clift

b. 5 January 1944, Boston, Massachusetts

Photograph collection: 26 fine prints

Highlights: Portfolios, *New Mexico*, 1975; *County Courthouses*, ca. 1976.

Alvin Langdon Coburn

11 June 1882, Boston – 23 November 1966, North Wales

Photograph collection: 84 fine prints, including 36 gravure prints from *Camera Work*; 2 albums of photogravures, *London*, 1909, and *New York*, 1910; and portfolio of gelatin silver prints, *Alvin Langdon Coburn: Photographs*, 1977

Alan Cohen

b. 28 August 1943, Harrisburg, Pennsylvania

Photograph collection: 14 fine prints, including 10 from the Collection of Aaron Siskind

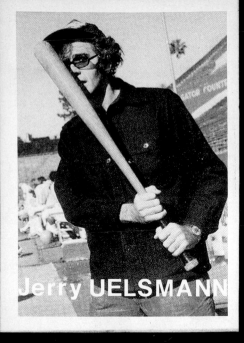

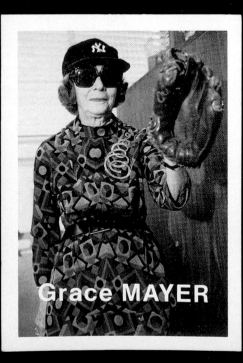

MIKE MANDEL:
Baseball Photographer Trading Cards, 1975 [Jerry Uelsmann, Naomi Savage, Grace Mayer, Edmund Teske], published by Clatworthy Colorvues
Robert Heinecken Archive

CLARENCE H. WHITE
School of Photography
Canaan, Connecticut

———

JULY SEVENTH TO AUGUST SIXTEENTH
TENTH SUMMER SESSION
1919

Brochure, Clarence H. White School of
Photography, Canaan, Connecticut, 1919
Alfred and Margaret Cohn Collection

Alfred Cohn

5 September 1897, Brooklyn, New York –
15 November 1972, Tucson, Arizona

Margaret Hummel Cohn

b. 27 February 1909, St. Paul, Minnesota

Photograph collection: 25 fine prints by Alfred
Cohn and 2 by Margaret Cohn, including some
platinum or palladium prints

Research collections: The Alfred and Margaret
Cohn Collection (AG 51) contains the papers
and photographic materials of Margaret
Hummel Cohn, a student of the Clarence H.

White School of Photography from 1937 to
1940, and her husband, Alfred Cohn, who
graduated from the White School in 1918
and taught there from 1939 until ca. 1943.
Margaret was an assistant to fashion photographer Louise Dahl-Wolfe beginning in 1945. In
1948 Alfred operated the Arizona School of
Photography in Tucson. The collection consists
of printed materials from the Clarence H.
White School of Photography; class notes,
assignments, equipment lists, negatives and
proof prints; tearsheets, contact prints, transparencies, and photographs from Margaret
Cohn's work with Dahl-Wolfe. (1 linear foot)

Highlight: Class assignments from the Clarence
H. White School of Photography.

Related information: Louise Dahl-Wolfe Archive
(AG 76). There are several other collections
related to the Clarence H. White School of
Photography at the CCP, including the Paul L.
Anderson Collection (AG 40) and the Ralph
Steiner Collection (AG 68). Anderson also
served as faculty at the School, and Steiner
was a student there ca. 1921 to 1922.

Van Deren Coke

b. 1 July 1921, Lexington, Kentucky

Photograph collection: 14 fine prints

Research materials: The Van Deren Coke Collection (AG 140) contains gallery announcements, clippings, publications, ephemera, and a few copies of letters from Minor White and Ansel Adams.

Allan D. Coleman

b. 19 December 1943, New York

Research materials: The A. D. Coleman Collection (AG 20) holds publications, correspondence, notes and manuscript materials, dating from 1968 to the present for this writer, photographer, and critic. Coleman was the CCP Distinguished Scholar-in-Residence in 1997. Also included are records of the Photography Media Institute, 1979 to 1988. (45 linear feet)

Highlights: Complete set of all Coleman's published writings organized by title of magazine and date. Extensive collection of ephemera documenting activities in the contemporary photography world has been interfiled with the CCP Library's information files.

CCP publications: *A.D. Coleman: A Bibliography of His Writings on Photography from 1968 to 1995* (2000); an essay by Coleman was included in "William Mortensen: A Revival," *The Archive* 33 (1998).

Eduardo Comesaña

b. 14 March 1940, Buenos Aires, Argentina

Photograph collection: 12 offset lithographs in portfolio, *Fotos poco conocidas de gente muy conocida*, 1972

Howard Conant

b. 1921

Research materials: The Howard Conant Collection (AG 113) consists of 6 letters to Conant regarding his work for the *Encyclopedia of Art*. Correspondents include Berenice Abbott, Margaret Bourke-White, Barbara Morgan, and others.

Gregory Conniff

b. 3 May 1944, Jersey City, New Jersey

Photograph collection: 17 fine prints

Related information: Water in the West Archive (AG 172)

LINDA CONNOR:
Seven Sacred Pools, Maui, Hawaii, 1978

Linda Connor

b. 18 November 1944, New York

Photograph collection: 85 fine prints, mostly on printing-out paper

Highlight: Portfolio, *Nepal*, 1986, created jointly with Mark Klett.

Maurice Constant

active 1930s to 1950s

Photograph collection: 72 fine prints, portraits of United States politicians and military figures

Thomas Joshua Cooper

b. 19 December 1946, San Francisco, California

Photograph collection: 33 fine prints

John Coplans

b. 24 June 1920, London, England

Photograph collection: 31 fine prints

Highlight: 24 prints from the series *A Body of Work*, 1984–87

Jim Cornfield

b. 6 November 1945, Chicago, Illinois

Photograph collection: Portfolio of 12 prints, *Fat Tuesday*, 1976

ABDULLAH FRÈRES: *Cuisinier ambulant,* ca. 1870s
Julia F. Corson Collection

Julia F. Corson Collection

Photograph collection: The Julia F. Corson Collection of travel photography has its origins in the nineteenth-century practice of commemorating travel by purchasing photographs from local businesses. Julia Corson lived in the vicinity of Camden, Maine, and her comfortable financial situation allowed her to travel extensively. She was apparently not a photographer herself, but rather gathered the images from commercial photographers and dealers in the various places visited in the course of her trips. Locations represented by the collection include Spain, Italy, Greece, Mexico, Turkey, Syria, Lebanon, Palestine, Egypt, India, China, and the South Pacific. Although there are some photographs that can't be attributed to known photographers, the impressive list of photographers who are identified indicates that Corson bought the best. There are over 300 photographs in the Corson Collection, including images by the following photographers and publishers: Abdullah Frères (9); Photographie Bonfils (103); Edizione Brogi (6); Edizione Esposito (17); Gulmez Frères (2); Suleiman Hakim (15); Giuseppe Incorpora (4); Josiah Martin (19); A. C. Santos (15); Alfred John Tattersall (20); and Zangaki Frères (21).

Related information: Several albums by British photographer Francis Frith of scenes from *Lower Egypt, Thebes and the Pyramids* (ca. 1860s) represent earlier examples of the same impulse to document travels in Egypt and the Middle East. A later version of travel photography may be seen in journals fashion photographer Louise Dahl-Wolfe kept from her travels in Europe and North Africa in the 1920s.

Kate Cory

8 February 1861, Waukegan, Illinois –
12 June 1958, Prescott, Arizona

Photograph collection: 62 gelatin silver prints, all dated 1905–12, printed in 1973 by Marc Gaede, used as plates for the 1986 book *The Hopi Photographs: Kate Cory, 1905–1912*

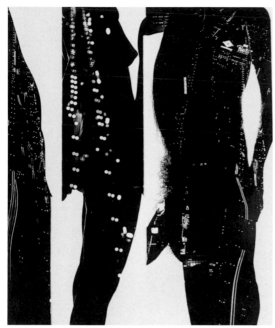

BARBARA CRANE: *City Lights, Chicago*, 1969

Barbara Crane

b. 19 March 1928, Chicago, Illinois

Photograph collection: 69 fine prints and unprocessed archive prints

Research materials: The Barbara Crane Archive (AG 176) contains negatives, contact prints, study prints, correspondence, book maquettes, lecture and teaching files, and memorabilia. (25 linear feet)

The Collection of Barbara Crane includes over 100 fine prints and group portfolios from the Institute of Design and the School of the Art Institute of Chicago.

Highlights: Portfolios, *Happy Birthday to Ansel Adams*, 1977; *Tucson Portfolio I*, 1979; *Tucson Portfolio II*, 1980; and 8 platinum/palladium prints from the *Objet trouvé* series, 1982–83.

CCP publication: *Barbara Crane: Photographs 1948–1980* (1981)

George M. Craven

1929, Philadelphia – July 1990, Cupertino, California

Photograph collection: 11 fine prints and many study prints

Research materials: The George M. Craven Archive (AG 132) contains personal papers and photographic materials of Craven, a photographer, teacher, and photohistorian. It includes letters, bibliography files on 3x5-inch cards, manuscripts for his book *Object and Image: An Introduction to Photography* (1975), teaching files, publications, negatives, transparencies, and work prints. (21 linear feet)

Highlights: Extensive research files compiled on Group *f*/64, including a postcard questionnaire sent out to all members of the Group still living in 1958. Letters from Imogen Cunningham, Clarence White, Jr., and others.

Creative Eye Gallery

Research materials: The Creative Eye Gallery Collection (AG 39) contains records of the gallery founded by Patricia and John Douglas Mercer in Sonoma, California. Includes exhibition files for more than 50 photographers, clippings, and correspondence, 1973 to 1977.

IMOGEN CUNNINGHAM:
Untitled [montage of Franklin Roosevelt, Herbert
  Hoover, and storm at the White House], ca. 1935

Imogen Cunningham

12 April 1883, Portland, Oregon –
28 June 1976, San Francisco, California

Photograph collection: 110 fine prints, including posthumous prints by the Imogen Cunningham Trust, ca. 1975

Research materials: Letters from Cunningham are found in the Ansel Adams Archive (AG 31), the Edward Weston Archive (AG 38), and other collections. The Judy Dater/Imogen Cunningham Collection (AG 41) contains transcripts of 38 interviews conducted by Dater in 1977.

Edward S. Curtis

1868, near White Water, Wisconsin –
21 October 1954, Los Angeles, California

Photograph collection: 303 fine prints, including 210 small gravure prints, primarily from volumes XII, XVII, XVIII, and XIX of *The North American Indian*

Research materials: 122 original copper gravure plates with annotated paper sleeves.

Highlights: 25 small cyanotypes of Cheyenne subjects made in the field; gravure plates used in printing the images in *The North American Indian* volumes I, II, XII, XVII and their accompanying portfolios.

Related information: Two complete sets of *The North American Indian* are found on the campus of the University of Arizona in the Arizona State Museum and in Special Collections, University of Arizona Library, within easy access to CCP researchers.

The CCP holds other photographs of Native Americans by Kate Cory, Timothy O'Sullivan, Jack Hillers, Ben Wittick, Ansel Adams, Laura Gilpin, Marion Palfi, Dan Budnik, and others.

LOUISE DAHL-WOLFE: *Dior Ball Gown, Paris*, 1950

Louise Dahl-Wolfe

19 November 1895, Alameda, California –
11 December 1989, Allendale, New Jersey

Photograph collection: 443 fine prints, including 83 printed in 1983–84 by Christopher Green

Research materials: The Louise Dahl-Wolfe Archive (AG 76) contains personal papers, photographic materials, and memorabilia documenting the career of fashion photographer Louise Dahl-Wolfe. Consists primarily of black-and-white negatives, contact prints, and tearsheets for Dahl-Wolfe's work at *Harper's Bazaar, Vogue, Sports Illustrated,* and for customers such as Saks Fifth Avenue and Bonwit Teller. Also includes portraits of her from childhood to old age and some biographical materials related to her family in San Francisco and Denmark, her marriage to painter Mike Wolfe, and her education at the San Francisco Art Institute. Letters from photographers such as Brassaï and Cecil Beaton, and from personalities in the fashion world such as Diana Vreeland and Carmel Snow, are included. (45 linear feet)

Highlights: Complete set of *Harper's Bazaar* magazine, 1938 to 1958. Visual index to Dahl-Wolfe's work for *Harper's*. More than 20 prints of Nashville sculptor William Edmondson, ca. 1933. Small travel journals created by Dahl-Wolfe when she traveled to Europe and Northern Africa with her friend Consuelo Kanaga, in the late 1920s.

Related information: Transparencies, prints, and tearsheets of Dahl-Wolfe's color work are at the Fashion Institute of Technology, New York.

Rights and permissions: Copyright to Louise Dahl-Wolfe's photography is held by the Center for Creative Photography, Arizona Board of Regents.

Judy Dater

b. 21 June 1941, Los Angeles, California

Photograph collection: 92 fine prints

Research materials: The Judy Dater/Imogen Cunningham Collection (AG 41) contains transcripts of 38 interviews conducted by Dater in 1977. The interviews were used in preparation for Dater's book *Imogen Cunningham: A Portrait,* 1979. Included are: Ansel Adams, Morley Baer, Laura Gilpin, Beaumont Newhall, Arnold Newman, Edmund Teske, and others. (1 linear foot)

Highlights: Portfolios, *Judy Dater – Ten Photographs*, 1974, *Men/Women: Portfolio II*, 1981, and *Hold Me!,* n.d.

Robert Davey

Photograph collection: 13 fine prints

Faurest Davis

24 July 1906, St. Louis, Missouri – 23 August 1991, Tucson, Arizona

Photograph collection: 20 fine prints

Research materials: The Faurest Davis Collection (AG 111) contains letters, papers, negatives, and photographs documenting Davis's career as a photographer in San Francisco and his friendships with Ansel Adams and Edward Weston. His work at the Carnegie Desert Laboratory near Tucson is also included.

LYNN DAVIS: *Dogon Village, Mali*, 1997

Joe Deal

b. 12 August 1947, Topeka, Kansas

Photograph collection: 20 fine prints, in portfolio, *The Fault Zone*, 1981

Lynn Davis

b. 1944, Minneapolis, Minnesota

Photograph collection: 43 fine prints, including 12 created for *Indivisible: Stories of American Community*, 2000

Phil Davis

b. 15 October 1921, Spokane, Washington

Photograph collection: 10 prints in *The Dexter Portfolio*, 1972

Robert Dawson

b. 1950, Sacramento, California

Photograph collection: 102 fine prints, part of the Water in the West project

Related information: Water in the West Archive (AG 172).

ROY DECARAVA:
Embroidered Blouse, Washington, D.C., 1975

Roy DeCarava

b. 9 December 1919, New York

Photograph collection: 28 fine prints

Liliane De Cock

b. 11 September 1939, Antwerp, Belgium

Photograph collection: 18 fine prints

Noel Deeks

b. 1904

Research materials: The Noel Deeks Collection (AG 24) consists of papers and photographic materials of Deeks, who worked as a printer for Edward Steichen. Includes pamphlets about the Raylo Camera and Deeks's Color Sheets.

Highlights: 2 color transparencies of *The Swedish Lotus* made by Hiram and Noel Deeks for Steichen; portraits of Steichen and Steichen's studio.

Jack Delano

1 August 1914, Kiev, Russia – 12 August 1997, Puerto Rico

Photograph collection: 10 fine prints from the Farm Security Administration project

Peter De Lory

b. 2 October 1948, Orleans, Massachusetts

Photograph collection: 10 fine prints

Robert Demachy

7 July 1859, Saint Germaine-en-Laye, France – 29 December 1936, Hennequeville, France

Photograph collection: 21 photogravures and offset lithographs, mostly from *Camera Work*

Adolf De Meyer

1868, Dresden, Germany – 6 January 1949, Los Angeles, California

Photograph collection: 39 fine prints

Highlight: 33 palladium prints printed by Richard Benson, bound in portfolio, *Nijinsky: L'Après-midi d'un faune, 1912*, published 1978 by Eakins Press Foundation.

Marius De Zayas

1880 – 1961

Photograph collection: 21 photogravures of his drawings, from *Camera Work,* numbers 39 and 46

Jim Dine and Lee Friedlander

Photograph collection: 16 fine prints, diptychs in portfolio *Photographs and Etchings,* 1969

John Divola

b. 6 June 1949, Santa Monica, California

Photograph collection: 12 fine prints, including 10 dye transfer prints in portfolio, *Zuma One,* 1982

Robert Doisneau

14 April 1912, Gentilly, France – 1 April 1994, Paris, France

Photograph collection: 34 fine prints, including 15 in portfolio *Robert Doisneau,* 1979

Jim Dow

b. 25 July 1942, Boston, Massachusetts

Photograph collection: 26 fine prints in two portfolios from 1982, *The National League Stadiums* and *The American League Stadiums*

Kenn Duncan

1928, Spring Lake, New Jersey – 27 July 1986

Photograph collection: 28 fine prints of New York dancers

MARK ALICE DURANT:
*We Want to Believe: White Handkerchiefs of
   Goodbye*, Chicago, 1996
Mark Alice Durant Collection

Mark Alice Durant

b. 1955

Research materials: The Mark Alice Durant Collection (AG 157) contains documentation of Durant's performance art, including his collaborative work as part of *Men of the World*, his writings, and other activities from the mid-1990s to the present.

Allen A. Dutton

b. 13 April 1922, Kingman, Arizona

Photograph collection: 11 fine prints in portfolio, *Hide and Seek*, 1979

Harold Edgerton

6 April 1903, Fremont, Nebraska –
4 January 1990, Boston, Massachusetts

Photograph collection: 154 fine prints, including 54 vintage prints from the Collection of Ansel and Virginia Adams and prints made by Gus Kayafas from original negatives, 1976–77

Highlights: Portfolios, *Seeing the Unseen*, 1977, and *Harold Edgerton: Ten Dye Transfer Photographs*, 1985.

Electronic Works of Art

Research materials: The Electronic Works of Art Collection (AG 160) contains art in electronic formats such as CD-ROM. Includes *3 Works* by MANUAL (Suzanne Bloom and Ed Hill), Esther Parada, and Stephen Axelrod.

Elliott Erwitt

b. 26 July 1928, Paris, France

Photograph collection: 28 fine prints, mostly in 2 portfolios, *Photographs: Elliott Erwitt*, 1977, and *Elliott Erwitt*, ca. 1979

Espejo

Research materials: The Espejo Collection (AG 81) contains papers related to the Espejo project and exhibition, 1977 to 1979. Includes project records, correspondence, clippings, publications, and writings by participants Louis Carlos Bernal, Morrie Camhi (project manager), Abigail Heyman, Roger Minick, and Neal Slavin. (2 linear feet)

Edizione Esposito

Photograph collection: 17 albumen prints of Pompei, from the Julia F. Corson Collection

---

Frederick H. Evans

26 June 1853, London, England – 24 June 1943, London, England

Photograph collection: 20 fine prints in portfolio of scenes from George Bernard Shaw play *Mrs. Warren's Profession*, ca. 1902, with overleaves written in Evans's hand

Research materials: The Frederick H. Evans Collection (AG 42) consists of lantern slides, 1887 to 1902, of photographs by Evans, Paul Martin, and others.

Highlights: 41-page typescript lecture notes with Evans's handwritten corrections for Lincoln Cathedral lantern slide presentation.

Terry Evans

b. 30 August 1944, Kansas City, Missouri

Photograph collection: 26 fine prints, including 9 from the Water in the West project, and 17 created for *Indivisible: Stories of American Community,* 2000

Related information: Water in the West Archive (AG 172.)

Walker Evans

3 November 1903, Saint Louis, Missouri – 10 April 1975, New Haven, Connecticut

Photograph collection: 53 fine prints

Highlights: 7 vintage prints from the 1930s from the Collection of Ansel and Virginia Adams. Portfolios: *Walker Evans,* 1971; *Walker Evans: Selected Photographs,* 1974; *Walker Evans, I,* 1978.

Related information: Walker Evans's archive is held at the Metropolitan Museum of Art, New York.

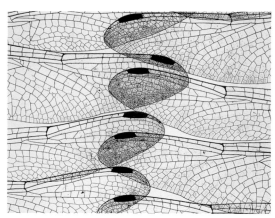

ANDREAS FEININGER:
Pattern Made of Dragonfly Wings [variant], ca. 1935

ADOLF FASSBENDER: *The Ice Serpent,* ca. 1933

Adolf Fassbender

3 May 1884, Grevenbroich, Germany –
2 January 1980, Newton, New Jersey

Photograph collection: approximately 400 fine prints and 400 study prints

Research materials: The Adolf Fassbender Archive (AG 168) contains papers and photographic materials related to the career of this teacher and leader in pictorialist photography. It includes letters, writings, teaching notes, publications, photographic journals, notebooks and diaries, artifacts, awards, scrapbooks, financial papers, negatives, lantern slides for teaching, transparencies, and photographs. Portraits of Fassbender teaching and a small bust are included. (60 linear feet)

Highlights: The correspondence files reveal his indefatigable lecture schedule and document the esteem in which he was held by his students.

Rights and restrictions: Copyright to Fassbender's writings and photographs is held by the Center for Creative Photography, The University of Arizona Foundation.

Andreas Feininger

27 December 1906, Paris, France –
18 February 1999, New York

Photograph collection: over 3000 fine prints

Research materials: The Andreas Feininger Archive (AG 53) contains personal papers and photographic materials. It includes biographical materials, correspondence, exhibition files, manuscripts and other writings, publication files, scrapbooks, appointment books 1930 to 1973, tearsheets, clippings, books, negatives 1928 to 1980s, transparencies, contact sheets, and study prints. The bulk of the collection documents Feininger's career as a photographer in Europe and the United States, especially his many photo essays for *Life* and other magazines. The photographic materials are organized according to Feininger's own subject headings.

Highlights: 76 unique vintage prints in *Hamburg Portfolio,* 1930–31; natural objects such as shells and feathers photographed by Feininger; scrapbooks 1929 to 1960 document his travels with maps, matchbook covers, ticket stubs, portraits of the artist, tearsheets, and correspondence.

Related information: Photograph by the artist's brother, T. Lux Feininger, is part of the Bauhaus Collection.

CCP publication: "Andreas Feininger: Early Work," *The Archive* 17 (March 1983).

Above: Exhibition of Fassbender's work, Pictorial Photographers of America, Chicago, 1966
Below: Adolf Fassbender teaching a class, 1960s
Adolf Fassbender Archive

Sandi Fellman

b. 24 January 1952, Detroit, Michigan

Photograph collection: 16 fine prints, most in portfolio *Scarlett and Other Women*, 1975

Antonio A. Fernandez

b. 31 October 1941, Havana, Cuba

Photograph collection: 45 fine prints

Highlight: 16 portraits made at the Miami racetrack between 1986–89, from the Aaron Siskind Collection.

Ben Fernandez

b. 5 April 1935, Nye, New York

Photograph collection: 12 fine prints in portfolio, *Countdown to Eternity: Photographs of Dr. Martin Luther King, Jr. in the 1960s,* 1989

Robert W. Fichter

b. 30 December 1939, Ft. Myers, Florida

Photograph collection: 15 fine prints

Research materials: The Robert Fichter Miscellaneous Acquisitions Collection (AG 109) contains material from various sources. Includes copies of mimeographed book by Fichter, *Confessions of a Silver Addic!* [sic] and other writings and research notes.

Highlight: 5 gelatin silver collages from 1976.

GEORGE FISKE: *Bridal Veil Fall. 900 feet,* ca. 1880s

George Fiske

22 October 1835, Amherst, New Hampshire – 20 October 1918, Yosemite, California

Photograph collection: 284 albumen prints, including 13 attributed to Fiske, a gift of Virginia Adams; and an album of 49 albumen prints, *Photographs, Yosemite, California,* n.d.

CCP publication: *George Fiske: Yosemite Photographer,* by Paul Hickman and Terence Pitts (Flagstaff, Arizona: Northland Press in cooperation with the Center for Creative Photography, 1980)

Judy Fiskin

b. 1 April 1945, Chicago, Illinois

Photograph collection: 16 gelatin silver prints, mostly from the series *Some Art*

Robbert Flick

b. 15 November 1939, Amersfoort, Holland

Photograph collection: 10 fine prints

Highlight: 3 boxes of study prints from *Midwest Diary* project.

W. P. Floyd

active 1870s

Photograph collection: 22 albumen prints in album, *The Typhoon – Hong Kong, September 1874*

Neil Folberg

b. 7 April 1950, San Francisco, California

Photograph collection: 15 fine prints, including 8 offset lithographs in *Portfolio One: We Are Thy People, Glimpses of Lubavitcher Life*, 1975

Jo Ann Frank

b. 11 April 1947, Philadelphia, Pennsylvania

Photograph collection: 18 fine prints, including 5 in *Design Portfolio*, 1981

Robert Frank

b. 9 November 1924, Zurich, Switzerland

Photograph collection: 23 fine prints

Research materials: Robert Frank Miscellaneous Acquisitions Collection (AG 102) contains materials from various sources. Includes audiotapes made at George Eastman House in 1967 and transcripts of interviews with 23 people. These were produced by the Museum of Fine Arts, Houston, and include comments by Lou Faurer, Ralph Gibson, Allen Ginsberg, June Leaf, Jonas Mekas, Duane Michals, John Szarkowski, and others.

Highlights: 9 prints from *The Americans*; 10 prints from *The Lines of My Hand*.

CCP Publication: *Robert Frank: A Bibliography, Filmography, and Exhibition Chronology 1946–1985*, by Stuart Alexander (CCP Bibliography Series 2, 1986).

Jim Frei

active 1970s

Photograph collection: 12 fine prints

Gisèle Freund

19 December 1912, Berlin, Germany – 31 March 2000, Paris, France

Photograph collection: 99 fine prints

Highlight: 10 dye transfer prints in portfolio, *Au pays des visages*, 1977.

Geoffrey Fricker

b. 1947

Photograph collection: 51 fine prints from Water in the West Project

Related information: Water in the West Archive (AG 172).

LEE FRIEDLANDER: *Sonora*, 1992

Lee Friedlander

b. 14 July 1934, Aberdeen, Washington

Photograph collection: 687 fine prints, including over 600 from *The American Monument* series (1970–1976) and 16 diptychs in portfolio, *Jim Dine, Etchings/Lee Friedlander, Photographs,* 1969

Research materials: The Lee Friedlander Collection (AG 117) contains dye transfer materials from the *Jazz & Blues* portfolio, and Friedlander's personal copy of *Fred Archer on Portraiture* (1948) with his juvenile signature.

Highlights: Portfolios: *15 Images by Lee Friedlander,* 1973; *Photographs of Flowers,* 1975; *Cherry Blossom Time in Japan,* 1986; *Jazz & Blues,* 1983; *The American Monument,* 1976; 11 images of the Sonoran Desert, part of the 1997 exhibition *An Excess of Fact.*

CCP publication: "Lee Friedlander: American Monuments," *The Archive* 25 (1988).

Francis Frith

1822, Chesterfield, England – 1898, Cannes, France

Photograph collection: 128 albumen prints in various published albums: *Upper Egypt & Ethiopia,* volume 1, 1860s; *Lower Egypt, Thebes and the Pyramids,* volume 1, 1860s; *Lower Egypt, Thebes and the Pyramids,* 1860s; *The Lake District,* n.d.; *The Gossiping Photographer at Hastings,* 1864; *The Gossiping Photographer on the Rhine,* 1864

William Fuller

b. 1948, Cleveland, Ohio

Photograph collection: 50 fine prints in portfolio, *Photographs: 1980–1990, Volume I,* 1990

Eric Futran

active 1970s

Photograph collection: 20 fine prints

Oliver Gagliani

b. 11 February 1917, Placerville, California

Photograph collection: 21 fine prints

Highlight: 16 prints from *The Italian Project: Sardinia,* 1980.

Christel Gang

1892 – ca. 1965

Research materials: The Christel Gang Collection (AG 47) contains correspondence, clippings, and brochures belonging to Gang, public stenographer and associate of Edward Weston. She assisted Weston by typing the pages from his Mexico daybook. The bulk of this collection is 66 letters and postcards from Weston.

Flor Garduño

b. 21 March 1957, Mexico City

Photograph collection: 13 fine prints

Paolo Gasparini

b. 15 March 1934, Italy

Photograph collection: 39 fine prints from the Collection of Paul Strand, including 13 on adult literacy in Venezuela, British West Indies, and Cuba

Arnold Gassan

2 May 1930 – 22 June 2001, Tucson, Arizona

Photograph collection: approximately 100 fine prints, including photogravures, photo-silkscreens, inkjet prints, and gelatin silver prints, many in portfolios

Research materials: The Arnold Gassan Archive (AG 58) contains personal papers and photographic materials of Gassan, photographer, poet, teacher, writer, and mental health professional. Includes letters from Ansel Adams, Walter Chappell, Syl Labrot, Minor White, and others; notes and writings; research notes and manuscripts from book projects such as *A Chronology of Photography*; negatives, transparencies, and study prints. (55 linear feet)

Highlights: Notes from a 1945 lecture given by Ansel Adams at the Museum of Modern Art, New York. Journal kept by Gassan during Yosemite Workshop with Ansel Adams in 1959.

Helen Gee/Limelight Gallery

b. 1926

Research materials: Helen Gee/Limelight Gallery Archive (AG 74) consists of the Helen Gee Papers and the Limelight Gallery Records. Gee, photographer, gallery owner, and writer, opened her New York gallery/coffeehouse in 1954. Records include correspondence from the many photographers represented by Limelight, including Ansel Adams, Bill Brandt, Imogen Cunningham, Eliot Porter, Minor White, and many others, as well as daybooks, ledgers, mailing lists, menus, printed materials, audiotapes, clippings, ephemera, and a scrapbook. Information about Gee's husband, painter Yun Gee, and her daughter, Li-lan, is included in her personal papers along with information about her work as an art dealer and author. (48 linear feet)

Related information: The CCP also has the records of other photography galleries: Witkin Gallery, Inc. (AG 62); correspondence with the Light Gallery, New York, in the Harry Callahan (AG 29), Aaron Siskind (AG 30), and Harold Jones (AG 67) collections.

RALPH GIBSON: *Sardinia*, 1980
From the series *Chiaroscuro*, 1974–80

Arnold Genthe

8 January 1869, Berlin, Germany – 9 August 1942, New Milford, Connecticut

Photograph collection: 63 fine prints

Highlights: 56 photographs were printed by Ansel Adams from Genthe's original negatives.

Stephen Gersh

b. 31 March 1942, Boston, Massachusetts

Photograph collection: 14 fine prints

Highlight: 10 prints in portfolio created with Nubar Alexanian, *Peruvian Portfolio*, 1975.

Ralph Gibson

b. 16 January 1939, Los Angeles, California

Photograph collection: 368 fine prints

Research materials: The Ralph Gibson Archive (AG 37) contains papers, photographic materials, and memorabilia from about 1959 to the present. Included are extensive files of incoming and outgoing business and personal correspondence, activity files, biographical materials, business receipts, clippings, date books and calendars, writings, interviews, publication and exhibition files, portraits of Gibson, audio- and videotapes. (63 linear feet)

Highlights: 42 Iris prints in series *Ex Libris*; portfolio, *France Near & Far*, 1992; 4 diptych etchings in portfolio created with Paolo Cotani, *Metafora*, ca. 1981; documentation of the activities of Lustrum Press, 1970 to the present.

CCP publication: "Ralph Gibson: Early Work," *The Archive* 24 (1987).

William Giles

b. 5 March 1934, Boston, Massachusetts

Photograph collection: 18 prints in portfolio, *Reflections*, 1977

Bernard Gille

b. 19 August 1952, Luxembourg

Photograph collection: 16 offset lithographs in portfolio, *Free People*, n.d.

LAURA GILPIN: *Navajos by Firelight*, 1932

Laura Gilpin

22 April 1891, Colorado Springs, Colorado – 30 November 1979, Santa Fe, New Mexico

Photograph collection: 58 fine prints, mostly platinum or palladium

Research materials: Correspondence from Gilpin appears in the Paul Strand Collection (AG 17) and in the Lee Witkin/Witkin Gallery, Inc. Collection (AG 62). The Laura Gilpin Miscellaneous Acquisitions Collection (AG 126) contains study prints and transparencies by Gilpin.

Related information: The CCP holds materials from other students of the Clarence H. White School of Photography such as Ralph Steiner and Alfred and Margaret Cohn. The Laura Gilpin archive is held by the Amon Carter Museum, Fort Worth, Texas.

CCP publication: "The Early Work of Laura Gilpin, 1917–1932," *Center for Creative Photography* 13 (April 1981).

Len Gittleman

b. 23 September 1932, Brooklyn, New York

Photograph collection: 17 fine prints

Highlight: 9 silkscreen prints in portfolio, *Lunar Transformations*, 1972.

Peter Goin

b. 1951, Madison, Wisconsin

Photograph collection: 188 fine prints, mostly from the Water in the West project

Related information: Water in the West Archive (AG 172).

Eugene O. Goldbeck

4 November 1892, San Antonio, Texas –
27 October 1986, San Antonio, Texas

Photograph collection: 16 fine prints, including 11 in panoramic format

---

Judith Golden

b. 29 November 1934, Chicago, Illinois

Photograph collection: 48 fine prints

Research materials: The Judith Golden Archive (AG 158) consists of papers and photographic materials, 1977 to the present, of the photographer and teacher Judith Golden. Includes correspondence, exhibition records, teaching materials, writings, biographical information, clippings, publications, financial records, and memorabilia. (10 linear feet)

Highlights: Artist's book, *Masks*, 1974–82; assemblage, *Butterfly Box*, 1985; portfolio of 18 Canon transfer prints, *Another Reality: Portraits of Oaxacan Artists*, 1994.

Barry Goldwater

1 January 1909, Phoenix, Arizona – 29 May 1998, Phoenix, Arizona

Photograph collection: 1 fine print

Research materials: The bulk of the Barry Goldwater Collection (AG 88) consists of negatives and small contact prints. Goldwater, in addition to serving as a United States senator and Republican nominee for president, was an aviator and photographer. His negatives, 1924 to 1972, document his wide-ranging travels throughout the Southwest photographing the land and the people. (6.5 linear feet)

Highlight: Images made during a float trip down the Green and Colorado Rivers in 1940 passing through Glen Canyon, later inundated when the river was dammed to form Lake Powell.

Emmet Gowin

b. 22 December 1941, Danville, Virginia

Photograph collection: 23 fine prints, including 9 from the *Working Landscape* series

---

George Alexander Grant

1891, Sunbury, Pennsylvania – 1964

Research materials: The George A. Grant Collection (AG 55) contains modern contact prints made from Grant's original 5x7-inch nitrate negatives in the collection of the Western Archaeological Center, Tucson. Subjects include missions in Sonora, California, Arizona, New Mexico, and Texas, as well as Boulder Dam, the Grand Canyon, and Hermosillo, Mexico. (3 linear feet)

Lauren Greenfield

b. 28 June 1966, Boston

Photograph collection: 35 fine prints, including 26 created for *Indivisible: Stories of American Community,* 2000, and 9 from the exhibition and book *Fast Forward: Growing Up in the Shadow of Hollywood* (1997)

Sidney Grossman

25 June 1913, New York – 31 December 1955, New York

Photograph collection: 4 fine prints and 8 contact prints mounted together

Research materials: The Sidney Grossman Collection (AG 56) consists primarily of negatives and modern contact prints documenting Grossman's career between 1934 and 1955. Subjects include Grossman's "Gruesomes," the Chelsea Document, Harlem, folksingers, the Midwest, Black Christ Festival, Panama, Central America, New York, Coney Island, American Legion, Mulberry Street, Provincetown, and ballet subjects. Also included are reference files, publications, teaching materials, and tearsheets. (20 linear feet)

Related information: The CCP has the work of other Photo League members such as Aaron Siskind and W. Eugene Smith. The Museum of Fine Arts, Houston, has the largest collection of Grossman's vintage prints.

Walter Gutman

1903 – 27 April 1986

Photograph collection: 14 fine prints, 13 of them from portfolio *Inspirations of Strong Women,* 1982

JOHN GUTMANN:
Machine Gunners, San Francisco, 1950

John Gutmann

28 May 1905, Breslau, Germany –
12 June 1998, San Francisco

Photograph collection: 2416 fine prints and an equal number of proof prints

Research materials: The John Gutmann Archive (AG 173) contains personal papers, audiovisual materials, memorabilia, artifacts, and photographic materials, 1930s to 1990s, of the photographer, teacher, painter, and collector, John Gutmann. Included are extensive files of correspondence, lecture notes from his tenure at San Francisco State University from 1936 to 1974, biographical information, clippings, publications, films, videotapes, proof prints, negatives, transparencies, and camera and movie equipment. (96 linear feet)

Related information: Gutmann's paintings and his collection of art are at the M. H. de Young Museum, San Francisco.

Rights and restrictions: Copyright to Gutmann's writings and photographs is held by the Center for Creative Photography, Arizona Board of Regents.

311

Contact prints from 4x5-inch negatives
From *Folksingers* series, 1940s
Sid Grossman Collection

JOHAN HAGEMEYER: *Trees on Telegraph Hill*, 1925

Johan Hagemeyer

1 June 1884, Amsterdam, the Netherlands – 1962, Berkeley, California

Photograph collection: 242 fine prints, including some platinum or palladium

Research materials: The Johan Hagemeyer Archive (AG 44) contains personal papers and photographic materials of this horticulturist, photographer, and close associate of Edward Weston. Included are letters, diaries, clippings, exhibition documentation, scrapbooks, publications, and artifacts. The bulk of the letters, mostly in Dutch, is between Hagemeyer and his brothers and friends in Holland. Diaries chronicle travels to Europe in 1912 and 1920, his trips around California, efforts at horticulture, meetings with Edward Weston, and poor health. Photographic materials include negatives, proof prints, portraits of Hagemeyer, and a view camera. (4.5 linear feet)

Highlights: Booklet containing 9 photographs of Albert Einstein, *Camera-portraits of Einstein*, 1931; letter from Einstein expressing his admiration for the portraits.

Related information: The Weston/Hagemeyer Collection (AG 5) and the Edward Weston Archive (AG 38) contain correspondence, scrapbooks, and other papers relevant to Hagemeyer's career.

CCP publications: "Weston to Hagemeyer: New York Notes," *Center for Creative Photography* 3 (November 1976); "Johan Hagemeyer Collection," *Guide Series* 11 (1985).

Betty Hahn

b. 11 October 1940, Chicago

Photograph collection: 16 fine prints

Suleiman Hakim

active late 1870s

Photograph collection: 15 albumen prints of Syria and Lebanon, in the Julia F. Corson Collection

Milton Halberstadt

b. 1919

Photograph collection: 15 fine prints, including 6 that Halberstadt printed from negatives of Ansel Adams with Kodalith treatment

Philippe Halsman

2 May 1906, Riga, Latvia – 25 June 1979, New York

Photograph collection: 52 fine prints

Highlights: Portfolios, *Halsman/Marilyn*, 1981; photoreproductions in Ky-vure process, *A Portfolio of Photographs by Philippe Halsman*, 1950s.

Hiroshi Hamaya

28 March 1915, Tokyo, Japan – 6 March 1999, Tokyo, Japan

Photograph collection: 22 photoreproductions in 2 portfolios: *Shizen* [Nature], 1971, and *Japanese Calligrapher Dr. Yaichi Aizu*, 1972, from the Collection of Ansel and Virginia Adams

---

Wanda Hammerbeck

b. 24 March 1945, Lincoln, Nebraska

Photograph collection: 14 prints, most from Water in the West project

Related information: Water in the West Archive (AG 172).

Charles Harbutt

b. 29 July 1935, Camden, New Jersey

Photograph collection: 304 fine prints, including many from the *Travelog* book project, 1960s–1970s; and the *Progreso* book project, 1970s–1980s

Research materials: The Charles Harbutt Archive (AG 144) contains the personal papers and photographic materials of the photojournalist and teacher, Charles Harbutt. Included are letters, research files, ephemera, publications, book maquettes, extensive negative files, and contact sheets. (60 linear feet)

Highlights: Letters from André Kertész; photographs made during the Cuban Revolution (1959), the Republican National Convention (1972), and Israel's 6 Day War (1967); Magnum story logs.

Robert S. Harrah

1925 – 1989

Research materials: The Robert S. Harrah Collection (AG 54) contains papers and photographic materials related to Harrah's work with W. Eugene Smith from 1945 to 1948. Harrah, also a photographer, collaborated with Smith on the *Country Doctor* photoessay for *Life* magazine.

Highlights: Unpublished 314-page manuscript *Gene and Me . . . and Photojournalism*

Lynne Harrison

Photograph collection: 12 fine prints, all portraits of photographers

---

Donald Scott Harter

b. 10 January 1950, West Bend, Wisconsin

Photograph collection: 10 prints from portfolio, *Land Extractions*, 1975

Paul B. Haviland

17 June 1880, Paris, France – 21 December 1950, Yzeures-sur-Creuse, France

Photograph collection: 13 plates from *Camera Work*, mostly photogravures, and 1 platinum print

---

David Heath

b. 27 June 1931, Philadelphia, Pennsylvania

Photograph collection: 10 gelatin silver prints

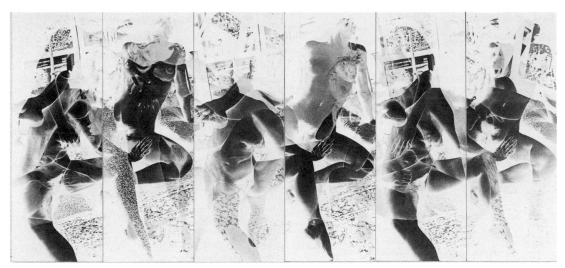

ROBERT HEINECKEN: *Cream Six*, 1970

Robert Heinecken

b. 29 October 1931, Denver, Colorado

Photograph collection: 440 fine prints

Research materials: The Robert Heinecken Archive (AG 45) holds papers, photographic materials, project and teaching files, and audiovisual materials from the 1950s to the present day. Personal papers include biographical materials, incoming and outgoing correspondence, activity files, exhibition files, documentation of teaching career at the University of California, Los Angeles, publications, and reference files about Heinecken and his career as artist, teacher, and member of the Society for Photographic Education. The photographic materials include extensive files of portraits of Heinecken from throughout his career. Also included are materials such as offset plates, prints, negatives, lithographs, contact sheets, transparencies, and tear sheets from periodicals from the 1960s to the present. These were used in the construction of reassembled figures, magazine collages and transfers, offset lithographs, photograms, solarized and bleached prints, and other multimedia works.

The audiovisual materials include slides used in lectures; exhibition installation views; audiotapes of Heinecken's lectures; videotaped interviews; and a film produced jointly with Robert Fichter. (ca. 65 linear feet)

Highlights: Works from Heinecken's earliest years as an artist, 1960s–70s; several versions of *Are You Rea*; and unique three-dimensional photo-sculptures.

Related information: The CCP also holds the official archive of the Society for Photographic Education (AG 78) and a small collection related to the career of Heinecken's wife, photographer Joyce Neimanas (AG 174).

Fritz Henle

9 June 1909, Dortmund, Germany –
31 January 1993, Christiansted, Virgin Islands

Photograph collection: 72 fine prints, including
some vintage prints and some printed from
original negatives in 1979

Florence Henri

28 June 1893, New York – 24 July 1982,
Compiègne, France

Photograph collection: 14 fine prints, most in
portfolio, *12 Fotografien*, 1974

Anthony Hernandez

b. 7 July 1947, Los Angeles, California

Photograph collection: 10 fine prints, from the
series *In Los Angeles, Landscapes for the
Homeless,* and *In America*

Abigail Heyman

b. August 1942, Danbury, Connecticut

Photograph collection: 30 fine prints from the
Espejo project, 1977–78

Gary Higgins

b. 22 March 1964

Photograph collection: 95 fine prints

Hill and Adamson

David Octavius Hill

1802, Perth, Scotland – 17 May 1870,
Edinburgh, Scotland

Robert Adamson

26 April 1821, St. Andrews, Scotland –
14 January 1848, St. Andrews, Scotland

Photograph collection: 66 fine prints, including
6 calotypes, 2 photogravures on tissue, and 47
carbon prints

Highlight: book of 47 carbon prints, *Calotypes
by D. O. Hill and R. Adamson, illustrating an
early stage in the development of photography,* 1928.

Jack Hillers

20 December 1843, Hanover, Germany –
14 November 1925, Washington, D.C.

Photograph collection: 8 platinum prints of
Southwest scenes, 1873 to ca. 1880

Research materials: Framed glass transparency
(34x30 inches) *Captains of the Cañon,* ca. 1879,
is part of the Lee Witkin/Witkin Gallery, Inc.
Collection (AG 62).

Lewis W. Hine

26 September 1874, Oshkosh, Wisconsin –
3 November 1940, Hastings-on-Hudson, New
York

Photograph collection: 12 fine prints, most in 2
copies of the portfolio, *Lewis W. Hine,
1874–1940,* 1942

Oscar Hofmeister

1871, Hamburg, Germany – 1937, Hamburg, Germany

Theodor Hofmeister

1868, Hamburg, Germany – 1943, Hamburg, Germany

Photograph collection: 12 prints, plates from 2 copies of *Camera Work* number 7

William Holgers

1904 – 1981

Research materials: The William Holgers Collection (AG 69) contains printed materials and photographs related to Edward Weston, Charis Wilson, and their family, friends, and colleagues, ca. 1930 to 1970s. Of special note are the many informal views of Weston taken at Point Lobos and Wildcat Hill.

WILLIAM HOLGERS:
Untitled [Edward Weston showing a dune photograph to visitors in his Wildcat Hill house], ca. 1945
William Holgers Collection

Emil Otto Hoppé

14 April 1878, Munich, Germany –
9 December 1972, London, England

Photograph collection: 9 fine prints, including 6 photogravures

Research materials: The Emil Otto Hoppé Collection (AG 14) contains handwritten and typescript reminiscences of friends and others photographed by Hoppé, biographical notes, and writings by and about the photographer.

Eikoh Hosoe

b. 18 March 1933, Tohoku, Yonezawa, Japan

Photograph collection: 25 fine prints

Thomas Houseworth & Company, San Francisco

Thomas Houseworth

21 June 1828, New York – 13 April 1915, San Francisco

Photograph collection: 47 stereoviews from the Virginia Adams Stereoview Collection; 7 others by or attributed to Charles L. Weed (distributed by Houseworth)

Herbert M. Howison

Photograph collection: 14 fine prints of pictorialist subjects

---

Philip Hyde

b. 15 August 1921, San Francisco, California

Photograph collection: 31 fine prints, including 2 copies of offset lithography portfolio, *Mountain and Desert*, 1973, from the Collection of Ansel and Virginia Adams

Michael Johnson

b. 1946

Photograph collection: 32 fine prints

Highlight: Portfolio, *Botanicals*, 1979

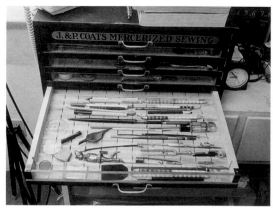

HAROLD JONES:
Untitled [view into drawer of small tools], 1999
From the series *A House Alone: Photographs of
Frederick Sommer's House*

Harold Jones

b. 29 September 1940, Morristown, New
Jersey

Photograph collection: 96 fine prints

Research materials: Photographer, curator, and
photoeducator Harold Jones was the founding
director of the CCP (1975–1977), a founder of
Light Gallery, New York (1973–1975), and a
long-term member of the faculty of the
University of Arizona. His archive contains correspondence, biographical materials, teaching
and exhibition files, records of the Society for
Photographic Education, publications and clippings, and ephemera covering his career from
the time he was a student at the University of
New Mexico. Correspondents include Robert
Heinecken, Jim Alinder, Robert Fichter,
Beaumont Newhall, Jerry Uelsmann, and many
others. (9 linear feet)

Highlights: *University: A Photographic Inquiry,*
1984–85: 2-volume maquette from project
titled *Universe City,* containing 44 gelatin silver
prints and 3 color prints. In 1999 the CCP
commissioned Jones to document Frederick
Sommer's house as it was shortly after Sommer's
death in a project titled *A House Alone.*

Pirkle Jones

b. 2 January 1914, Shreveport, Louisiana

Photograph collection: 24 fine prints, including 12 in *Portfolio Two*, 1968

Kenneth Josephson

b. 1 July 1932, Detroit, Michigan

Photograph collection: 16 fine prints

Richard L. Julian

b. 1915

Photograph collection: 51 fine prints

Highlights: Portfolios, *The Little Portfolio (Malé Portfolio)*, 1973; *Fourteen Photographs*, 1971.

Blake Justice

b. 1956, Wichita, Kansas

Photograph collection: 12 fine prints

Frederick "Fritz" Kaeser

3 July 1910, Greenville, Illinois – 6 June 1990, Tucson, Arizona

Photograph collection: 22 fine prints, including carbro prints, bromoil transfers, and gelatin silver prints

Research materials: Photographer Fritz Kaeser was an assistant to William Mortensen from 1932 to 1933, was a participant in Ansel Adams's 1945 workshop, and later opened the k2 Studio and Gallery in Aspen, Colorado. The Kaeser Collection (AG 86) contains personal papers, correspondence, portraits, and publications, 1933–1986. (fraction of a linear foot)

Highlights: Materials from the Aspen Institute Conference on Photography, 26 September – 6 October 1951, a key event in the founding of *Aperture* magazine.

Tamarra Kaida

b. 6 July 1946, Lienz, Austria

Photograph collection: 12 fine prints

Brian Katz

active 1960s –1970s

Photograph collection: 17 fine prints, nude abstractions

Gus Kayafas

b. 1947

Photograph collection: 19 fine prints, including 18 in the bound portfolio, *Miami: Photographs by Gus Kayafas*, 1984

Joseph T. Keiley

26 July 1869, Maryland – 21 January 1914, New York

Photograph collection: 10 prints, mostly plates from *Camera Work*, including 1 platinum print with selective glycerine toning

---

Ron Kelley

b. 1950, Detroit, Michigan

Photograph collection: 37 fine prints

Highlight: 31 prints in portfolio, *Winogrand Are Beautiful*, 1981–82. Created as maquette for a book that was never published, it is a spoof and critique of Garry Winogrand's *Women are Beautiful.*

Related information: Letters from Kelley regarding the portfolio are found in the Robert Heinecken Archive (AG 45).

Michael Kenna

b. 20 November 1953, Widnes, England

Photograph collection: 11 fine prints

David Hume Kennerly

b. 9 March 1947, Oregon

Photograph collection: 23 fine prints from President Gerald Ford's administration, 1974–76

André Kertész

2 July 1894, Budapest, Hungary – 27 September 1985, New York

Photograph collection: 31 fine prints from 3 portfolios—*Photographs, André Kertész, Volume I: 1913–1929; Photographs, André Kertész, Volume II: 1930–1972; André Kertész/Still Life*, 1981

Keystone View Company, Meadville, Pennsylvania

Photograph collection: 14 stereoviews from the Virginia Adams Stereoview Collection

---

Sant Khalsa

b. 3 January 1953, New York

Photograph collection: 58 gelatin silver prints from the Water in the West project

Related information: Water in the West Archive (AG 172).

Kilburn Brothers, Littleton, New Hampshire

Benjamin West Kilburn

10 December 1827 – 15 January 1909, Littleton, New Hampshire

Photograph collection: 50 stereoviews, 9 by B. W. Kilburn, from the Virginia Adams Stereoview Collection

Chris Killip

b. 11 July 1946, Douglas, Isle of Man, England

Photograph collection: 11 fine prints

Ryuzo Kitahara

b. 12 January 1936

Photograph collection: 50 fine prints

MARK KLETT:
*Stop Sign near Open Shooting Range, Reach 10,
    Granite Reef Aqueduct, North Phoenix, 10/20/84*
From the *Central Arizona Project Photographic
    Survey*

Mark Klett

b. 9 September 1952, Albany, New York

Photograph collection: 65 fine prints, including work from the *Central Arizona Project Photographic Survey* and the Water in the West project; portfolio *Nepal*, 1986, created jointly with Linda Connor

Highlight: The CCP commissioned Klett to photograph *Martian Test Landscape at the University of Arizona, Tucson, 11/13/98*. It was shown in the exhibition *Imag(in)ing Mars*, 1998–99.

Related information: Water in the West Archive (AG 172).

Philip Knight

b. [?] – d. 1953

Photograph collection: 21 fine prints, from the Collection of Ansel and Virginia Adams

---

Norio Kobayashi

b. 1952, Akita, Japan

Photograph collection: 10 fine prints

Lewis S. Kostiner

b. 4 April 1950

Photograph collection: 34 fine prints, from the Collection of Aaron Siskind

---

Leslie Krims

b. 16 August 1942, Brooklyn, New York

Photograph collection: 23 fine prints

Highlights: Portfolios, *Porsche Rainbow*, 1973, and *Please!*, 1978.

Heinrich Kühn

25 February 1866, Dresden, Germany – 9 October 1944, Birgitz, Austria

Photograph collection: 13 prints, including 9 plates from *Camera Work*

Yasuo Kuniyoshi

1889, Japan – 1953, New York

Research materials: The Yasuo Kuniyoshi Collection (AG 85) contains 35 mm black-and-white negatives, 1935 to 1941, and work prints of portraits and scenes in Woodstock, New York. (fraction of a linear foot)

Ellen Land-Weber

b. 16 March 1943, Rochester, New York

Photograph collection: 87 fine prints, digital photo collages and gelatin silver prints done for the Water in the West project

Related information: Water in the West Archive (AG 172).

Victor Landweber

b. 11 September 1943, Washington, D.C.

Photograph collection: 40 fine prints

Highlights: Portfolio of 17 Polaroid diptychs, *Sweet Stuff*, 1979.

Dorothea Lange

26 April 1895, Hoboken, New Jersey – 13 October 1965, San Francisco, California

Photograph collection: 13 fine prints

William Larson

b. 14 October 1942, North Tonawanda, New York

Photograph collection: 63 fine prints, including portfolios: *The Figure in Motion, 1966–70*, 1980; and *Aprille*, 1980; and the *Tucson Gardens* series, ca. 1982

Highlights: 6 electro-carbon prints, transmitted by the Graphic Sciences Teleprinter, 1971–1975.

Jacques-Henri Lartique

29 June 1894, Courbevoie, France – 13 September 1986, Nice, France

Photograph collection: 22 fine prints, mostly from portfolios, *A Portfolio of Photographs by Jacques-Henri Lartigue*, 1972, and *Jacques-Henri Lartigue: A Collector's Portfolio, 1903 to 1916*, 1978

CLARENCE JOHN LAUGHLIN:
Light as Protagonist, 1949
From the series *Group K: Visual Poems*

Clarence John Laughlin

14 August 1905, Lake Charles, Louisiana –
2 January 1985, New Orleans, Louisiana

Photograph collection: 54 fine prints

Research materials: Letters in Edward Weston
Archive (AG 38) relate to their meeting during
Weston's 1941 *Leaves of Grass* project.

CCP publication: "Clarence John Laughlin,"
Center for Creative Photography 10 (October
1979).

Jean (Juan) Laurent (y Cía., Madrid)

23 July 1816, Garchizy, France – before 1892

Photograph collection: 58 albumen prints

Related information: A selection of Laurent's
photographs was exhibited at the CCP July
through October, 2001. A website in English
and Spanish was created by the curator, Sara
Badía-Villaseca, with extensive bibliography
and texts.

Alma Lavenson

20 May 1897, San Francisco – 20 May 1989,
Piedmont, California

Photograph collection: 14 fine prints

Joseph LeConte

1823, Georgia – 1901, Yosemite Valley,
California

Photograph collection: 12 stereoviews from the
Virginia Adams Stereoview Collection

Lectures, Writings, Interviews, and Manuscripts

Research materials: This collection (AG 101) holds miscellaneous materials documenting the lives and careers of photographers and various institutions of photography. Materials are acquired from a wide variety of sources. Types of materials in the collection include academic papers, theses and dissertations, papers delivered at conferences, interviews, poems, and details of photographic processes. Among the subjects of this collection are Frederick Sommer, Ralph Steiner, O. Winston Link, Garry Winogrand, Ansel Adams, Louise Dahl-Wolfe, Hans Namuth, Pictorialism, the Witkin Gallery, the Center for Creative Photography, the Master Photo Dealers and Finishers Association, and the Museum of Modern Art. (1 linear foot)

Russell Lee

21 July 1903, Ottawa, Illinois – 28 August 1986, Austin, Texas

Photograph collection: 32 fine prints, the bulk of which were made for the Farm Security Administration

Cy Lehrer

b. 6 September 1933, Philadelphia, Pennsylvania

Photograph collection: 17 fine prints, most of which are from the series, *Places of Ha'Shoah,* 1994/1995

Ron Leighton

b. 8 August 1944, New York

Photograph collection: 15 fine prints in untitled bound portfolio, 1976

Maurice Lemaître

b. 1929, Paris, France

Photograph collection: 24 fine prints in portfolio, *Au-Delà du Déclic,* 1965, examples of his "lettrist" experimentation with text

Nathan Lerner

b. 30 March 1913, Chicago, Illinois

Photograph collection: 23 fine prints

Joel D. Levinson

b. 24 April 1953, Bridgeport, Connecticut

Photograph collection: 15 fine prints in portfolio, *California Flea Markets,* 1981

Leon Levinstein

20 September 1910, Buckhannon, West Virginia – December 1988, New York

Photograph collection: 45 fine prints

DAVID LEVINTHAL: Untitled, 1994 [original in color]
From the series *Mein Kampf*, 1994–95

David Levinthal

b. 8 March 1949, San Francisco

Photograph collection: 56 fine prints, including 35 gelatin silver prints on Kodalith paper from *Hitler Moves East* series, 1972–75; 20 Polaroid 20x24-inch Land prints from the *Mein Kampf* series, 1994–95

Research materials: The David Levinthal Collection (AG 177) documents the *Hitler Moves East* series with miniature toy soldiers, vehicles, and other props the artist used to create the tableaux he photographed. Also included is his collection of research publications about World War II and photographs of Levinthal creating the tableaux. (6 linear feet)

HELEN LEVITT: *Halloween, New York*, ca. 1942

Helen Levitt

b. 31 August 1913, Brooklyn, New York

Photograph collection: 63 fine prints

Highlights: Collection includes a number of views made in Mexico in 1941, as well as modern dye transfer and incorporated color coupler prints made from the artist's transparencies.

Jerome Liebling

b. 16 April 1924, New York

Photograph collection: 13 fine prints, 10 of them in portfolio, *Jerome Liebling: Photographs*, 1976

Joan Liftin

b. 1935, Teaneck, New Jersey

Photograph collection: 23 fine prints, including 18 created for *Indivisible: Stories of American Community*, 2000

Ken Light

b. 16 March 1951, New York

Photograph collection: 45 fine prints, from the projects *Images of New York*, 1978; *With These Hands*, 1986; and *To the Promised Land*, 1988

John Loengard

b. 1934, New York

Photograph collection: 18 fine prints from the series *Celebrating the Negative*, 1992–93

Highlights: The hands of various CCP staff members are shown holding original negatives in the collections.

Reagan Louie

b. 1951, San Francisco, California

Photograph collection: 16 photographs created for *Indivisible: Stories of American Community*, 2000

Marshall Lupp

b. 1949, Sebewaing, Michigan

Photograph collection: 13 fine prints, most from *Portfolio III, Metasight*, 1988

George Platt Lynes

15 April 1907, East Orange, New Jersey – 1955, New York

Photograph collection: 56 fine prints and 42 attributed to him

Highlights: Fine prints are evenly split between portraits and fashion photography, mostly from his work with *Vogue*, and include two self-portraits.

DANNY LYON:
Bus Stop, Tehuantepec, Oaxaca, 1978
From the portfolio *Danny Lyon*, 1979

Danny Lyon

b. 16 March 1942, Brooklyn, New York

Photograph collection: 206 fine prints, including portfolios: *Danny Lyon*, 1979; *Conversations with the Dead*, 1983; *Haiti*, 1988. 20 photographs including 4 original montages created for *Indivisible: Stories of American Community*, 2000

Research materials: 8 Bleak Beauty 16 mm motion pictures, 1969 to 1985, constitute the Danny Lyon Collection (AG 161). Included are *Little Boy, Los Niños Abandonados, Llanito, Willie I and II, Born to Film, Dear Mark,* and *Social Science 127*.

Highlights: 8 photographs of events of the Southern Civil Rights Movement, early 1960s, printed by Chuck Kelton, 1996.

JOAN LYONS:
Patio, Fountain / Pavilion, New York, 1982

Joan Lyons

b. 6 March 1937, New York

Photograph collection: 14 fine prints

Highlight: 11 offset lithographs in portfolio, *Presences*, 1980.

Alen MacWeeney

b. 1 September 1939, Dublin, Ireland

Photograph collection: 12 fine prints in portfolio, *Alen MacWeeney*, 1979

Ben Maddow

1909 – 9 October 1992, Hollywood, California

Research materials: The Ben Maddow Collection (AG 108) contains correspondence with Willard Van Dyke and a manuscript about their trip to South America, ca. 1941 to 1942 while filming *The Bridge*.

Magnum Photos

Research materials: The Magnum Collection (AG 104) contains research files assembled during work on the book and exhibition *In Our Time: The World as Seen by Magnum Photographers*. These files were brought together by Stuart Alexander from 1986 to 1990. Included are copies of Magnum publications, memos, biographical materials, bibliographies, chronologies, correspondence, and clippings pertaining to the history of Magnum Photos and its members.

Joe Maloney

b. 28 October 1949, Worcester, Massachusetts

Photograph collection: 11 fine prints, 10 of them in portfolio *Joe Maloney/Dye Transfer*, 1982

Man Ray (Emmanuel Radnitzky)

27 August 1890, Philadelphia, Pennsylvania – 18 November 1976, Paris, France

Photograph collection: 11 fine prints, including 10 photogravures of photograms or "rayographs" in portfolio, *Électricité*, 1931

Mike Mandel

b. 24 November 1950, Los Angeles, California

Photograph collection: 21 gelatin silver prints and 2 uncut offset sheets for the *Baseball Photographer Trading Card Series* (1975); 81 prints collected by Mandel and Larry Sultan for the *Evidence* project; collaborative photo silkscreen billboard with Sultan; 2 time-lapse cibachromes

Research materials: Samples of the *Baseball Photographer Trading Card Series* (1975) are in several archival collections, including Robert Heinecken Archive (AG 45) which also contains letters from Mandel.

ROBERT MAPPLETHORPE: *Lisa Lyon*, 1982

Robert Mapplethorpe

4 November 1946, Floral Park, New York –
9 March 1989, Boston

Photograph collection: 12 fine prints

Highlights: 8 photogravures in book *A Season in Hell* with text by Arthur Rimbaud (Limited Editions Club, 1986).

Josiah Martin

1843, London – 1916, Auckland, New Zealand

Photograph collection: 19 collodion chloride and albumen prints of Fiji and Samoa, ca. 1900, from the Julia F. Corson Collection

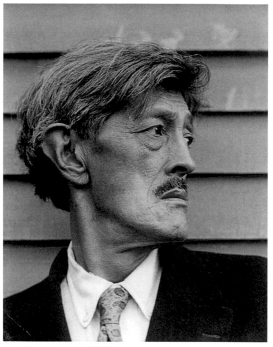

MARGRETHE MATHER:
Sadakichi Hartmann, ca. 1935

Margrethe Mather

1885, Salt Lake City, Utah – 1952, Glendale, California

Photograph collection: 156 fine and study prints

Research materials: The Edward Weston Archive (AG 38), the Edward Weston Miscellaneous Acquisitions Collection (AG 6), and the Edward Weston and Johan Hagemeyer Collection (AG 5) contain correspondence with and about Mather. The William Justema Miscellaneous Acquisitions Collection (AG 120) contains information about Mather's artistic collaborator Justema.

Highlights: Love letters from Mather to Weston from the 1920s, several including pressed flowers. Platinum portraits of Johan Hagemeyer and Edward Weston, 1921. Many portraits of William Justema and 17 photographs of Justema's drawings of Mather.

CCP publication: "Margrethe Mather," *Center for Creative Photography* 11 (December 1979).

Neil E. Matthew

Research materials: The Neil E. Matthew Collection (AG 131) contains materials documenting the career of Matthew, Associate Professor Emeritus, Herron School of Art, Indiana University. These were collected by Matthew while he was a student of Henry Holmes Smith at Indiana University in the 1950s. Includes 2 essays written by Robert Forth, also a student of Smith, in 1963. (fraction of a linear foot)

Ben Maxey

b. [?] – d. 1987

Research materials: The Ben Maxey Collection (AG 112) contains personal papers and photographic materials of Maxey, a Tucson studio photographer and student of William Mortensen. Included are newspaper advertisements, notes on facial expressions, and photographs used as "glamour photography." (fraction of a linear foot)

Allan B. McCoy

1900, Rhode Island – 1972, Cranston, Rhode Island

Photograph collection: 14 gelatin silver prints prepared for pictorialist salon, ca. 1950s

---

Robyn Stoutenburg McDaniels

b. 1958

Photograph collection: 13 fine prints, including 12 toned gelatin silver prints in self-published artist's book, *Images, 12 Years*, 1994

LAWRENCE MCFARLAND:
Petrogylph on Hill Overlooking Site of Picacho Pumping Plant, 1985
From the *Central Arizona Project Photographic Survey*

Lawrence McFarland

b. 1 September 1942, Wichita, Kansas

Photograph collection: 46 fine prints

Highlights: 18 prints created for the *Central Arizona Project Photographic Survey* project, 1980s; portfolio, *Lawrence McFarland: Twelve Photographs*, 1983.

Maynard McFarlane

b. 1895, London, England – d. [?]

Research materials: The Maynard McFarlane Collection (AG 23) contains memorabilia and papers related to the invention and use of the Bartlane System of Picture Telegraphy invented by McFarlane and Harry Guy Bartholomew. Includes photographs, patents, clippings, and publications. (fraction of a linear foot)

Richard McGraw

1905, Sioux City, Iowa – 1978, Carmel, California

Photograph collection: 309 fine prints

Research materials: The Richard McGraw Archive (AG 59) holds personal papers, scrapbooks, clippings, publications, transparencies, negatives, a large number of study prints, stereo photographs, and photographic equipment of this Carmel-based photographer and patron of the arts. (ca. 34 linear feet)

Highlight: Correspondence with Ansel Adams, 1952–62, 1969–73, and with Edward Weston, 1950–53

McGraw Colorgraph Company
(ca. 1944–1969)

Research materials: The McGraw Colorgraph Collection (AG 22) documents the company, initially in business as Devin Colorgraph and then as Devin-McGraw, manufacturer of the Devin Tri-Color one-exposure camera and McGraw carbro color printing materials. Offers insight into the technique and process of tri-color carbro printing and the use of tricolor one-shot cameras, which were in use from the 1930s until they were superseded by Kodak's dye transfer process in the 1950s. The collection includes business and laboratory records, customer files, fine prints and work prints relating to the photographic processes, formulas, research programs, patents, and equipment used by the company in its production of carbro prints, tricolor commercial processing, and one-shot tricolor cameras. (ca. 37 linear feet)

Mildred Mead

b. [?] – d. 2000, Tucson, Arizona

Research materials: The Mildred Mead Collection (AG 179) contains biographical and photographic materials of this Chicago-based documentary photographer. Included are study prints, clippings, publications, and awards. Mead spent 20 years photographing Chicago for public and private agencies. The University of Chicago Library and the Chicago Historical Society have collections of her photographs, 1948 to 1959. (1 linear foot)

2385599

THE UNITED STATES OF AMERICA

TO ALL TO WHOM THESE PRESENTS SHALL COME:

Whereas JOSEPH ARTHUR BALL, of Los Angeles, and LAWRENCE PLOTIN, of North Hollywood, California, assignors to MAX McGRAW, doing business as McGRAW COLORGRAPH COMPANY, of Burbank, California,

PRESENTED TO THE **Commissioner of Patents** A PETITION PRAYING FOR THE GRANT OF LETTERS PATENT FOR AN ALLEGED NEW AND USEFUL IMPROVEMENT IN

COLOR PHOTOGRAPHY,

A DESCRIPTION OF WHICH INVENTION IS CONTAINED IN THE SPECIFICATION OF WHICH A COPY IS HEREUNTO ANNEXED AND MADE A PART HEREOF, AND COMPLIED WITH THE VARIOUS REQUIREMENTS OF LAW IN SUCH CASES MADE AND PROVIDED, AND **Whereas** UPON DUE EXAMINATION MADE THE SAID CLAIMANT s are ADJUDGED TO BE JUSTLY ENTITLED TO A PATENT UNDER THE LAW.

NOW THEREFORE THESE **Letters Patent** ARE TO GRANT UNTO THE SAID

Max McGraw, doing business as McGraw Colorgraph Company, his heirs

OR ASSIGNS

FOR THE TERM OF **SEVENTEEN** YEARS FROM THE DATE OF THIS GRANT

THE EXCLUSIVE RIGHT TO MAKE, USE AND VEND THE SAID INVENTION THROUGHOUT THE UNITED STATES AND THE TERRITORIES THEREOF.

In testimony whereof, I have hereunto set my hand and caused the seal of the Patent Office to be affixed at the City of Washington this twenty-fifth *day of* September, *in the year of our Lord one thousand nine hundred and* forty-five, *and of the Independence of the United States of America the one hundred and* seventieth.

Attest:

E. L. Reynolds
Law Examiner.

Casper W. Ooms
Commissioner of Patents.

Patent awarded to the McGraw Colorgraph Company for process to form color prints with color separation negatives and carbon tissue, 1945
McGraw Colorgraph Collection

Ralph Eugene Meatyard

15 May 1925, Normal, Illinois – 7 May 1972, Lexington, Kentucky

Photograph collection: 10 gelatin silver prints in *Portfolio Three: The Work of Ralph Eugene Meatyard*, 1974

Héctor M. Méndez Caratini

b. 1949, Puerto Rico

Photograph collection: 20 gelatin silver prints in portfolio, *Petriglifos de Boriquén*, 1978

Roger Mertin

9 December 1942, Bridgeport, Connecticut – 7 May 2001, Rochester, New York

Photograph collection: 11 fine prints

Alan D. Metnick

active 1960s – 1980s

Photograph collection: 27 fine prints, including lithographic portfolios: *Swingers*, 1973, and *Metnick, Ten Prints*, 1985, both from the Collection of Aaron Siskind

Pedro Meyer

b. 6 October 1935, Madrid, Spain

Photograph collection: 25 fine prints

Joel Meyerowitz

b. 6 March 1938, New York

Photograph collection: 28 fine prints

Research materials: Videotape of Meyerowitz commenting on a selection of Garry Winogrand's color transparencies and describing Winogrand's style of working on street photography is in the CCP Library.

Highlights: Portfolios: *French Portfolio*, 1983; *Toscana: Selected Images of Joel Meyerowitz*, ca. 1996.

J. M'Ghie

active ca. 1860s

Photograph collection: 35 albumen prints in album, *Photographs of Lanarkshire Scenery*, ca. 1870

Duane Michals

b. 18 February 1932, McKeesport, Pennsylvania

Photograph collection: 15 fine prints, including 13 in *Duane Michals: Album No. 8, December 7, 1976*

OTTO HAGEL OR HANSEL MIETH: *Automobile Graveyard*, 1937

Hansel Mieth

9 April 1909, Fellbach, Germany –
14 February 1998, Santa Rosa, California

Otto Hagel

12 March 1909, Fellbach, Germany –
8 January 1973, San Francisco, California

Photograph collection: ca. 2000 fine prints

Research materials: The Hansel Mieth/Otto Hagel Archive (AG 170) contains the photographic materials and personal papers of these two socially conscious photographers who lived and worked together from the time they were teenagers in their native Germany. Includes biographical documentation, correspondence, writings, exhibition materials, tear sheets, clippings, publications, and audiovisual materials. Correspondents include many photographers and people in the world of photojournalism such as Horace Bristol, Imogen Cunningham, Cornell Capa, Edward K. Thompson, John G. Morris, and Wilson Hicks. Breadth of subject matter is documented through seven decades of writings and their 150,000 negatives produced for *Life* magazine and other employers. Hagel's photographic essay *Men and Machines* documents the mechanization of the longshoreman's world. Other projects "We Return to Fellbach," "The Simple Life," and photographs of the Heart Mountain internment camp in Wyoming are also represented. (48.25 linear feet)

Rights and restrictions: Copyright to Mieth's and Hagel's writings and photographs is held by the Center for Creative Photography, The University of Arizona Foundation.

Tom Millea

b. 30 September 1944, Bridgeport, Connecticut

Photograph collection: 55 platinum/palladium prints

Roger Minick

b. 13 July 1944, Ramona, Oklahoma

Photograph collection: 46 fine prints

Highlights: 31 gelatin silver prints from group exhibition, *Espejo*, 1977–78; selections from the *Delta Portfolio* and the *Ozark Portfolio.*

Arno Rafael Minkkinen

b. 4 June 1945, Helsinki, Finland

Photograph collection: 41 fine prints, mostly in 2 copies of the portfolio, *White Underpants,* 1973

RICHARD MISRACH:
Playboy #90 (hole in mouth), 1990
From the series *Desert Canto XI: Violence (The playboys)*

Richard Misrach

b. 11 July 1949, Los Angeles, California

Photograph collection: 31 fine prints

Highlights: 12 dye transfer prints in portfolio, *Graecism*, 1982; 12 incorporated color coupler prints from the *Desert Cantos* series.

Kozo Miyoshi

b. 2 November 1947, Chiba, Japan

Photograph collection: 111 fine prints, including images from the series *Conservatory, Picture Show, Innocents, Chapel, Southwest (landscape), Southwest (humanscape), Roots <NE>, and Conservatory U.S.A.*

Highlight: While Miyoshi was a visiting artist in residence at the CCP from 1992 to 1996, he regularly made portraits of visiting scholars—John Szarkowski, Allan Sekula, Sally Stein, David Peeler, M. Darsie Alexander, David Levi Strauss, and Antonella Pelizzari—and visiting artists—Robert Heinecken, Paul and Linda McCartney.

CCP publication: *Far East and Southwest: The Photography of Kozo Miyoshi* (1994).

Lisette Model

10 November 1906, Vienna, Austria –
30 March 1983, New York

Photograph collection: 53 fine prints, including 40 vintage prints acquired as part of the Collection of Ansel and Virginia Adams, and portfolio *Lisette Model: Twelve Photographs*, 1977

CCP publication: "Lisette Model," *Center for Creative Photography* 4 (May 1977).

Tina Modotti

16 August 1896, Udine, Italy – 5 January 1942, Mexico City, Mexico

Photograph collection: 68 fine prints, 2 platinum. The attribution of 44 fine prints of murals and folk arts is uncertain; some may be by Weston; some have Modotti's stamp on the verso. 21 prints are from the Louis Bunin marionette series.

Research materials: The Edward Weston Archive (AG 38) is the CCP's richest source of information on Tina Modotti. It contains letters from Modotti plus fragments of letters and enclosures associated with the letters, a copy of her will in which she leaves her photographs to Weston, pressed flowers, original negatives of portraits of Modotti, and clippings spanning the years 1922–1931. Weston's original daybook manuscript of over 1000 pages and his scrapbooks contain references and ephemera related to Modotti. The Johan Hagemeyer Archive (AG 44) contains a few letters from Modotti and diary entries referring to meetings with Modotti in San Francisco in the late 1920s. The Louis Bunin Collection includes prints of the puppeteer's creations photographed by Modotti in the late 1920s. The Edward Weston Miscellaneous Acquisitions Collection (AG 6) contains a variety of letters and papers by and related to Modotti.

Highlights: 31 letters from Modotti to Weston. Weston's Mexico scrapbook documents Modotti's exhibitions with installation views and clippings.

CCP publication: "The Letters from Tina Modotti to Edward Weston," *The Archive* 22 (January 1986).

RUTHE MORAND:
Preparing Canal for Lining at Apache Junction, 1985
From the *Central Arizona Project Photographic Survey*

Ruthe Morand

b. 2 April 1953, Harrisburg, Pennsylvania

Photograph collection: 28 fine prints including a 12-part polyptych

Highlight: 21 gelatin silver prints made for the *Central Arizona Project Photographic Survey* project, 1985

Inge Morath

27 May 1923, Graz, Austria –
30 January 2002, New York

Photograph collection: 11 fine prints

Barbara Morgan

8 July 1900, Buffalo, New York – 17 August 1992, North Tarrytown, New York

Photograph collection: 12 fine prints

Research materials: Letters from Morgan illustrating her friendship and support are in the Robert Heinecken Archive (AG 45).

Highlights: Photomontages *Use the Litter Basket,* 1943, and *Spring in Madison Square,* 1938.

Charles W. Morris

1903 – 1979

Research materials: The Charles W. Morris Collection (AG 116) contains photocopies of correspondence and other documentation related to the New Bauhaus, American School of Design, Chicago, collected by Morris, one of the instructors. Included are letters from Laszlo Moholy-Nagy, class outlines, clippings, and original manuscripts. (1 linear foot)

Earl H. Morris

1889 – 1956

Photograph collection: 20 fine prints in *Earl H. Morris Photographic Portfolio,* 1985, printed by Billy Moore and Steve Fitch from original negatives, 1910–40, documenting archaeological work in the Southwest

John G. Morris

b. 1916

Research materials: The John G. Morris Collection (AG 127) contains the typescript of a lecture with slides dealing with his work as a photo editor for *Life, Washington Post, New York Times,* and Magnum. (fraction of a linear foot)

Wright Morris

6 January 1910, Central City, Nebraska – 25 April 1998, Mill Valley, California

Photograph collection: 13 fine prints

Brochure for Mortensen School of Photography, Laguna Beach, California, 1937
William Mortensen Archive

William Mortensen

27 January 1897, Park City, Utah –
12 August 1965, Laguna Beach, California

Photograph collection: 294 prints including bromoil transfers, pigment prints, photogravures, Metalchromes, and gelatin silver prints

Research materials: The William Mortensen Archive (AG 147) holds a wide variety of papers and photographic materials, 1890s–1986, related to Mortensen, photographer, teacher, and author. The bulk of the collection dates from 1950 to 1965, and includes biographical incoming and outgoing correspondence with publishers, personal letters, family photographs, clippings, tear sheets, documentation about the Mortensen School of Photography, Mortensen's student sketchbooks, and posthumous correspondence between his widow and biographers and researchers, including Deborah Irmas and Robert Balcomb. Documentation of the 1979 retrospective exhibition *The Photographic Magic of William Mortensen* is also included. (ca. 18 linear feet)

The Mortensen/Dunham Collection (AG 43), acquired from the estate of George Dunham (1896–1976), friend, frequent model, collaborator, and co-author, is another rich source of information about Mortensen. The bulk of this collection consists of 37 original manuscripts of Mortensen's writings, ca. 1933 to 1965, some with handwritten annotations or corrections. It also includes tear sheets, publications, and work prints of figure and landscape studies. (3.5 linear feet)

Additional information on Mortensen as well as additional fine prints are found in collections acquired from students of Mortensen: Robert Balcomb (AG 180), Fritz Kaeser (AG 86), and Grey Silva (AG 134). Researchers also can consult the Adolf Fassbender Archive (AG 168) for information about an East Coast pictorialist who established his own school and curriculum.

Highlights: 2 portfolios: 17 gelatin silver prints in *Pictorial Photography*, ca. 1935; and 25 gelatin silver prints in an undated, untitled portfolio. Early drawings and engravings done by Mortensen while a student in New York, ca. 1917. Original, annotated manuscript drafts of Mortensen's many books and articles. Small work prints from the 1920s illustrating Mortensen's multiple printing techniques, thematic investigations, use of elaborate tableaux, and work on Hollywood movie sets.

CCP publication: "William Mortensen: A Revival," *The Archive* 33 (1998).

Workprints from multiple negatives, annotated by Mortensen
Gray Silva Archive

STEFAN MOSES:
Krabbenfischer, Travemunde, 1963–64
From the series *Deutsch*

Stefan Moses

b. 29 August 1928, Liegnitz, Silesia (now Legnica, Poland)

Photograph collection: 98 fine prints from *Deutsche* series, 1963–64

David Muench

b. 25 June 1936, Santa Barbara, California

Research materials: The David Muench Collection (AG 178) contains a nearly complete set of the books he has published since 1970.

Eadweard Muybridge

9 April 1830, Kingston-on-Thames, England – 8 May 1904, Kingston-on-Thames, England

Photograph collection: 119 albumen prints, 100 in album, plus 10 modern albumen prints in *Eadweard Muybridge, Yosemite Photographs 1872* (Chicago Albumen Works, 1977). Also includes 8 stereoviews from the Virginia Adams Stereoview Collection and a self-portrait of 36 poses, plate 521 from *Animal Locomotion* (1887)

Highlight: One of only 8 known versions (each one unique) of album, *Photographic Studies of Central America and the Isthmus of Panama*, 1876. Title page: *The Pacific Coast of Central America and Mexico: The Isthmus of Panama; Guatemala; and the Cultivation and Shipment of Coffee.*

Nagatani and Tracey

Patrick Nagatani

b. 19 August 1945, Chicago, Illinois

Andrée Tracey

b. 1948, La Jolla, California

Photograph collection: 41 Polaroid 20x24-inch prints, many of them diptychs and triptychs, created collaboratively; more than half were shown in 2001 at the CCP exhibition *Nagatani/ Tracey Collaboration, 1983–1989*

Research materials: Printed materials related to the collaborations between Nagatani and Tracey. Includes exhibition catalogs, announcements, and brochures, magazines, newspaper clippings, installation photographs, views of the artists at work, artifacts, and videotapes. (1 linear foot)

HANS NAMUTH:
Marcos Pablo Jeronimo, 57 Years Old, Bagmaker and Carpenter, 1978
From the series *Todos Santos Cuchumatán*

Hans Namuth

17 March 1915, Essen, Germany –
13 October 1990, East Hampton, New York

Photograph collection: 18 fine prints, 9 of them posthumous exhibition prints created in 1995; extensive print files are on extended loan to the CCP

Rights and restrictions: Copyright of Namuth's photographs is managed for the Hans Namuth Estate by the Center for Creative Photography.

Enrico Natali

b. 10 August 1933, Utica, New York

Photograph collection: 30 fine prints, 26 from the *Subway* series

Carlo Naya

1816, Tronzano Vercellese, Italy –
29 May 1882, Venice, Italy

Photograph collection: 12 albumen prints

Joyce Neimanas

b. 22 January 1944, Chicago, Illinois

Photographic collections: 22 fine prints, including photograms and altered gelatin silver prints; one print is a collaboration with Robert Heinecken

Research materials: The Joyce Neimanas Collection (AG 174) contains biographical and manuscript materials related to her career and marriage to Robert Heinecken. (1 linear foot)

ESTA NESBITT: *Selenium Songs*, 1972

Esta Nesbitt

19 November 1918, New York –
30 November 1975, New York

Photograph collection: approximately 120 art works

Research materials: The Esta Nesbitt Collection (AG 60) holds documentation of the career of this teacher, performance artist, photographer, book artist, and trailblazing xerographic artist. Included are records of her exhibitions, such as the 1973 exhibition *Xerography—Extensions in Art* and the performance piece *Walk Up Tape-On*. (3 linear feet)

Bea Nettles

b. 17 October 1946, Gainesville, Florida

Photograph collection: 31 fine prints, including Kwik prints, collages, and cyanotypes

Highlights: Artist's books, *Bruises and Other Collections* (1970) and *Escape* (1972).

Floris M. Neusüss

b. 3 March 1937, Lennep, Germany

Photograph collection: 30 fine prints, studies of life-size photograms, 1960s to 1980s

Beaumont and Nancy Newhall

Beaumont Newhall

22 June 1908, Lynn, Massachusetts –
26 February 1993, Santa Fe, New Mexico

Nancy Wynne Newhall

9 May 1908, Swampscott, Massachusetts –
7 July 1974, Jackson Hole, Wyoming

Photograph collection: 20 fine prints by
Beaumont Newhall; 9 fine prints by Nancy
Newhall

Research materials: The Beaumont and Nancy
Newhall Collection (AG 48) holds correspondence, writings, and subject files, 1930–1983,
related to the careers of these two writers,
curators, and photographers. Included is
incoming correspondence from many noted
photographers such as Ansel Adams and
Edward Weston. The bulk of the collection
relates to Nancy's career and includes letters
and published and unpublished manuscripts
concerning Ansel Adams, such as *Death Valley*
(1953), *The Eloquent Light* (1963), and "The
Enduring Moment" (ca. 1971), the unfinished
second volume of Adams's biography. Some
manuscripts for Beaumont's writings, such as
Photography: Essays and Images (1980) and
his revised and enlarged edition of *The History
of Photography* (1982) are included. (9.5 linear
feet)

The Beaumont Newhall Miscellaneous
Acquisitions Collection (AG125) contains a
variety of materials acquired from many
sources. (fraction of a linear foot)

Highlights: Of particular interest is the 243-
page photocopy of Beaumont's typed class
notes from his Harvard course in "Museum
Work and Museum Problems" taught by Paul
Sachs, 1930. Voluminous files of letters from
Ansel Adams are included and complement
the corresponding letters from the Newhalls,
found in the Ansel Adams Archive.

Related information: Additional references to
the Newhalls can be found in: Paul Strand
Collection (AG 17), Edward Weston Archive
(AG 38), Wynn Bullock Archive (AG 10), and
others. The Images and Words Collection (AG
121) holds materials regarding the Images and
Words workshop taught by the Newhalls, Ansel
Adams, and Robert Katz at the University of
California, Santa Cruz in the summer of 1967.
The Newhall archive is at the Getty Research
Institute, Getty Center, Los Angeles, California.

Arnold Newman

b. 3 March 1918, New York

Photograph collection: 24 fine prints

Nineteenth-Century Photographic Formats

Research materials: The CCP holds a small but
interesting selection of nineteenth-century
photographic formats including daguerreotypes, tintypes, ambrotypes, cartes de visite,
cabinet cards, and over 700 stereoviews.

Lorie Novak

b. 1954, Los Angeles, California

Photograph collection: 31 incorporated color coupler prints mounted on Plexiglas, most acquired for 2001 exhibition *Lorie Novak: Photographs, 1983–2000*

P. H. Oelman

7 July 1880, Dayton, Ohio – 7 August 1957, Cincinnati, Ohio

Photograph collection: 12 fine prints in two portfolios, both titled *Nudes,* ca. 1940s

---

Arthur E. Ojeda

1901 – 1985

Research materials: The Arthur E. Ojeda Collection (AG 122) contains biographical materials documenting the career of Ojeda, businessman and stereophotographer. Included are articles published by the Photographic Society of America, 1984 to 1985, and one obituary. (fraction of a linear foot)

Oracle Conference

Research materials: The Oracle Conference is an international group of photography museum professionals that has met in annual conference since 1983. Taking its name from the location of its first meeting at the University of Arizona's Oracle Conference Center north of Tucson, the venue for the conference has changed yearly. The Oracle Conference Collection (AG 110) holds records and documentation of the conferences, including lists of attendees, conference schedules, and topics of discussion. (fraction of a linear foot)

Ted Orland

b. 1941, San Francisco, California

Photograph collection: 11 fine prints

Timothy H. O'Sullivan

1840?, New York – 14 January 1882, Staten Island, New York

Photograph collection: 34 albumen prints

Highlights: Prints are from the Wheeler surveys of 1871 and 1873–74. Album of 25 albumen prints (7 by William Bell) titled *Photographs Showing Landscapes, Geological and Other Features, of Portions of the Western Territory of the United States* was acquired with the Collection of Ansel and Virginia Adams.

Bill Owens

b. 25 September 1938, San Jose, California

Photograph collection: 10 fine prints, including *Bill Owens Portfolio,* 1977

Pacific Press Service

Research materials: The Pacific Press Service Collection (AG 141) contains the *Spectrum* portfolio issued in 1990 to celebrate the 25th anniversary of the Pacific Press Service with 10 halftone plates of photographs by Hiroshi Hamaya, Tadahiko Hayasaki, Eikoh Hosoe, Takeji Iwamiya, Takeshi Mizokoshi, Ikko Narahara, Kazuyoshi Nomachi, Akira Sato, Teiji Saga, and Yoshio Watanabe.

MARION PALFI:
Chaim Gross—Working in His Studio Alone, 1944
From the series *Great American Artists of Minority Groups*

Marion Palfi

21 October 1907, Berlin, Germany –
4 November 1978, Los Angeles, California

Photograph collection: 1133 fine prints

Research materials: The Marion Palfi Archive (AG 46) documents her activities as a photographer, teacher, researcher, and social critic during the period from 1945 to 1978. There is little documentation of her first career in Germany as an actress, model, and dancer, but once she immigrated to the United States, information about her career increases. The collection contains correspondence between Palfi and friends, photographers, scholars, writers, publishers, and governmental and private institutions on subjects ranging through personal matters, her philosophy of using photography to influence social change, her sales of photographs, and her often unsuccessful efforts to publish her work. Correspondents include Langston Hughes, Eleanor Roosevelt, and Edward Steichen. Activity files contain biographical and exhibition information, correspondence, brochures, handwritten and typed

manuscripts, articles, books, catalogs, clippings, résumés, scrapbooks, research notes, and other items. Project files contain letters, field notes, draft manuscripts, and book maquettes. Photographic materials include negatives, contact sheets, and study prints. (51 linear feet)

The Marion Palfi Miscellaneous Acquisitions Collection (AG 130) contains a variety of materials acquired from different sources. Of special note are documents about Palfi obtained from the United States government through the Freedom of Information Act.

Related information: The CCP holds the archives of a number of European artists who immigrated to the United States before and during World War II: Josef Breitenbach, Andreas Feininger, John Gutmann, Otto Hagel and Hansel Mieth, Hans Namuth.

CCP publications: "Marion Palfi," *The Archive* 19 (1983); "Marion Palfi Archive," *Guide Series* 10 (1985).

MIICKEY PALLAS: *Sugar Ray Robinson and Abe Saperstein, Paris*, n.d.

Mickey Pallas

21 March 1916, Belvidere, Illinois –
8 August 1997, Scottsdale, Arizona

Photograph collection: 90 fine prints

Research materials: The Mickey Pallas Archive (AG 145) contains biographical materials, correspondence, publications, awards, memorabilia, exhibition files, financial papers, catalogs, and audiovisual materials related to Pallas's career as a photographer in the Chicago area. Also documented are Pallas's businesses—Gamma Photo labs, the Center for Photographic Arts, and Pallas Photographica Gallery. The bulk of the collection consists of study prints, photographs, and negatives. (45 linear feet)

Highlights: Nearly complete set of proof prints made by assistant Janet Ginsburg; and index to subject matter created by CCP staff.

Rights and restrictions: Copyright to Pallas's photographs is held by the Center for Creative Photography, The University of Arizona Foundation.

Igor Palmin

b. 1933, Russia

Photograph collection: 10 fine prints

Richard Pare

b. 20 January 1948, Portsmouth, England

Photograph collection: 10 fine prints, including a 9-part polyptych

Ann Parker

b. 6 March 1934, London, England

Photograph collection: 40 fine prints

Highlights: 30 prints from portfolio, *Itinerant Images of Guatemala*, 1983; gravestone rubbing made in collaboration with Avon Neal.

Fred R. Parker

b. 11 June 1938, Compton, California

Photograph collections: 10 cliché-verre gelatin silver prints in portfolio, *Connotations*, 1984–85

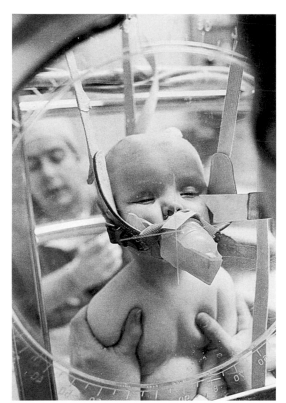

MITCHELL PAYNE: Untitled, 1970–72
From the series *Neurosurgeons in Action*

Mitchell Payne

31 March 1944, Shawnee Mission, Kansas –
19 August 1977, Kansas

Photograph collection: approximately 500 fine prints

Research materials: The Mitchell Payne Collection (AG 49) documents both Payne's student and professional photography in Rochester, New York, and San Francisco, from ca. 1940 to 1977. Included are personal papers, biographical information, project files, negatives, transparencies, dye transfer materials, and study prints for the projects *Strippers* (1968–1970), *Lisa* (1969–1972), *Hospital Pictures* (1970–1972), *High School Youth* (1973–1975), *Tammy* (1973–1976), and *American Snapshots*. (6 linear feet)

Brian C. Pelletier

b. 1941, Newport, Rhode Island

Photograph collection: 12 gelatin silver prints in portfolio, *Twelve Old Photographs: New Prints Made from Negatives Three-Quarters of a Century Old*, 1970.

Gilles Peress

b. 29 December 1946, Paris

Photograph collection: 12 fine prints in portfolio *Flashpoints: Selected Images of Gilles Peress*, ca. 1996

Leon Pescheret

b. [?] – 1971

Research materials: The Leon Pescheret Collection (AG 92) contains photographic materials and equipment of stereophotographer Pescheret. Includes 6 cases of stereo slides and one stereo projector. (3 linear feet)

Thomas Petrillo

b. 3 February 1949, McKees Rock, Pennsylvania

Photograph collection: 10 gelatin silver stereoviews in handmade book, *Mound: Ten Views*, ca. 1975

John Pfahl

b. 17 February 1939, New York

Photograph collection: 56 fine prints, including 48 dye transfer prints in portfolio, *Altered Landscapes: The Photographs of John Pfahl*, 1981

The Philadelphia Photographer

Photograph collection: 10 volumes of this journal, 1867 to 1875, illustrated with 11 fine prints, mostly albumen, by I. W. Taber, J. H. Kent, and others

Photographic Literature

Research material: The Photographic Literature Collection (AG 82) contains ephemeral publications from a wide variety of sources. Included are brochures, manuals, and leaflets about camera, film, lenses, and photographic technique published by Agfa, Kodak, Rollei, Zeiss and many other companies. (4 file drawers)

Photographic Mats

Research material: The Photographic Mat Collection (AG 100) contains vintage mats and trimmed mat board from photographs in the CCP photograph collection. These mats were separated from their original prints when photographic conservation was carried out.

Signatures of artists, quality of original paper stock, and exhibition labels are of interest.

Ave Pildas

b. 16 September 1939, Cincinnati, Ohio

Photograph collection: 12 gelatin silver prints in portfolio, *Bijou: 12 L. A. Box Offices*, 1975

Sylvia Plachy

b. 24 May 1943, Budapest, Hungary

Photograph collection: 14 fine prints created for *Indivisible: Stories of American Community*, 2000

Bernard Plossu

b. 26 February 1945, Dalat, South Vietnam

Photograph collection: 122 fine prints

Research materials: The Bernard Plossu Collection (AG 71) contains letters, writings, exhibition announcements, clippings, and publications documenting the artist's personal life and career. (3 linear feet)

Highlights: 52 gelatin silver prints used in the production of Plossu's book *The African Desert* (1987).

David Plowden

b. 9 October 1932, Boston, Massachusetts

Photograph collection: 66 fine prints

Alan Pogue

b. 3 April 1946, Corpus Christi, Texas

Photograph collection: 20 fine prints in portfolio, *Agricultural Workers of the Rio Grande and Rio Bravo Valleys*, 1984

Peter Pollack

21 March 1909, Wing, North Dakota –
13 May 1978

Photograph collection: 12 fine prints, portraits of Mexican artists

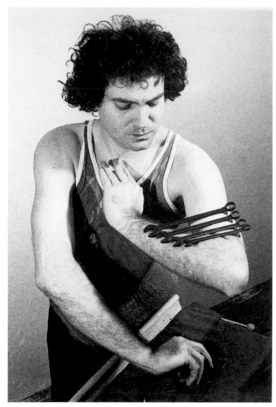

YURA ADAMS:
Jim Pomeroy, Performing Mechanics Music, 1979
Jim Pomeroy Archive

Jim Pomeroy

21 March 1945, Reading, Pennsylvania –
6 April 1992, Arlington, Texas

Photograph collection: 9 prints from *It's Only a Baby Moon* series, 1983–90; and additional art works as yet uncataloged

Research materials: The Jim Pomeroy Archive (AG 155) contains the personal papers and photographic materials of Pomeroy, a photographer and performance artist who worked in a wide variety of media incorporating sound, motion, optical effects, computer and photographic technology. Included are biographical materials and portraits of the artist in his various personae; sketches and plans for installations; clippings, publications, and reviews; slide sets; objects collected and sometimes used in installations; and a large collection of artists'

books and books about performance art. (180 linear feet)

Related information: The Bender/Nordby Collection contains documentation of multimedia installation art in the 1970s.

C. L. Pond

ca. 1832, New York [state] – 7 June 1891, Buffalo, New York

Photograph collection: 53 stereoviews, from the Virginia Adams Stereoview Collection

Postcard [original in color], *Assassination Site - John F. Kennedy, November 22, 1963. Dealey Plaza; Dallas, Texas.* © 1981 A. W. Distributors
Postcard Collection

Eliot Porter

6 December 1901, Winnetka, Illinois –
2 November 1990, Santa Fe, New Mexico

Photograph collection: 29 fine prints

Highlights: Portfolios, 12 dye transfer prints in *Portfolio Two: Iceland,* 1975; 8 dye transfer prints in *Birds in Flight,*1978.

Related information: The Eliot Porter archive is held by the Amon Carter Museum, Fort Worth, Texas.

Postcards

Research materials: The Postcard Collection contains hundreds of examples of photographic imagery in postcard format from the mid-nineteenth century to the present day. Items are arranged primarily geographically and, when appropriate, by subject matter including headings such as jokes, politics, restaurants, hotels, artworks, transportation, and events. The collection was begun by Harold Jones, the CCP's first director, and since then has been acquired from a variety of sources.

CHARLES PRATT: *Roxbury, Connecticut*, 1964

Charles Pratt

13 April 1926, New York – 25 May 1976, New York

Photograph collection: 87 fine prints and many study prints

Research materials: The Charles Pratt Archive (AG 133) contains personal papers and photographic materials, 1950–1976, from the career of Charles Pratt. Includes extensive files of photographs, negatives, transparencies, and contact sheets documenting the artist's numerous exhibition and book projects, including *At Night*, *Here on the Island: Being an Account of a Way of Life Several Miles Off the Maine Coast*, and *The Garden and the Wilderness*. Among the correspondents in this collection are Beaumont Newhall, Ralph Steiner, Lisette Model, David Vestal, and Lilo Raymond. (24 linear feet)

Highlights: Letters from Rachel Carson, whose influential books *A Sense of Wonder* and *Rocky Coast*, were illustrated by Pratt.

Doug Prince

b. 2 January 1943, Des Moines, Iowa

Photograph collection: 12 fine prints

Herb Quick

b. 7 November 1925, Manistique, Michigan

Photograph collection: 34 fine prints

Achille Quinet

1831 – 1900

Photograph collection: 40 albumen prints in album, *Paris en photographies*, ca. 1860s

T. Rago

b. ca. 1927

Photograph collection: 24 fine prints, from the collections of Harry Callahan and Aaron Siskind

Eli Reed

b. 4 August 1946, Linden, New Jersey

Photograph collection: 18 fine prints created for *Indivisible: Stories of American Community*, 2000

Linda Rich

b. 9 August 1949

Photograph collection: 21 fine prints in hand-made book, *I Do* (1975); 18 fine prints in handmade book, *Skin Deep* (1973)

Walter Rosenblum

b. 1 October 1919, New York

Photograph collection: 14 fine prints

Donald Ross

10 March 1912, Oakland, California – 4 June 1999, San Pablo, California

Photograph collection: 98 fine prints

Arthur Rothstein

17 July 1915, New York – 11 November 1985, New Rochelle, New York

Photograph collection: 83 fine prints

Highlights: Portfolios, *Arthur Rothstein*, 1981, and *A Portfolio of Photographs by Arthur Rothstein*, 1983.

Steve Rowles

Photograph collection: 10 fine prints in untitled portfolio, n.d.

Yolla Niclas Sachs

24 February ca. 1915, Berlin, Germany – December 1977, Manchester, Connecticut

Photograph collection: 34 fine prints

Philippe Salaün

b. 4 March 1943, Plonevez-du-Faou, France

Photograph collection: 26 fine prints, including 10 in untitled portfolio, ca. 1978

Mario Samarughi

Italy, active 1970s – 80s

Photograph collection: 10 Cibachrome prints, from the Collection of Aaron Siskind

---

Jesús Sánchez Uribe

b. 24 August 1928, Mexico City, Mexico

Photograph collection: 15 fine prints, from the collections of W. Eugene Smith and Aaron Siskind

---

A. C. Santos

Photograph collection: 15 albumen prints of the Madeira Islands, ca. 1900, from the Julia F. Corson Collection

NAOMI SAVAGE: *Roman Profile*, 1969–80

Naomi Savage

b. 25 June 1927, Princeton, New Jersey

Photograph collection: Approximately 60 fine prints including gum prints, photo-intaglio prints, and photo-engravings

Highlight: 8 gelatin silver prints in *Portfolio No. XVI*, 1980.

JOHN P. SCHAEFER:
St. Anthony and the Christ Child, Mission San Xavier del Bac, Tucson, Arizona, 1977
From the portfolio *Bac: Where the Waters Gather*

John P. Schaefer

b. 17 September 1934, New York

Photograph collection: 44 fine prints, including some in platinum

Research materials: The John P. Schaefer Collection (AG 27) contains manuscript materials related to the publication of *Bac: Where the Waters Gather*.

Highlights: 14 gelatin silver prints in portfolio, *Bac: Where the Waters Gather*, 1977.

David Scheinbaum

b. 1951, Brooklyn, New York

Photograph collection: 11 fine prints, including 10 in *Portfolio One, Bisti*, 1985

Diana Schoenfeld

b. 3 September 1949, Knoxville, Tennessee

Photograph collection: 15 fine prints in bound portfolio, *Illusory Arrangements*, 1978

J. Keith Schreiber

b. 13 August 1959, New Orleans, Louisiana

Photograph collection: 10 prints, mostly palladium panoramas of Alaska

George H. Seeley

1880, Stockbridge, Massachusetts –
1955, Stockbridge, Massachusetts

Photograph collection: 12 prints, mostly plates from *Camera Work*, and 1 self-portrait attributed to him

John Sexton

b. 22 May 1953, Maywood, California

Photograph collection: 25 fine prints

David Seymour (Chim)

20 November 1911, Warsaw, Poland –
10 November 1956, Suez, Egypt

Photograph collection: 12 prints in portfolio, *David Seymour, Chim*, 1982

Toshio Shibata

b. 1949, Tokyo, Japan

Photograph collection: 10 fine prints

Stephen Shore

b. 8 October 1947, New York

Photograph collection: 24 fine prints

Research materials: The Stephen Shore Collection (AG 50) contains papers and publications relating to Shore's career, 1973 to 1978. (2.5 linear feet)

Irene Shwachman

30 July 1915, New York – August 1988

Research materials: The Irene Shwachman Archive (AG 91) contains correspondence, monographs, book maquettes, writings, clippings, book project materials, exhibition files, negatives, transparencies, proof prints, and contact sheets, ca. 1930–1988. Photographer and book artist Shwachman is known for her *Boston Document*, extensively documenting portions of the city before they were destroyed by urban renewal over the period 1959–68. Her artist's books include *Temple of Knowledge* (1980), *Photography for Girls* (1982), *We Grew Up in Manhattan: Notes for an autobiography* (1984), and *Now You Know: This Is Serious Photography* (1987).

Highlight: Shwachman kept a journal recording her long friendship with Berenice Abbott. That journal, maintained over the period 1959–1986, contains much material related to Abbott's photography and writing, as well as materials concerning photographic exhibitions at the Carl Siembab Gallery in Boston.

Arthur Siegel

2 August 1913, Detroit, Michigan –
1 February 1978, Chicago, Illinois

Photograph collection: 11 fine prints

Grey Silva

23 July 1911 – 1 May 1997

Photograph collection: approximately 400 fine prints

Research materials: The Grey Silva Collection (AG 134) contains materials documenting Silva's career and that of his teacher, William Mortensen. It includes correspondence, publications, technical notes, exhibition and salon records, Silva's negatives, proof prints, and fine prints. His friendship with Mortensen is documented through copies of Mortensen's books, original work prints, and finished fine prints. Silva, who made his home in San Diego, was an active member of the Photographic Society of America. He was also an authority on the processes used by Mortensen, particularly the Metalchrome process, about which he wrote and published several articles. (15 linear feet)

Highlights: Mortensen's original instructions on the Metalchrome process and Silva's notes on that technique.

Related information: Additional materials on the life and work of William Mortensen are found in the William Mortensen Archive (AG 147), the William Mortensen/George Dunham Collection (AG 43), the Ben Maxey Collection (AG 112), and the Robert Balcomb Collection (AG 180).

Vivienne Silver

Research materials: The Vivienne Silver Collection (AG 106) contains 19 audiocassettes of interviews taped by Silver in 1979 for her master's thesis on Manuel Alvarez Bravo. Also includes typescripts with annotations. (fraction of a linear foot)

ANN SIMMONS-MYERS:
Blast Foreman Trey Gardner with Blasting Compound at Site of Picacho Pumping Plant, 1984
From the *Central Arizona Project Photographic Survey*

Ann Simmons-Myers

b. 10 July 1953, Berkeley, California

Photograph collection: 37 fine prints

Highlight: 29 prints from the *Central Arizona Project Photographic Survey*, 1984–85.

Roland Sinclair

active 1960s

Photograph collection: 15 fine prints

Clara Sipprell

31 October 1885, Tillsonburg, Ontario, Canada – 15 April 1975, Bennington, Vermont

Photograph collection: 59 fine prints, including some photogravures and platinum prints

Highlights: 40 portraits of Peter Strauss Kaufman in album, *Portraits of Peter*, 1927–31.

AARON SISKIND: *Harlem*, 1940
From the *Harlem Document*, 1932–40

Aaron Siskind

4 December 1903, New York – 8 February
1991, Providence, Rhode Island

Photograph collection: 904 fine prints

Research materials: The Aaron Siskind Archive
(AG 30) contains the artist's personal papers,
photographic materials, audiovisual materials,
and memorabilia, ca. 1925–1991. It includes
correspondence with other photographers,
curators, writers, friends, and family; handwritten and typed drafts of writings; exhibition and
business files; materials related to the Photo
League; publications files including book dum-
mies, galleys, and proof prints; photographic
materials including contact sheets, negatives,
work prints, and transparencies; audiovisual
material including film, video, and audiotaped
interviews; and memorabilia relating to his
career. (ca. 50 linear feet)

**The Aaron Siskind Miscellaneous Acquisitions
Collection** (AG 26) contains a variety of materials from various sources. It includes correspondence, research materials, and publications.
(1 linear foot)

Highlights: notes from meetings of the Photo
League along with story assignments.

Related information: Other collections at the
CCP that offer insight into Siskind's work and
relationships with other photographers include:
Harry Callahan Archive (AG 29), Max Yavno
Archive (AG 136), Frederick Sommer Archive
(AG 28), Barbara Crane Archive (AG 176), and
Carl Chiarenza Collection (AG 87).

The Collection of Aaron Siskind includes 870
fine prints, including 14 group portfolios from
the Rhode Island School of Design, and photographs by Antonio A. Fernandez, Lewis
Kostiner, Arno Rafael Minkkinen, Gus Kayafas,
Todd Walker, Charles Swedlund, Jesús Sánchez
Uribe, Alex Traube, and many others.

CCP publication: "Aaron Siskind and His
Critics," *Center for Creative Photography* 7/8
(September 1978)

Neal Slavin

b. 19 August 1941, Brooklyn, New York

Photograph collection: 43 fine prints

Highlights: 39 prints from *Espejo* project, ca. 1978

Scott L. Slobodian

b. ca. 1942

Photograph collection: 10 fine prints in portfolio, . . . *And a Whole World Dwelleth by the Sea*, n.d.

Herbert Small

1913 [?] – 1978 [?]

Photograph collection: Small's personal photograph collection includes *Camera Work* numbers 8, 11–13, 39, and 46 as well as nearly 100 images by a variety of photographers including Alfred Stieglitz, Gertrude Käsebier, Judy Dater, Kathryn Paul, and Karen Truax.

Research materials: The Herbert Small Collection (AG 4) contains materials from the Stieglitz and Small families, including a Stieglitz family genealogy, a biography of Alfred Stieglitz's younger brother Julius Oscar Stieglitz (1867–1937), and family photographs. Herbert Fedor Small (1881–1931), the father of the donor, was a friend and younger cousin of Alfred Stieglitz (1864–1946). (1.5 linear feet)

Highlight: 12 small photographs, taken ca. 1896–99, by Alfred Stieglitz showing New York streets following a snowstorm, on Easter Sunday, and several other street scenes.

Related information: Stieglitz photographs in the Small Collection were published in "Alfred Stieglitz: Photographs from the Herbert Small Collection," *Center for Creative Photography* 6 (April 1978).

Henry Holmes Smith

23 October 1909, Bloomington, Illinois – 24 March 1986, Marin County, California

Photograph collection: 43 fine prints, including many dye transfers and photosilkscreens

Research materials: The Henry Holmes Smith Archive (AG 32) holds correspondence, writings, research files, activity files, audiotapes, and photographic materials, 1920s–1980s. The bulk of the collection consists of personal papers documenting Smith's career as an educator at the New Bauhaus School (Chicago), his long tenure at Indiana University (Bloomington), his activities as a founding member of the Society for Photographic Education, his relationships with colleagues in the field of photographic education, and his participation in numerous conferences and workshops. Included are manuscripts and revisions of articles, his writings for *Minicam* magazine, transcripts of lectures, and records of the Photographer's Exhibition Service, a project to encourage exhibitions and exchanges of information within the photographic community. There is also information on the exhibition and sale of his early paintings, drawings, and cartoons; texts for his short stories and poems; biographical information; and reference files on photography. (19 linear feet)

Highlights: 12 dye transfer prints in the *Royal Pair* series; 10 gelatin silver prints in portfolio, *Henry Holmes Smith*, 1973; copies of Smith's short stores, poems, and cartoons, some of which were sold to *The New Yorker* magazine.

Related information: The Charles Morris Collection (AG 116) contains catalogs and course outlines from the New Bauhaus in Chicago, where Smith taught in 1937–38. The Neil E. Matthew Collection (AG 131) contains materials from Smith's courses at Indiana University in the 1950s. The archive of the Society for Photographic Education (AG 78) contains references to his involvement.

CCP publications: "Henry Holmes Smith: Selected Critical Articles," *Center for Creative Photography* 5 (October 1977); "Henry Holmes Smith Papers," *Guide Series* 8 (1983).

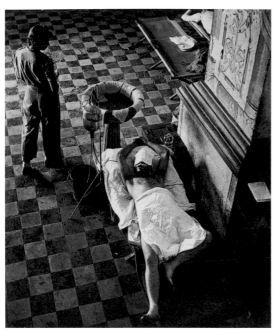

W. EUGENE SMITH:
*Holy Water Font in Leyte Cathedral, Used as
  Hospital*, 1944
From "Hospital on Leyte"

W. Eugene Smith

30 December 1918, Wichita, Kansas –
15 October 1978, Tucson, Arizona

Photograph collection: approximately 3500
fine prints and hundreds of study prints

Research materials: The W. Eugene Smith
Archive (AG 33) holds personal papers, audiovisual materials, and photographic materials,
1910–78, documenting the life and career of
this photojournalist. The bulk of the collection
consists of photographic essay project files,
activity files, correspondence, writings, financial records, and exhibition files from 1935 to
1978. They document Smith's work as photographer for *Life* magazine, Black Star Publishing,
Magnum, and other agencies; his extensive
freelance projects; membership in the Photo
League; his writings and project materials
including layouts and revisions; his exhibitions;
and his educational activities. Smith's own
paintings and his tape recordings of jazz ses-
sions in his New York loft are also included. His
extensive files of photographs, study prints,

contact sheets, negatives, and transparencies
represent his entire career. The collection also
includes some camera and darkroom equipment and photographic materials from Smith's
mother, Nettie Lee Smith (ca.1890–1955).
(300 linear feet)

**The W. Eugene Smith Miscellaneous
Acquisitions Collection** (AG 79) contains
various materials about Smith's life and career
received from diverse sources. Included are
correspondence, manuscripts about Smith,
publications, photographic materials, audiovisual
materials, clippings, materials related to the
book and exhibition *Let Truth Be the Prejudice*
(1985), and notes and maquette for William
Johnson's book *W. Eugene Smith: Master of
the Photographic Essay* (1981). (3.5 linear feet)

Highlights: Maquettes documenting Smith's
efforts over many years to create his definitive
book project, *The Big Book*; paintings, plays,
short stories, and poems by Smith; many portraits of Smith from childhood through his last
years.

Related information: The Ben Maddow
Collection (AG 108) contains letters and other
writings concerning Smith. The Robert Harrah
Collection (AG 54) contains information about
the "Country Doctor" essay.

CCP publications: "W. Eugene Smith: Early
Work," *Center for Creative Photography* 12
(July 1980); "W. Eugene Smith: Middle Years,"
The Archive 20 (July 1984). "W. Eugene Smith:
A Chronological Bibliography 1934–1980, Part
II," by William S. Johnson (*Bibliography Series*
1, 1981). [Part I was included in *Center for
Creative Photography Photography* 12 (1980)].
"W. Eugene Smith: A Chronological Bibliography
1934–1980, Addendum," by William S. Johnson
(*Bibliography Series* 1, 1981).

Society for Photographic Education

The Society for Photographic Education (SPE) was founded in 1963 as a nonprofit, professional organization with the goal of supporting teachers of photography. The organization is concerned with the practice, analysis and history of photography and related media as means for creative expression. SPE membership includes all areas of the photographic community, including teachers, collectors, archivists, critics, curators, historians, and gallery directors.

Research materials: The SPE Archive (AG 78) holds records for the organization from 1963 to date. These materials include correspondence, minutes of board and executive committee meetings, treasurer's reports, budgets, questionnaires, membership files and directories, conference materials, and national and regional publications, including the SPE quarterly journal *Exposure*. The bulk of the material documents the period 1975–91. (32 linear feet)

Related information: The CCP also holds other collections on photographers and educators who have long been active in SPE. These include the papers of Henry Holmes Smith (AG 32), one of the founding members of SPE, and whose collection contains materials concerning the process through which SPE was created; Robert Heinecken; Harold Jones, and others.

Rosalind Solomon

b. 2 April 1930, Highland Park, Illinois

Photograph collection: 41 fine prints

FREDERICK SOMMER: Untitled, 1991

Frederick Sommer

7 September 1905, Angri, Italy – 23 January 1999, Prescott, Arizona

Photograph collection: 88 fine prints

Research materials: The Frederick Sommer Archive (AG 28) holds the personal papers and photographic materials of Sommer, photographer, writer, and designer. Included in the papers are extensive files of correspondence with photographers, friends, family, and others; portraits of Sommer and his wife, Frances; manuscripts of Sommer's essays and poetry; clippings related to his career; and documentation of his exhibitions and publications. Among the photographic materials are a variety of sizes and types of negatives and some photographic equipment and small tools. (68 linear feet)

Highlights: 12 collages along with pieces never used and the original medical and scientific antiquarian books Sommer used as sources for his collages; the original paper constructions photographed by Sommer for his cut paper works; the original negatives for smoke (soot) on glass photographs.

Related information: Correspondence from Sommer is found in the archives of Aaron Siskind (AG 30) and Edward Weston (AG 38), among others. The CCP commissioned Harold Jones to photograph Sommer's house in Prescott shortly after his death. The resulting series of photographs, *A House Alone*, was exhibited in the CCP library in 2000. The prints are in the Harold Jones Collection (AG 67).

CCP publication: *Sommer · Words, Sommer · Images* (1984)

Giorgio Sommer

2 September 1834, Frankfurt, Germany – 1914, Naples, Italy

Photograph collection: 110 undated albumen prints of Naples and Pompei

Highlight: 48 hand-colored albumen prints in album, *Costumi di Napoli*, ca. 1870.

Eve Sonneman

b. 14 January 1946, Chicago, Illinois

Photograph collection: 15 fine prints

John P. Soule

9 October 1828, Phillips, Maine – 1904, Boston, Massachusetts

Photograph Collection: 46 stereoviews from the Virginia Adams Stereoview Collection

OJU MO OLA PHOTO SERVICE, ILA, NIGERIA: Portrait of unknown Yoruba man Collected by Stephen Sprague, 1975

Stephen Sprague

7 June 1942, Roslyn, New York – 2 May 1979, West Lebanon, Indiana

Photograph collection: approximately 100 fine prints

Research materials: The Stephen Sprague Archive (AG 65) holds activity files, photographic and audiovisual materials, and elements of the personal library of this photographer and educator. Sprague was teaching photography, film and video at Purdue University when he was killed in an automobile accident in 1979. His projects included studies of Yoruba photography in Nigeria, a study of the photography of C. J. Pansirna, the Mr. and Miss Nude America contest, and the Maxwell Street Flea Market in Chicago. Included in his archive are letters, negatives, transparencies, prints, films, videotapes and audiotapes from his documentary, artistic and ethnographic projects. The black-and-white and color negatives and contact prints span the years 1964 to 1978. (20 linear feet)

Highlight: Sprague collected the work of Yoruba portrait photographers in Nigeria and used some of it in his project *How I See the Yoruba See Themselves* (1975–78).

PETER STACKPOLE:
Rita Hayworth and Orson Welles, 1945

Peter Stackpole

15 June 1913, San Francisco, California –
11 May 1997, Novato, California

Photograph collection: approximately 400 fine prints

Research materials: The Peter Stackpole Collection (AG 169) contains what personal papers and photographic materials survived the devastating Oakland, California, fires of 1991. The few materials that were saved were rescued by Stackpole and his friend and neighbor, Floyd Winter, moments before the conflagration consumed the house. The bulk of the archive is photographic materials that document the work of the photographer from 1930 to 1950. These include negatives of the construction of the San Francisco Bay bridges and of other early photographic work as well as negatives of many of his Hollywood assignments. A comparison of Stackpole's *Life* assignment cards with negatives surviving in his archive indicates that many negatives have not survived or are today in the Picture Collection of Time Inc. Also included in the archive are personal papers, a partial autobiography, exhibition

367

materials, activity files, audiovisual materials, and works by others. (12 linear feet)

Rights and restrictions: Copyright of Stackpole's photographs is managed for the Peter Stackpole Estate by the Center for Creative Photography.

John Lewis Stage

b. 1925

Photograph collection: 17 fine prints from 2 photoessays published in *International Harvester's Today* magazine, bound in portfolio, 1950s, from the Collection of W. Eugene Smith

EDWARD STEICHEN:
Dana, n.d.

Edward Steichen

27 March 1879, Luxembourg – 25 March 1973, West Redding, Connecticut

Photograph collection: 218 fine prints, including some in color and many plates from *Camera Work*

Research materials: The Edward Steichen Collection (AG 24) consists of 205 lantern slides. Most of these are aerial views taken during World War I; the rest are commercial, theatrical, and portraits made between 1920 and 1934. (1.5 linear feet)

Highlights: 107 Type R Technicolor prints of shadblow tree and landscapes; 12 prints in the 1981 portfolio, *Edward Steichen: The Early Years, 1900–1927.*

Related information: The Noel Deeks Collection (AG 24) contains information collected by Deeks, who worked as a printer for Steichen. Includes 2 color transparencies of *The Swedish Lotus* made for Steichen; portraits of Steichen, and Steichen's studio.

RALPH STEINER: *Ham and Eggs*, 1929–30

Ralph Steiner

8 February 1899, Cleveland, Ohio – 13 July 1986, Thetford Hill, Vermont

Photograph collection: 187 fine prints

Research materials: The Ralph Steiner Collection (AG 68) holds a selection of Steiner's personal papers, negatives, motion picture films, and sound tracks, 1940–1975. The bulk of the collection consists of motion pictures from *The Joy of Seeing* series, 1960 to 1975. Also included are correspondence; negatives and transparencies from Steiner's personal and commercial work; and tear sheets from *PM* magazine. There are also fragments of the early film *Café Universal* (1934), still images from the making of *The Plow that Broke the Plains* (1936), and stills made by Marion Post Wolcott of Steiner at work on the film *The People of the Cumberland* (1937). (20.5 linear feet)

Highlights: Portfolios: *Ten Photographs from the Twenties and Thirties & One from the Seventies*, ca. 1978, and *Portfolio: Twenty-two Little Contact Prints from 1921–1929 Negatives*, 1981, and a number of vintage prints.

Related information: Letters and other materials concerning Ralph Steiner may also be found in the Willard Van Dyke Archive (AG 77), Paul Strand Collection (AG 17), and Ansel Adams Archive (AG 31). The Lectures, Writings, Manuscripts Collection (AG 101) contains a copy of Joel Stewart Zuker's Ph.D. dissertation "Ralph Steiner: Filmmaker and Still Photographer" (New York University, June 1976).

Jay Sternberg

2 November 1900 – 11 March 1957, Tucson, Arizona

Grace Sternberg

1 August 1902 – 23 December 2000, Tucson, Arizona

Photograph collection: 23 fine prints by Jay Sternberg and 5 fine prints by Grace Sternberg, his wife. Together, they owned and operated a photography studio in Tucson for many years.

Albert W. Stevens

13 March 1886, Belfast, Maine – 26 March 1949, Redwood City, California

Photograph collection: 34 gelatin silver prints, aerial views around California in the 1920s

Virginia Stevens

b. 1912

Research materials: The Virginia Stevens Collection (AG 107) contains the papers, 1930s–1980s, of the actress and writer Virginia Stevens, who was Paul Strand's wife from 1936 to 1949. The collection includes 22 letters from Paul Strand, a pamphlet on Frontier Films, pencil drawing of darkroom by Strand, clippings, and autobiographical notes by Stevens regarding Strand's break with Stieglitz. (fraction of a linear foot)

Sharon Stewart

b. 20 April 1955, Edinburg, Texas

Photograph collection: 81 fine prints from the Water in the West project

Related information: Water in the West Archive (AG 172).

ALFRED STIEGLITZ: Untitled, 1896–99

Alfred Stieglitz

1 January 1864, Hoboken, New Jersey – 13 July 1946, New York

Photograph collection: 117 fine prints, 81 of them plates from *Camera Work*, 4 collaborations with Clarence H. White

Highlights: Satista print portrait of Paul Strand, 1916; 18 offset lithographs in *Stieglitz Memorial Portfolio 1864–1946*; 12 gelatin silver prints, 1896 to 1925, from the Herbert Small Collection.

CCP publications: "Alfred Stieglitz: A Talk," *Center for Creative Photography* 1 (March 1976); "Alfred Stieglitz: Photographs from the Herbert Small Collection," *Center for Creative Photography* 6 (April 1978).

Dennis Stock

b. 24 July 1928, New York

Photograph collection: 40 dye transfer prints, from the *Brother Sun Collection*

Lou Stoumen

15 July 1917, Springtown, Pennsylvania – 20 September 1991, Sebastopol, California

Photograph collection: 47 fine prints

Highlight: Portfolio, *Times Square, 1940: A Paper Movie*, 1977.

Hazel Kingsbury Strand

Photograph collection: 73 fine prints, mostly portraits of her husband Paul Strand

Research materials: Letters to and from Hazel Strand are found in the Paul Strand Collection (AG 17). Some information concerning her employment as Louise Dahl-Wolfe's assistant is found in the Louise Dahl-Wolfe Archive (AG 76).

Paul Strand

16 October 1890, New York – 31 March 1976, Orgeval, France

Photograph collection: 806 fine and study prints

Research materials: The Paul Strand Collection (AG 17) contains the personal papers of Paul Strand. Included are activity files, biographical information, extensive incoming and outgoing correspondence files, clippings and published materials, miniature book maquettes, information about Strand's films including *The Wave*, and 9 scrapbooks, 1902–1975. The bulk of the collection is correspondence with many individuals in the worlds of photography and the arts including Ansel Adams, Henri Cartier-Bresson, Waldo Frank, Laura Gilpin, Lotte Jacobi, John Marin, Elizabeth McCausland, Beaumont and Nancy Newhall, Dorothy Norman, Georgia O'Keeffe, Alfred Stieglitz, Edward Weston, Clarence White, and many others. (30.5 linear feet)

The Paul Strand Miscellaneous Acquisitions Collection (AG 94) contains documents from a variety of sources and includes correspondence, clippings, and photographic materials. (fraction of a linear foot)

Highlights: Strand's scrapbooks are a rich source of ephemera documenting events in the art world from 1902 to 1975. Strand's collection of photographs at the time of his death is documented in transparencies.

Related information: Other collections relevant to a study of Strand include: Kurt Baasch Collection (AG 137); Virginia Stevens Collection (AG 107); Beaumont and Nancy Newhall Collection (AG 48); and Dorothy Norman Collection (AG 164).

Rights and permissions: The Paul Strand Archive, held by the Aperture Foundation, New York, includes Strand's negatives, contact sheets, and personal library, as well as the largest collection of Strand's prints and the copyright to his work.

CCP publications: "Paul Strand Archive," *Guide Series* 2 (1980); "Paul Strand and Ansel Adams: Native Land and Natural Scene," *The Archive* 27 (1990).

Strohmeyer & Wyman

(offered by Underwood & Underwood)

active 1890s

Photograph collection: 13 stereoviews from the Virginia Adams Stereoview Collection

---

Karl Struss

30 November 1886, New York –
15 December 1981, Los Angeles, California

Photograph collection: 30 fine prints

Highlights: 15 hand-coated platinum prints, printed by Phil Davis under the supervision of Struss in *Karl Struss: A Portfolio, 1909/29*, 1979.

Related information: The Karl Struss archive is held by the Amon Carter Museum, Fort Worth, Texas.

Martin Stupich

b. 1949

Photograph collection: 23 fine prints from the Water in the West project

Related information: Water in the West Archive (AG 172).

Roger Sturtevant

26 January 1903, Alameda, California –
3 July 1982, Oakland, California

Photograph collection: 10 fine prints

Jean-Pierre Sudre

27 September 1921, Paris, France –
September 1997, Aix-en-Provence, France

Photograph collection: 10 toned, chemically altered gelatin silver prints, from the *Végétal & Insectes* series

---

Hiroshi Sugimoto

b. February 1948, Tokyo, Japan

Photograph collection: 52 fine prints, including 50 laser scanned tri-tone photolithographs in the portfolio *Time Exposed*, 1991

Larry Sultan

b. 13 July 1946, Brooklyn, New York

Photograph collection: 81 prints collected by Sultan and Mike Mandel for the *Evidence* project

---

H. Y. Summons

active 1900s – 1940s

Photograph collection: 11 fine prints, from the Collection of Paul L. Anderson

---

Soichi Sunami

1885 – 1971

Photograph collection: 18 gelatin silver prints of dancers, including Martha Graham and Gertrude Shurr

---

Charles Swedlund

b. 1935, Chicago, Illinois

Photograph collection: 26 fine prints, including 5 offset lithographs in *A Portfolio of Color Prints by Charles Swedlund*, 1973

Dick Swift

b. 24 October 1936

Photograph collection: 15 portraits of W. Eugene Smith

William Henry Fox Talbot

11 February 1800, Melbury, England –
17 September 1877, Wiltshire, England

Photograph collection: 1 calotype, ca. 1845

Research materials: The William Henry Fox Talbot Collection (AG 13) contains 3 printed documents dated 1841 and 1854 relating to the calotype (or Talbotype) process.

Alfred John Tattersall

1861, Auckland, New Zealand – 1951, Samoa

Photograph collection: 20 albumen prints of Samoa in the Julia F. Corson Collection

---

John Tellaisha

Photograph collection: 4 fine prints

Research materials: The John Tellaisha Collection (AG 8) contains correspondence and biographical information pertaining to Edward Weston. Includes letters from Edward and Brett Weston, 1944–51. (fraction of a linear foot)

Saturday, March 9, 1996 at 7:00 pm
712 S. Santa Fe Avenue, Studio 103
Los Angeles, CA 90021
Secured parking on 7th Place
Please r.s.v.p. by March 2, 1996
213.627.2067

Invitation to birthday party for Edmund Teske
Robert Heinecken Archive

Edmund Teske

7 March 1911, Chicago, Illinois –
22 November 1996, Los Angeles, California

Photograph collection: 12 fine prints

Research materials: The Edmund Teske Miscellaneous Acquisitions Collection (AG 15) contains materials from a variety of sources. Includes text, dummy and layout for catalog of exhibition at Los Angeles Municipal Art Gallery, 1974. Ephemera and small work prints from Teske are found in the Robert Heinecken Archive (AG 45).

John Thomson

14 June 1837, Edinburgh, Scotland –
October 1921, London, England

Photograph collection: 58 fine prints, including
16 albumen prints in *The Antiquities of
Cambodia: A series of photographs taken on
the spot* (1867); and 21 Woodburytype prints
in 2 copies of *Street Incidents* (1881)

RUTH THORNE-THOMSEN:
Parable, Wisconsin, 1991
From the series *Songs of the Sea*

Ruth Thorne-Thomsen

b. 13 May 1943, New York

Photograph collection: 13 gelatin silver pinhole
prints

Jacqueline Thurston

b. 27 January 1939, Cincinnati, Ohio

Photograph collection: 17 fine prints, mostly in
portfolio, *Circus Series*, ca. 1980

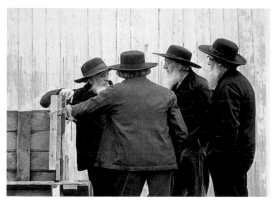

GEORGE A. TICE:
Old Amish Men, Lancaster, Pennsylvania, 1966
From *The Amish Portfolio*, ca. 1968

George A. Tice

b. 13 October 1938, Newark, New Jersey

Photograph collection: 69 fine prints, including portfolios I through V: *Amish Portfolio*, 1968; *Trees*, 1969; *Bodie*, 1971; *Peekamoose*, 1972; *George A. Tice: Portfolio V*, 1976

Research materials: The George A. Tice Collection (AG 63) includes documentation of the Artie Van Blarcum project, correspondence, photographic equipment, ephemera, and carefully assembled book production materials. (1 linear foot)

Charles Traub

b. 6 April 1945, Louisville, Kentucky

Photograph collection: 20 fine prints, and 2 made in collaboration with Douglas Baz for the Cajun project, 1974

Alex Traube

b. 5 June 1946, New York

Photograph collection: 25 fine prints, including 10 in portfolio, *Letters to My Father*, 1976

ARTHUR TRESS: *Initiations 8:5*, 1974

Arthur Tress

b. 24 November 1940, Brooklyn, New York

Photograph collection: 155 fine prints

Research materials: The Arthur Tress Collection (AG 149) contains materials that uniquely document this artist's creative process. Annotations in books and pamphlets record his interest in symbolic imagery of dreams and legends, homoerotic subtexts, and the power of metaphor in art. His carefully organized card catalog is an artifact of intrinsic interest as well as a source of information on Tress's dreams and readings. Small found and collected objects such as toys, decorative figurines, and salt/pepper shakers used as props in the series *Fish Tank Sonata* and *Teapot Opera* are labeled by the artist. Other materials include publications and the raw materials and notes used in *Shadow: A Novel in Photographs*. (20 linear feet)

Highlights: Tress's personal collection of mounted original political cartoons by Thomas Nast and other artists from journals published in the United States and France. *The Wurlitzer Trilogy* is represented by 24 prints from the *Fish Tank Sonata*, 21 prints from the *Teapot Opera*, and 9 prints from *Requiem for a Paperweight*. The complete series (94 prints) of *Shadow: A Novel in Photographs* (1974) is included.

Henry Troup

b. 1924

Photograph collection: 21 fine prints, from the Collection of Aaron Siskind

---

Tseng Kwong Chi

6 September 1950, Hong Kong – 10 March 1990, New York

Photograph collection: 95 fine prints, including 12 in portfolio, *Costumes at the Met*, 1997

Highlight: The CCP holds the most complete set of Tseng's series, *The Expeditionary Works*, in a public institution.

JERRY N. UELSMANN: *Equivalent*, 1964

Jerry N. Uelsmann

b. 11 June 1934, Detroit, Michigan

Photograph collection: 136 fine prints

Research materials: The Jerry N. Uelsmann Collection (AG 35) contains personal papers and photographic materials, ca. 1955 to the present, of photographer and instructor Jerry Uelsmann. Included are correspondence, writings, book maquettes, publications, clippings, posters, videotapes, memorabilia, and portraits of the artist. Files of announcements and catalogs document most of Uelsmann's exhibitions and books from 1964 to 1998. Contact sheets and proof prints are of particular interest in tracing how the artist derives his imagery. (36 linear feet)

Highlight: Carbon copy of Minor White's dissertation, "Fundamentals of Style in Photography and the Elements of Reading Photographs," ca. 1955.

Related information: Correspondence from Uelsmann, a dedicated and inspired letter-writer, can be found in numerous other collections including: Society for Photographic Education Archive (AG 78); Henry Holmes Smith Archive (AG 32); Frederick Sommer Archive (AG 28); and Robert Heinecken Archive (AG 45).

Bea Ullrich-Zuckerman

1907 – 30 April 1987

Research materials: The Bea Ullrich-Zuckerman Collection (AG 75) contains correspondence to her from Edward and Charis Weston and other papers relating to their friendship. Included in some letters are work prints and negatives. (fraction of a linear foot)

Highlight: 34-page typescript manuscript describing meeting Weston in Louisiana in 1941 and visiting him in California in 1942.

Doris Ulmann

29 May 1882, New York – 28 August 1934, New York

Photograph collection: Palladium portrait of Carl Van Vechten, ca. 1933

Research materials: The Doris Ulmann Collection (AG 84) holds photographic equipment used by Ulmann, and includes a 4x5-inch Korona view camera with several lenses, film holders, tripods, focusing cloth and miscellaneous accessories. (3 linear feet)

Umbo (Otto Umbehr)

18 January 1902, Dusseldorf, Germany – 13 May 1980, Hannover, Germany

Photograph collection: 25 fine prints

Highlight: *Umbo, Portfolio of Ten Silver Prints*, 1980.

Underwood & Underwood

Bert Underwood

1862, Oxford, Illinois – 27 December 1943, Tucson, Arizona

Elmer Underwood

1860, Fulton County, Illinois – 18 August 1947, St. Petersburg, Florida

Photograph collection: 14 stereoviews from the Virginia Adams Stereoview Collection, and 1 portrait

---

Burk Uzzle

b. 4 August 1938, Raleigh, North Carolina

Photograph collection: 94 fine prints

Artie Van Blarcum

b. 4 July 1925, Newark, New Jersey

Photograph collection: 12 fine prints

James Van Der Zee

29 June 1886, Lenox, Massachusetts – 15 May 1983, New York

Photograph collection: 19 fine prints, including portfolio, *James Van Der Zee: Eighteen Photographs*, 1974

Research materials: Letters from Van Der Zee are contained in the Lee Witkin/Witkin Gallery Collection (AG 62).

WILLARD VAN DYKE: *Ventilators*, ca. 1933

Willard Van Dyke

5 December 1906, Denver, Colorado – 23 January 1986, Jackson, Tennessee

Photograph collection: 17 fine prints

Research materials: The Willard Van Dyke Archive (AG 34) holds personal papers, photographic materials, and audiovisual materials of Van Dyke from 1915 to 1986. Included are correspondence, biographical materials, writings, film scripts, exhibition announcements, publications, negatives, study and contact prints, and files relating to his career at the Museum of Modern Art. (17 linear feet)

The Willard Van Dyke Miscellaneous Acquisitions Collection (AG 97) holds a variety of materials acquired from diverse sources. It includes correspondence dated 1984-85.

Related information: Several other collections hold materials relevant to a study of Van Dyke:

Edward Weston Archive (AG 38); Ansel Adams Archive (AG 31); Ralph Steiner Collection (AG 68); and William Holgers Archive (AG 69).

Related Information: The Ben Maddow Collection (AG 108) contains materials concerning a trip to South America that he and Van Dyke made for the film *The Bridge* in 1941–42, as well as correspondence with Van Dyke dating 1976–85.

CCP publications: "Willard Van Dyke Archive," *Guide Series 14* (1992) and "The Letters between Edward Weston and Willard Van Dyke," *The Archive* 30 (1992).

Annette Gest Very

active 1950s–60s, d. 1970s, Tucson, Arizona

Photograph collection: 15 fine prints

David Vestal

b. 21 March 1924, Menlo Park, California

Photograph collection: 24 gelatin silver prints, 14 made at the Gila River Indian Community, Sacaton, Arizona, 1966

André Villers

b. 1930, Beaucourt, France

Photograph collection: 30 collotypes of Pablo Picasso's decoupages superimposed on Viller's photographs in portfolio of collaborative images, *Diurnes*, 1962

Christian Vogt

b. 12 April 1946, Basle, Switzerland

Photograph collection: 12 fine prints in portfolio, *Christian Vogt*, 1981

Laura Volkerding

16 October 1939, Louisville, Kentucky –
3 September 1996, San Francisco, California

Photograph collection: Over 1000 fine prints

Research materials: The Laura Volkerding Archive (AG 162) contains the personal papers and photographic materials of Volkerding, printmaker, photographer, and instructor. Included are letters, teaching files, exhibition records, diaries, and ephemera. Extensive files of negatives and study prints document the artist's entire career including her work in the panoramic format and her late project with the Compagnons du Devoir. (72 linear feet)

The Collection of Laura Volkerding consists of 50 fine prints by a variety of photographers, including Eugène Atget, Richard D. Pare, Aaron Siskind, and Jock Sturges.

Rights and restrictions: Copyright to Volkerding's photographs is held by the Center for Creative Photography, The University of Arizona Foundation.

Adam Clark Vroman

15 April 1856, La Salle, Illinois – 24 July 1916, Altadena, California

Photograph collection: 74 fine prints, including 70 in the album, *Southern California and Yosemite Valley*, 1900–01

Bob Wade

b. 6 January 1943, Austin, Texas

Photograph collection: 150 color xerographic prints in handmade book, *Bob Wade's Texas*, 1976

Catherine Wagner

b. 31 January 1953, San Francisco, California

Photograph collection: 13 fine prints

Max Waldman

2 June 1919, New York – 8 March 1981, New York

Photograph collection: 10 fine prints of New York theatrical performances, 1966 to 1974

Todd Walker

25 September 1917, Salt Lake City, Utah –
13 September 1998, Tucson, Arizona

Photograph collection: 87 fine prints in a wide variety of media, including gelatin silver prints, offset prints, photolithographs, and photo-silkscreens

Research materials: The Todd Walker Collection (AG 83) holds a selection of Walker's self-published books and booklets, as well as other books, periodicals and clippings documenting his career. Photographer and photoeducator Harold Todd Walker was an innovator in non-silver and photomechanical printing processes and in his later years conducted in-depth experiments with computer imaging. From 1965 until his death in 1998, Walker published his own artist's books under the Thumbprint Press imprint in California, Florida, and Tucson. (3 linear feet)

Highlights: 15 offset lithographs in *Portfolio Three*, 1969; and *Fragments of Melancholy* (1980), a portfolio of offset lithographs with texts taken from Robert Burton's "Anatomy of Melancholy."

John Ward

b. 23 March 1943, Washington, D.C.

Photograph collection: 11 of the original 12 prints in *John Ward: Landscape, Portfolio One*, 1981

Bradford Washburn

b. 7 June 1910, Cambridge, Massachusetts

Photograph collection: 48 fine prints, aerial views of mountains, taken from 1937 to 1978

Research materials: 3 study prints of Mount Everest, prints by Swiss Air Photo Surveys, 1984.

Water in the West

Photograph collection: over 700 fine prints

Research materials: The Water in the West Archive (AG 172) holds biographical materials about the project directors Robert Dawson and Ellen Manchester, and about the participants Laurie Brown, Gregory Conniff, Terry Evans, Geoff Fricker, Peter Goin, Wanda Hammerbeck, Sant Khalsa, Mark Klett, Ellen Land-Weber, Sharon Stewart and Martin Stupich. The collection also holds notes, research materials, press coverage, clippings, catalogs, contact sheets, and other records related to the individual and collaborative projects undertaken by the participants in documenting water issues in the American West.   (6 linear feet)

Related information: The CCP also holds a complete set of photographs from the *Central Arizona Project Photographic Survey*, undertaken by Mark Klett, Ruthe Morand, Lawrence McFarland, and Ann Simmons-Myers in 1984–86. The Central Arizona Project (CAP) was constructed by the Department of the Interior's Bureau of Reclamation to divert water from the Colorado River for use in central and southern Arizona. A number of stereoviews made by Sierra Club activist Joseph LeConte in the Collection of Ansel and Virginia Adams depict the Hetch Hetchy Valley. Hetch Hetchy, just north of Yosemite, was inundated when the Tuolumne River was dammed in 1923 to create a reservoir serving San Francisco and the Bay Area 160 miles away. The Barry M. Goldwater Collection (AG 88) includes views made while on a float trip down the Green and Colorado Rivers in 1940. This trip, also documented in the book *A Trip Down the Green and Colorado Rivers, 1940* (Phoenix, AZ: H. Walker, 1940), included Glen Canyon, which was later inundated to form Lake Powell. The Mieth/Hagel Archive (AG 170) holds notes, negatives, transparencies, and contact sheets from Otto Hagel's 1961 extensive essay on water issues in California for *Life* magazine under the working title "California Water Story."

Carleton E. Watkins

11 November 1829, Oneonta, New York –
23 June 1916, Imola, California

Photograph collection: 53 albumen prints and 143 stereoviews

Highlight: 50 albumen prints in album, *Yo-Semite Valley: Photographic Views of the Falls and Valley of Yo-Semite in Mariposa County, California* (1863)

TODD WEBB: *Masie, "Queen of the Bowery"*, 1946

Todd Webb

15 September 1905, Detroit, Michigan –
15 April 2000, Auburn, Maine

Photograph collection: 1421 fine prints

Research materials: The Todd Webb Archive (AG 2) contains personal papers and photographic materials related to Webb's long career as a photographer. It includes personal and business letters, biographical files, exhibition documentation, manuscripts, journals, printed materials, extensive files of negatives, and contact sheets. Webb's Guggenheim fellowship and United Nations projects that took him across the United States in 1955 and 1956, the Texas Architecture Survey he worked on from 1962 to 1967, his years in New Mexico, in Europe, and finally in Maine are documented in the archive. (20 linear feet)

Highlights: Small album of photographs made in New Guinea during the war years; letters from Georgia O'Keeffe, 1957 to 1985, and many portraits of O'Keeffe for Webb's book *Georgia O'Keeffe: The Artist's Landscape*, 1984

WEEGEE:
"Lost Children," June 9, 1941

Weegee (Arthur Fellig)

12 June 1899, Zloczew (formerly Austria, now Poland) – 26 December 1968, New York

Photograph collection: 172 fine prints

BRIAN WEIL:
Transvestite Safe-Sex Outreach Worker, Dominican Republic, 1987

Brian Weil

1954, Chicago – 3 February 1996, New York

Photograph collection: Over 300 fine prints

Research materials: The Brian Weil Collection (AG 175) contains personal papers as well as photographic materials of Brian Weil, a photographer who founded the City Wide Needle Exchange and who worked with the World Health Organization establishing community-based AIDS organizations in Haiti, South Africa, and Thailand. Included are some of his personal papers, videotapes, negatives, and numerous study prints. Weil's work was published by Aperture in 1992 in the book *Every Seventeen Seconds: A Global Perspective on the AIDS Crisis* with essay by Simon Watney. (24 linear feet)

DAN WEINER: Untitled, 1954
From the book *South Africa in Transition*,
  text by Alan Paton, 1956

Dan Weiner

12 October 1919, New York City – 26 January
1959, Versailles, Kentucky

Photograph collection: over 1000 fine prints

Research materials: The Dan Weiner Archive
(AG 150) contains the papers and photographic materials of Dan Weiner, photographer
and writer. Includes correspondence, pocket
calendars, project files, publications, negatives,
color transparencies, negatives, and contact
sheets. Of special note are materials related to
the Photo League and to Weiner's book projects. A broad selection of American popular
magazines of the 1950s such as *McCall's,
Collier's, Sports Illustrated,* and *Life* is included.
(33 linear feet)

Jack Welpott

b. 27 April 1923, Kansas City, Kansas

Photograph collection: 15 fine prints

Eudora Welty

13 April 1909, Jackson, Mississippi – 23 July
2001, Jackson, Mississippi

Photograph collection: Portfolio, *Twenty
Photographs*, 1980, includes images made in
Mississippi while employed by the Works
Progress Administration in the 1930s

BRETT WESTON: Untitled, ca. 1985

Brett Weston

16 December 1911, Los Angeles – 22 January 1993, Paradise Park, Hawaii

Photograph collection: over 1400 fine prints

Research materials: The Brett Weston Collection (AG 143) contains negatives in a variety of formats, 1911 to 1993. (2 linear feet)

Highlight: 106 gelatin silver prints, 1926 to 1975, comprising the entire *Fiftieth Anniversary Exhibition,* curated by Beaumont Newhall.

Related information: Letters and other documentation of Brett's life and career are present in several collections including the Edward Weston Archive (AG 38) and the Wynn Bullock Archive (AG 10).

Chandler Weston

29 April 1910, Los Angeles – 3 December 1995

Photograph collection: 10 gelatin silver prints (4 are study prints) from the Collection of Edward Weston

Research materials: Letters from Chandler are contained in the Edward Weston Archive (AG 38).

EDWARD WESTON: *Excusado, Mexico*, 1925

Edward Weston

24 March 1886, Highland Park, Illinois –
1 January 1958, Carmel, California

Photograph collection: 2260 fine prints

Research materials: The Edward Weston
Archive (AG 38) contains personal papers and
photographic materials along with some artifacts and memorabilia belonging to the photographer. Included are letters from and to
Weston, original manuscripts for his daybooks,
financial and studio records, exhibition and
publication files, documentation of his
Guggenheim project, trips to Mexico, and
other photographic activities. Of particular
importance are letters from photographers
such as Ansel Adams, Tina Modotti, Charles
Sheeler, Willard Van Dyke, and Brett Weston.
Included are 6 scrapbooks with clippings,
ephemera, and snapshots from the 1920s to
1940s. Financial records document business
and household expenses and income as well as
political contributions and medical bills.
Artifacts include one camera, several suitcases,
and many original film and photographic paper
boxes. The archive also contains nearly 7000
small format portrait negatives, 3000 8x10-inch
negatives, and a small number of glass negatives and color transparencies. (75 linear feet)

**The Edward Weston and Johan Hagemeyer
Collection** (AG 5) consists mainly of letters
from Weston to Hagemeyer between 1918 and
1938. There are also published and unpublished manuscripts, clippings, notes, and
brochures. Notable are manuscript fragments
sent as enclosures with letters written in New
York in 1922 and Mexico in 1923. Other correspondents include Tina Modotti, Dorothea
Lange, and Margarethe Mather. (fraction of a
linear foot)

**The Edward Weston Miscellaneous
Acquisitions Collection** (AG 6) contains materials from a variety of sources. Of special note
are letters from figures in Weston's circle to
Betty Brandner; Weston's manuscript
"Photography in America;" and a questionnaire by Beaumont and Nancy Newhall.

Highlight: Original autograph and typescript
manuscripts for Weston's daybooks.

Related information: Letters and other docu-
mentation of Edward Weston's life and career
can be found in a number of other collections:
Ansel Adams Archive (AG 31), Wynn Bullock
Archive (AG 10), Beaumont and Nancy Newhall
Collection (AG 48), Frederick Sommer Archive
(AG 28), Sonya Noskowiak Archive (AG 3),
Johan Hagemeyer Archive (AG 44), Leon
Wilson Collection (AG 165), Helen Caddes
Collection (AG 171), John Tellaisha Collection
(AG 8), and Bea Ullrich-Zuckerman Collection
(AG 75).

The Collection of Edward Weston includes 157
fine prints including photographs by Ansel
Adams, Manuel Alvarez Bravo, Daniel Masclet,
Tina Modotti, Sonya Noskowiak, Arthur Siegel,
John Tellaisha, Brett Weston, Minor White, and
Max Yavno.

Rights and restrictions: Copyright to Weston's
writings and photographs is held by the Center
for Creative Photography, Arizona Board of
Regents.

89 Sunday—

I have on my desk before me, a halved red onion which is so absolutely marvellous as to bring desire to start still-life again! indeed I would, but where the time? Xmas only a month away, and orders must be kept moving to make ready for last moment rush. Then I may go to the city: several sittings await me, and I could be there for the opening of my exhibit. But I dread "home Portraits,"— I can't use my formula! I waste too much time for the money.

Work at the point yesterday was most satisfactory. The tide was higher than I have ever seen it, and then correspondingly lower. The gravel washed out, revealing eight inches of base I had never seen before, offering new forms to work with, or variations of old forms. I made seven negatives,— eight, but I don't count

The last one of an abalone which moved during a prolonged exposure at 5⁰⁰ o'clock. Arriving upon my scene of action, a number of sea-gulls took off, rather reluctantly I noted. Descending to the beach, I found eight or more enormous abalones washed ashore. Why, I cannot guess, for there had been no storm, and it seems to me a terrific force necessary to loosen the grip of an abalone. Several were very much alive, and I was spellbound with the beauty of their form and rhythm of movement, not to mention colour. One, who had given up, and lay half slid off his shell was too fine to resist, but during exposure slid some more.

All afternoon the gulls sat upon rocks above me or sailed overhead, angrily squeaking at me for spoiling their feast.

flagrant examples of municipal bad taste all over Mexico City.
Statues to every sort of hero abound, line the Paseo de la Reforma,
and dot the Alameda; gilded statues, some as vulgar as our own Goddess
of Liberty. So, after all, middle class minds and aspirations are the
same everywhere, one can only hope for no further increase in their
power.

LLewellyn is here, at last, with his police dog, Panurge.
Recounting his trip, brings back my own: the unforgettable train
ride from Manzanillo to Mexico City, and those beautiful cities,
C olima and Guadalajara. I should like to hve lived a while in
Colima, but we spent only one day in each place, just enough to ø
excite our fancies. These cities were less spoiled than Mexico
City, the natives more genuine. From Manzanillo to Colima was a
touch of the tropics, luxuriant vegetation with stretches of tangled
vines, dense growth amounting to ⁀ jungle. The Indians sold strange
nad delicious fruits at every stop, the mango, fresh coconuts and ban-
anas, aguacates, sugar cane. In these foods I indulged, they seemed
safe enough, but tempting as they looked, I hesitated over the tamales
and other steaming dishes and sweets. Later, I learned that the tamales were not chicken as advertised but iguana, the giant lizard----
well, why not? A tender iguana might be more palatable than a
tough old hen!
We wandered through the streets of Colima after a well-cooked
savory repast. It was there we met little Carmen; she sat on the
cement walk, leaning against a pillar under long corridors of
arches, in front of her a tray of pumpkin seeds. She dozed, awakening now and then to dish out automatically a dozen seeds or so for
un centavo. Again, her heavy lids would droop, once more her pale
profile would assume its tenderly poignant outline in the

fakes which hid them. Our friends, too, are dubious as to our moving so far from the city and expecting our clientele to come out. Well, surely I have not come all the way to Mexico to open a commercial studio on Main Street! I hardly dare look ahead.

A few days ago, Tina took me to see the work of Diego Rivera---murals for a public building. It was the work of a great artist which we viewed. Later We met him, and he was great in another way, tall and of striking girth. I regret not being able to converse with him. He has lived among the foremost contemporary artists in Paris, Picasso, Matisse, and others.

The murals of Rivera have raised a storm of protest, but the work continues. I cannot imagine his having the opportunity to start such paintings in any American building. Government of the people, by the people, and for the people does not seem to foster great art.

Llewellyn (Bixby a pupil) friend is here at last, with his police dog, Panurge.

August 27

Roberto Turnbull, a Mexican cinematographer, very much Americanized, took us to La Tapatia, a place famous for its cooking, where down and outs rub elbows with

CCP publications: "Weston to Hagemeyer: New York Notes," *Center for Creative Photography* 3 (November 1976); "The Letters from Tina Modotti to Edward Weston," *The Archive* 22 (January 1986); *Edward Weston: Color Photography* (1986); "Edward Weston Papers," *Guide Series* 13 (1986); "The Letters between Edward Weston and Willard Van Dyke," *The Archive* 30 (1992); *Edward Weston: Photographs from the Collection of the Center for Creative Photography* by Amy Conger (1992).

MINOR WHITE:
Gallery Cove, Point Lobos, California, 1953

Clarence H. White

8 April 1871, West Carlisle, Ohio – 8 July 1925, Mexico City, Mexico

Photograph collection: 19 prints, many of them from *Camera Work* numbers 3 and 9, and plates from *Camera Work* number 25 of images made in collaboration with Alfred Stieglitz

Minor White

9 July 1908, Minneapolis, Minnesota – 24 June 1976, Boston

Photograph collection: 148 fine prints, including portfolios: *Song without Words*, 1947; *Fourth Sequence*, 1950; *Sequence 17*, 1963; *Jupiter Portfolio*, 1975

Research materials: The Minor White Miscellaneous Acquisitions Collection (AG 9) includes materials related to Minor White acquired from a variety of sources. Includes many letters between White and Ansel Adams. (fraction of a linear foot)

Highlight: "Notebook Resume," prepared by Arnold Gassan at a photography workshop conducted by White in 1962.

Leon Wilson

b. 1912 [?]

Research materials: The Leon Wilson Collection (AG 165) contains 18 letters from Edward Weston, 1945 to 1956, to Wilson, the brother of Weston's wife, Charis Wilson Weston. (fraction of a linear foot)

Geoff Winningham

b. 4 March 1943, Jackson, Tennessee

Photograph collection: 18 fine prints, from the Collection of Wynn Bullock

---

Garry Winogrand

14 January 1928, New York – 19 March 1984, Tijuana, Mexico

Photograph collection: approximately 30,000 fine and work prints

Research materials: The Garry Winogrand Archive (AG 72) consists of the personal papers and photographic materials of the photographer. Included are complete files of negatives, contact sheets, color transparencies, home movies, Polaroid prints, work prints, and tear sheets, ca. 1947 to 1980s. A detailed index has been prepared to assist access to the ca. 400 contact sheets. Negatives developed and printed posthumously are also included. Papers include letters, exhibition records, and ephemera. (144 linear feet)

Highlights: approximately 30,500 35 mm color transparencies of commercial and personal work; early black-and-white commercial work for Henrietta Brackman and other agents.

CCP publication: "Garry Winogrand: Early Work," *The Archive* 26 (1999).

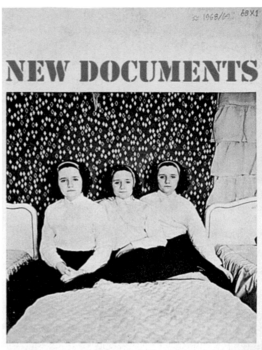

Two-fold brochure from *New Documents: Diane Arbus, Lee Friedlander, Garry Winogrand* exhibition, Museum of Modern Art, 1967
Garry Winogrand Archive

Joel-Peter Witkin

b. 13 September 1939, Brooklyn, New York

Photograph collection: 16 fine prints

Highlight: Artist's book of photogravures, *Twelve Photographs*, 1993.

MARION POST WOLCOTT:
A Member of the Wilkins Family Making Biscuits for Dinner on Corn-Shucking Day, at the Home of Mrs. Fred Wilkins, near Tallyho & Stem, N.C., 1939

Marion Post Wolcott

7 June 1910, Montclair, New Jersey –
24 November 1990, Santa Barbara, California

Photograph collection: 172 fine prints, most printed later from negatives made for the Farm Security Administration in the 1930s

Research materials: The Marion Post Wolcott Collection (AG 114) consists of files assembled by Wolcott during the last decade of her life to document her work with the Farm Security Administration and exhibition of her work in the 1970s and 1980s. Included are photocopies of letters from Roy Stryker and other research materials used by Wolcott in lectures and interviews. The strength of this collection resides in biographical reference materials and correspondence with Jack Delano, Ralph Steiner, Arthur Rothstein, and Russell Lee. (6 linear feet)

Highlight: Copy of letter from Paul Strand to Stryker recommending Wolcott.

John Wood

b. 10 July 1922, Delhi, California

Photograph collection: 13 fine prints, including 12 in *John Wood: A Portfolio of Offset Lithographs*, 1980

Willard E. Worden

20 November 1868, Philadelphia, Pennsylvania – 6 September 1946, Palo Alto, California

Photograph collection: 17 fine prints of San Francisco area subjects, 1904 to 1913

Don Worth

b. 2 January 1924

Photograph collection: 64 fine prints, including portfolio, *Twelve Photographs*, 1957

Cedric Wright

1889 – 1959

Photograph collection: 38 fine prints

Wu Dazhen

b. 25 June 1944, Chunchen, China

Photograph collection: 22 fine prints

Mihoko Yamagata

b. 1949, Zushi-shi, Kanagawa-ken, Japan

Photograph collection: 20 dye transfer prints in portfolio, *Kaiso*, 1986

Mariana Yampolsky

b. 6 September 1925, Chicago

Photograph collection: 19 fine prints

MAX YAVNO:
Mayan Indians and Photographer, 1981

Max Yavno

26 April 1911, New York – 4 March 1985,
San Francisco, California

Photograph collection: 734 fine prints

Research materials: The Max Yavno Archive
(AG 136) consists of the personal papers and
photographic materials of the photographer
Max Yavno. Included are correspondence files,
records of commercial assignments, exhibition
materials, publications about Yavno, books
from his personal library, financial records,
ceramic and bronze sculpture, and extensive
files of negatives, transparencies, contact
sheets, proof prints, and study prints. Yavno's
book projects, *The San Francisco Book* (1948)
and *The Los Angeles Book* (1950), are documented in the archive. (63 linear feet)

Highlights: Documentation of Yavno's collabo-
ration with M. F. K. Fisher on the book *The
Story of Wine in California,* 1962; files of *TV
Guide* magazine, one of Yavno's corporate
accounts; information regarding the Photo
League and Aaron Siskind.

Rights and restrictions: Copyright to Yavno's
writings and photographs is held by the Center
for Creative Photography, The University of
Arizona Foundation.

Animaux **des Indes**

Texte et photographies d'Ylla

Mise en pages de Luc Bouchage

Editions Clairefontaine   Lausanne

Title page spread in Ylla's last book, published posthumously by Editions Clairefontaine in 1958
Ylla Archive

Ylla (Camilla or Kamilla Koffler)

1911, Vienna – 30 March 1955, Bharatpur, India

Photograph collection: over 1000 fine and work prints

Research materials: The Ylla Archive (AG 138) contains papers and photographs documenting Ylla's career as an animal photographer and author of ten books, including several children's classics such as *The Sleepy Little Lion* and *The Small Little Bear*. Includes correspondence, writings, biographical and exhibition information, clippings, photographic materials, and copies of the books she published, 1937 to 1985. (7.5 linear feet)

Ruiko Yoshida

b. 1939, Hokkaido, Japan

Photograph collection: 17 gelatin silver prints selected by W. Eugene Smith for unrealized magazine *Sensorium*

P. Z. [name unknown]

active 1890s

Photograph collection: 13 Photocrom prints of Switzerland and Windsor Castle

C. and G. Zangaki (Adelphoi Zangaki, Zangaki Brothers)

active 1870s to ca. 1900

Photograph collection: 21 albumen prints of Egypt, ca. 1880s, from the Julia F. Corson Collection

Zaslavsky [first name unknown]

Photograph collection: 16 gelatin silver prints made while serving in the Lincoln Brigade during the Spanish Civil War, 1936 to 1939

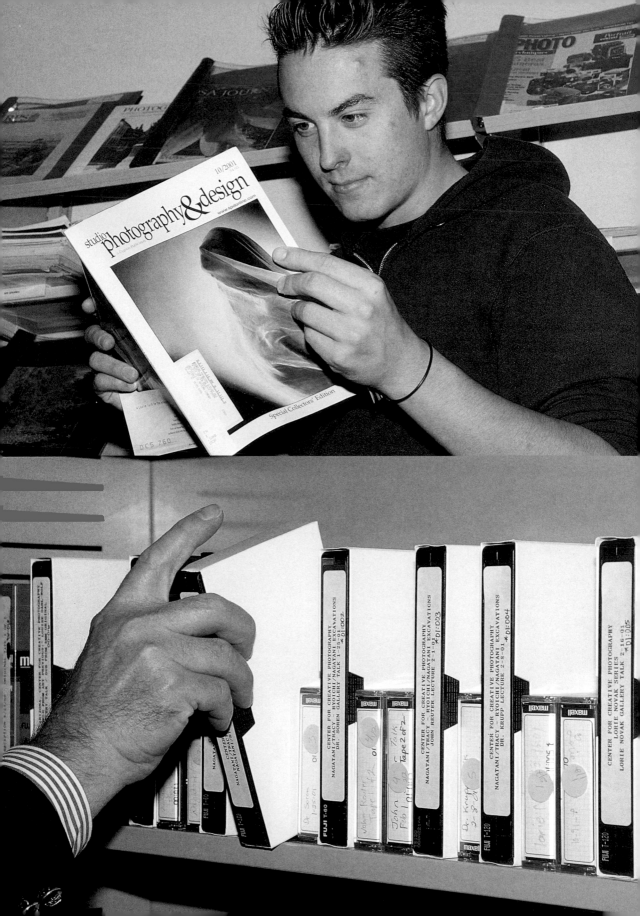

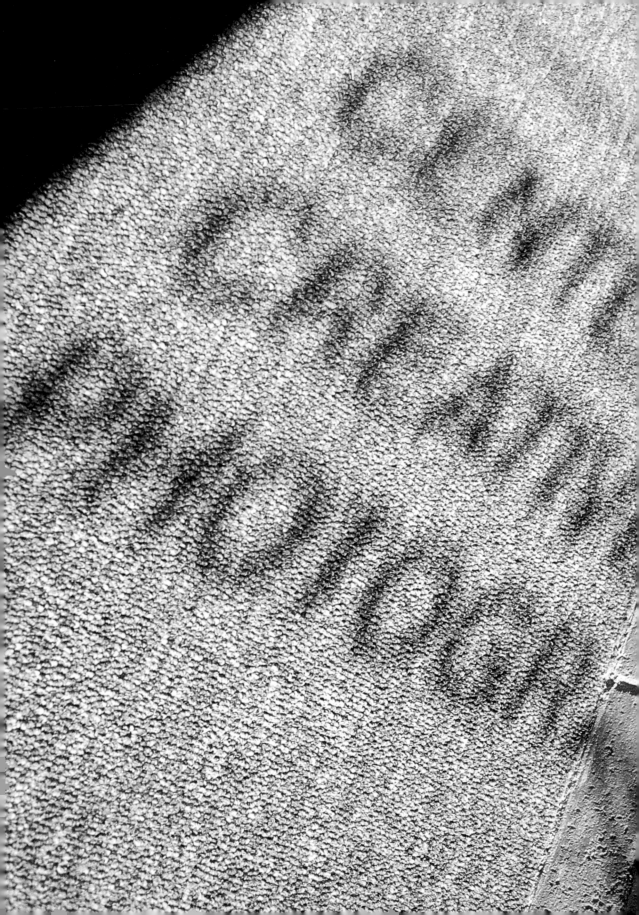

List of Illustrations:

Images from the CCP Photograph Collection

Abdullah Frères

Page 290   *Cuisinier ambulant*, ca. 1870s
Albumen print, 19.3 x 25.7 cm
Purchase
78:120:001

[albums]

Pages 206–07   *Greece*, 1880s
Assembled by Alice Maude Bovyer Cowell
Various photographers
Gift of Charles T. Mason and Pat Bovyer Mason
79:217:000

Pages 204–05   *Pacific Islands*, 1917
Parrish family album
Purchase
83:125:000

Ansel Adams

Page 36   *White Branches, Mono Lake,
California*, 1947
Gelatin silver print, 34.4 x 26.6 cm
Ansel Adams Archive
© 1985 Ansel Adams Publishing Rights Trust
78:152:112

Page 38   *Gravestone Carving and Lichens,
New England Cemetery, Concord,
Massachusetts*, ca. 1965
Gelatin silver print, 26.7 x 25.7 cm
Ansel Adams Archive
© 1985 Ansel Adams Publishing Rights Trust
84:090:229

Page 107   *Boards and Thistles, South San
Francisco*, 1932
Gelatin silver print, 22.8 x 16.7 cm
Ansel Adams Archive
© 1985 Ansel Adams Publishing Rights Trust
84:090:094

Page 262   *Leaves, Glacier Bay, Alaska,
ca. 1947
Gelatin silver print, 31.7 x 24.2 cm
Ansel Adams Archive
© 1985 Ansel Adams Publishing Rights Trust
84:092:215

Lola Alvarez Bravo

Page 42   *En su propia cárcel*, ca. 1950
Gelatin silver print, 18.4 x 21.2 cm
Lola Alvarez Bravo Archive
© 1995 Center for Creative Photography,
The University of Arizona Foundation
93:006:049

Page 264   *San Isidro Labrador*, n.d.
Gelatin silver print, 16.7 x 21 cm
Lola Alvarez Bravo Archive
© 1995 Center for Creative Photography,
The University of Arizona Foundation
93:006:039

Manuel Alvarez Bravo

Page 265   *La visita*, 1935
Gelatin silver print, 12.2 x 17.2 cm
Purchase
© 1935 Manuel Alvarez Bravo
78:095:013

Paul L. Anderson

Page 266   *M.G.A. with Camera Work*, 1909
Platinum print, 24.3 x 19.1 cm
Gift of Mrs. Raymond C. Collins
80:170:090

Dick Arentz

Page 267   *Chairs II, Vichy, France*, 1994
Palladium print, 16.3 x 41.9 cm
Purchase
© 1994 Dick Arentz
95:012:002

Richard Avedon

Page 50   *Cesar Chavez, Founder, United Farm Workers, Keene, California, 6-27-76*
From the portfolio *Rolling Stone: The Family*, 1976
Gelatin silver print, 25.5 x 20.1 cm
Richard Avedon Archive, Gift of the artist
© 1976 by Richard Avedon Inc., all rights reserved
89:109:031

Page 52   *Ezra Pound, Poet, June 30, 1958, Rutherford, New Jersey*, 1958
Gelatin silver print, 55.8 x 50.9 cm
Richard Avedon Archive, Gift of the artist
© 1958 by Richard Avedon Inc., all rights reserved
89:107:008

Page 268   *Elise Daniels, Turban by Paulette, Pré-Catelan, Paris, August 1948*
From the portfolio *Avedon/Paris*, 1978
Gelatin silver print, 35.7 x 44.8 cm
Purchase
© 1948 by Richard Avedon Inc., all rights reserved
89:110:009

Herbert Bayer

Page 271   *View from Pont Transbordeur*, 1928
Gelatin silver print, 36.1 x 23.2 cm
Gift of the Herbert Bayer Estate
© 2002 Herbert Bayer Estate
86:105:005

Lotte Beese

Page 93   *Untitled* [Hannes Meyer], ca. 1928
Gelatin silver print, 22.7 x 16.9 cm
Purchase
82:032:023

Louis Carlos Bernal

Page 54   *Dos Mujeres, Douglas, Arizona*, 1978
From the group exhibition *Espejo*
Incorporated color coupler print, 23 x 23 cm
Gift of the Mexican American Legal Defense and Educational Fund
© 1993 Lisa Bernal Brethour and Katrina Bernal
82:077:087

Page 271   *Cómoda*, 1977
From the series *Benitez Suite*
Gelatin silver print, 22.9 x 22.8 cm
Purchase
© 1993 Lisa Bernal Brethour and Katrina Bernal
79:087:003

Lucienne Bloch

Page 273   *Father* [Ernest Bloch] *with Mushrooms, Roveredo, Switzerland*, 1928
Gelatin silver print, 17.1 x 25 cm, printed 1974 by Eric Johnson
Purchase
© 1997 Old Stage Studios, Gualala, California
78:167:002

Karl Blossfeldt

Page 273   *Blumenbachia hieronymi. Geschlossene Samenkapsel, 18mal ver-grössert*, 1900–1928
From the portfolio *Karl Blossfeldt— 12 Photographien*, 1975
Gelatin silver print, 26 x 21 cm
Purchase
© Karl Blossfeldt Archiv, Ann and Jürgen Wilde, Cologne and Zülpich, Germany
76:209:012

Félix Bonfils

Page 274   *Les pyramides prises de Gizeh*, n.d.
Albumen print, 21.9 x 27.9 cm
Purchase
78:123:001

Brassaï

Page 90   *Le passage cloute*, 1937
Gelatin silver print, 29.3 x 22.7 cm
Gift of Ansel and Virginia Adams
© 1937 Estate Brassaï – Gilberte Brassaï
76:305:002

Josef Breitenbach and Henri Devaux

Page 60   *Rose Petal Exhaling Its Fragrance*, 1937–39
Selectively colored gelatin silver print, 27.1 x 22.2 cms
Josef Breitenbach Archive
© The Josef Breitenbach Trust, New York
89:088:077

Josef Breitenbach

Page 56   *Sybille Binder and Paul Robeson, Role Portrait in Othello*, ca. 1932
Toned gelatin silver print, 29.8 x 39.4 cm
Josef Breitenbach Archive
© The Josef Breitenbach Trust, New York
89:090:133

Page 61   Untitled [back view of young nude woman in the woods], ca. 1950
Gelatin silver print, 35.3 x 28 cm
Josef Breitenbach Archive
© The Josef Breitenbach Trust, New York
89:091:123

Page 275   *Josef Albers, Black Mountain College, North Carolina*, 1944
Gelatin silver print
Josef Breitenbach Archive
© The Josef Breitenbach Trust, New York

Dean Brown

Page 277   Untitled [sphinx-like sculpture in winter garden], 1969
From the series *Berlin*, 1969
Gelatin silver print, 15.5 x 10.6 cm
Dean Brown Archive, Gift of Carol Brown
© 2001 Dean Brown (with the permission of Carol Brown)
78:217:010

Laurie Brown

Page 233   *Convergence #9*, 1995
From the series *Divining Western Waters*
Iris print, 30.5 x 55.9 cm (irregular)
Water in the West Archive
© 2002 Laurie Brown
98:071:008

Francis J. Bruguière

Page 64   *Experiment* [multiple images, female face], ca. 1925
Gelatin silver print, 13.3 x 11.6 cm, printed 1982 by James Enyeart
Gift of James Enyeart
84:067:199

Page 65   *"Few Are Chosen"* [cut paper abstraction], 1931
Gelatin silver print, 11 x 9.1 cm, printed 1982 by James Enyeart
Gift of James Enyeart
84:067:040

Wynn Bullock

Page 279   *Old Typewriter*, 1951
Gelatin silver print, 18.9 x 24 cm
© 2002 Bullock Family Photography LLC, All Rights Reserved
76:051:022

Debbie Fleming Caffery

Page 280   Untitled [ghosting image], October 1985
From the series *Polly*
Gelatin silver print, 47.9 x 48.2 cm
Gift of the artist
© 1985 Debbie Fleming Caffery
92:157:021

Harry Callahan

Page 66   *Chicago*, ca. 1952
Dye transfer print, 22.4 x 34.1 cm
Harry Callahan Archive
© 1980 The Estate of Harry Callahan
79:082:009

Page 70   *Eleanor*, 1949
Gelatin silver print, 19.4 x 24.3 cm
© 1964 The Estate of Harry Callahan
76:031:006

Page 70   *Eleanor and Barbara, Chicago*, 1954
Gelatin silver print, 23.6 x 23.0 cm
Gift of Irving W. Rose
© 1996 The Estate of Harry Callahan
92:104:023

Page 281　*Detroit*, 1943
Gelatin silver print, 22.4 x 30.6 cm
© 1996 The Estate of Harry Callahan
79:029:005

Jo Ann Callis

Page 200　*Goldfish and Stringbeans*, 1980
From the portfolio *Jo Ann Callis*, 1984
Dye transfer print, 43.9 x 59.2 cm
Purchase
© 1980 Jo Ann Callis
86:016:007

Lucy Capehart

Page 282　*Sarah Natani in Her Sheep Corral,
　　Table Mesa near Shiprock, New Mexico,
　　1999*
Incorporated color coupler print, 37.9 x 46.6 cm
Indivisible Archive
© 2001 Lucy Capehart
2000:059:003

Koldo Chamorro

Page 191　Untitled [man with twisted face,
　　children in street], 1980s
From the series *España Mágica*
Gelatin silver print, 29.2 x 19.5 cm
Purchase
© 1986 Koldo Chamorro
90:018:001

Carl Chiarenza

Page 283　*Noumenon 256*, 1984/85
Gelatin silver print, 38.2 x 47.7 cm
Purchase
© 1985 Carl Chiarenza
86:013:001

William Christenberry

Page 72　*Church, between Greensboro and
　　Marion, Alabama*, 1973
From *The Alabama Box*, 1980
Incorporated color coupler print, 8.3 x 12.2 cm
Purchase
© 1973 William Christenberry
95:045:005

Page 75　*5¢ Sign, Demopolis,
　　Alabama*, 1976
From *The Alabama Box*, 1980
Incorporated color coupler print, 8.3 x 12.2 cm
Purchase
© 1976 William Christenberry
95:045:009

Larry Clark

Page 284　Untitled [Billy Mann], 1963
From the portfolio *Tulsa*, 1980
Gelatin silver print, 20.8 x 31.6 cm
Gift of Mimi and Ariel Halpern
© 1963 Larry Clark. Courtesy of the artist and
　　Luhring Augustine, New York
82:092:005

Linda Connor

Page 289　*Seven Sacred Pools, Maui,
　　Hawaii*, 1978
Gelatin silver printing-out paper print,
　　24.3 x 19.3 cm
Gift of the artist
© Linda S. Connor
88:038:012

Barbara Crane

Page 291　*City Lights, Chicago*, 1969
Gelatin silver print, 35 x 27.8 cm
Gift of Ansel and Virginia Adams
© 1969 Barbara Crane
76:312:004

Imogen Cunningham

Page 292　Untitled [montage of Franklin
　　Roosevelt, Herbert Hoover, and storm at
　　the White House], ca. 1935
Gelatin silver print, 24.5 x 19.3 cm
Purchase
© 1978 Imogen Cunningham Trust
88:055:003

Edward S. Curtis

Page 76　*Cheyenne*, ca. 1900–1910
Cyanotype, 19.9 x 14.3 cm (irregular)
Gift of Manford Magnuson
78:003:025

Louise Dahl-Wolfe

Page 80   *Japanese Bath, Betty Threat, Model*, 1954
Gelatin silver print, 46 x 35.9 cm
Louise Dahl-Wolfe Archive/Gift of the artist
© 1989 Center for Creative Photography, Arizona Board of Regents
85:017:008

Page 84   *Edward Hopper, Standing*, 1933
Gelatin silver print, 33.1 x 22.8 cm
Louise Dahl-Wolfe Archive/Gift of the Louise Dahl-Wolfe Trust
© 1989 Center for Creative Photography, Arizona Board of Regents
85:102:013

Page 293   *Dior Ball Gown, Paris*, 1950
Gelatin silver print, 29.8 x 25.2 cm
Louise Dahl-Wolfe Archive
© 1989 Center for Creative Photography, Arizona Board of Regents
93:072:052

Lynn Davis

Page 295   *Dogon Village, Mali*, 1997
Gelatin silver print, 48.2 x 48.2 cm
Gift of Steve Rifkin
© 1997 Lynn Davis
2000:087:001

Roy DeCarava

Page 296   *Embroidered Blouse, Washington, D.C.*, 1975
Gelatin silver print, 32.9 x 24.1 cm
Purchase
© 2002 Roy DeCarava
81:095:015

Robert Doisneau

Page 90   *Les animaux supérieurs*, 1954
Gelatin silver print, 33.5 x 49.6 cm
Purchase
© Robert Doisneau/Rapho
78:130:011

Juan Dolcet

Page 190   *Empalao*, 1968
Gelatin silver print, 25.8 x 33.4 cm
Gift of the artist
© 2002 Elias Dolcet del Almo
87:052:002

Terry Evans

Page 231   *Wheel That Raises Gate for Water Regulation, Cheyenne Bottoms, August 1992*
From the series *Western Waters*, No. 21
Gelatin silver print, 38.4 x 37.9 cm
Water in the West Archive
© 1992 Terry Evans
99:067:002

Adolf Fassbender

Page 300   *The Ice Serpent*, ca. 1933
Gelatin silver print, 41.2 x 33.5 cm
Adolf Fassbender Archive
©1998 Center for Creative Photography, The University of Arizona Foundation

Andreas Feininger

Page 85   *The Photojournalist Dennis Stock, Winner of the LIFE Young Photographers Contest*, 1951
Gelatin silver print, 34.5 x 26.6 cm
Andreas Feininger Archive
© Andreas Feininger / TimePix
81:030:001

Page 86   *Midtown Manhattan Seen from Weehawken, New Jersey*, 1942
Gelatin silver print, 25.6 x 34.1 cm
Andreas Feininger Archive
© Andreas Feininger / TimePix
81:040:037

Page 300   *Pattern Made of Dragonfly Wings* [variant], ca. 1935
Gelatin silver print, 18.1 x 23.5 cm
Andreas Feininger Archive
© 1935 Andreas Feininger
81:056:003

George Fiske

Page 302   *Bridal Veil Fall, 900 feet*, ca. 1880s
Albumen print, 18.3 x 11 cm
Gift of Virginia Adams
79:127:154

Gisèle Freund

Page 91   *Hôtel du Châtelet, Paris*, 1952
Gelatin silver print, 26.1 x 18.5 cm
Purchase
© 1952 Gisèle Freund
80:043:057

Geoffrey Fricker

Page 234   *Hamakuapoko Mill*, 1979
From the series *Sugar Mills*
Gelatin silver print, 45.7 x 58.1 cm
Water in the West Archive
© 1979 Geoff Fricker
98:046:001

Lee Friedlander

Page 304   *Sonora* [large saguaro with
    curving limb], 1992
Gelatin silver print, 37.8 x 37.5 cm
Purchase
© 1992 Lee Friedlander
98:022:003

Cristina García Rodero

Page 191   *Virgen y mártir, Brión*, 1978
Gelatin silver print, 23.7 x 36 cm
Gift of the artist
© 1978 Cristina Garcia Rodero
91:013:001

Flor Garduño

Page 126   *Arból de Yalalag, Yalalag, Mexico*,
    1983
Gelatin silver print, 34.4 x 44.4 cm
Purchase
© 2002 Flor Garduño
95:022:003

Ralph Gibson

Page 94   *Complutensian Polyglot Bible,
    Pierpont Morgan Library*, 2000
Iris print, 96.5 x 64.4 cm
On loan to the Ralph Gibson Archive
© 2000 Ralph Gibson
2001:002:037

Page 98   *Hands Over Prow*, 1969
Gelatin silver print, 45.3 x 30.4 cm
Ralph Gibson Archive / Gift of David and Lois
    Kuniansky
© 1969 Ralph Gibson
99:056:015

Page 308   *Sardinia*, 1980
From the series *Chiaroscuro*, 1974–80
Gelatin silver print, 31.4 x 20.6 cm
Purchase
© 1980 Ralph Gibson
81:149:003

Laura Gilpin

Page 102   *Cornice—Temple of Kukulcan,
    Chichen Itza, Yucatan*, 1932
Platinum print, 16.9 x 11.5 cm
Purchase
© 1979 Amon Carter Museum, Fort Worth,
    Texas, Bequest of Laura Gilpin
77:023:018

Page 309   *Navajos by Firelight*, 1932
Platinum print, 24.2 x 19.1 cm
Purchase
© 1979 Amon Carter Museum, Fort Worth,
    Texas, Bequest of Laura Gilpin
79:098:004

Peter Goin

Page 230   *Hot Springs at The Needles,
    Pyramid Lake, Nevada*, 1990
Incorporated color coupler print, 26.8 x 34.7 cm
Water in the West Archive
© 1990 Peter Goin
98:080:045

Judith Golden

Page 104   *Masks*, 1974–1982
Artist's book of gelatin silver prints with oil
    painting and applied sequins, glitter, beads
    and feathers, machine-stitched in plastic
    sleeves with black leather-texture cover
    (sizes vary)
Purchase
© 1982 Judith Golden
84:003:000

Page 106   *Persona #10*, 1983
From the *Persona Series*, 1982-85
Polaroid Polacolor ER 20 x 24 inch Land print,
    70 x 53 cm
Purchase
© 1983 Judith Golden
83:080:001

John Gutmann

Page 24   *"Good Luck" Toes*, 1945
Gelatin silver print, 28.4 x 25.9 cm
John Gutmann Archive
© 2000 Center for Creative Photography,
    Arizona Board of Regents

Page 311   *Machine Gunners,*
    San Francisco, 1950
Gelatin silver print, 27.2 x 25.9 cm
John Gutmann Archive
© 2000 Center for Creative Photography,
    Arizona Board of Regents

Otto Hagel

Page 130   *New York Stock Exchange*, 1938
Gelatin silver print, 34.2 x 26.3 cm
Hansel Mieth and Otto Hagel Archive / Gift of
    Hansel Mieth Hagel
©1998 Center for Creative Photography,
    The University of Arizona Foundation
98:110:020

Page 335   *Automobile Graveyard*, 1937
Gelatin silver print, 26.4 x 34.2 cm
Hansel Mieth and Otto Hagel Archive / Gift of
    Hansel Mieth Hagel
©1998 Center for Creative Photography,
    The University of Arizona Foundation
91:045:010

Johan Hagemeyer

Page 313   *Trees on Telegraph Hill*, 1925
Gelatin silver print, 22.6 x 16.8 cm
Purchase
81:111:112

Charles Harbutt

Page 111   *Riverdale Balcony, Riverdale,*
    New York, 1968
Gelatin silver print, 30.6 x 45.8 cm
Charles Harbutt Archive / Gift of Sarah Harbutt
© 1968 Charles Harbutt
97:055:028

Page 112   *Scrivener, Wall Street,*
    New York, 1970
Gelatin silver print, 30.3 x 45.9 cm
Charles Harbutt Archive / Gift of Sarah Harbutt
© 1970 Charles Harbutt
97:028:006

Page 113   *Boys Smoking in Car, Reform*
    School, New York, 1963
Gelatin silver print, 30.4 x 45.6 cm
Charles Harbutt Archive / Gift of Sarah Harbutt
© 1963 Charles Harbutt
97:028:004

Robert Heinecken

Page 114   *Recto/Verso #3*, 1989
From the portfolio *Recto/Verso*, 1989
Silver dye bleach print, 27.7 x 20.0 cm
Robert Heinecken Archive/Purchase
© 1989 Robert Heinecken
91:014:003

Page 315   *Cream Six*, 1970
Photo emulsion and chalk on canvas in 6 panels,
    103.3 x 226 cm
© 1970 Robert Heinecken
79:046:006

Lewis W. Hine

Page 161   *Bowery Mission Bread Line,*
    2 A.M., 1907
From the portfolio *Lewis W. Hine, 1874–1940*,
    1942
Gelatin silver print, 11.8 x 15 cm
Gift of W. Eugene Smith
78:038:030

Eikoh Hosoe

Page 118   *Man and Woman, #24*, 1960
From the series *Man and Woman*, 1959–60
Gelatin silver print, 30.9 x 54.4 cm
Gift of Eugene and Susan Spiritus
© 1960 Eikoh Hosoe
86:063:003

Graciela Iturbide

Page 125   *El Sacrificio, La Mixteca*, 1992
Gelatin silver print, 44.1 x 31.4 cm
Gift of the artist
© 1990–92 Graciela Iturbide
95:019:010

Harold Jones

Page 320   Untitled [view into drawer of small
    tools], 1999
From the series *A House Alone: Photographs
    of Frederick Sommer's House*
© 1999 Harold Jones
Harold Jones Collection

Mark Klett

Page 323   *Stop Sign near Open Shooting
    Range, Reach 10, Granite Reef Aqueduct,
    North Phoenix, 10/20/84*
From the *Central Arizona Project Photographic
    Survey*
Gelatin silver print, 27.8 x 35.5 cm
Gift of the artist
© 1984 Mark Klett
86:044:001

Clarence John Laughlin

Page 325   *Light as Protagonist*, 1949
From the series *Group K: Visual Poems*
Gelatin silver print, 24.5 x 19.6 cm
Gift of Wynn Bullock
© 1981 The Historic New Orleans Collection
76:246:011

David Levinthal

Page 327   Untitled [Hitler doll saluting
    soldiers], 1994
From the series *Mein Kampf*, 1994–95
Polaroid Polacolor ER 20 x 24 in Land print,
    61 x 51 cm
Purchase
© 1994 David Levinthal
95:062:017

Helen Levitt

Page 327   *Halloween, New York*, ca. 1942
Gelatin silver print, 16.2 x 23.8 cm
Purchase
© 1965 Helen Levitt
92:083:001

Jerome Liebling

Page 160   *Boy and Car, New York City*, 1949
From the portfolio *Jerome Liebling
    Photographs*, 1976
Gelatin silver print, 25.4 x 25.4 cm
Purchase
© 1961 Jerome Liebling
77:060:001

Heinz Loew

Page 269   *Bits*, 1928
Gelatin silver print, 11.3 x 9.3 cm
Purchase
82:032:002

Danny Lyon

Page 328   *Bus Stop, Tehuantepec,
    Oaxaca*, 1978
From the portfolio *Danny Lyon*, 1979
Gelatin silver print from paper negative,
    33.5 x 22.3 cm
Gift of Robert Callaway
© 1978 Danny Lyon
86:064:028

Joan Lyons

Page 329   *Patio, Fountain / Pavilion,
    New York*, 1982
Vandyke print, 40.4 x 48.0 cm
Purchase
© 1982 Joan Lyons
84:013:001

Robert Mapplethorpe

Page 330   *Lisa Lyon*, 1982
Gelatin silver print, 48.9 x 38.7 cm
Gift of the Robert Mapplethorpe Foundation,
    Inc., MAP# 767
© 1982 The Estate of Robert Mapplethorpe.
    Used with permission.
91:011:002

Margrethe Mather

Page 122   *Semi-nude* [Billy Justema wearing
    kimono], ca. 1923
Gelatin silver print, 9.3 x 11.8 cm
78:150:001

Page 330   *Sadakichi Hartmann*, ca. 1935
Gelatin silver print, 24.0 x 18.7 cm
Purchase
79:013:021

Lawrence McFarland

Page 331   *Petroglyph on Hill Overlooking
    Site of Picacho Pumping Plant*, 1985
From the *Central Arizona Project Photographic
    Survey*
Gelatin silver print, 26.4 x 43.1 cm
Gift of the artist
© 1985 Lawrence McFarland
86:046:004

Pedro Meyer

Page 126   *La boda en Coyoacán*, 1983
Gelatin silver print, 20.3 x 30.4 cm
Purchase
© 1983 Pedro Meyer
84:012:001

Hansel Mieth

Page 128   *Young Man Sleeping in Box
    Car*, 1936
Gelatin silver print, 25.0 x 33.4 cm
Hansel Mieth and Otto Hagel Archive
©1998 Center for Creative Photography,
    The University of Arizona Foundation
98:106:069

Richard Misrach

Page 336   *Playboy #90 (hole in mouth)*, 1990
From the series *Desert Canto XI: Violence
    (The playboys)*
Incorporated color coupler print, 73.7 x 92.4 cm
Purchase
© 1990 Richard Misrach
97:075:001

Kozo Miyoshi

Page 132   *B-6*, 1987–91
From the series *Roots <NE>*
Gelatin silver print, 55.4 x 44.9 cm
Gift of the artist
© 1992 Kozo Miyoshi
96:040:002

Tina Modotti

Page 136   *Circus Tent*, 1924
Platinum print, 23.3 x 17.6 cm
Purchase
85:082:001

Page 280   *Lou Bunin, Puppet Master,
    producer of "Hairy Ape," with Marionettes*,
    ca. 1929
Gelatin silver print, 23.3 x 19.0 cm
Purchase
93:027:006

Ruthe Morand

Page 337   *Preparing Canal for Lining at
    Apache Junction*, 1985
From the *Central Arizona Project Photographic
    Survey*
Gelatin silver print, 29.7 x 44.3 cm
Gift of the artist
© 2002 Ruthe Morand
86:043:009

Jun Morinaga

Page 120   Untitled [shadows on water],
    ca. 1963
From book *River, Its Shadow of Shadows*, 1978
Gelatin silver print, 19.3 x 28.7 cm
Purchase
© 1978 Jun Morinaga
80:004:001

Daido Moriyama

Page 120   *Ferryboats, Tsugaru Strait*, 1971
Gelatin silver print, 23.4 x 34.4 cm
Purchase, with matching funds from Hitachi
    America, Ltd.
© 2002 Daido Moriyama
90:009:003

William Mortensen

Page 138   *Torse*, ca. 1935
From the portfolio *Pictorial Photography*,
    ca. 1935
Gelatin silver print, 13.1 x 16.6 cm
Gift of Fritz Kaeser
76:251:004

Page 142   Untitled [George Dunham], n.d.
Gelatin silver print, 33.3 x 22.6 cm
Purchase
81:093:017

Stefan Moses

Page 340   *Krabbenfischer, Travemunde*,
    1963–64
From the series *Deutsche*
Gelatin silver print, 33.0 x 27.2 cm
Purchase
© 1963 Stefan Moses
82:018:047

Eadweard Muybridge

Page 203   *Panama Bay by Moonlight*,
    1875–76
From the album *Photographic Studies of
    Central America and the Isthmus of Panama*,
    1876
Albumen print, 13.6 x 23.7 cm
76:253:041

Hans Namuth

Page 341   *Marcos Pablo Jeronimo, 57 Years
    Old, Bagmaker and Carpenter*, 1978
From the series *Todos Santos Cuchumatán*
Gelatin silver print, 39.6 x 35.1 cm
Purchase
© 1990 Hans Namuth Ltd.
81:188:002

Ikko Narahara

Page 119   *Japanesque #46,
    Sojiji, Japan*, 1969
From the series *Zen*
Gelatin silver print, 45.9 x 33.2 cm
Purchase, with matching funds from Hitachi
    America, Ltd.
© 1969 Ikko Narahara
90:012:002

Esta Nesbitt

Page 342   *Selenium Songs*, 1972
Xerographic prints, 21.3 x 84.8 cm
Esta Nesbitt Archive / Gift of Saul and
    Meryl Nesbitt
© 2002 Esta Nesbitt
83:203:003

Floris M. Neusüss

Page 92   *Engel*, 1967
Gelatin silver photogram, 32.5 x 15 cm
Gift of the artist
© 1967 Floris M. Neusüss, Kassel
93:052:001

Beaumont Newhall

Page 146   *Henri Cartier-Bresson,
    New York*, 1946
Gelatin silver print, 23.7 x 35.4 cm
Purchase
© 1946 Beaumont Newhall, The Estate of
    Beaumont Newhall and Nancy Newhall,
    Courtesy of Scheinbaum and Russek, Ltd.,
    Santa Fe, New Mexico
78:030:002

Sonya Noskowiak

Page 150   *Calla Lily*, 1930
Gelatin silver print, 17.7 x 23.2 cm
Gift of Arthur Noskowiak
© 1930 Arthur F. Noskowiak
76:009:248

Page 152   Untitled
    [Golden Gate Bridge], 1930s
Gelatin silver print, 24.2 x 18.8 cm
Gift of Arthur Noskowiak
© 1930 Arthur F. Noskowiak
76:009:229

Page 345   *Water Lily Leaves*, 1931
Gelatin silver print, 16.6 x 22 cm
Gift of Arthur Noskowiak
© 1931 Arthur F. Noskowiak
76:009:211

Marion Palfi

Page 153   Untitled [three men in boat on
    river, bridge in background], 1967–69
From the series *First I Liked the Whites, I Gave
    Them Fruits*
Gelatin silver print, 30.7 x 42.2 cm
Marion Palfi Archive /Gift of the Menninger
    Foundation and Martin Magner
© Martin Magner
83:110:083

Page 154   Untitled [elderly woman, head on
    her arms, in bedroom], 1955–57
From the series *You Have Never Been Old*
Gelatin silver print, 23.7 x 34.6 cm
Marion Palfi Archive /Gift of the Menninger
    Foundation and Martin Magner
© Martin Magner
83:108:027

Page 155   Untitled [man seated outside
    storefronts], 1949
From the series *There Is No More Time*
Gelatin silver print, 34.5 x 41.9 cm
Marion Palfi Archive /Gift of the Menninger
    Foundation and Martin Magner
© Martin Magner
83:105:039

Page 347   *Chaim Gross—Working in His
    Studio Alone*, 1944
From the series *Great American Artists of
    Minority Groups*
Gelatin silver print, 20.7 x 19.6 cm
Marion Palfi Archive /Gift of the Menninger
    Foundation and Martin Magner
© Martin Magner
83:102:071

Mickey Pallas

Page 158   *Hula Hoopers, Chicago*, 1958
Gelatin silver print, 32 x 48 cm
Mickey Pallas Archive / Gift of the artist
    and Pat Pallas
© 1995 Center for Creative Photography,
    The University of Arizona Foundation
94:057:053

Page 348   *Sugar Ray Robinson and Abe
    Saperstein, Paris*, n.d.
Gelatin silver print, 26.7 x 26.4 cm
Mickey Pallas Archive / Gift of the artist
    and Pat Pallas
© 1995 Center for Creative Photography,
    The University of Arizona Foundation
94:057:039

Mitchell Payne

Page 349   Untitled [infant in surgery],
    1970–72
From the series *Neurosurgeons in Action*
Gelatin silver print, 20.7 x 14.0 cm
Mitchell Payne Archive
© 1979 Linda M. Montano
81:134:003

Bernard Plossu

Page 89   *Fulani Nomad, Niger*, 1975
Gelatin silver print, 29.9 x 20.1 cm
Purchase
© 1975 Bernard Plossu
79:138:002

Marta Povo

Page 190   *Campanet, Mallorca*, 1984
From the series *Light*, 182/8
Gelatin silver print, 41.8 x 41.9 cm
Purchase
© 1984 Marta Povo
90:007:002

Charles Pratt

Page 353   *Roxbury, Connecticut*, 1964
Gelatin silver print, 22.5 x 34.1 cm
Gift of John Gossage
© 1980 Julie Pratt Shattuck
92:079:014

Werner Rohde

Page 93 *Karneval*, ca. 1928
Gelatin silver print, 24.3 x 17.9 cm (irregular)
Purchase
82:030:007

Walter Rosenblum

Page 161 *Women and Baby Carriage,
     Pitt Street, New York*, 1938
Gelatin silver print, 26.7 x 34.2 cm
Gift of Nina Rosenblum
© 1938 Walter Rosenblum
94:031:008

Naomi Savage

Page 357 *Roman Profile*, 1969–80
Photo-intaglio, 22 x 15 cm
Gift of Gordon Braine
© 1980 Naomi Savage
83:119:005

John P. Schaefer

Page 357 *St. Anthony and the Christ Child,
     Mission San Xavier del Bac, Tucson, Arizona,
     1977*
From the portfolio *Bac: Where the Waters
     Gather*
Gelatin silver print, 18.5 x 13.5 cm
Gift of the artist
© 1978 John P. Schaefer
78:036:010

Ann Simmons-Myers

Page 359 *Blast Foreman Trey Gardner
     with Blasting Compound at Site of Picacho
     Pumping Plant*, 1984
From the *Central Arizona Project Photographic
     Survey*
Gelatin silver print, 26.5 x 24.9 cm
Gift of the artist
© 1984 Ann Simmons-Myers
86:045:009

Aaron Siskind

Page 164 *Remembering Joseph Cornell in
     Merida 12*, 1975
Gelatin silver print, 24.7 x 23.6 cm
Aaron Siskind Archive
© 1991 Aaron Siskind Foundation
80:165:052

Page 166 *Terrors and Pleasures of
     Levitation 94*, 1961
Gelatin silver print, 25.1 x 24.2 cm
Aaron Siskind Archive
© 1991 Aaron Siskind Foundation
90:019:211

Page 360 *Harlem*, 1940
From the *Harlem Document*, 1932–1940
Gelatin silver print, 24.6 x 21.7 cm
Aaron Siskind Archive
© 1991 Aaron Siskind Foundation
90:019:058

Henry Holmes Smith

Page 168 *Royal Pair*, 1951/1982
Dye transfer print, 8.7 x 5.7 cm
Gift of the Estate of Henry Holmes Smith
© 1982 Ted Smith, Smith Family Trust
88:046:003

Page 170 *Royal Pair, 8*, 1951/1982
Dye transfer print, 8.7 x 5.7 cm
Purchase
© 1982 Ted Smith, Smith Family Trust
82:076:004

Keith Smith

Page 363 *Book No. 81*, 1981
Artist's book of various processes
Purchase
© 1981 Keith Smith
84:021:000

W. Eugene Smith

Page 172 *Untitled [Haiti]*, 1958–59
Gelatin silver print, 49.0 x 32.0 cm
W. Eugene Smith Archive
© The Heirs of W. Eugene Smith, courtesy
     Black Star, Inc., New York
82:127:008

Page 175 *Earl Hines*, 1964
Gelatin silver print, 24.3 x 32.4 cm
W. Eugene Smith Archive
© The Heirs of W. Eugene Smith, courtesy
     Black Star, Inc., New York
82:131:004

Page 364   *Holy Water Font in Leyte Cathedral, Used as Hospital*, 1944
From the essay "Hospital on Leyte"
Gelatin silver print, 32.0 x 26.9 cm
W. Eugene Smith Archive
© The Heirs of W. Eugene Smith, courtesy Black Star, Inc., New York
82:102:112

Frederick Sommer

Page 178   *Smoke on Glass*, 1962
Gelatin silver print, 33.9 x 26.5 cm
Frederick Sommer Archive
© 1962 Frederick and Frances Sommer Foundation
76:032:037

Page 180   *Valise d'Adam*, 1949
Gelatin silver print, 24.1 x 19.2 cm
Frederick Sommer Archive
© 1949 Frederick and Frances Sommer Foundation
76:032:029

Page 182   *Paracelsus (Paint on Cellophane)*, 1959
Gelatin silver print, 33.7 x 25.8 cm
Frederick Sommer Archive
© 1959 Frederick and Frances Sommer Foundation
76:032:035

Page 365   Untitled [collaged medical illustrations, including veins, female reproductive organs, tailbone, and pelvis], 1991
Paper collage, 29.5 x 36.2 cm
Frederick Sommer Archive/ Gift of the artist
© 1991 Frederick and Frances Sommer Foundation
92:062:005

Albert Sands Southworth & Josiah Johnson Hawes

Page 186 and 188   *Sleeping Baby*, 1860
Daguerreotype, 16.0 x 13.7 cm
Gift of Ansel and Virginia Adams
76:351:002

Peter Stackpole

Page 192   *Watching a load of rivets coming up against the backdrop of San Francisco*, 1935
Gelatin silver print, 17.6 x 23.7 cm
Peter Stackpole Archive / Gift of the Stackpole Family
© Kathie Stackpole Bunnell, for the Stackpole Family
98:038:065

Page 194   *Alfred Hitchcock at Academy Awards Banquet*, 1941
Gelatin silver print, 26.8 x 27.9 cm
Peter Stackpole Archive / Gift of the Stackpole Family
© Peter Stackpole / TimePix
98:035:059

Page 367   *Rita Hayworth and Orson Welles*, 1945
Gelatin silver print, 32.0 x 26.7 cm
Peter Stackpole Archive / Gift of the Stackpole Family
© Peter Stackpole / TimePix
98:035:003

Edward Steichen

Page 368   *Dana*, n.d.
Gelatin silver print, 24.6 x 19.4 cm
Bequest of Edward Steichen by direction of Joanna T. Steichen and International Museum of Photography at George Eastman House
Reprinted with permission of Joanna T. Steichen
© Joanna T. Steichen
82:069:002

Ralph Steiner

Page 369   *Ham and Eggs*, 1929–30
Gelatin silver print, 24 x 19 cm
Purchase
© 2002 Ralph Steiner
81:135:004

Sharon Stewart

Page 232   *El Cerrito y La Acequia Madre: Diggin' Ditch*, 1993
Gelatin silver print, 31.7 x 31.4 cm
Water in the West Archive / Purchased in part with funds from the Gay Block and Malka Drucker Philanthropic Fund of The Endowment Fund of the Jewish Community of Houston; and Joan Morgenstern
© 1993 Sharon Stewart
98:087:008

Alfred Stieglitz

Page 370   Untitled [New York City street scene], 1896-99
Gelatin silver print, 8.3 x 10.8 cm
Gift of Herbert Small
© Courtesy The Georgia O'Keeffe Foundation
76:049:003

Paul Strand

Page 195   *Toadstool and Grasses, Maine*, 1928
Platinum print, 24.6 x 19.4 cm
Purchase
© 1950 Aperture Foundation, Inc., Paul Strand Archive
76:011:036

Page 196   *White Sheets, New Orleans, Louisiana*, 1918
Palladium print, 23.3 x 18.8 cm
Purchase
© 1981 Aperture Foundation, Inc., Paul Strand Archive
76:011:008

Page 198   *The Family, Luzzara, Italy* [three small variants], 1953
Gelatin silver study prints, each 14.9 x 11.7 cm
Gifts of the Paul Strand Foundation in honor of Ansel Adams
© 2001 Aperture Foundation, Inc., Paul Strand Archive
81:082:002, 81:082:004, 81:082:017

Jean-Pierre Sudre

Page 91   Untitled [butterflies and grasses], 1979
From the series *Végétal & Insectes*
Chemically altered and toned gelatin silver print, 30.4 x 23.9 cm
Purchase
© 2002 Jean-Pierre Sudre
79:112:004

Ruth Thorne-Thomsen

Page 374   *Parable, Wisconsin*, 1991
From the series *Songs of the Sea*
Gelatin silver print, 11 x 12.8 cm
Purchase
© 2002 Ruth Thorne-Thomsen
96:051:009

George A. Tice

Page 375   *Old Amish Men, Lancaster, Pennsylvania*, 1966
From *The Amish Portfolio*, ca. 1968
Gelatin silver print, 11.3 x 15.1 cm
Gift of the artist
© 1970 George A. Tice
77:025:011

Arthur Tress

Page 210   *Whiteface Mountain, New York*, 1989.
  Howls echo over the hills
  As the lone wolf beckons a friend;
  In this wide open country,
  Solitude may in fact be his end.
From the series *Fish Tank Sonata*
Silver dye bleach print, 38.6 x 38.6 cm
Purchase
© 1989 Arthur Tress
94:034:021

Page 375   *Initiations 8:5*, 1974
Gelatin silver print, 18.8 x 18.9 cm
Gift of the artist
© 1974 Arthur Tress
86:032:003

Tseng Kwong Chi
Page 212   *New York, New York,* 1979
From *The Expeditionary Series*
Gelatin silver print, 91.5 x 91.5 cm
Purchase
© 1979 Muna Tseng Dance Projects, Inc.,
    New York City
94:052:081

Jerry N. Uelsmann
Page 214   Untitled [framed tree photograph
    over couch with floating leaves], 1987
Gelatin silver print, 38.2 x 48.2 cm
Purchase
© 1987 Jerry N. Uelsmann
2000:061:001

Page 216   Untitled [cube over surf], 1979
Gelatin silver print, 39.6 x 49.7 cm
On extended loan from the artist
© 1979 Jerry N. Uelsmann
82:056:004

Page 376   *Equivalent,* 1964
Gelatin silver print, 34.6 x 24.1 cm
© 1964 Jerry N. Uelsmann
76:007:005

Willard Van Dyke
Page 218   Untitled [detail of hay rake and
    window], 1967
Polaroid 4 x 5-inch Land print, 8.9 x 10.5 cm
Gift of the artist
© 2001 Willard Van Dyke Estate
87:035:003

Page 378   *Ventilators,* ca. 1933
Gelatin silver print, 24.0 x 16.2 cm
Purchase
© 2001 Willard Van Dyke Estate
84:074:001

Laura Volkerding
Page 222   *Louisiana,* 1972
Gelatin silver print, 19.9 x 29.8 cm
Laura Volkerding Archive
© 1996 Center for Creative Photography,
    The University of Arizona Foundation
96:090:061

Page 224   *Coubertin,* 1986
Gelatin silver print, 31.9 x 40.1 cm
Laura Volkerding Archive
© 1996 Center for Creative Photography,
    The University of Arizona Foundation
96:102:065

Page 225   *Folly at Santa Rosa Ranch,*
    Coachella Valley, 1986
Gelatin silver print, 19.4 x 73.1 cm
Laura Volkerding Archive
© 1996 Center for Creative Photography,
    The University of Arizona Foundation
96:099:011

Todd Walker
Page 226   Untitled [view of road through
    windshield], 1969
Gelatin silver print with Sabattier effect and
    selective toning, 18 x 24.7 cm
Gift of the artist
© 1969 Melanie Walker
78:054:003

Page 229   *Chris, Veiled,* 1970
Gelatin silver print with Sabattier effect,
    24.8 x 18.5 cm
Gift of the artist
© 1970 Melanie Walker
86:027:002

Todd Webb
Page 236   *Detail, Wall Opposite My Studio*
    Door, Paris, 1950
Gelatin silver print, 24.1 x 19.1 cm
Todd Webb Archive
© 1950 Todd Webb
85:108:044

Page 381   *Masie, "Queen of the Bowery,"*
    1946
Gelatin silver print, 29.3 x 23.1 cm
Todd Webb Archive /Purchase
© 1946 Todd Webb
97:039:001

Weegee
Page 382   *"Lost Children," June 9, 1941*
Gelatin silver print, 33.8 x 26.8 cm
Purchase
© Weegee/ International Center of
    Photography/ Getty Images
78:107:003

Brian Weil
Page 382   *Transvestite Safe-Sex Outreach
    Worker, Dominican Republic*, 1987
Gelatin silver print, 16.6 x 16.4 cm
Gift of the Weil Family
© 1992 Brian Weil

Dan Weiner
Page 383   Untitled [men in blankets walking
    on busy street, South Africa], 1954
From the book *South Africa in Transition*, text
    by Alan Paton, 1956
Gelatin silver print, 34.1 x 22.6 cm
Dan Weiner Archive
© 1956 Sandra Weiner

Sandra Weiner
Page 163   *East 26th Street,
    New York, NY*, 1948
Gelatin silver print, 16.1 x 23.9 cm
Gift of the artist
© 1948 Sandra Weiner
96:031:001

Brett Weston
Page 109   *Three Fingers and an Ear*, 1929
Gelatin silver print, 18.1 x 24.3 cm
Gift of Arthur Noskowiak
© The Brett Weston Archive
76:045:001

Page 238   Untitled [leaf, Hawaii], ca. 1980s
Gelatin silver print, 29.8 x 27.1 cm
© The Brett Weston Archive

Page 240   *Skylight, Midtown*, 1947
From the portfolio *New York: Twelve
    Photographs*, n.d.
Gelatin silver print, 24.4 x 19.2 cm
© The Brett Weston Archive
76:036:005

Page 384   Untitled [leaf, Hawaii], ca. 1985
Gelatin silver print, 32.9 x 26.8 cm
© The Brett Weston Archive

Edward Weston
Page 242   *The White Iris*, 1921
Platinum or palladium print, 24.1 x 19.0 cm
Purchase
© 1981 Center for Creative Photography,
    Arizona Board of Regents
76:005:027

Page 244   *Nude Floating*, 1939
Gelatin silver print, 19.1 x 24.4 cm
Edward Weston Archive
© 1981 Center for Creative Photography,
    Arizona Board of Regents
81:110:044

Page 244   *Winter Zero Schwartzel's "Bottle
    Farm," Farmersville, Ohio*, 1941
Gelatin silver print, 19.5 x 24.6 cm
Edward Weston Archive/Gift of the Heirs of
    Edward Weston
© 1981 Center for Creative Photography,
    Arizona Board of Regents
81:280:046

Page 248   Verso of *Pepper No. 30*, 1930
Gelatin silver print, 24.4 x 19.3 cm
Gift of Arthur Noskowiak
© 1981 Center for Creative Photography,
    Arizona Board of Regents
76:010:006

Page 385   *Excusado, Mexico*, 1925
Gelatin silver print, 24.1 x 19.2 cm
Edward Weston Archive
© 1981 Center for Creative Photography,
    Arizona Board of Regents
81:252:049

Minor White
Page 25   *Lake Almanor, California,
    April 4, 1947*
Gelatin silver print, 9.4 x 11.9 cm
Gift of Ansel and Virginia Adams
© 2002 The Trustees of Princeton University.
    All Rights Reserved.
76:040:015

Page 390   *Gallery Cove, Point Lobos,
    California*, 1953
Gelatin silver print, 7.3 x 11.5 cm
Gift of the Heirs of Edward Weston
© 2002 The Trustees of Princeton University.
    All Rights Reserved.
84:017:001

Garry Winogrand

Page 250   [New York—women in coats
    among sidewalk crowd], ca. 1960-61
Gelatin silver print, 22.7 x 34.1 cm
Garry Winogrand Archive/Gift of the artist
© 1984 The Estate of Garry Winogrand
83:205:021

Page 251   [Texas—steer with wild eyes in
    corral], 1964
Gelatin silver print, 22.8 x 34.1 cm
Garry Winogrand Archive/Gift of the artist
© 1984 The Estate of Garry Winogrand
83:211:069

Marion Post Wolcott

Page 394   *A Member of the Wilkins Family
    Making Biscuits for Dinner on Corn-
    Shucking Day, at the Home of Mrs. Fred
    Wilkins, near Tallyho & Stem, N.C.*, 1939
Gelatin silver print, 22.6 x 30.8 cm
Gift of Ansel and Virginia Adams
© 1975 Linda Wolcott-Moore
85:125:049

Max Yavno

Page 395   *Mayan Indians and Photographer*,
    1981
Gelatin silver print, 25.4 x 34.1 cm
Max Yavno Archive
© 1998 Center for Creative Photography,
    The University of Arizona Foundation
92:152:061

Darsie Alexander is Associate Curator in the Department of Prints, Drawings, and Photographs at the Baltimore Museum of Art. She was awarded the Ansel Adams Research Fellowship in 1994 for her study of Sonya Noskowiak. Since then, she has organized numerous exhibitions including *Sets and Situations* (2000) and *Anatomically Incorrect* (1999) while assistant curator in the Department of Photography at The Museum of Modern Art.

Stuart Alexander is an independent curator and photo historian based in New York City since 1997. In 1980 he organized the Andreas Feininger Archive and curated an exhibition from its riches. He is the archivist to the Brassaï Estate, and author of *Robert Frank: A Bibliography, Filmography and Exhibition Chronology, 1946–1985*, and numerous other scholarly and critical articles. He was a Guest Scholar at the J. Paul Getty Museum in 2001.

Cristina Cuevas-Wolf is an art historian with a Ph.D. from Northwestern University. She received an Ansel Adams Research Fellowship from the CCP in 1998 to support her work on Lola Alvarez Bravo. The first chapter of her dissertation was published in 1996 under the title *Guillermo Kahlo and Casasola: Architectural Form and Urban Unrest,* in the journal *History of Photography*. She is currently researching a book on photomontage in the 1930s.

Jennifer S. Edwards is the Curator of

Visual Resources at the Bowdoin College Art Department. She earned a Master's degree in art history from the University of Arizona where her thesis on Louise Dahl-Wolfe grew out of the work she did while an Ansel Adams Intern at the CCP.

James Enyeart is the Anne and John Marion Professor and Director of the Marion Center for Photographic Arts at The College of Santa Fe. He served from 1977 to 1989 as the second director of the CCP. Since then, he has been Director of George Eastman House, 1989 to 1995, and then designer of the new, innovative photographic program at The College of Santa Fe. In the mid-1970s, he was director of the Friends of Photography. He has received numerous international awards and honors, authored many articles and books, and is himself a photographer.

Cass Fey has been Curator of Education at the CCP since 1993. She promotes life-long learning through the aesthetic and historical appreciation of original works of art. She is a frequent presenter at national photography and arts education conferences, has published in *Art Education*, the *Journal of the National Art Education Association*, and has served on the Publications Committee of the Society for Photographic Education.

Carol Flax is an Assistant Professor in the Department of Art at the University of Arizona where she teaches photography and digital media. She received her M.F.A.

from the California Institute of the Arts and now works primarily with digital technologies, making art ranging from print to interactive installation to publication on the World Wide Web. Her work has been extensively exhibited and published internationally in Paris, Scotland, and the Netherlands as well as in the United States. She has received numerous awards and arts residencies.

William S. Johnson was trained as a professional librarian. For the past thirty-odd years he has attempted to bring the best attributes of that profession (service, quality, maintenance of standards of responsibility) to the varied activities of teaching, writing, expostulating about, and facilitating the study of the disciplines of photography and the visual arts. He admires H. H. Paul's 1851 description of the aspirations of the forthcoming Crystal Palace Exhibition: "The records of all time will be consulted, and the secrets of every region searched out, to enrich this peaceful gathering together of the fruits of human perseverance."

Harold Jones is the Associate Director of Academic Affairs, School of Art, University of Arizona. He received an M.F.A. from the University of New Mexico where he worked with Van Deren Coke. Later he worked at George Eastman House with Nathan Lyons and Beaumont Newhall. In 1971 he was the first director of Light Gallery in New York City, and in 1975 became the first director of the CCP. He was the coordinator of the photography program at the University of Arizona for over eighteen years. His photographs have appeared in numerous one-person and group exhibitions.

Dustin W. Leavitt is the Museum Preparator at the CCP. He has worked variously in libraries and on horse ranches, as a freelance writer, and as a sailor in the Pacific, the Caribbean, and the Bering Sea. His essays on boat building, travel, tattoos, and other topics have been published widely. Currently he is completing his Master's degree in creative writing at the University of Arizona.

Stephanie Lipscomb studied the history of photography as a graduate student at the School of the Art Institute of Chicago and chose Robert Heinecken as the subject of her thesis. She researched and organized exhibitions for the Art Institute of Chicago from 1996 to 1999. She is a regular contributor of biographies to the *Encyclopedia Americana*, specializing in the lives of photographers and women artists. She is currently Associate Director of Continuing Studies at Northwestern University in Evanston, Illinois.

Larry Lytle has been a fine art and commercial photographer in Los Angeles since 1978. His vocation of making art led him into thinking, writing, and teaching about its historic aspects. He is currently at work on a book about William Mortensen.

Dena McDuffie is Archivist at the Arizona Historical Society. She is also an editor, author, and artist. She has degrees in art and library science and has worked for publishers and museums throughout the United States. While a graduate student at the University of Arizona, she worked at the CCP with the Pallas Archive funded by a grant from the Institute of Museum and Library Services. During the course of the project, she interviewed Mickey and

Pat Pallas, an experience that allowed her to get to know the artist as well as his work.

Keith McElroy, Associate Professor of Art History at the University of Arizona, has taught the history of photography since 1977. As Beaumont Newhall's first doctoral student, he was present during Beaumont's early years at the University of New Mexico. McElroy's own research has focused on nineteenthth-century photography in the non-industrial world and especially in Latin America.

Betsi Meissner, Acting Registrar at the CCP, has taught the history of photography at Pima Community College and at Prescott College. In 1999, she completed a master's program at the University of Arizona. Her thesis was titled *Marion Palfi: The Early Years in Context*. Employed at the CCP since 1993, she has been a recipient of the Ansel Adams Internship and curated a number of small exhibitions including *Automania: The Cult of the Car* and *In Concert: Photographers and Musicians*.

Sarah J. Moore is on the art history faculty at the University of Arizona where she teaches nineteenth- and twentieth-century art and culture. Her primary research area is art of the United States at the turn of the twentieth century, looking in particular at the construction of national identity in art created for the public sphere and in critical discourse.

While attending the University of Oregon in the fall of 1975, **Dianne Nilsen** was introduced to Brett Weston by her photography professor, Bernie Freemesser. She later moved to Carmel where, as Brett's apprentice, she refined her printing skills and large format photographic technique. She also contributed to the selection process and production of Brett's portfolio *Twenty Photographs*. A CCP staff member for twenty years, Nilsen now manages the Center's Rights and Reproductions Department, dividing her time between traditional photography, digital imaging and copyright management.

Alison Nordström has been Director and Senior Curator of the Southeast Museum of Photography since 1992, having previously held positions at the Peabody Museum, Harvard, and the Brattleboro Museum in Vermont. She holds a Ph.D. in Cultural and Visual Studies. In addition to the the Ansel Adams Fellowship in 1998, she has received fellowships from the National Endowment for the Humanities, International Partnerships Amongst Museums, and the William Darrah Award for Excellence in Writing on Historical Photography.

Ellwood C. Parry III, received his B.A. from Harvard in 1964 and his M.A. from the University of California at Los Angeles in 1966. After earning a Ph.D. in the history of art from Yale in 1970, he taught at Columbia University and then the University of Iowa. Since 1981, he has been a professor in the Art History Program at the University of Arizona. His major publications include *The Image of the Indian and the Black Man in American Art, 1590–1900* (1974) and *The Art of Thomas Cole: Ambition and Imagination* (1988).

David Peeler specializes in American intellectual and cultural history and is a professor at the United States Naval Academy. He received the first Ansel Adams Visiting Fellowship in 1991. He is the author of *The Illuminating Mind in American Photography: Stieglitz, Strand, Weston, Adams,* and *Hope Among Us Yet: Social Criticism and Social Solace in Depression America.* Together with a small pack of greyhounds and whippets, he and his wife live in central Maryland.

Maria Antonella Pelizzari is Assistant Curator of Photography at the Canadian Centre for Architecture. She earned her Ph.D. from the University of New Mexico and has published numerous articles in *History of Photography, Visual Resources, Afterimage, Casabella, Fotologia, Performing Arts Journal,* and *Millenium Film Journal.* She has contributed to the books *Picturing Place: Photography and Imaginative Geographies, America: The New World in Nineteenth-Century Painting* (1999), and *Alto Adige: Ritratti del territorio* (1992). She was the 1995 recipient of the Ansel Adams Research Fellow-ship and the 1997 recipient of the Lisette Model/Joseph G. Blum Fellowship at the National Gallery of Canada, Ottawa.

Terence Pitts is Executive Director of the Cedar Rapids Museum of Art. Previously, he spent twenty-four years at the Center for Creative Photography in various positions, including ten years as its third director. As an art historian and curator, he has focused primarily on the evolution of twentieth-century photography in the United States and Mexico. His Master's thesis in art history for the University of Arizona was on the nineteenth-century American photographer William Bell and the photography of the Wheeler Surveys, 1871–1873.

Roxane Ramos is the Museum Store Manager at the CCP and writes fiction.

Amy Rule, Archivist at the CCP, served as Acting Director from 2000 to 2001. During her twenty-year tenure, research collections covering photography's many cultural manifestations grew to over 3000 linear feet. Her experience with photographers and researchers taught her to scrutinize how we get our knowledge about photography and to expand rather than to restrict the view. She has an M.L.S. from University of California, Berkeley, was the co-editor of the *World Photographers Reference Series* for ABC/Clio Press from 1989 to 1997, and has published in numerous photography, art, and historical journals.

John P. Schaefer is President of the Research Corporation, the only United States foundation wholly dedicated to the advancement of science. While President of the University of Arizona from 1971 to 1982, he was responsible for the founding of the Center for Creative Photography, now in a building bearing his name. He took up photography thirty years ago as a hobby and later studied with several well-known photographers. His work has been exhibited in Florence, Italy; the Photography Southwest Gallery in Scottsdale, Arizona; and the Tucson Museum of Art. A frequent contributor to professional photographic journals, he has also been published in *Arizona Highways* magazine.

Nancy Solomon worked at the Center for Creative Photography for twenty years as Director of Publications and Public Information. She is currently a freelance publishing consultant and an artist who makes bookworks and video art and uses alternative photographic processes.

Sally Stein is an Associate Professor in the Department of Art History and the Ph.D. Program in Visual Studies at the University of California, Irvine. She has published numerous essays on twentieth-century documentary photography and mass media, and is co-author of *Official Images: New Deal Photography* (Smithsonian), and co-curator and co-author of *Montage and Modern Life*. She received the Ansel Adams Research Fellowship in 1992 and was also a guest curator at the CCP for the exhibition *Harry Callahan/Color Photography*.

Marcia Tiede has been the Curatorial Associate/Cataloger at the CCP since 1986. She has an M.A. in Cultural Anthropology from the University of Arizona, Tucson. Her interests are: languages (including French and Malinké); culture and history (African and Diaspora, the Middle East, the classical world); artisanship and design; native plants and gardening. She contributed an essay on Josef Breitenbach's photographs in Asia for *Josef Breitenbach Photographien* (Schirmer/Mosel, 1996).

Timothy Troy was Librarian at the CCP for ten years before joining the staff of the San Francisco Public Library. Previously, he was Bibliographer for American Indian Materials and Research Librarian at the New York Public Library. He is the recipient of the Edward H. Spicer Award for writing from the Southwest Center at the University of Arizona. He continues his research and writing in the area of cultural anthropology and is currently collaborat-ing with the Regional Oral History Office, Bancroft Library, on an oral history of J. Desmond Clark, paleoarchaeologist and Africanist.

April Watson is currently the Curatorial Assistant in the Department of Photographs, National Gallery of Art. She has an M.F.A. in the History of Photography from the University of New Mexico. While a graduate student at UNM, she assisted with the exhibition *For My Best Beloved Sister Mia: An Album of Photographs by Julia Margaret Cameron*. She taught studio art and photography at The Baylor School in Chattanooga, Tennessee. As an NEA intern at the CCP (1994–95), she met Bill Christenberry while assisting curator Trudy Wilner Stack on the artist's first major retrospective.

Mark Williams was Associate Registrar at the CCP for eleven years, where he had responsibility for the shipment, organizing, and documenting of the Richard Avedon Archive.

Leon Zimlich is a graduate of Spring Hill College in Mobile, Alabama, and the University of Arizona, and is currently completing a dissertation on photography in the American Southwest at the close of the nineteenth century in the Department of the History of Art and Architecture at the University of California, Santa Barbara. While a graduate student at the University of Arizona, he held the position of graduate student assistant and later served as Project Researcher for this book.

Index

5 ans de régime hitlérien, exhibition (1938), 275

5 Associates, 262

5¢ Sign, Demopolis, Alabama (Christenberry), *75*

20 Photographs by Eugène Atget (Atget/Abbott), 89, 267

30–30 (magazine), 135, 137

291 gallery, New York, 195

683 Brockhurst Gallery, Oakland, 151, 219

Abbott, Berenice, 16, 25, 89, 161, 162, 163, 223, 267, 358

ABC-TV, 159

Abdullah Frères, *Cuisinier ambulant* (ca. 1870s), *290*

abstract expressionism, 74, 157, 165

Ackerman, Gerald S., 262

Adams, Ansel, 16, 22, 34–41, 67, 77, 89, 90, 107, 108, 109, 110, 147, 149, 162, 163, 170, 184, 187, 188, 189, 215, 216, 219, 220, 227, 229, 237, 244, 248, 275, 306; archive, 262–63; books, *Ansel Adams: Letters and Images, 1916–1984*, 39; *Taos Pueblo*, 39; collection, 89–90, 93, 148, 262, 274. Works: *Boards and Thistles, South San Francisco* (1932), *107*; *Clearing Winter Storm*, printing instructions, 41; *Gravestone Carving and Lichens, New England Cemetery, Concord, Massachusetts* (ca. 1965), *38*; *Leaves, Glacier Bay, Alaska* (ca. 1947), *262*; *Monolith, The Face of Half Dome, Yosemite Valley*, *37*; *Parmelian Prints of the High Sierras*, 263; *White Branches, Mono Lake, California* (1947), *36*

Adams, Virginia, 22, 24

Adams, Yura, *Jim Pomeroy, Performing Mechanics Music* (1979), *351*

Adamson, Robert, 316

aerial photography, 368, 380

The African Desert (Plossu), 91, 350

Airfields (Miyoshi), 133

AIZ (magazine), 127

Akeley camera, 195

Akiba, David, 263

The Alabama Box series (Christenberry), *72*,

Albers, Josef, 57, 143, 275

Album (magazine), 318–19

albumen photographs, 89, 202, 204, 206, 263, 266, 270, 274, 303, 304, 313, 330, 334, 340, 341, 346, 353, 356, 366, 373, 374, 381, 396

albums, 204–08

Alexander, Darsie, 19

Alexander, Stuart, 19, 329

Alexanian, Nubar, 263; *Peruvian Portfolio* (Alexanian and Stephen Gersh), 263, 308

Alfred Hitchcock at Academy Awards Banquet (Stackpole), *194*

Alfred Stieglitz (Norman), *344*

Alice in Wonderland portfolio (Avedon), 268

Alinari and Cook, 206

Alinari Fratelli, 206, 207, 263; *Ricordi di Firenze*, 206

Alland, Alexander, 163

Allen, Casey, 264; *In and Out of Focus*, 264

Alternity (Bender), 270

Alvarez Bravo, Lola, 42–45, 126, 264; collection, 264. Works: *En su propia cárcel* (ca. 1950), *42*; *San Isidro Labrador* (n.d.), *264*

Alvarez Bravo, Manuel, 43, 44, 125, 265, 359; *La visita* (1945), *265*

ambrotypes, 343

America in Crisis (Harbutt), 113

An American Exodus (Lange and Taylor), 127

The American League Stadiums (Dow), 297

American Legends (Feininger), 88

American Monument series (Friedlander), 304

Amero, Emilio, 44

AMICO *see* Art Museum Image Consortium

Amish Portfolio (Tice), 375

Amon Carter Museum, 237, 352, 372

anaglyph stereo photography, 49

Anderson, James, 265

Anderson, Margaret, 121

Anderson, Paul L., 101, 266, 276; collection, 266; *M. G. A. with Camera Work* (1909), *266*

Anderson, Sherwood, *Winesburg, Ohio* (1919), 197

Angel Rodríguez, José, 126

Animal Photographs by Ylla exhibition, New York, 254

animal photography, 253

Animals in Africa (Ylla), 253

Animals in India (Ylla), 255

Animaux des Indes (Ylla), *396*

Les animaux supérieurs (Doisneau), *90*

Annan, Thomas J., 266
Ansel Adams: Letters and Images, 1916–1984, 39
Ansel Adams Gallery, San Francisco, 151
Ansel Adams Publishing Rights Trust, 263
Anthony, Edward and Henry T., & Company, 263, 266
Aperture (magazine), 25, 61, 170, 179
Apollinaire, Guillaume, *Zone*, 184
Apollo Jest: An American Mythology (in depth) (Pomeroy), *48, 49*
Apple computer, 229
Aramasa, Taku, 119
Arból de Yalalag, Yalalag, Mexico (Garduño), *126*
Arbus, Diane, 202, 249, 266, 391
Arches Galerie paper, 225
architectural photography, 101
archives at CCP, 262, 268, 273, 275, 277, 278, 279, 281, 291, 293, 300, 305, 308, 310, 311, 313, 314, 315, 318, 335, 339, 345, 347, 348, 351, 353, 358, 360, 361, 364, 365, 366, 378, 379, 380, 381, 383, 385, 391, 392, 395, 396
ARCO, 92
Are You Rea (Heinecken), 116
Arensberg, Walter, 248
Arentz, Dick, 267; *Chairs II, Vichy, France* (1994), *267*
Arid Waters: Photographs from the Water in the West Project (1992), 231, 232
Arizona School of Photography, 287
Arizona State Museum, 78
Arizona State University, Tempe, 53
Arles Photo Festival, 89
Armitage, Merle, 248
Armory Exhibition, New York, 195
Armstrong, Louis, 241
Arnold, Eve, 267

Art Center School, New York, 63
Art Institute of Chicago, School, 105, 170
Art Museum Image Consortium [AMICO], 23
L'Art Vivant (magazine), 137
artists' books, 46–49, 202, 227, 229, 282, 310, 331, 342, 351, 358, 363, 379
Aspen Institute of Humanistic Studies, 25
Aspen Photographers Conference (1951), 25, 321
Aspen Photographers Conference, Hotel Jerome, Aspen, Colorado, 1951 (Bishop), *16*
assemblage, 116
Association of Arts and Industries, 169
Atget, Eugène, 89, 97, 202, 223, 267. Works: *20 Photographs by Eugène Atget* (1970), 89, 267; *Le Parc de Saint-Cloud* (1982), 89, 267
Athanassiou, Constantin, *Panorama d'Athènes* (n.d.), *206, 207*
Automobile Graveyard (Hagel or Mieth), *335*
Avance (magazine), 44
Avedon, Richard, 50–52, 163, 268; archive, 268. Works: *Alice in Wonderland* portfolio, 268; *Avedon/Paris* portfolio, 268; *The Beatles* portfolio, 268; *Cesar Chavez, Founder, United Farm Workers, Keene, California (6-27-76)* from the portfolio *Rolling Stone: The Family*, *50*; *Elise Daniels, Turban by Paulette, Pré-Catelan, Paris, August* (1948), *268*; *Ezra Pound, Poet, June 30, 1958, Rutherford, New Jersey, 52*; *Jacob Israel Avedon* portfolio, 268; *Minneapolis* portfolio, 268; *Rolling Stone: The Family* portfolio, *50*, 268

Avedon/Paris portfolio (Avedon), 268
Axelrod, Stephen, 298

B-6 from the series *Roots <NE>* (Miyoshi), *132*
Baasch, Kurt, 268
Bac: Where the Waters Gather (Schaefer), 357
Bacall, Lauren, 84
Badía-Villaseca, Sara, 325
Baedecker travel guides, 207
Bailly-Maître-Grand, Patrick, *Les Nipponnes d'eau*, 90
Baker, Ray Jerome, 283
Balcomb, Robert, 142n1, 268
Baldessari, John, 116
Baltz, Lewis, 268
Bandolier, Corn, Sickle (Modotti), *135*
Barakei (Ordeal by Roses) series (Hosoe), 118
Bard College, Annandale-on-Hudson, 211
Barnbaum, Bruce, 268
Barron, Susan, 269
Barrow, Thomas, 269
Bartholomew, Harry Guy, 332
Bartlane System of Picture Telegraphy, 332
Baruch, Ruth-Marion, 93
baseball, 285, 286, 297
Baseball Photographer Trading Cards (Clatworthy Colorvues), 285, *286*, 329
bas-relief prints, 60
Bauhaus, 85, 169
Bauhaus Collection, 92, 269
Bayer, Herbert, 16, 92, 270; *View from Pont Transbordeur* (1928), *270*
Bayer, Joella, 16
The Beatles portfolio (Avedon), 268
Beato, Felice Antonio, 205
Becher, Bernd and Hilla, 93
Becher, Max, 93
Beese, Lotte, 92, 269; Untitled [Hannes Meyer] (ca. 1928), *93*
Bell, William, 77, 270, 346
Bellmer, Hans, 90; *Les Jeux de la Poupée* series (1930), 90

Beman, Anson, 142n1
Bender, Rudy, 270; *Alternity,* 270
Benitez Suite (Bernal), 53, 271
Benor-Kalter, J., 271
Bergasa, Miguel, 190
Bergman, Ingrid, 84
Berko, Ferenc, 16, 271
Berlin series (Dean Brown), 277
Berman, Wallace, 116
Bernal, Louis Carlos, 53-55, 271. Works: *Cómoda* from the *Benitez Suite* (1977), 271; *Dos Mujeres, Douglas, Arizona* (1978) from the *Espejo* series, 54
Bernhard, Ruth, 93, 272
Bernstein, Lou, 163
Bey, Dawoud, 272
Beyond This Point (Bruguière), 65
Bierstadt, Charles, 263, 272
Big Bend Photo Club, 272
The Big Book (W. Eugene Smith), 364
Binder, Sybille, 56
Bing, Ilse, 272
Bishop, Robert C., *Aspen Photographers Conference, Hotel Jerome, Aspen, Colorado,* 1951, *16*
Bits (Loew), *269*
Blache, Philippe, 89, 272
Black Bird series (Fukase), 119
Black Mountain College, 57, 143, 167, 275
blacklisting, 163
Blake, William, 165
Blast Foreman Trey Gardner with Blasting Compound at Site of Picacho Pumping Plant (Simmons-Myers), *359*
Bleak Beauty, 328
Bloch, Ernest, 273; archive, 273; portrait, *273*
Bloch, Lucienne, *Father [Ernest Bloch] with Mushrooms, Roveredo, Switzerland* (1928), *273*
Bloom, Suzanne, 298

Blossfeldt, Karl, 93, 273. Works: *Blumenbachia hieronymi. Geschlossene Samenkapsel, 18mal vergrössert* (1900–28), *273*; *Karl Blossfeldt—12 Photografien* portfolio (1975), 273
The Blue Four, 239
Blumann, Sigismund, 124n3
Blumenbachia hieronymi. Geschlossene Samenkapsel, 18mal vergrössert (Blossfeldt), *273*
Boards and Thistles, South San Francisco (Adams), *107*
Boas, Franz, 78
La Boda en Coyoacán (Meyer), *126*
Bodine, A. Aubrey, 274
Boeing Company, 101
Bohnen, Blythe, 274
Bond, Howard, 274
Bonfils, Félix, 89, 205, 207, 274, 290; *Les pyramides prises de Gizeh* (n.d.), *274*
Bonfoey, Kay, gallery, 148
Book 81 (Keith Smith), *363*
Book 91 (Keith Smith), 48
Book 118 (Keith Smith), 48
Both, Katt, 92
Boubat, Edouard, 89, 274
Boughton, Alice, 274
Bourke-White, Margaret, 84, 127, 162, 193
Bourne, Samuel, 205
Bowers, Harry, 274
Bowery Mission Bread Line, 2 A.M. (Hine), *161*
A Box of Ku series (Yamamoto), 119
Boy and Car, New York City (Liebling), *160*
Boys Smoking in Car, Reform School, New York (Harbutt), *113*
Brackman, Henrietta, 264
Brady, Mathew, 275
Brancusi, Constantin, 239
Brandt, Bill, 38
Brassaï, 38, 89, 90, 275; *Le passage cloute* (1937), *90*

Breakey, Kate, 203
Brecht, Bertolt, 57, 275
Breitenbach, Josef, 56–62, 93, 275–76; archive, 275. Works: *Josef Albers, Black Mountain College, North Carolina* (1944), *275*; *Rose Petal Exhaling Its Fragrance* (1937–39), *60*; *Sybille Binder and Paul Robeson, Role Portrait in Othello* (ca. 1932), *56*; "This Beautiful Landscape," *61*; Untitled [back view of nude in woods]; *61*; *Women of Asia* (1968), *61*
Breitenbach Foundation, 62
Brenner, Anita, 137; *Idols Behind Altars* (1929), 137
Bridal Veil Fall, 900 feet (Fiske), *302*
Brigman, Anne W., 79, 219, 276
Brihat, Denis, 90
Bristol, Horace, 127
British International News Agency, 57
Brodovitch, Alexey, 81, 249, 264
Brogi Edizione, 290
bromoil prints, 92
Brown, Carol, 277
Brown, Dean, 277; archive, 277; Untitled [sphinx-like sculpture in winter garden] from series *Berlin* (1969), *277*
Brown, John Mason, 65
Brown, Laurie, 230, 232, 277. Works: *Convergence #9* (1995) from the series *Divining Western Waters,* 233; *Earth Edges* portfolio (1984), 277; *Recent Terrains: Transforming the American West* (2000), 232
Brown, Margaret Wise, 253
Brownie camera, 74, 75
Bruehl, Anton, 277
Bruguière, Francis Joseph, 63–65, 170, 278; archive, 278; book, *Beyond This*

Point (1929), 65. Works:
Experiment, (ca. 1925), *64;*
"Few Are Chosen", 1931,
65; Light Rhythms, 65; *The*
Way, 63
Brumfield, John, 201
Budnik, Dan, 278
Bullock, Edna, 278
Bullock, Wynn, 20, 21, 22, 24,
34, 35, 39, 65, 270, 279;
archive, 279; *Old Typewriter*
(1951), *279*
Bunin, Louis, 280
Bureau of American
Ethnology, 78
Burke, Bill, 47, 280; *I Want to*
Take Picture, 47
Burkhardt, Rudolph, 163
Burkhart, Kenneth, 159
Burr, B. G., 147
Burroughs, John, 278
Bus Stop, Tehuantepec,
Oaxaca (Lyon), *328*

cabinet cards, 343
Cactus (Miyoshi), 134
Caddes, Helen, 385
Caffery, Debbie Fleming, 280;
Untitled [ghosting image
from the *Polly* series]
(October 1985), *280*
Cage, John, 143
Caisse Nationale des
Monuments Historiques et
des Sites, 89
California Institute of the Arts,
201
California Museum of
Photography, 49
California State University,
Northridge, 201
California State University, San
Bernardino, 233
"California Water Story"
(Hagel), 380
Calla Lily (Noskowiak), *150*
Callahan, Harry, 22, 34, 35,
39, 66–71, 97, 167, 169,
227, 237, 281; archive, 281.
Works: *Chicago* (1952), 66;
Detroit (1943), *281; Eleanor*

(1949), *70; Eleanor and*
Barbara, Chicago (1954), *70;*
portrait of Aaron Siskind
(1951), *22*
Callis, Jo Ann, 201, 282;
Goldfish and Stringbeans
(1980) from the portfolio *Jo*
Ann Callis, 1984, *200*
calotypes, 316, 373
Camargo Foundation, 225
camera clubs, 161
Camera Craft Publishing
Company, 140
Camera Pictorialists of Los
Angeles, 121, 123
Camera Work (magazine), 92,
195, 266, 282
Camera-portraits of Einstein
(Hagemeyer), 313
cameras: Akeley, 195;
Brownie, 74, 75; Century
Universal, 179; Deardorff,
75, 133, 134, 223, 224;
Devin Tri-Color, 332;
Graflex, 193, 239; Korona,
377; Leica, 193; Polyscop,
273; Raylo, 296; Rolleicord,
268; Speed Graphic, 193;
Widelux, 223
Cameron, Carol, 282
Camhi, Morrie, 53, 282
Campanet, Mallorca (Povo), *190*
Capa, Robert, *Death of a*
Loyalist Soldier, 117
Capehart, Lucy, 282; *Sarah*
Natani in Her Sheep Corral,
Table Mesa near Shiprock,
New Mexico (1999), *282*
Caponigro, Paul, 282
Captains of the Cañon
(Hillers), 316
carbon prints, 277, 316
carbro prints, 332, 354
CARE (Cooperative for
Assistance and Relief
Everywhere), 91
Carl Siembab Gallery, Boston,
358
Carpenter, William J., 282
Carrillo, Manuel, 126, 283

Carson, Rachel, 353. Works:
A Sense of Wonder, 353;
Rocky Coast, 353
cartes-de-visite, 343
Cartier-Bresson, Henri, 44, 89,
111, 146, 239, 283
cartoons, 361, 375
Casanovas, Marti, 135, 137
Castanho, Eduardo, 283
Català-Roca, Francesc, 190
Center for Creative
Photography, 17–25, 34–35,
53, 67, 95, 105, 139, 147,
148, 159, 184, 220, 229,
240, 251; archives, 262,
268, 273, 275, 277, 278,
279, 281, 291, 293, 300,
305, 308, 310, 311, 313,
314, 315, 318, 335, 339,
345, 347, 348, 351, 353,
358, 360, 361, 364, 365,
366, 378, 379, 380, 381,
383, 385, 391, 392, 395,
396; collections, 15, 125,
187, 201; galleries, 105;
founding of, 34–35; Laura
Volkerding Reading Room,
225; Library, 46, 98, 139;
PrintViewing, 48, 105;
Research Center, 48, 96,
139, 142
Center for Photographic Arts,
Chicago, 159
Central Arizona Project
Photographic Survey, 230,
323, 331, 337, 359, 380
A Century of Progress (Hagel),
127
Century Universal view cam-
era, 179
El Cerrito y la Acequia Madre:
Diggin' Ditch (Stewart), *232*
Cesar Chavez, Organizer,
United Farm Workers,
Keene, California, 6-27-76
(Avedon), *50*
Chaim Gross—Working in His
Studio Alone (Palfi), *347*
Chairs II, Vichy, France
(Arentz), *267*
Chameleon series (Golden),
106

Chamorro, Koldo, 191; Untitled [from the series *España Mágica*] (1980s), *191*
Chanel, Gabrielle (Coco), 84
Chapel (Miyoshi), 133–34
"Chaplin at Work" essay (W. Eugene Smith), 174
Chappell, Walter, 283
Charlot, Jean, 248
Chats (Ylla), 253
Chavez, Cesar, 50–51, *50*
chemigrammes, 90
Cheyenne (Curtis), 76
Chiarenza, Carl, 165, 283; *Noumenon 256* (1984/85), *283*
Chiaroscuro series (Gibson), 308
Chicago (Callahan), 66
Chicago Office of Fine Art, 159
Chicanismo, 53
Chief Joseph, 77
Chiens (Ylla), 253
chin collé, 225
chlorobromide prints, 266
Chris, Veiled (Walker), *229*
Christenberry, William, Jr., 72–75, 284. Works: *5¢ Sign, Demopolis, Alabama* (1976), *75*; *The Alabama Box* series (1980), *72*; *Building Constructions*, 75; *Church, Between Greensboro and Marion* (1973), *72*; *Dream Buildings*, 75; *Hate I* and *Hate II*, 74; *The Klan Room*, 74; *Southern Monuments*, 75
Christopher, Frank, 274
A Chronology of Photography (Gassan), 305
Church, Between Greensboro and Marion (Christenberry), *72*
Circus Tent (Modotti), *136*
Citizen Kane (Welles), 227
Citret, Mark, 284
The City (Steiner and Van Dyke), 219
City College of New York, 249
City Lights, Chicago (Crane), *291*

Clarence H. White School of Photography, 101, 287
Clark, Larry, 284; *Tulsa* series 1963, *284*
Clatworthy Colorvues, 285–86. Works: *Baseball Photographer Trading Cards*, 286; *Evidence*, 329
Clearing Winter Storm (Adams), printing instructions, *41*
Clergue, Lucien, 89, 90, 285
cliché-verre, 65, 184,185, 348
Clift, William, 285
A Closer Look: Four Photographers, exhibition, New York, 1948, 155
Cloth Folds (Modotti), 135
Coburn, Alvin Langdon, 38, 285
Cocteau, Jean, 38, 84
Cohen, Allan, 285
Cohen, Susan E., 229
Cohn, Alfred and Margaret, 287
Coke, Van Deren, 125, 288
Cold War, 129, 155, 157, 173
Coleman, Allan D., 139, 288
collage, 105, 216, 365
Collier, John, Jr., 103
Collier, John, Sr., 155
Collier's (magazine), 253
collotypes, 282
Colombe, Denise, 90
color photography, 131, 169, 209, 227
Columbia University, 249
Comesaña, Eduardo, 288
Cómoda (Bernal), *271*
Compagnons du Devoir, 224
Complutensian Polyglot Bible, Pierpont Morgan Library (Gibson), *94*
Conant, Howard, 288
Confessions of a Silver Addic! [sic] (Fichter), 302
Connell, Will, 16
Conniff, Gregory, 230, 231, 232, 288
Connor, Linda, 125, 289; *Seven Sacred Pools, Maui, Hawaii* (1978), *289*
Consemüller, Erich, 269

Conservatory series (Miyoshi), 133
Constant, Maurice, 289
constructivism, 44
Los Contemporaneos, 43
Contemporary Photographer (magazine), 283
Contemporary Photography in Mexico: 9 Photographers, exhibition, Tucson, 125
Convergence #9 from the *Divining Western Waters* series (Laurie Brown), *233*
Cooper, Thomas Joshua, 289
Cooper Union, New York, 60
Coplans, John, 289
Corcoran School of Art, Washington, D. C., 74
Cordier, Pierre, 90
Cornfield, Jim, 289
Cornell, Joseph, 164, 166
Cornell University, Ithaca, 179
Cornice–Temple of Kukulcan, Chichen Itza, Yucatan, (Gilpin), *102*
Corson, Julia F., 22, 290
Cory, Kate, 290
Costumes at the Met (Tseng), 213
Costumi di Napoli (Giorgio Sommer), 336
Coubertin (Volkerding), *224*
Coubertin foundry, 224
"Country Doctor" essay (W. Eugene Smith), 174, 177
Cowell, Alice Maude Bovyer, 206–07
Crane, Barbara, 291; archive, 291; *City Lights, Chicago* (1969), *291*
Craven, George M., 108, 291; archive, 291; *Object and Image: An Introduction to Photography* (1975), 291
Cream Six (Heinecken), *315*
Creative Arts (magazine), 137
Creative Camera (magazine), 318
Creative Eye Gallery, Sonoma, 292
Crowninshield, Frank, 79

Crumpler, Jonathan, 202
Cualladó, Gabriel, 190
Cuevas-Wolfe, Cristina, 19
Cuisinier ambulant (Abdullah Frères), *290*
Cunningham, Imogen, 107, 108, 109, 152, 219, 229, 292, 294; Untitled [montage of Franklin Roosevelt, Herbert Hoover, and storm at the White House] (ca. 1935), *292*
Cunningham, Merce, 143
Curtis, Edward S., 76–78, 103, 293. Works: *Cheyenne* (1900–1910), *76*; *In the Land of the Headhunters*, 77; *The North American Indian*, 77, 78, 293; *The Vanishing Race and Other Illusions: Photographs of Indians by Edward Curtis* (1982), 78
cyanotypes, 76, 293, 342
Cycles series (Golden), 106

Daguerre, Louis-Jacques-Mandé, 189
daguerreotypes, 186–89, 202, 319, 343
Dahl-Wolfe, Louise, 79–84, 287, 293–94; archive, 293. Works: *Dior Ball Gown, Paris* (1950), *293*; *Edward Hopper, Standing* (1933), *84*; *Japanese Bath, Betty Threat, Model* (1954), *80*
Daily Worker (newspaper), 110, 160
Daitz, Evelyn, 392
Dali, Salvador, 57
Dana (Steichen), *368*
Dance of the Casts (Volkerding), 224
Dancy, Wallace Edwin, 266
Daniels, Elise, 268
Danysh, Joseph, 108
Dater, Judy, 294; holiday card (1969), *21*
Davey, Robert, 294
Davis, Ben, 272
Davis, Faurest, 294

Davis, Lynn, 295; *Dogon Village, Mali* (1997), *295*
Davis, Phil, 295
Dawson, Robert, 230, 232, 233, 295
Daybooks (Weston), 121, 248, 305, 337, 386–89
Deal, Joe, 295
Deardorff view camera, 75, 133, 134, 223, 224
Death of a Loyalist Soldier (Capa), 117
Debroise, Olivier, 45
DeCarava, Roy, 202, 296; *Embroidered Blouse, Washington, D.C.* (1975), *296*
De Cock, Liliane, 296
Deeks, Hiram and Noel, 296
Delano, Jack, 163, 296
De Lory, Peter, 296
Demachy, Robert, 296
De Meyer, Adolf, 297
Denny-Watrous Gallery, 151
de Richey, Robo, 121
Deschamps, F., 47; *Life in a Book*, 47
Desert Canto XI: Violence series (Misrach), 336
Detail, Wall Opposite My Studio Door, Paris (Webb), *236*
Detroit (Callahan), *281*
Deutsche series (Moses), *340*
Devaux, Henri, 57; *Rose Petal Exhaling Its Fragrance* (1937–39), *60*
Devin Colorgraph (Devin-McGraw) Company, 332
Devin Tri-Color Camera, 332
de Young Memorial Museum *see* M. H. de Young Memorial Museum (San Francisco)
De Zayas, Marius, 297
digital photography, 217, 225, 227, 229, 234, 251
Diller, Stefan, 93
Dine, Jim, 297
Dior Ball Gown, Paris (Dahl-Wolfe), *293*
Diurnes (Picasso and Villers), 90

Divining Western Waters series (Laurie Brown), 232, *233*
Divola, John, 201, 297
Dixon, Dean, 155
documentary filmmaking, 127, 160, 219–20
Dogon Village, Mali (Lynn Davis), *295*
Doisneau, Robert, 89, 297; *Les animaux supérieurs* (1954), *90*
Dolcet, Juan, 190; *Empalao* (1968), *190*
Doniz, Rafael, 126
Dos Mujeres, Douglas, Arizona (Bernal), *54*
Dove, Arthur, 195
Dow, Jim, 297. Works: *The National League Stadiums*, 297; *The American League Stadiums*, 297
Downey, Laura, 202
Droste, Sebastian, 63
Duchamp, Marcel, 95
Duncan, Kenn, 297
Dunham, George, 139, 142
Durant, Mark Alice, 298. Works: *Men of the World*, 298; *We Want to Believe: White Handkerchiefs of Goodbye, Chicago* (1996), *298*
Dutton, Allen A., 298
dye transfer photographs, 171, 267, 349, 354

Earl Hines (W. Eugene Smith), *175*
Earth Edges portfolio (Laurie Brown), 277
East 26th Street, New York, NY (Weiner), *163*
East Meets West series (Tseng), 213
Eastman Kodak Company, 248
Ebony (magazine), 156, 159
Edgerton, Harold, 298
Edizione Brogi, 290
Edizione Esposito, 290, 299
Edmondson, William, 294
Edward Hawes, Asleep, with Hands Together (Southworth & Hawes), 187

Edward Hawes, Asleep, with One Arm Raised (Southworth & Hawes), 187
Edward Hopper, Standing (Dahl-Wolfe), *84*
Edwards, Jennifer, 19
Edwards, John Paul, 107, 219
Edwards, Mary Jeannette, 219
Einstein, Albert, 313
Eisenstaedt, Alfred, 127, 193
Eisenstein, Sergei, 44
Eleanor (Callahan), *70*
Eleanor and Barbara, Chicago (Callahan), *70*
Électricité (Man Ray), *90, 329*
electro-carbon prints, 324
Electronic Works of Art Collection, 298
Elements series (Golden), 106
Eliot, T. S., 165
Elise Daniels, Turban by Paulette, Pré-Catelan, Paris, August 1948 (Avedon), *268*
Elisofon, Eliot, 163
The Eloquent Light (Nancy Newhall), 38
Embrace series (Hosoe), 118
Embroidered Blouse, Washington, D.C. (De Carava), *296*
émigrés, 57, 93, 127, 153, 169
Empalao (Dolcet), *190*
En su propia cárcel (Lola Alvarez Bravo), *42*
Encyclopedia Britannica, 159
The Enduring Navaho (Gilpin), 103
Engel (Neusüss), *92*
Engel, Morris, 155, 163
Enthusiasm Strengthens (Walker), 47, *228, 229*
Enyeart, James, 19, 37, 96, 97, 179, 278
"Epicure Corner" (Newhall), 147
Equivalent (Uelsmann), *376*
Ernst, Max, 57, 179
Erwitt, Elliott, 298
The Esau Jenkins Story (Palfi), 156
Espacio (magazine), 44

España Mágica series (Chamorro), *191*
Espejo: Reflections of the Mexican American, 53, 271, 298
Esposito Edizione, 290, 299
etchings, 48
ethnographic photography, 76–78
Eugene, Frank, 63, 278
Evans, Frederick H., 299
Evans, Terry, 230, 231, 232, 299; books, *The Inhabited Prairie* (1998), 233; *No Mountains in the Way* (1975), 230; *Prairie: Images of Ground and Sky* (1986), 233. Work: *Wheel That Raises Gate for Water Regulation, Cheyenne Bottoms (August 1992) from the series Western Waters, No. 21, 231*
Evans, Walker, 74, 223, 249, 299; *Let Us Now Praise Famous Men*, 74
Evidence (Mandel and Sultan), 329
Ex Libris exhibition (Gibson), 95, 100
Excusado, Mexico (Edward Weston), *385*
Expeditionary Series (Tseng), *212, 213*
Experiment (Bruguière), *64*
experimental film, 44, 65
Exposé of Form (Mather/Justema), 124
Ezra Pound, Poet, June 30, 1958, Rutherford, New Jersey (Avedon), *52*

f/64 *see* Group f/64
Face to Face series (Suzuka), 119
Facing Eden: 100 Years of Landscape Art in the Bay Area (1995), 232
family albums, 204
The Family, Luzzara [three small variants] (Strand), 23, *198*

Family of Man, exhibition (New York), 61, 129
FAP *see* Federal Art Project
Farm Security Administration, 151, 155, 162, 296, 326
fashion photography, 79–84
Fassbender, Adolf, 93, 300–01; archive, 300; *The Ice Serpent* (ca. 1933), *300*
Father with Mushrooms, Roveredo, Switzerland (Lucienne Bloch), *273*
Faulkner, William, 74
Federal Art Project, 151, 152
Feigenbaum, David, 187
Feininger, Andreas, 57, 85–88, 93, 300; archive, 300. Works: *American Legends* (1945), 88; *Hamburg Portfolio* (1930–31), 300; *Man-Made Landscapes* (1945), 88; *Midtown Manhattan Seen from Weehawken, New Jersey* (1942), *86*; *The Photojournalist Dennis Stock, Winner of the LIFE Young Photographers Contest* (1951), *85*; *Pattern Made of Dragonfly Wings* [variant] (ca. 1935), *300*
Feininger, Lyonel, 85
Feininger, T. Lux, 269
Fellig, Arthur *see* Weegee
Fellman, Sandi, 302
Fernandez, Antonio A., 302
Fernandez, Ben, 302
Fernández Ledesma, Gabriel, 44
Ferryboats, Tsugaru Strait (Moriyama), *120*
"*Few Are Chosen*" (Bruguière), *65*
A Few Notes: Selected from Lesson A of Wilson's Photographics (Walker), 47
Fey, Cass, 19
Fichter, Robert, 171, 272, 302; *Confessions of a Silver Addict!* [sic], 302
Film and Photo League, 160, 165–66, 197

Film und Foto exhibition (Stuttgart), 123

First I Liked the Whites, I Gave Them Fruits (Palfi), *153*

First International Photographic Exhibition, Grand Central Palace, New York (1938), 189

Fish Tank Sonata (Tress), 211

Fisher, M. F. K., 395

Fiske, George, 302; *Bridal Veil Fall, 900 feet* (ca. 1880s), *302*

Fiskin, Judy, 201, 203, 303; *Some Art*, 203

Flax, Carol, 19

Flick, Robbert, 303

Florida State University, 229

Floyd, W. P., 303

Focus (Beaumont Newhall), 143

Folberg, Neil, 303

"Folk Singers" essay (W. Eugene Smith), 174

Folksingers series (Grossman), *312*

Folly at Santa Rosa Ranch, Coachella Valley (Volkerding), *225*

Fonssagrives, Lisa, 84

Fontcuberta, Joan, 191

For Nothing Changes: Democritus, on the Other Side, Burst Laughing (Walker), 47, 229

Forster, Elizabeth (Betsy), 101, 103

Försterling, Hermann, 93

Forth, Robert, 285

Fortune (magazine), 57, 74, 127, 131, 237

Fraissenet, 89

La France de Profil (Strand), 197

Frank, Jo Ann, 303

Frank, Robert, 61, 113, 162, 249, 303

Frei, Jim, 303

Frei Deutsche Kunst exhibition (1938), 275

French photography, 89–91

Frente a Frente (magazine), 44

Fresson prints, 91, 262, 276, 285

Freund, Gisèle, 89, 303; *Hôtel du Châtelet, Paris* (1952), *91*

Fricker, Geoffrey, 230, 233, 303; *Hamakuapoko Mill* from series *Sugar Mills* (1979), *234*

Friedlander, Lee, 249, 251, 297, 304, 391. Works: *American Monument* series (1970–76), 304; *Jim Dine, Etchings/Lee Friedlander, Photographs* portfolio with Jim Dine (1969), 297, 304; *Sonora* (1992), *304*

Friends of Photography, 262, 279

Frith, Francis, 205, 304

Frocheur, Nichole, 202

Frontier Films, 160, 369

FSA *see* Farm Security Administration

Fukase, Masahisa, 119; *Black Bird* series, 119

Fulani Nomad, Niger (Plossu), *89*

Fuller, Buckminster, 38, 143

Fuller, Rosalinde, 63, 65

Fuller, William, 304

funk art, 105

Futran, Eric, 304

futurists, 63

Futuro (magazine), 44

Gagern, Verena von, 93

Gagliani, Oliver, 304

Galerie Wilde, Cologne, 93

galleries: 291 gallery, 195; Ansel Adams, 151; Carl Siembab, 358; Creative Eye, 292; Denny-Watrous, 151; Galerie Wilde, 93; Hallmark, 70, 71; Halsted, 92; Julie Saul, 213; k2 Studio and Gallery, 321; Kay Bonfoey, 148; Light Gallery, New York, 67, 281; Limelight, 61, 307–08; El Mochuelo, 67

Gallery Cove, Point Lobos, California (Minor White), *390*

Gamma Photo Labs, Chicago, 159

Gang, Christel, 305

Garcia Rodero, Cristina, 190; *Virgen y mártir, Brión* (1978), *191*

Garduño, Flor, 126, 305; *Arból de Yalalag, Yalalag, Mexico* (1983), *126*

Garson, Greer, 194

Gasparini, Paolo, 305

Gassan, Arnold, archive, 305; *A Chronology of Photography*, 305

Gates of Hell (Rodin), 224

Gatewood, Charles, 264

Gee, Helen, 61, 307–08; archive, 308

Genthe, Arnold, 308

Geographical and Geological Explorations and Surveys West of the 100th Meridian (1871, 1872, 1873), 270

George Eastman House, Rochester, 143, 187, 249

German photography, 92–93

Geronimo, 77

Gerrard, Charles, 121

Gersh, Stephen, 308; *Peruvian Portfolio* (Gersh and Nubar Alexanian), 263, 308

Getty Research Institute, 147, 343

Ghana: An African Portrait (Strand), 199

GI Bill, 115, 169

Gibson, Ralph, 94–100, 308; portrait, 96. Works: *Complutensian Polyglot Bible, Pierpont Morgan Library* (2000), *94*; *Ex Libris*, 95, 100; *Hands Over Prow* (1969), *98*; *Sardinia* (1980) from the *Chiaroscuro* series, *308*; *The Somnambulist*, 95, 96

Giles, William, 309

Gille, Bernard, 309

Gilpin, Laura, 16, 101–103, 309; books, *The Enduring Navaho* (1968), 103; *The Pueblos: A Camera Chronicle* (1941), 101; *The Rio Grande: River of Destiny* (1949), 101; *Temples in Yucatan: A Camera Chronicle of Chichen Itza* (1948), 101. Works: *Cornice—Temple of Kukulcan, Chichen Itza, Yucatan* (1932), *102*; *Navajos by Firelight* (1932), *309*

Ginsburg, Janet, 159

Gittings, Elisa C., 48; *Rock's Words*, 48

Gittleman, Len, 310

Giving Fear a Proper Name: Detroit (Susan kae Grant), *47*

Gladding McBean company, 224

Gloeden, Wilhelm von, 92

Goin, Peter, 230, 232, 233, 310; books, *Humanature* (1996), 233; *Nuclear Landscapes* (1991), 233; *A Rephotographic Survey of Lake Tahoe* (1992), 233. Work: *Hot Springs at The Needles, Pyramid Lake, Nevada* (1990), *230*

The Gold Rush Trail (Webb), 237

Gold Strikes and Ghost Towns (Webb), 237

Goldbeck, Eugene O., 310

Golden, Judith, 24, 47, 48, 104–106, 310; archive, 310. Works: *Chameleon* series, 106; *Cycles* series, 106; *The Elements* series, 106; *Magazine Make-Over* series, 106; *Masks* (1974–82), 48, 105–106, *104*; *Persona #10* (1983), *106*; *Persona* series, 106

Goldfish and Stringbeans (Callis), *200*

Goldman, Emma, 121

Goldschmidt, Lucien, 275

Goldwater, Barry, 310; *A Trip Down the Green and Colorado Rivers* (1940), 380

"Good Luck" Toes (Gutmann), *24*

Gowin, Emmet, 310

Grabhorn Press, 39

Graflex camera, 193, 239

Grant, George A., 310

Grant, Susan kae, 47; *Giving Fear a Proper Name: Detroit* (1984), 47

Graphic Sciences Teleprinter, 324

Gravestone Carving and Lichens, New England Cemetery, Concord, Massachusetts (Adams), *38*

Great American Artists of Minority Groups (Palfi), 155, 347

"Great Britain" essay (W. Eugene Smith), 174

The Great Central Valley: California's Heartland (Stephen Johnson), 230

Great Depression, 109, 159

Greece (album), *206, 207*

Greenfield, Lauren, 311

Gregor, Arthur, 253

Gropius, Walter, 143

Gross, Chaim, 155, 347

Grossman, Sidney, 163, 311–12; *Folksingers* series (1940s), *312*

Group f/64, 107–110, 149, 187, 189, 193, 216, 219, 220, 244, 291, 345

Group K: Visual Poems series (Laughlin), *325*

Guggenheim Fellowship *see* John Simon Guggenheim Foundation Fellowship

Gulmez Frères, 207, 290

gum bichromate prints, 48, 266

Guthrie, Woody, 162

Gutman, Walter, 311

Gutmann, John, 23, 57, 93, 311; archive, 311. Works: *"Good Luck" Toes* (1945), *24*; *Machine Gunners, San Francisco* (1950), *311*

Hagel, Otto, 57, 93, 127–31, 335; archive, 335. Works: *Automobile Graveyard* (1937), *335*; *"California Water Story"* (1961), 380; *A Century of Progress* (1930s), 127; *Men and Machines* (1964), 129; *Men and Ships* (1937), 127; *New York Stock Exchange* (1938), *130*; *Return to Fellbach* (1950), 129; *A Simple Life* (1955), 129

Hagemeyer, Dora, 151

Hagemeyer, Johan, 121, 123, 149, 143, 248, 313; archive, 313. Works: *Trees on Telegraph Hill* (1925), *313*; *Camera-portraits of Einstein* (1913), 313

Hahn, Betty, 171, 313

Haiti series (W. Eugene Smith), *172, 175*

Hakim, Suleiman, 290, 313

Halberstadt, Milton, 313

Hallmark Gallery, 70, 71

Halloween, New York (Levitt), *327*

Halsman, Philippe, 57, 264, 313

Halsted Gallery, 92

Halston, 213

Ham and Eggs (Steiner), *369*

Hamakuapoko Mill (Fricker), *234*

Hamaya, Hiroshi, 314

Hamburg Portfolio (Feininger), 300

Hammerbeck, Wanda, 230, 231, 233, 314

Hands Over Prow (Gibson), *98*

Harbutt, Charles, 111–13, 314; archive, 314; books: *America in Crisis* (1969), 113; *Travelog* (1973), 111. Works: *Boys Smoking in Car, Reform School, New York* (1963), *113*; *Riverdale Balcony, Riverdale, New York* (1968), *111*; *Scrivener, Wall Street, New York* (1970), *112*

Harlem (Siskind), 360

Harlem Document, (Siskind), 166, *360*

Harlem Globetrotters, 159

Harper, Maria, 202

Harper, Toy, 155

Harper's Bazaar (magazine), 79, 81, 82, 83, 84, 93, 293–94

Harrah, Robert S., 163, 314

Harrison, Lynne, 314

Harter, Donald Scott, 314

Hartmann, Sadakichi, 63, 121, 278, 330

Harvard College, 188

Haviland, Paul B., 314

Hawes, Edward Southworth, 186–89

Hawes, Josiah Johnson, 187

Hawes, Nancy Southworth, 188

He:/She: (Heinecken), 117

Heartfield, John, 127, 161

Heath, David, 314

Heinecken, Robert, 18, 24, 114–17, 315, 341; archive, 315. Works: Altered Time magazine "150 Years of Photojournalism" (1989), *117*; *Cream Six* (1970), *315*; holiday card (ca. 1975), *20*; "Manipulative Photography," 116; *Recto/Verso #3* (1989) from the *Recto/Verso* series, *114*; *Are You Rea,* 116; *He:/She:* series, 117; *Shiva* series, 117

Helguera, Leon, 155

Henle, Fritz, 93, 163, 316

Henri, Florence, 89, 316

Henri Cartier-Bresson (Newhall), *146*

Henry Street Settlement (Palfi), *156*

Hernandez, Anthony, 316

Hessemans, Matthias Van, 241

Heyman, Abigail, 53, 316

Hicks, Wilson, 85

Higgins, Gary, 316

Hill, David Octavius, 316

Hill, Ed, 298

Hill and Adamson, 276, 316

Hillers, Jack, 316; *Captains of the Cañon,* 316

Hine, Lewis Wickes, 161, 162, 163, 316; *Bowery Mission Bread Line, 2 A.M.* (1907) from the portfolio *Lewis W. Hine,* 1874–1940, *161*

Hines, Earl, 175

History of Photography (Newhall), 147

Hitachi America, Ltd., 118, 175

Hodge, Frederick Webb, 78

Hoffman, Bernard, 127

Hofmeister, Theodor and Oscar, 92, 317

Holder, Preston, 107, 219

Holgers, William, 317; Untitled [Edward Weston showing a dune photograph to visitors in his Wildcat Hill house] (ca. 1945), *317*

Hollywood portfolio (Stackpole), 194

Holman's Print Shop, 189

Holy Water Font in Leyte Cathedral, Used as Hospital (W. Eugene Smith), *364*

Hoover, Herbert, 292

Hoppé, Emil Otto, 317

Hopper, Edward, 84, 113

Hosoe, Eikoh, 118, 317. Works: *Barakei* (Ordeal by Roses) series, 118; *Embrace* series, 118; holiday card (1975), *20*; *Kamaitachi* series, 118; *Kimono* series, 119; *Man and Woman* series, 118; *Man and Woman, #24* (1960), *118*

Hosoe, Kenji, 119

Hospital on Leyte (W. Eugene Smith), 174, *364*

Hot Springs at The Needles, Pyramid Lake, Nevada (Goin), *230*

Hôtel du Châtelet (Freund), *91*

A House Alone: Photographs of Frederick Sommer's House (Jones), *320*

House Un-American Activities Committee, 129

Houseworth, Thomas, 263, 317

Howison, Herbert M., 317

Hughes, Langston, 155, 156

Hula Hoopers, Chicago (Pallas), *158*

Humanature (Goin), 233

Humboldt State University, 234

Hyde, Philip, 317

I Want to Take Picture (Burke), 47

IBM, 61

The Ice Serpent (Fassbender), *300*

Idols Behind Altars (Brenner), 137

Ilha da Madeira (anonymous album), 206

Illinois State Normal University, 170

"Image, Obscurity, and Interpretation," (H. H. Smith), 170

Imager for Mars Pathfinder (IMP), 318

Images and Words Collection, 343

Images and Words Workshop, 262

Immisch, T. O., 62

IMP *see* Imager for Mars Pathfinder

In and Out of Focus (Allen), 264

In Our Time: The World as Seen by Magnum Photographers, 329

In Plain Sight (Newhall), 148

In the Land of the Headhunters (Curtis), 77

Incorpora, Giuseppe, 290

Index to American Photographic Collections, 139

Indiana University, 169, 216

Indivisible: Stories of American Community (2000), 272, 280, 282, 295, 311, 327, 328, 350, 353

The Inhabited Prairie (Evans), 233

Initiations 8:5 (Tress), *375*

Innocents (Miyoshi), 134

Institute of Design, Chicago, 143, 167, 223
intaglio prints, 48, 225
International Surrealism Exhibition, Paris (1938), 57
Iris prints, 225
Ishimoto, Yasuhiro, 119
Ishiuchi, Miyako, 119
Ito, Yoshihiko, 119
Iturbide, Graciela, 126, 318; *El Sacrificio, La Mixteca* (1992), *125*
Iwo Jima (Rosenthal), *117*

J. Paul Getty Research Institute *see* Getty Research Institute
Jachna, Joseph, 123, 318; holiday card (1970s), *20*
Jackson, William Henry, 77
Jacob Israel Avedon portfolio (Avedon), 268
Jansen, Arno, 93
Japan: A Chapter of Image (W. Eugene Smith), 120, 175
Japanese Bath, Betty Threat, Model (Dahl-Wolfe), *80*
Japanese Camera Pictorialists of California, 123
Japanese photography, 118–20, 123–24
Japanesque #46, Sojiji, Japan (Narahara), *119*
Jay, Bill, 318–19; archive, 318
Jeffers, Robinson, 248
Les Jeux de la Poupée (Bellmer), 90
Jim Pomeroy, Performing Mechanics Music (Yura Adams), 351
Jim Pomeroy: Stereo View (Pomeroy), 49
John D. and Catherine T. MacArthur Foundation Fellowship, 148
John Reed Club, 110
John Simon Guggenheim Foundation Fellowship, 124, 143, 155, 179, 225, 237, 248, 249
Johnson, Michael, 320

Johnson, Stephen, 230; *The Great Central Valley: California's Heartland* (1993), 230
Johnson, William S., 19, 229
Joint Committee for Cultural and Educational Cooperation, 190
Jones, Harold, 19, 34, 35, 95, 320, 352; *A House Alone: Photographs of Frederick Sommer's House* (1999), *320*
Jones, Pirkle, 321, 393
Josef Albers, Black Mountain College, North Carolina (Breitenbach), *275*
Josephson, Kenneth, 321
Joslyn, Carolyn, 202
Joyce, James, 57, 165
Julia F. Corson Collection, 89, 274, 290
Julian, Richard L., 321
Julie Saul Gallery, New York, 213
Julius Rosenwald Fellowship, 155
Justema, William (Billy), 121–24, 330; "The Exposé of Form," 124
Justice, Blake, 321

k2 Studio and Gallery, Aspen, Colorado, 321
Kaeser, Frederick (Fritz), 16, 321
Kaeser, Milly, 16
Kahlo, Frida, 264
Kaida, Tamarra, 321
Kaiso (Yamagata), 119
Kales, Arthur F., 121, 123
Kamaitachi series (Hosoe), 118
Kammerichs, Klaus, 93
Kanaga, Consuelo, 79, 107, 110, 163, 294
Karl Blossfeldt – 12 Photographien portfolio (Blossfeldt), *273*
Karneval (Rohde), *93*
Kattelson, Sy, 163
Katz, Brian, 321
Katz, Robert, 343

Kawada, Kikuji, 119
Kay Bonfoey Gallery, Tucson, 148
Kayafas, Gus, 321
Keiley, Joseph T., 322
Kelley, Ron, 322; *Winogrand Are Beautiful* (1981–82), 322
Kenna, Michael, 322
Kennedy, John F., 111, 352
Kennerly, David Hume, 322
Kepes, Gyorgy, 169
Kertész, André, 57, 113, 322
Keystone View Company, 322
Khalsa, Sant, 230, 233, 322
Kikai, Hiroh, 119
Kilburne Brothers, 263, 322
Killip, Chris, 323
Kimono series (Hosoe), 119
Kitahara, Ryuzo, 118, 323
The Klan Room (Christenberry), 74
Klein, Franz, 166
Klett, Mark, 230, 234, 323. Works: *Martian Test Landscape at the University of Arizona, Tucson, 11/13/98*, 323; *Stop Sign near Open Shooting Range, Reach 10, Granite Reef Aqueduct, North Phoenix* (1984) from the *Central Arizona Project Photographic Survey*, 323
Knight, Philip, 323
Kobayashi, Norio, 119, 323
Koffler, Kamilla or Camilla *see* Ylla
Kon, Michiko, 119
Konica Prize, 119, 134
Korona view camera, 377
Kostiner, Lewis S., 324
Krabbenfischer, *Travemunde* (Moses), 340
Kreymborg, Alfred, 121
Krims, Leslie, 324
Kruger, Barbara, 216
Ku Klux Klan, 74, 176
Kühn, Heinrich, 92, 324
Kuniyoshi, Yasuo, 324

Laffoon, Jennifer, 202
Laird, W. David, 35

Lake Almanor, California
(Minor White), *25*
Landau, Ergy, 253
Land-Weber, Ellen, 230, 234,
324
Landweber, Victor, 324
Lange, Dorothea, 16, 25, 97,
108, 127, 152, 163, 193, 253,
324; *Migrant Mother, 117*
lantern slides, 299, 368
Larson, William, 324
Lartigue, Jacques-Henri, 89,
202, 324
Laughlin, Clarence, 272, 325;
Light as Protagonist (1949)
from the series *Group K:*
Visual Poems, 325
Laurent, Jean (Juan), 89, 191,
325
Lavenson, Alma, 107, 152, 325
Leakey, L. S. B., 253
LEAR *see* Liga de escritores y
artistas revolucionarios
Leaves, Glacier Bay, Alaska
(Adams), *262*
Leaves of Grass (Whitman),
197, 248
Leavitt, Dustin W., 19
LeConte, Joseph, 263, 325, 380
Lectures, Writings, Interviews,
and Manuscripts Collection,
326
Lee, Russell, 326
Lehrer, Cy, 326
Leica camera, 193
Leighton, Ron, 326
Lemaître, Maurice, 326
Lenz, Herm, 108
Lerner, Nathan, 326
Let Truth Be the Prejudice (W.
Eugene Smith), 364
Let Us Now Praise Famous
Men (Walker Evans), 74
Levinson, Joel D., 326
Levinstein, Leon, 326
Levinthal, David, 327; Untitled
from the series *Mein Kampf*
(1994–95), *327*
Levitt, Helen, 327; *Halloween,*
New York (ca. 1942), *327*

Levy, Julien, 392
Lewis Hine Memorial
Collection, 162
Librairie Godtfurneau, 206
Library of Congress,
Washington, D. C., 77
Liebling, Jerome, 160, 163,
327. Works: *Boy and Car,*
New York City (1949) from
the portfolio *Jerome*
Liebling: Photographs, 160;
Jerome Liebling:
Photographs (1976), 327
Life (magazine), 57, 85, 93,
127, 131, 174, 193, 194
Life in a Book (Deschamps), 47
Liftin, Joan, 327
Liga de escritores y artistas
revolucionarios, 43, 44
Light, Ken, 328
Light as Protagonist (Laughlin),
325
Light Gallery, New York, 67, 281
Light Rhythms (Bruguière), 65
Light (Povo), *190*
Limelight Gallery, New York,
61, 307–08; archive, 308
Limited Editions Club, 248
Lipscomb, Stephanie, 19
Lisa Lyon (Mapplethorpe), *330*
lithocollotypes, 206
lithography, 225, 227, 229
Living Egypt (Strand), 199
Loengard, John, 328
Loew, Heinz, 92, 269; *Bits*
(1928), *269*
London, Jack, 129
Longshoreman's Union of the
Pacific, 129
Look (magazine), 253
Loren, Sophia, 221
Lorenz, Pare, 219; *The River,*
219
Los Angeles Camera Club, 121
"Lost Children," (Weegee), *382*
Lou Bunin, Puppet Master,
Producer of "Hairy Ape,"
with Marionettes (Modotti),
280
Louie, Reagan, 328
Louisiana (Volkerding), *222*

Lowe, Sarah, 137
Luce, Henry, 193
Lupp, Marshall, 328
Lustrum Press, 96, 98
Lyman, Christopher, 78
Lynes, George Platt, 328
Lyon, Danny, 125, 328; *Bus*
Stop, Tehuantepec, Oaxaca
(1978) from the portfolio
Danny Lyon, 1979, *328*
Lyon, Lisa, 330
Lyons, Joan, 329; *Patio,*
Fountain / Pavilion, New
York (1982), *329*
Lyons, Naomi, 181, 183
Lytle, Larry, 19

M. H. de Young Memorial
Museum (San Francisco),
107, 124, 149, 151, 232, 244
MacArthur Foundation
Fellowship *see* John D. and
Catherine T. MacArthur
Foundation Fellowship
El Machete (magazine), 44,
135, 137
Machine Gunners, San
Francisco (Gutmann), *311*
MacWeeney, Alen, 329
Maddow, Ben, 329
Mademoiselle (magazine), 253
El Maestro Rural (magazine),
44, 45
Magazine Make-Over series
(Golden), 106
Magnum Photos, 111, 113, 329
Maharaja of Bharatpur, 253
Maillol, Aristide, 57
MALDEF *see* Mexican
American Legal Defense
and Educational Fund
Malone, Roxanne, 65
Maloney, Joe, 329
Man and Woman series
(Hosoe), 118
Man and Woman, #24
(Hosoe), *118*
"A Man of Mercy" essay (W.
Eugene Smith), 174
Man Ray, 57, 65, 81, 90, 329;
Électricité (1931), 90, 329

Manchester, Ellen, 230, 231, 232

Mandel, Mike, 285–86, 329; *Baseball Photographer Trading Card Series* (1975), *286*; Clatworthy Colorvues, 285; *Evidence*, 329, 372

Manhatta (Strand and Sheeler), 197

"Manipulative Photography" (Heinecken), 116

Man-Made Landscapes (Feininger), 88

Mann, Thomas, 74

Mannahatta (Whitman), 197

MANUAL, 298

Mapplethorpe, Robert, 330. Works: *Lisa Lyon* (1982), *330*; *A Season in Hell* (1986), 330

Marcos Pablo Jeronimo, 57 Years Old, Bagmaker and Carpenter (Namuth), *341*

Marin, John, 195

Marshall Field Department Store, Chicago, 169

Martian Test Landscape at the University of Arizona, Tucson, 11/13/98 (Klett), 323

Martin, Josiah, 290, 330

Masclet, Daniel, 90

Masie, "Queen of the Bowery" (Webb), *381*

Masks (Golden), *104*, 105–106

Mason, Pat Bovyer, 208n5

Masters, Edgar Lee, 197; *Spoon River Anthology*, 197

Mather, Margrethe, 18, 24, 121–24, 243, 330. Works: "The Exposé of Form", 124; *Sadakichi Hartmann* (ca. 1935), *330*; *Semi-Nude* [Billy Justema wearing kimono] (ca. 1923), *122*, 123

Matter, Herbert, 155

Matthew, Neil E., 331

Maxey, Ben, 331

Mayan Indians and Photographer (Yavno), *395*

Mayer, Grace, 275, 286

McAvoy, Thomas, 127, 193

McCarthy, Joseph, 163

McCarthyism, 155

McCartney, Paul and Linda, 336

McCoy, Allan B., 331

McCullers, Carson, 74, 84

McDaniels, Robyn Stoutenburg, 331

McDuffie, Dena, 19

McElroy, Keith, 19

McFarland, Lawrence, 331; *Petroglyph on Hill Overlooking Site of Picacho Pumping Plant* from *Central Arizona Project Photographic Survey* (1985), *331*

McFarlane, Maynard, 332

McGehee, Clarence B. (Ramiel), 121, 243

McGraw, Richard, 332

McGraw Colorgraph Company, 332–33

McMillan, Jerry, 201

Mead, Mildred, 332

Meatyard, Ralph Eugene, 334

Mein Kampf series (Levinthal), 327

Meissner, Betsi, 19

Mella, Julio Antonio, 137

Member of the Wilkins Family Making Biscuits for Dinner on Corn-Shucking Day, at the Home of Mrs. Fred Wilkins, near Tallyho & Stern, N.C. (Wolcott), *394*

Memphis State University, 74

Men and Machines (Hagel), 129, 131

Men and Ships (Hagel), 127

Men of the World (Durant), 298

Méndez Caratini, Héctor M., 334

Mercer, Patricia and John, 292

Meridan Press, 70

Mertin, Roger, 334

metalchrome prints, 268

Metnick, Alan D., 334

Metropolitan Museum of Art, New York, 187, 189, 213

Mexican American Legal Defense and Educational Fund, 53

Mexican Folkways (magazine), 135, 137

Mexican photography, 125–26

Meyer, Hannes, 92, *93*

Meyer, Pedro, 126, 334; *La boda en Coyoacán* (1983), *126*

Meyerowitz, Joel, 334

mezzotint, 49

M. G. A. with Camera Work (Paul Anderson), *266*

M'Ghie, J., 334

Michals, Duane, 334

Mickey Pallas: Photographs 1945 to 1960 exhibition, Chicago, 159

Mickey Pallas and His International Famous Orchestra, 159

Midtown Manhattan Seen from Weehawken, New Jersey (Feininger), *86*

Mieth, Hansel, 93, 127–31, 335; archive, 335. Works: *Return to Fellbach* (1950), 129; *The Simple Life* (1955), 129; *Young Man Sleeping in Box Car* (1936), *128*

Migrant Mother (Lange), *117*

Millea, Tom, 335

Millet, Laurent, 90; *Petite Machine Littorale,* 90

Miller, Wayne, 16

"Minamata" essay (W. Eugene Smith), 175

Minicam (magazine), 170

Minick, Roger, 53, 223, 335

Minkkinen, Arno Rafael, 335

Minneapolis portfolio (Avedon), 268

Misrach, Richard, 336; *Playboy #90 (hole in mouth)* from series *Desert Canto XI: Violence* (1990), *336*

Miyoshi, Kozo, 119, 132–34, 336. Works: *Airfields,* 133; *B-6* from the series *Roots <NE>* (1987–91), *132*; *Cactus,* 134; *Chapel,* 133–34; *Conservatory* series, 133; *Innocents,* 134;

Picture Show, 134; *Roots <NE>* series, 133–34; *Route 66*, 134; *Southwest*, 134
El Mochuelo Gallery, Santa Barbara, 67
Model, Lisette, 57, 60, 155, 161, 163, 336
Modern Photography (magazine), 87
modernist photography, 121, 124, 220
Modotti, Tina, 44, 121, 135–37, 243, 248, 280, 337. Works: *Bandolier, Corn, Sickle*, 135; *Circus Tent* (1924), *136*; *Cloth Folds*, 135; *Lou Bunin, Puppet Master, producer of "Hairy Ape," with Marionettes* (ca. 1929), *280*; *Telegraph Wires*, 135; *Texture and Shadow*, 135; *Worker Reading* El Machete, 135, 137; *Workers' Parade*, 135
Moholy-Nagy, László, 143, 169, 170
Moholy-Nagy, Lucia, 269
Monolith, The Face of Half Dome, Yosemite Valley (Adams), 37
Monroe, Marilyn, 268
montage, 57, 215
Moore, Charles Le Roy, 188
Moore, Henry, 239
Moore, Marianne, 24
Moore, Pamela, 48; *Wooden Book*, 48
Moore, Sarah, 19
Morand, Ruthe, 337; *Preparing Canal for Lining at Apache Junction* from *Central Arizona Project Photographic Survey* (1985), *337*
Morath, Inge, 337
Morgan, Barbara, 57, 163, 338
Morgan, J. Pierpont, 77
Morgan and Morgan, 262
Morinaga, Jun, 118, 120; Untitled from *River, Its Shadow of Shadows* (1978), *120*
Morishita, Ittetsu, 119

Moriyama, Daido, 119, 120; *Ferryboats, Tsugaru Strait* (1971), *120*
Morris, Charles W., 338
Morris, Earl H., 338
Morris, John G., 16, 338
Morris, Wright, 338
Morris B. Sachs' Amateur Hour, 159
Mortensen, Myrdith, 139, 142
Mortensen, William, 23, 109, 138–42, 268, 321, 331, 339, 359; archive, 339. Works: *Torse* (ca. 1935) from the portfolio *Pictorial Photography*, *138*; Untitled [George Dunham] (n.d.), *142*
Mortensen School of Photography, 142, 338
Moses, Stefan, 340; *Krabbenfischer; Travemunde*, (1963–64) from the series *Deutsche*, *340*
Mother and Son (H. H. Smith), 171
motion pictures, 65, 77, 369
Müller-Pohle, Andreas, 93
Muench, David, 340
Münchner Stadtmuseum, 61
Muhr, Adolph, 78
Muniz, Vik, 217
Munkacsi, Martin, 81
murals in Mexico, 43, 137
Murphy, Michaela Allan, 270
Museum of Contemporary Art, Chicago, 115
Museum of Fine Arts, Boston, 187
Museum of Modern Art, New York, 60, 79, 81, 143, 144, 148, 219, 220, 249, 253
Museum of Natural History, New York, 254
Muybridge, Eadweard, 202, 263, 340. Works: *The Pacific Coast of Central America and Mexico*, 202; *Panama Bay by Moonlight* (1875–76), *203*; *Photograph Studies of Central America and the Isthmus of Panama* (1876), *340*
Mydans, Carl, 127

Nadeau, Luis, 277
Nagatani, Patrick, 340
Nagatani/Tracey Collaboration, 340
Nakahashi, Kenji, 119
Namuth, Hans, 57, 60, 93, 341; *Marcos Pablo Jeronimo, 57 Years Old, Bagmaker and Carpenter* from the series *Todos Santos Cuchumatán* (1978), *341*
Narahara, Ikko, 119; *Japanesque #46, Sojiji, Japan* (1969), *119*
Nash, Roderick, 231
Nash Editions, 225
Nast, Thomas, 375
Natali, Enrico, 341
National Endowment for the Arts, 48, 155, 211, 230
The National League Stadiums (Dow), 297
Native Land (Strand), 197
Navajo, 101, 103, 309
Navajos by Firelight (Gilpin), *309*
Naya, Carlo, 341
negatives in collections, 185, 202, 220, 239–41, 263, 264, 273, 276, 278, 279, 281, 293, 310, 311, 313, 314, 324, 328, 332, 339, 345, 349, 353, 354, 360, 364, 365, 367, 369, 378, 379, 384, 385, 391
Neimanas, Joyce, 115, 251, 341
Nesbitt, Esta, 342; *Selenium Songs* (1972), *342*
Nettles, Bea, 342
Neurosurgeons in Action (Payne), 349
Neusüss, Floris M., 93, 342; *Engel* (1967), *92*
Neutra, Richard, 248
New Bauhaus, American School of Design, Chicago, 169, 338
New Documents exhibition, New York, 249, 391
New England Conservatory of Music, 101

New Masses (magazine), 110, 137, 160
New Mexico Portfolio (Newhall), 148
New School for Social Research, New York, 60, 249
[New York], ca. 1960–61 (Winogrand), *250*
New York, New York (Tseng), *212*
New York Graphic Society, 262
New York Herald Tribune (newspaper), 153
New York Stock Exchange (Hagel), *130*
New York World's Fair (1939), 82
Newhall, Beaumont, 16, 35, 38, 79, 143–48, 163, 170, 188, 189, 237, 248, 343; *Henri Cartier-Bresson* (1946), *146*. Writings: "Epicure Corner," 147; *Focus* (1993), 143; *History of Photography*, 147; *In Plain Sight* (1983), 148; *New Mexico Portfolio* (1976), 148; *Photography: Essays and Images* (1980), 148
Newhall, Christi Yates, 148
Newhall, Nancy, 16, 38, 41, 143–48, 163, 170, 237, 248, 343. Writings: *The Eloquent Light*, 38; *Time in New England* (1950), 143
Newman, Arnold, 155, 163, 343
Nexus Press, 47
Nigerian photography, 366
Nilsen, Dianne, 19
Nineteenth-Century Photographic Formats Collection, 343
Les Nipponnes d'eau (Bailly-Maître-Grand), 90
No Mountains in the Way (Terry Evans), 230
Nordby, Will, 270
Nordström, Alison, 19
Norman, Dorothy, 23, 237, 344–45; *Alfred Stieglitz* (1930s–40s), *344*
North, Kenda, 345

North American Indian (Curtis), 77, 78, 293
Noskowiak, Sonya, 93, 107, 149–52, 219, 248, 345; archive, 345. Works: *Calla Lily* (1930), *150*; *Untitled [Golden Gate Bridge]* (1930s), *152*; *Water Lily Leaves* (1931), *345*
Noumenon 256, 1984/85 (Chiarenza), *283*
Novak, Lorie, 346
Now You Know: This Is Serious Photography (Shwachman), 48–49, *49*
Nuclear Landscapes (Goin), 233
Nude Floating (Edward Weston), *244*
nudist camps, 60
"Nurse Midwife" essay (W. Eugene Smith), 174

Object and Image: An Introduction to Photography (Craven), 291
Oelman, P. H., 346
offset lithographs, 47, 227, 229, 288, 296, 303, 309, 317, 329, 354, 379, 394
Ohio State University, 169, 170
Ojeda, Arthur E., 346
Oju Mo Olas Photo Service, Ila, Nigeria, 366
O'Keeffe, Georgia, 195, 237, 239, 381
Old Amish Men, Lancaster, Pennsylvania (Tice), *375*
Old Typewriter (Bullock), *279*
Olympic Organizing Committee, Los Angeles, 1984, 53
One Thing Just Sort of Led to Another (Walker), 229
O'Neill, Eugene, 280
Oracle Conference, 346
Ordeal by Roses (Hosoe) *see Barakei* series
Orkin, Ruth, 163
Orland, Ted, 346
Ortiz Rubio, Pascual, 137
Osato, Sono, 155

O'Sullivan, Timothy, 77, 346
Overseas Training Program for Artists (Japan), 119
Owens, Bill, 346

The Pacific Coast of Central America and Mexico (Muybridge), 202
Pacific Islands (album), *204–05, 207–08*
Pacific Maritime Federation, 127
Pacific Press Service, 346
Paepcke, Walter, 16
Un paese (Strand), 197
Palfi, Marion, 57, 60, 93, 153–57, 163, 347; archive, 347. Works: *Chaim Gross—Working in His Studio Alone* from the series *Great American Artists of Minority Groups and Democracy at Work* (1944), 155, *347*; *The Esau Jenkins Story* (1964/66), 156; *First I Liked the Whites, I Gave Them Fruits* (1967–69), *153*; *Henry Street Settlement* (1945), *156*; *Suffer Little Children*, 153; *There Is No More Time* (1949), *155*; *You Have Never Been Old* (1955–57), *154*
palladium prints, 297
Pallas, Mickey, 158–59, 348; archive, 348. Works: *Hula Hoopers, Chicago* (1958), *158*; *Mickey Pallas: Photographs 1945 to 1960*, 159; *Sugar Ray Robinson and Abe Saperstein, Paris* (n.d.), *348*
Pallas, Millie, 159
Pallas Photographica Gallery, Chicago, 159
Palmin, Igor, 348
Panama Bay by Moonlight (Muybridge), *203*
Panama Pacific International Exposition, 38; ticket book, *40*
Panorama d'Athenes (Athanassiou), *206, 207, 207*

437

panoramic photography, 207, 223, 225, 232, 310, 354

Pansirna, C. J., 366

Parable, Wisconsin (Thorne-Thomsen), *374*

Paracelsus (paint on cellophane) (Frederick Sommer), *182*

Parada, Esther, 298

Le Parc de Saint-Cloud (Atget), 89, 267

Pare, Richard D., 348

Paris en photographies (Quinet), 89

Parker, Ann, 348

Parker, Fred R., 348

Parmelian Prints of the High Sierras (Adams), 263

Parrish Family albums, 207–08

Parry, Ellwood C. III, 19

Le passage cloute (Brassaï), *90*

Patio, Fountain / Pavilion, New York (Lyons), *329*

Paton, Alan, 383; *South Africa in Transition* (1956), *383*

Pattern Made of Dragonfly Wings [variant] (Feininger), *300*

Patterns by Photography exhibition (San Francisco), 124

Payne, Mitchell, 349; Untitled from series *Neurosurgeons in Action* (1970–72), *349*

Peeler, David, 19

Pelizzari, Maria Antonella, 19

Pelletier, Brian C., 349

Pepper No. 30 [verso] (Edward Weston), *248*

Peress, Gilles, 349

Pérez Martinez, Héctor, 44

performance art, 351

Persona #10 (Golden), *106*

Persona series (Golden), 106

Peruvian Portfolio (Alexanian and Gersh), 263, 308

Pescheret, Leon, 349

Peterhans, Walter, 269

Petite Machine Littorale (Millet), 90

Petrillo, Thomas, 349

Petroglyph on Hill Overlooking Site of Picacho Pumping Plant (McFarland), *331*

Pfahl, John, 349

Philadelphia Photographer (magazine), 350

Photo League, 155, 160–63, 173, 230, 360, 383

Photo Notes (magazine), 162

Photocrom prints, 396

photograms, 60, 90, 170, 329

"The Photograph and Its Readers" (H. H. Smith), 170

The Photographer (Van Dyke), 220

Photographers Baseball Series (Mandel), *286*

photographic education, 167, 169, 171, 201–203, 216

Photographic Literature Collection, 350

Photographic Mat Collection, 350

Photographic Studies of Central America and the Isthmus of Panama (Muybridge), 340

Photography: Essays and Images (Newhall), 148

Photography 1839 – 1937 exhibition (New York), 79, 143

Photography Media Institute, 288

photography of animals, 253

photography of Native Americans, 76–78, 101–103, 155

photography schools, 101, 142, 287, 338

photogravure prints, 271, 285, 293, 296, 314, 316, 329, 330, 359

photojournalism, 127, 193, 215, 249

The Photojournalist Dennis Stock, Winner of the LIFE Young Photographers Contest (Feininger), *85, 86*

photomontage, 170, 217

Photo-Secession, 63, 219

photo-silkscreen, 229

Picasso, Pablo, 90

Picasso, Paloma, 213

Pictorial Photographers of America, 121, 301

Pictorial Photography in America (magazine), 121

Pictorial Photography portfolio (Mortensen), *138*

pictorialist photography, 101, 108, 109, 121, 123, 124, 139, 160, 239, 243, 274, 331

Picture Show (Miyoshi), 134

Pildas, Ave, 350

Pima Community College, 53

pinhole photography, 225, 374

Pitts, Terence, 19

"Pittsburgh" essay (W. Eugene Smith), 174

Plachy, Sylvia, 350

platinum photographs, 101, 144, 179, 262, 266, 267, 274, 276, 277, 313, 314, 316, 330, 359, 372

Playboy (magazine), 159

Playboy #90 (hole in mouth) (Misrach), *336*

Plossu, Bernard, 89, 90, 91, 350. Works: *The African Desert* (1987), 91, 350; *Fulani Nomad, Niger* (1975), *89*

Plowden, David, 350

Pogue, Alan, 350

Pokemon, 134

Polaroid photography, 148, 392

Polke, Sigmar, 93

Pollack, Peter, 350

Polly series (Caffery), 281

Polyscop stereo camera, 273

Polytechnic Preparatory Country Day School, Brooklyn, 188

Pomeroy, Jim, 48–49, 351; archive, 351. Works: *Apollo Jest: An American Mythology (in depth)* (1983), *48*; *Jim Pomeroy: Stereo View,* 49; *Seeing Double,* 49

Pond, C. L., 263, 351
Ponti, Carlo, 221
pop art, 74
Porter, Aline, 16
Porter, Eliot, 16, 352
Portrait of a Woman (Southworth & Hawes), 187, 189
Portrait of a Young Man (Southworth & Hawes), 187, 189
portrait photography, 50–52, 57, 101, 152, 153, 197
Postcard Collection, 22, 352
postmortem photography, 187
post-visualization, 216
Pound, Ezra, *52*
Povo, Marta, 191; *Campanet, Mallorca* (1984) from the series *Light, 190*
Powell, John Wesley, 231, 233
Prairie: Images of Ground and Sky (Terry Evans), 233
Pratt, Charles, 353; archive, 353. Works: *A Sense of Wonder*, 353; *Rocky Coast*, 353; *Roxbury, Connecticut* (1964), *353*
Preparing Canal for Lining at Apache Junction (Morand), *337*
Prestini, 63
pre-visualization, 35, 216
Price, Melville, 74
Prince, Doug, 353
printing-out paper prints, 225
printmaking, 223, 225
Prisma Graphic Company, 184
Profile of a Young Girl (Southworth & Hawes), 187, 189
Prologue to a Sad Spring (Edward Weston), 123
Proust, Marcel, 165
Pueblo Indians, 101
The Pueblos: A Camera Chronicle (Gilpin), 101
Pultz, John, 231, 232
Puritans, 243
Les pyramides prises de Gizeh (Bonfils), *274*

Quadravision, 270
Quick, Herb, 353
Quinet, Achille, 89, 353; *Paris en photographies*, 89

Radnitzky, Emmanuel *see* Man Ray
Rago, T., 353
Ramirez, Monica, 202
Ramos, Roxane, 19
Rauschenberg, Robert, 115
Raylo Camera, 296
rayographs, 329
La Raza, 55
reading photographs, 170, 179, 376
Recent Terrains: Transforming the American West (Laurie Brown), 232
"Recording Artists" essay (W. Eugene Smith), 174
Recto/Verso #3 (Heinecken), *114*
Reed, Eli, 353
Reilly, J. J., 263
Reisner, Marc, 231, 232
relief printing, 65
Relocation Continued (Wehr), 47
Rembrandt, 185
Remembering Joseph Cornell in Merida 12 (Siskind), *164*
Rephotographic Survey Project, 230, 234
Requiem for a Paperweight (Tress), 211
Rhode Island School of Design, 167
Ribalta, Jorge, 191
Rice, Leland, 270
Rich, Linda, 353
Richter, Hans, 65
Ricordi di Firenze (Alinari), 206
Riebesehl, Heinrich, 93
Rimbaud, Arthur, 330; *A Season in Hell*, 330
The Rio Grande: River of Destiny (Gilpin), 101
Rita Hayworth and Orson Welles (Stackpole), *367*
The River (Lorenz), 219

River, Its Shadow of Shadows (Morinaga), *120*
A River Too Far: The Past and Future of the Arid West (1991), 231
Rivera, Diego, 43, 137, 193, 264
Riverdale Balcony, Riverdale, New York (Harbutt), *111*
The Road to Oregon (Webb), 237
Robbins, Andrea, 93
Robeson, Paul, 56, 84
Robinson, Sugar Ray, 348
Roche, John P., 354
Rochester Institute of Technology, 143, 216
Rock's Words (Gittings), 48
Rocky Coast (Carson and Pratt), 353
Rodin, Auguste, *Gates of Hell*, 224
Roh, Franz, 92
Rohde, Werner, 92; *Karneval* (ca. 1928), *93*
Roitz, Charles, 354
Rolleicord camera, 268
Rolling Stone: The Family portfolio (Avedon), 50, 268
Roman Profile (Savage), *357*
Romeike, Carla, 354
Roosevelt, Eleanor, 155
Roosevelt, Franklin D., 292
Roosevelt, Theodore, 77
Roots <NE> (Miyoshi), *132, 133–34*
Rose, Ben, 354–55
Rose Petal Exhaling Its Fragrance (Breitenbach and Devaux), *60*
Rosenblum, Walter, 163, 356; *Women and Baby Carriage, Pitt Street, New York* (1938), *161*
Rosenthal, Joe, *Iwo Jima, 117*
Rosenwald *see* Julius Rosenwald Fellowship
Ross, Donald, 356
Rothstein, Arthur, 163, 356
Route 66 (Miyoshi), 134
Rowles, Steve, 356

Roxbury, Connecticut (Pratt), *353*

Roy, Claude, 197

Royal Pair (H. H. Smith), *168*, 171

Royal Pair 8 (H. H. Smith), *170*

Royal Photographic Society, 57

Rubenstein, Meridel, 147

Rudolf Kicken Galerie, Cologne, 92

Ruff, Thomas, 93

Rule, Amy, 185n6

Ruscha, Edward, 49, 116; *Various Small Fires and Milk*, 49

Ruzicka, Drahomir, 276

Sabattier effect, 65, 227, 229

Sachs, Morris B., 159

Sachs, Paul, 343

Sachs, Yolla Niclas, 93, 163, 356

Sacred Wood (Sommer), 179

El Sacrificio, La Mixteca (Iturbide), *125*

Sadakichi Hartmann (Mather), *330*

Salaün, Philippe, 91, 356

Samarughi, Mario, 356

San Francisco Art Institute, 79

San Francisco Chronicle, 241

San Francisco City College, 232

San Francisco General Strike (1934), 109, 127

San Francisco Society of Women Artists, 345

San Isidro Labrador (Lola Alvarez Bravo), *264*

Sánchez, América, 191

Sánchez Uribe, Jesús, 126, 356

Sandburg, Carl, 121

Sander, August, 92

Sandweiss, Martha, 103

Santos, A. C., 290, 356

Saperstein, Abe, 348

Sarah Natani in Her Sheep Corral, Table Mesa near Shiprock, New Mexico (Capehart), *282*

Sardinia (Gibson), *308*

Savage, Naomi, 286, 357; *Roman Profile* (1969–80), *357*

Schaefer, John P., 19, 34, 357; *St. Anthony and the Christ Child, Mission San Xavier del Bac, Tucson, Arizona* from the portfolio *Bac: Where the Waters Gather* (1977), *357*

Scheinbaum, David, 148, 358

Schmidt, Bastienne, 93, 113; *Vivir la Muerte*, 93

Schoenberg, Arnold, 248

Schoenfeld, Diana, 358

Schrag, Karl, 57

Schrager, Victor, 272

Schreiber, J. Keith, 358

Schweitzer, Albert, 174

Scrivener, Wall Street, New York (Harbutt), *112*

Seagrams Corporation, 223

Sea Change exhibition, Tucson, 119

A Season in Hell (Rimbaud and Mapplethorpe), 330

See (Walker), 47, 229

Seeger, Pete, 162

Seeing Double (Pomeroy), 49

Seeley, George H., 358

Seghers, Hercules, 185

Seidenstucker, Friedrich, 92

Sekiguchi, Takashi, 119; *Uzura* series, 119

Selenium Songs (Nesbitt), *342*

Selkirk, Neil, 266

Semi-nude [Billy Justema wearing kimono] (Mather), *122*

A Sense of Wonder (Carson and Pratt), 353

Sensorium (magazine), 120

sentimentalism in Japanese art, 133–34

Sepia (magazine), 159

Seven Fifty Studio, Chicago, 69

Seven Sacred Pools, Maui, Hawaii (Connor), *289*

Sexton, John, 358

Seymour, David (Chim), 358

Shadow: A Novel in Photographs (Tress), 209

Shahn, Ben, 163

Sheeler, Charles, 179, 197, 239, 248; *Manhatta* (1920); 197

Shibata, Toshio, 119, 358

Shiva series (Heinecken), 117

Shore, Stephen, 358

Shwachman, Irene, 48–49, 358; archive, 358; *Now You Know, This is Serious Photography* (1987), *49*

Sidney Janis Gallery, 89

Siegel, Arthur, 169, 237, 359

Sierra Club, 39, 211, 262

Sieveking, Lance, 65

Silva, Grey, 142n1, 339, 359

Silver, Vivienne, 265, 359

Simmons-Myers, Ann, 359; *Blast Foreman Trey Gardner with Blasting Compound at Site of Picacho Pumping Plant* from *Central Arizona Project Photographic Survey* (1984), *359*

The Simple Life (Mieth and Hagel), 129

Sinclair, Roland, 359

Sinsabaugh, Art, 223

Sipprell, Clara, 359

Siqueiros, David Alfaro, 135

Siskind, Aaron, 22, 35, 97, 125, 163, 164–67, 169, 223, 229, 283, 360; archive, 360; collection, 90; portrait by Harry Callahan (1951), *22*. Works: *Harlem* (1940) from the *Harlem Document*, 1932–40, *360*; *Remembering Joseph Cornell in Merida 12* (1975), *164*; *Terrors and Pleasures of Levitation 94* (1961), *166*

skipreading, 184

Skoglund, Sandy, 217

Skylight, Midtown (Brett Weston), *240*

Slavin, Neil, 53, 361

Sleeping Baby (Southworth & Hawes), 186–89, *186*, *188*

Sligh, Clarissa, 47; *What's Happening with Momma?* (1988), 46, 47
Slobodian, Scott L., 361
Small, Herbert, 361
Small, Herbert Fedor, 361
Smith, Aileen Miyoko, 118, 175
Smith, Henry Holmes, 65, 168–71, 179, 216, 331, 361–62; archive, 361. Works: *Mother and Son*, 171; *Royal Pair* (1951), *168*, 171; *Royal Pair 8* (1951/82), *170*; "Xi Zero in Photography" (1959), *362*
Smith, Keith, 18, 24, 48, 105, 363. Works: *Book no. 81* (1981), *363*; *Book 91* (1982), 48; *Book 118* (1986), 48; envelope to Robert Heinecken, *18*
Smith, Lauren, 363
Smith, Michael A., 363
Smith, Nettie Lee, 364
Smith, W. Eugene, 35, 60, 89, 118, 120, 162, 163, 172–77, 215, 253, 364; archive, 364. Works: *The Big Book*, 364; "Chaplin at Work," 174; "Country Doctor (1948)", 174, *177*; *Earl Hines* (1964), *175*; "Folk Singers," 174; "Great Britain," 174; *Haiti* (1958–59), *172*, 175; *Holy Water Font in Leyte Cathedral* from series *Hospital on Leyte* (1944), 174, *364*; *Japan: A Chapter of Image*, 120, 175; *Let Truth Be the Prejudice*, 364; "A Man of Mercy," 174; "Minamata," 175; "Nurse Midwife," 174; "Pittsburgh," 174 ; "Recording Artists," 174; "Spanish Village," 174; "Taft and Ohio," 174
Smithsonian Institution, Washington, D. C., 60, 78
Smoke on Glass (Frederick Sommer), *178*

Snow, Carmel, 81
social documentary, 153–57
Société française de la photographie, 57
Society for Photographic Education, 116, 167, 169, 171, 365
solarization, 170
Solomon, Nancy, 184
Solomon, Rosalind, 125, 365
Solomon's Temple: The European Building-Crafts Legacy (Volkerding), 225
Some Art (Fiskin), 203
Sommer, Frances, 364
Sommer, Frederick, 16, 22, 25, 34, 35, 65, 93, 97, 178–85, 245–47, 229, 320, 365–66; archive 365. Works: *Paracelsus (paint on cellophane)* (1959), *182*, *183*; *Sacred Wood*, 179; *Smoke on Glass* (1962), *178*, *183*; *Sommer · Images / Sommer · Words* (1984), 179, 184–85; *Untitled [collaged medical illustrations]* (1991), *365*; *Valise d'Adam* (1949), *180*, *181*, 185
Sommer, Giorgio, 206, 207, 366. Works: *Costumi di Napoli* (ca. 1870), 366; *Souvenir de Pompei*, 206
Sommer · Images / Sommer · Words (Sommer), 179, 184–85
The Somnambulist (Gibson), 95, 96–98, 99
Songs of the Sea series (Thorne-Thomsen), 374
Sonneman, Eve, 366
Sonora (Friedlander), *304*
Sotheby's, 187
Soule, John P., 263, 366
South Africa in Transition (Weiner and Paton), 383
Southwest (Miyoshi), 134
Southworth & Hawes, 186–89. Works: *Edward Hawes, Asleep, with Hands*

Together, 187; *Edward Hawes, Asleep, with One Arm Raised*, 187; *Portrait of a Woman*, 187, 189; *Portrait of a Young Man*, 187, 189; *Profile of a Young Girl*, 187, 189; *Sleeping Baby* (1860), *186*, 187, *188*; *Unidentified Female*, 187
Souvenir de Pompei (Giorgio Sommer), 206
Spanish Civil War, 396
Spanish photography, 190–91
"Spanish Village" essay (W. Eugene Smith), 174
Speed Graphic camera, 193
Spoon River Anthology (Masters), 197
Sports Illustrated (magazine), 84, 253
Sprague, Stephen, 366–67; archive, 366–67
St. Anthony and the Christ Child, Mission San Xavier del Bac, Tucson, Arizona (Schaefer), *357*
Staatliche Galerie Moritzburg Halle, 62
Stackpole, Peter, 127, 192–94, 367–68. Works: *Alfred Hitchcock at Academy Awards Banquet* (1941), *194*; *Hollywood* portfolio, 194; *Rita Hayworth and Orson Welles* (1945), *367*; *Watching a Load of Rivets Coming Up Against the Backdrop of San Francisco* (1935), *192*
Stage, John Lewis, 368
Standard Oil Company, 61, 159, 237
Stanford University, 223, 224, 225
State University of New York, Buffalo, 143
State University of New York, Purchase, 220
Steele, Mrs. [secretary to Walter Paepcke], 16

Stegner, Wallace, 231

Steichen, Edward, 61, 65, 71, 129, 143, 155, 296, 368. Works: *Dana* (n.d.), *368*; *Swedish Lotus*, 296

Stein, Sally, 19

Steiner, Ralph, 160, 219, 220, 369. Works: *Ham and Eggs* (1929–30), *369*; *The City* (1938), 219

stereo photography, 49, 232, 266, 272, 317, 322, 325, 332, 340, 343, 346, 351, 366, 372, 377, 381

stereopticon, 73

Sternberg, Grace and Jay, 369

Stettner, Louis, 163

Stevens, Albert W., 369

Stevens, Virginia, 369

Stewart, Jimmy, 194

Stewart, Sharon, 230, 234, 370. Works: *El Cerrito y la Acequia Madre: Diggin' Ditch* (1993), *232*; *Toxic Tour of Texas* (1989–91), 234

Stieglitz, Alfred, 23, 35, 63, 109, 110, 145, 148, 162, 179, 195, 199, 237, 248, 344–45, 361, 370; Untitled [New York street scene] (1896–99), *370*

Stieglitz, Julius Oscar, 361

Stillman, Andrea, 39n1

Stock, Dennis, 85, 371

Stock Exchange (Hagel), *130*

Stokes, I. N. Phelps, 189

Stone Pine Inn, Carmel, 240

Stop Sign near Open Shooting Range, Reach 10, Granite Reef Aqueduct, North Phoenix (Klett), *323*

Stoumen, Lou, 163, 371

Stoutenburg, Robyn *see* McDaniels, Robyn Stoutenburg

Strand, Hazel Kingsbury, 269, 371

Strand, Paul, 23, 35, 44, 63, 91, 109, 125, 143, 148, 160, 161, 162, 163, 195–99, 220, 239, 269,

369, 371; books: *La France de Profil*, 197; *Ghana: An African Portrait*, 199; *Living Egypt*, 199; *Time in New England*, 143, 197; *Tir a'Mhurain*, 199; *Un paese*, 197; films: *Manhatta* (1920), 197; *Native Land* (1942), 197. Works: *The Family, Luzzara* [three small variants] (1953), 23, *198*; *Toadstool and Grasses, Maine* (1928), *195*; *The Wave* (1937), 197; *White Sheets, New Orleans, Louisiana* (1918), *196*

stroboscopic photography, 355

Strohmeyer & Wyman, 372

Struss, Karl, 266, 372

Stryker, Roy, 101, 155, 253

Stupich, Martin, 230, 234, 372

Sturtevant, Roger, 372

Suda, Issei, 119

Sudre, Jean-Pierre, 372; Untitled (1979) from the series *Végétal & Insectes*, 90, *91*

Suffer Little Children (Palfi), 153

Sugar Mills series (Fricker), 234

Sugar Ray Robinson and Abe Saperstein, Paris (Pallas), *348*

Sugimoto, Hiroshi, 119, 372; *Time Exposed* (1991), 119

Sultan, Larry, 285, 372. Works: Clatworthy Colorvues, 285, *286*; *Evidence*, 372

Summons, H. Y., 372

The Sun Is Longing for the Sea series (Yamazaki), 119

Sunami, Soichi, 372

surrealists, 216

Suzuka, Yoshiyasu, 119, *Face to Face* series, 119

Swedish Lotus (Steichen), 296

Swedlund, Charles, 372

Swift, Dick, 219, 373

Swift, Henry, 107

Sybille Binder and Paul Robeson, Role Portrait in Othello (Breitenbach), *56*

SynAesthetics, 270

Szarkowski, John, 39, 249, 264

Tabard, Maurice, 90

Taconic Foundation, 155

"Taft and Ohio" essay (W. Eugene Smith), 174

Talbot, William Henry Fox, 373

Taos Pueblo (Adams), 39

Tattersall, Alfred John, 290, 373

Taylor, Elizabeth, 194

Taylor, Paul, 127

teaching photography, 116, 143, 147–48, 167, 169, 171, 201–203, 216

Teapot Opera (Tress), 211

Telegraph Wires (Modotti), 135

telephoto lens, 87

television, 157, 229

Tellaisha, John, 373

Temples in Yucatan: A Camera Chronicle of Chichen Itza (Gilpin), 101

Terkel, Studs, 159

Terrors and Pleasures of Levitation 94 (Siskind), 165, *166*

Teske, Edmund, 286, 373

[*Texas*], *1964* (Winogrand), *251*

Texture and Shadow (Modotti), 135

There Is No More Time (Palfi), *155*

Third View, 234

"This Beautiful Landscape" (Breitenbach), 61

Thomson, John, 374

Thoreau, Henry David, 243

Thorne-Thomsen, Ruth, 202, 374; *Parable, Wisconsin* from series *Songs of the Sea* (1991), *374*

Three Fingers and an Ear (Brett Weston), *109*

Thumbprint Press, 47, 227, 229, 379

Thurston, Jacqueline, 374

Tice, George, 375; *Old Amish Men, Lancaster, Pennsylvania* from *The Amish Portfolio* (1968), *375*

Tico, Tico (Ylla), 254

Tiede, Marcia, 19

Time Exposed (Sugimoto), 119

Time in New England (Strand and Newhall), 143, 197

442

Time-Life, 74, 129
tintypes, 343
Tir a'Mhurain (Strand), 199
Toadstool and Grasses, Maine (Strand), *195*
Todd Walker in the Litho Studio (1980s), 229
Todos Santos Cuchumatán series (Namuth), 341
Tomatsu, Shomei, 119
Torse (Mortensen), *138*
Toward a Social Landscape exhibition, New York, 249
Toxic Tour of Texas series (Stewart), 234
Tracey, Andrée, 340
Transvestite Safe-Sex Outreach Worker, Dominican Republic (Weil), *382*
Traub, Charles, 375
Traube, Alex, 375
travel, 166
travel albums, 204–08
Travelog (Harbutt), 111
Tree in Yalalag (Garduño), *126*
Trees on Telegraph Hill (Hagemeyer), *313*
Treinta-Treintista, 43, 135
Tress, Arthur, 209–11, 375. Works: *Fish Tank Sonata,* 211; *Initiations 8:5* (1974), *375*; *Requiem for a Paperweight,* 209, 211; *Shadow: A Novel in Photographs,* 209; *Teapot Opera,* 211; *Whiteface Mountain, New York* (1989), *210*; *The Wurlitzer Trilogy* (exhibition installation view), *211*
A Trip Down the Green and Colorado Rivers (Goldwater), 380
Troup, Henry, 376
Troy, Timothy, 19
Tseng Kwong Chi, 213, 376. Works: *Costumes at the Met* (1997), 213; *East Meets West,* 213; *Expeditionary Series,* 213; *New York, New York* (1979) from the *Expeditionary Series, 212*

Tucker, Anne, 163n1
Tulsa portfolio (Clark), 284
Turnage, William A., 35
TV Guide (magazine), 394
typewriters, 16, 37, 38, 39, *279*
typography, 227

U. S. Camera (magazine), 193, 253
Uelsmann, Jerry, 171, 214–17, 286, 376. Works: *Equivalent* (1964), *376*; holiday card (1972), *21*; Untitled [cube over surf] (1979), *216*; Untitled [framed tree photograph over couch with floating leaves] (1987), *214*
Ullrich-Zuckerman, Bea, 377
Ulmann, Doris, 377
Umbo (Otto Umbehr), 92, 269, 377
Underwood & Underwood, 377
UNESCO (United Nations Educational, Scientific and Cultural Organization), 61
UNICEF (United Nations Children's Fund), 61
Unidentified Female (Southworth & Hawes), 187
United Nations, 237
United States Air Force, 249
United States Attorney General, 163, 173
United States Department of Housing and Urban Development, 211
United States Information Agency, 220
United States Office of War Information, 101, 202
University of Alabama, Tuscaloosa, 74
University of Arizona, 35, 78, 106, 201, 229
University of California, Davis, 105
University of California, Los Angeles, 115, 116
University of Chicago, 223
University of Nevada, Reno, 233

University of New Mexico, 143, 147
UNKRA (United Nations Korean Relief Agency), 61
Uzura series (Sekiguchi), 119
Uzzle, Burk, 377

Vachon, John, 163
Valise d'Adam (Frederick Sommer), *180, 181,* 185
Van Blarcum, Artie, 375, 377
Vanderbilt, Mr. and Mrs. Paul, 16
Van Der Zee, James, 377
Van Dyke, Barbara, 220
Van Dyke, Willard, 107, 108, 110, 151, 193, 218–21, 378; archive, 378. Works: *The City* (1938), 219; *The Photographer* (1947), 220; Untitled [detail of hay rake and window] (1967), *218*; *Ventilators* (ca. 1933), *378*
The Vanishing Race and Other Illusions: Photographs of Indians by Edward Curtis (Curtis), 78
Vanity Fair (magazine), 79
Various Small Fires and Milk (Ruscha), 49
Vea (magazine), 44
Végétal & Insectes series (Sudre), 90, *91*
Ventilators (Van Dyke), *378*
Vertov, Dziga, 44
Very, Annette Gest, 378
Vestal, David, 163, 378
Victoria and Albert Museum, London, 148
View from Pont Transbordeur (Bayer), *270*
View Master, 49
Villers, André, 90, 378; *Diurnes* (1962), 90
Virgen y mártir, Brión (García Rodero), *191*
Virginia Adams Stereoview Collection, 263, 266, 272, 317, 322, 325, 340, 351, 366, 372, 377
Vishniac, Roman, 392

La visita (Manuel Alvarez Bravo), *265*

Visual Studies Workshop, 47

Vivir la Muerte (Schmidt), 93

Vogt, Christian, 378

Vogue (magazine), 84

Volkerding, Laura, 222–25, 379; archive, 379; collection, 89, 223. Works: *Coubertin* (1986), *224*; *Dance of the Casts*, 224; *Folly at Santa Rosa Ranch, Coachella Valley* (1986), *225*; *Louisiana* (1972), *222*; *Solomon's Temple: The European Building-Crafts Legacy*, 225; *White Pictures*, 224

von zur Muehlen, Peter, 93

Voz (magazine), 44

Vroman, Adam Clark, 379

Vues d'Ostende (anonymous album), 206

Wade, Bob, 379

Wagner, Catherine, 379

Wagstaff, Sam, 65

Waldman, Max, 379

Walker, Melanie, 272

Walker, Todd, 47, 49, 226–29, 272, 379. Works: *Chris, Veiled* (1970), *229*; *Enthusiasm Strengthens* (1987), 47, *228*, 229; *A Few Notes: Selected from Lesson A of Wilson's Photographics* (1976), 47; *For Nothing Changes*, 229; *Fragments of Melancholy* (1980), 379; holiday card (1972), *20*; *One Thing Just Sort of Led to Another*, 229; *Portfolio Three* (1969), 379; *See*, 229; *Todd Walker in the Litho Studio*, 229; *Untitled [view of road through windshield]* (1969), *226*

Ward, John, 380

Warehouseman's Union of the Pacific, 129

Warhol, Andy, 194

Washburn, Bradford, Jr., 380

Watching a Load of Rivets Coming Up Against the Backdrop of San Francisco (Stackpole), *192*

Water in the West, 39, 230–34, 380; archive, 380

Water Lily Leaves (Noskowiak), *345*

Watkins, Carleton E., 25, 263, 381. Works: *Yosemite Falls* (1861), *24*; *Yo-Semite Valley: Photographic Views of the Falls and Valley* (1863 album), 381

Watkins' Pacific coast series, 24

Watson, April, 19

The Wave (Strand), 197

The Way (Bruguière), 63

We Want to Believe: White Handkerchiefs of Goodbye, Chicago (Durant), *298*

Webb, Lucille, 237

Webb, Todd, 67, 125, 163, 235–37, 381; archive, 381. Works: *Detail, Wall Opposite My Studio Door, Paris* (1950), *236*; *The Gold Rush Trail*, 237; *Gold Strikes and Ghost Towns*, 237; *Masie, "Queen of the Bowery"* (1946), *381*; *The Road to Oregon*, 237

Weber, Max, 101

Weed, Charles L., 317

Weegee (Arthur Fellig), 215, 382; *"Lost Children,"* (June 9, 1941), *382*

Wehr, Beata, 47; *Relocation Continued*; 47

Weil, Brian, 382; *Transvestite Safe-Sex Outreach Worker, Dominican Republic* (1987), *382*

Weiman Company, 159

Weiner, Dan, 163, 383; archive, 383; *Untitled from South Africa in Transition* (1956), *383*

Weiner, Sandra, *East 26th Street, New York, NY* (1948), *163*

Welles, Orson, *Citizen Kane*, 367

Welpott, Jack, 171, 383; holiday card (1972), *21*

Welty, Eudora, 73, 75, 383

West Coast photography, 109–110

Western Waters: Photographs by Gregory Conniff, Terry Evans, and Wanda Hammerbeck (1996), 231, 232, 233

Weston, Brett, 39, 107, 125, 238–41, 243, 384. Works: *Fiftieth Anniversary Exhibition* (1976), 384; holiday card (1975), *21*; *Skylight, Midtown* (1947), *240*; *Three Fingers and an Ear* (1929), *109*; *Untitled [leaf, Hawaii]* (ca. 1985), *384*; *Untitled [detail of leaf, Hawaii]* (ca. 1980s), *238*

Weston, Chandler, 243, 384

Weston, Charis Wilson, 248, 391

Weston, Cole, 240, 243

Weston, Edward, 18, 23, 24, 35, 39, 43, 107, 108, 109, 110, 121, 123, 125, 135, 137, 144, 145, 148, 149, 162, 163, 179, 185, 193, 216, 219, 220, 239, 240, 242–48, 305, 317, 373, 377, 385–90; archive, 385; collection, 90; daybooks, 121, 248, 305, 337, 386–89; letters, 245. Works: *Excusado, Mexico* (1925), *385*; *Nude Floating* (1939), *244*; *Pepper No. 30* [verso], 248; *Prologue to a Sad Spring* (1920), *123*; *The White Iris* (1921), *242*; *Winter Zero Schwartzel's "Bottle Farm," Farmersville, Ohio* (1941), *244*

Weston, Erica, 240

Weston, Flora Chandler, 243
Weston, Neil, 243
What's Happening with Momma? (Sligh), 46
Wheel That Raises Gate for Water Regulation, Cheyenne Bottoms, August 1992 (Evans), *231*
Wheeler Survey (1871–1873), 346
White, Clarence H., 390
White, Minor, 16, 25, 163, 170, 216, 376, 390. Works: *Gallery Cove, Point Lobos, California* (1953), *390; Lake Almanor, California* (1947), *25*
White Branches, Mono Lake, California (Adams), *36*
The White Iris (Edward Weston), *242*
White Pictures (Volkerding), 224
White Sheets, New Orleans, Louisiana (Strand), *196*
Whiteface Mountain, New York (Tress), *210*
Whitman, Walt, 197, 248; *Leaves of Grass,* 197, 248; *Mannahatta,* 197
Widelux panoramic camera, 223
Wilder, Mitchell, 237
Willard Van Dyke Fund for Documentary Photography, 119
Williams, Mark, 19
Wilson, Leon, 391
Winesburg, Ohio (Anderson), 197
Winningham, Geoff, 391
Winogrand, Garry, 223, 249–52, 334, 391; archive, 391. Works: [El Morocco nightclub, New York, contact sheet] (1955), *252;* [New York] (ca. 1960–61), *250;* [Texas] (1964), *251*
Winogrand Are Beautiful (Kelley), 322

Winter Zero Schwartzel's "Bottle Farm," Farmersville, Ohio (Edward Weston), *244*
WIR *see* Workers International Relief
Witkin, Joel-Peter, 202, 391
Witkin, Lee, 65, 392; archive, 392
Witkin Gallery, New York, 93, 392; archive, 392
Wittick, Ben, 77
Wolbarst, John, 392–93
Wolcott, Marion Post. 394; *Member of the Wilkins Family Making Biscuits for Dinner on Corn-Shucking Day, at the Home of Mrs. Fred Wilkins, near Tallyho & Stern, N.C.* (1939), *394*
Wolfe, Meyer (Mike), 79, 81
Woman's Day (magazine), 253
Women and Baby Carriage, Pitt Street, New York (Rosenblum), *161*
Women of Asia (Breitenbach), 61, 275
Wood, Beatrice, 248
Wood, John, 394
Woodburytypes, 374
Wooden Book (Pamela Moore), 48
Worden, Willard, 394
Worker Reading El Machete (Modotti), 135, 137
Workers Camera Leagues, 160
Workers International Relief (WIR), 160
Workers' Parade (Modotti), 135
Works Progress Administration, 151
World War II, 174, 194, 220, 248
Worster, Donald, 231, 232
Worth, Don, 394
Wright, Cedric, 394
Wu Dazhen, 394
The Wurlitzer Trilogy (Tress), 211
The Wurlitzer Trilogy (exhibition installation view), *211*

xerography, 342, 379
"Xi Zero in Photography" (Henry Holmes Smith), 362

Yamagata, Mihoko, 119, 394; *Kaiso* (1986), 119
Yamamoto, Masao, 119; *A Box of Ku* series, 119
Yamazaki, Hiroshi, 119; *The Sun Is Longing for the Sea* series, 119
Yampolsky, Mariana (Marianne), 44, 126, 394
Yañez Polo, Miguel Angel, 191
Yavno, Max, 125, 163, 395; archive, 395; *Mayan Indians and Photographer* (1981), *395*
Ylla (Camilla or Kamilla Koffler), 163, 253–255, 396; archive, 396. Works: *Animals in Africa,* 253; *Animals in India,* 255; *Animaux des Indes* (1958), *396; Chats* (1953), 253; *Chiens* (1953), 253; *Tico Tico,* 254
Yosemite Falls (Watkins), *24*
Yo-Semite Valley: Photographic Views of the Falls and Valley (Watkins) 381
You Have Never Been Old (Palfi), *154*
Young Man Sleeping in Box Car (Mieth), *128*
Yoshida, Ruiko, 120, 396

Z., P. [name unknown], 396
Zabalza, Ramon, 190
Zangaki, C. and G., 207, 290, 396
Zaslavsky, [?], 396
Zavattini, Cesare, 197
Zimmerman, Pat, 159
Zone (Apollinaire), 184
Zone System, 184

DESIGNED BY NANCY SOLOMON

COPY PHOTOGRAPHY BY DIANNE NILSEN AND DENISE GOSÉ

PRINTING BY PRISMA GRAPHIC CORPORATION

BINDING BY ROSWELL BOOKBINDING

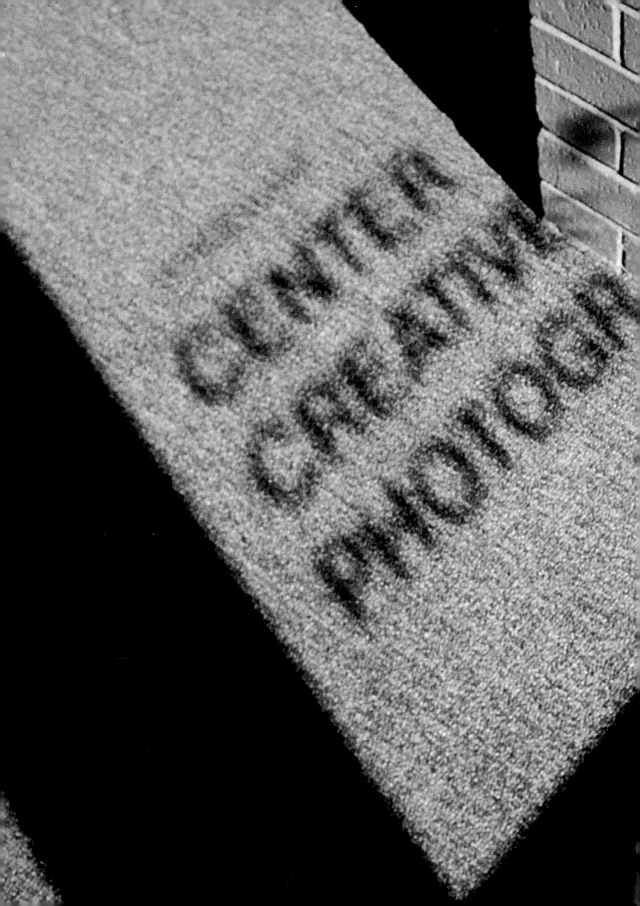